Sally Socolich's

Bargain
Hunting
in the
Bay Area

Sally Socolich's

Bargain
Hunting
in the
Bay Area

CHRONICLE BOOKS

San Francisco

Copyright © **1995**
by Sally Socolich.
All rights reserved. No part of this book may be reproduced in any form without written permission from the publisher.

Printed in the United States of America.

ISBN 0-8118-1143-3
ISSN available

Distributed in Canada by Raincoast Books,
8680 Cambie Street,
Vancouver, B.C. V6P 6M9

10 9 8 7 6 5 4 3 2 1

Chronicle Books
275 Fifth Street
San Francisco, CA 94103

Contents

How to Be a Bargain Hunter

I've been writing and reporting on the bargain scene for more than twenty years. You've heard the saying, "the more things change, the more they stay the same." It's true. There's been an evolution and revolution in retailing, in off-price and outlet retailing. Yet, for all the changes, consumers haven't changed— they still want bargains. Fortunately, there are still manufacturers and companies who manage to meet the challenge and save you money. And because I've done the footwork and made the calls, my book will save you time as well—an equally important consideration. *Bargain Hunting in the Bay Area* is designed to be a quick and reliable reference that serves your shopping needs.

Like the rest of the country, the Bay Area has had its share of store openings, closings, expansions, contractions, and moves, all of which are reflected in this new edition. My standards haven't changed. Outlets and off-price stores must still measure up in price and integrity. Each store must offer greater savings than its competitors in the overall Bay Area retail marketplace. I'm not bothered by the lack of retail amenities found in many outlets or warehouse-style businesses, but I do try to warn you when this is the case so that you'll approach the business with the right expectations. It's not my intention to tell you what to buy (I leave that to product-buying guides like *Consumer Reports* and other publications). Rather, my mission is to direct you to those sources where, whatever you buy, you'll be getting the best value for the money you spend. Many of these stores and outlets are well known to consumers by now; others benefit from the high-profile brands they stock. I've limited or eliminated my comments regarding many of the well-known bargain sources, giving more space to those that are more obscure.

Remember that bargains are relative. Your income level, value system, and exposure to merchandise in all price ranges and qualities will provide you with your uniquely personal perception of a "bargain." Bargain hunting appeals to shoppers at all income levels, but you must often think in terms of trade-offs. To capture savings you may have to drive forty to ninety miles north or south to one of the outlet centers or to a community on another side of the bay: is it worth it? At some stores and outlets, the hours may be inconvenient, the inventory unpredictable, the service indifferent, the parking nonexistent, or the neighborhood plagued by SWAT-team-like meter maids. Only you can decide how much inconvenience equals the trade-off—saving money. Don't confuse "cheap" with "value." A $10,000 dining room suite purchased for $6,700 is as good a "value" as a $1,500 dining room suite purchased for $900. Likewise, a $300 cashmere sweater purchased for $150 is as good a "value" as a $40 cotton sweater purchased for $20. It's the savings that count, more than just the final price. And remember: nothing is a bargain if you don't need it. One of the biggest problems at outlets and discount stores is the compulsion to buy simply because everything seems so cheap. To truly save money, quit while you're ahead.

While I hope that this book will save you some time when it comes to comparison shopping, it can still be worth your while. It always helps to know your market. Timing, overhead, special promotions, stock liquidations, and other factors can be reflected in the prices offered by particular outlets. Please refer to the Glossary of Bargain-Hunting Terms on page 343 for a full explanation. It's time to admit that there's a lot of outlet merchandise being sold at phantom values—labels that once denoted quality are now trading on long-lost reputations. It appears that some manufacturers have a two-tiered distribution system: one quality for major full-price retailers, a knock-off and lesser quality for outlet stores. Those swayed by "labels" should know that by now labels do not necessarily indicate quality or value. Likewise, don't be fooled by "suggested retail prices"; some appear to have been arbitrarily chosen to create the illusion of a greater discount. Caveat emptor should be a part of all your buying decisions.

Fortunately, there are still many "only-in-the-Bay-Area" outlets that showcase the talents and diversity of local manufacturers and businesses. May they thrive forever! In addition, major companies (outside the Bay Area) have instituted "outlet divisions," which has led to the "factory stores" that show up in regional outlet centers across the country. They may not always meet the expectations of consumers who first cut their bargain-hunting teeth shopping at the original and unique factory outlets (many have vanished from the scene) that were profiled in earlier editions of this book. Yet, factory stores located far from the company's factory or distribution sites provide an opportunity to buy quality goods at modest to maximum discounts that were unavailable to Bay Area consumers before these companies went into the outlet business.

This edition of *Bargain Hunting in the Bay Area* includes more than 700 stores offering solid values. With few exceptions, I expect a store or outlet to offer at least 20% off the retail price, though most entries offer far greater reductions. When possible, I have quoted prices to indicate the kinds of bargains available at the various stores. These prices are based on research conducted in the late spring of 1995. This book is intended as a guide, not an endorsement of the stores listed. I have no affiliation with the stores reviewed; no one paid to be in this book; no "printing charges" were assessed (a practice sometimes utilized by other guidebooks); nor were my comments subject to store approval.

A Word of Warning Before You Set Out

Since store hours—and even locations—are subject to change, I recommend that you call those shops you intend to visit before driving miles across town. (One clearance center relocated twice while I was compiling this manuscript.) It's always frustrating when outlets or centers are scheduled to open after the book is published. I have included "coming attractions" listings (based on interviews with the people or companies involved) for yet-to-open stores that I considered too important to ignore or of particular interest to readers of this book. Addresses and phone numbers were correct at the time of publication, but these may change. Subsequent printings will include corrections, and readers are encouraged to notify me in care of the publisher of any such changes. Also, don't hesitate to let me know when a store doesn't measure up to my description. I want to know whether you were satisfied with the experience. Be fair—I need your name in case I have to contact you to establish that your letter is not an envious competitor's sour grapes. Be assured I will keep your name in confidence if I believe it's important to pass along your criticisms to the store involved. Your "happy reports" are appreciated, as well—I love them! And I would be delighted to hear from other bargain hunters regarding new listings for future editions or other suggestions you may have. Please send any and all comments to my publisher:

Chronicle Books
275 Fifth Street
San Francisco, CA 94103

Happy hunting!

How to Use This Book

Bargain Hunting in the Bay Area is arranged by general merchandise category. Under each subject heading, store names are listed in alphabetical order. Some subjects, such as Apparel/Fashion, House and Home, and others, have been divided into subcategories. For each store, I give the address, phone number, hours, parking availability, and means of payment accepted (cash only, cash or check, and/or credit cards). If a store takes credit cards, it will also take checks unless otherwise noted. Credit card codes: MC—MasterCard, AE—American Express, DIS—Discovery, DC—Diners Club, CB—Carte Blanche, and VISA. Note listings under Other Outlet Centers and Other Store(s), where branch stores or similar services are offered.

Because many stores sell a wide variety of merchandise, I have made a limited number of cross-references that I thought would be helpful to a bargain hunter. These appear at the end of each section. And please consult the indexes at the end of the book: Store listings on 351, arranged alphabetically; Geographical listings on page 360, arranged by city; and Subject listings on page 374, arranged by product or service supplied.

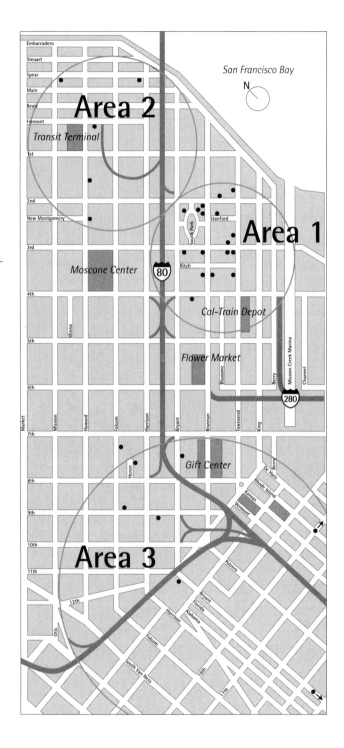

Area 1

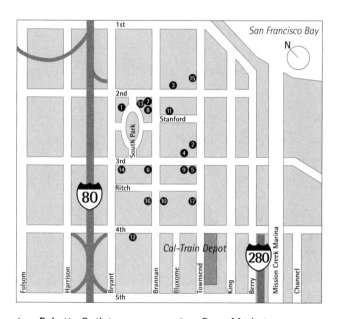

1	Babette Outlet	9	Dress Market
2	Bo Bo Kidz		Heat
3	Bridal Warehouse	10	Golden Rainbow
	Go Silk Outlet	11	Gunne Sax/Jessica
	2nd Street Kids		McClintock Outlets
4	Carole's Shoe Warehouse	12	Harper Greer
	Designer Co-Op	13	Isda & Co. Outlet
5	Cut Loose Factory Outlet	14	Jeanne Marc Outlet
6	Deja Vu A Paris	15	N. E. Wear
7	Designer's Outlet	16	New West
8	Discount Bridal Outlet	17	Secret Oasis

Area 2

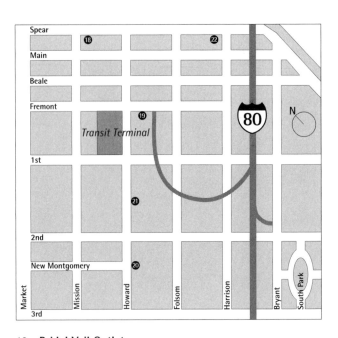

18 **Bridal Veil Outlet**
19 **Fritzi Factory Outlet**
20 **Kutler Clothiers**
   Spaccio
21 **Marguerite Rubel Raincoats/Jackets**
22 **Rock Express**

Area 3

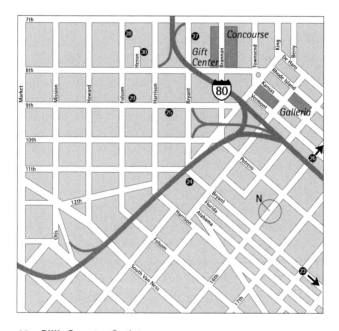

San Francisco's Factory Outlets and Off-Price Stores

Covering South of Market (SOMA), Parts of the Mission and Potrero Districts, and Surrounding Areas

Rather than follow an alphabetical arrangement for all apparel, I've listed all categories in women's apparel first, followed by men's, then general/family, which includes children's. Next come fashion-related sections (cosmetics, jewelry, shoes, etc.).

I've divided the women's apparel listings into several sections so that you can locate the resources that best meet your shopping needs. The first is devoted to all the outlet and off-price stores in the South of Market and surrounding areas of San Francisco. It's a focal point for bargain hunters, so you can plan shopping days in the City by quickly perusing the listings. For special sizes, manufacturers' outlets elsewhere, and off-price, chain, and specialty stores, please refer to the sections that follow.

The recent changes South of Market reflect the current state of the economy. A generally soft retail environment has resulted in the relocation or demise of many established outlet stores. The glory days of SOMA shopping may have passed, but, fortunately, there are still some important outlets and new outlets have opened. Caveat emptor! Don't assume that just because a store is located South of Market and purports to offer bargains, you will find good values. The merchandise of some businesses (not listed) I would describe with the words "cheap," "junk," or "schlock."

Factory outlets: Many of the stores listed here and throughout the Apparel/Fashion chapter are factory stores or factory outlets, typically owned and operated by clothing manufacturers, importers, or distributors, and often located on or near the manufacturers' plants. Some offer little in the way of retail store amenities; others have gone high-tech. Some may not take credit cards, have unconventional hours, or have difficult parking resulting in very limited hours of operation. Be sure to call ahead to verify hours and addresses. I've noted in parentheses which stores are factory outlets.

Note: Some outlets have additional locations at various outlet centers around the perimeter of the Bay Area. These centers are mentioned in the outlet's listing. For the locations and hours of these centers, please refer to the Guide to Outlet Centers in the Appendix.

Babette Outlet (Factory Outlet)

28 S. Park, San Francisco. (415) 267-0280.
M–F 11–5, Sat Noon–5. MC, VISA. Parking: street.
For those of you who search out the unusual, this slightly off-beat outlet is a great place to start. Babette's unusual rainwear, outerwear, and sportswear is sold at stores like Barney's and Bendels back East (can't name the locals). The sophisticated styles are hard to describe—distinctive fashions in microfibers; pleated tops, bottoms, and raincoats; plus fleece coats. Overall, a rather exotic and unconventional selection of styles at 50–70% off retail, sold from four or five racks. Babette's little outlet is proof positive that the best things come in small packages.

Bill's Sweater Outlet (Factory Outlet)

2101 Bryant Street, San Francisco. (415) 285-9999.
M–F 8:30–5:30, Sat 10–4. Cash/Check.
Parking: street, 20 minutes in rear lot.
This company's outlet is somewhat primitive and small (shelves mounted around its small lobby are overflowing), but it's stocked with choice goods. You'll find mostly women's sweaters, a limited number of very special men's sweaters, and a few wonderful children's styles. The sweaters are fully fashioned, woven to shape and size before the sides and sleeves are stitched together—the way all quality sweaters should be made. Most of the sweaters are made under private labels

for designers, fashion houses, department stores, or catalog companies, which accounts for the fashion styling and the wonderful textures and yarns (cashmere, mohair, cotton, and silk). A special "Bill & Penny" label has been created for the outlet. Prices hover around wholesale, with greater discounts on prototype samples. Give a holler if no one's around, and presto, someone will appear to give you the lowdown on prices and willingly take your money.

Byer Factory Outlet (Factory Outlet)

1300 Bryant Street, San Francisco. (415) 626-1228.
W–Sat 10–5. MC, VISA. Parking: lot.
(Other outlets: BFO/Byer Factory Outlet, Mervyn's Plaza,
Santa Clara; Great Mall, Milpitas.)
Byer California manages to satisfy legions of budget shoppers, many of whom consider regular pilgrimages to its factory stores a must—most prices at $8–$49 are too hard for teens and their moms to resist! At the outlet, discounts are usually 40–60% off original retail. These aren't seconds but first quality. Younger working gals stretch dollars on blouses, pants, and sophisticated coordinates or dresses; they can save on a New Year's Eve knockout prior to the holidays. Byer offers modestly priced lines of Junior, Misses, and Petite dresses and related sets, jackets, and sportswear (sizes 3–18); Large fashions (1X–3X); Girls sportswear and dresses (4–6X and 7–14). Some of the labels you'll recognize: Byer Too, Pacquette Too, Ms. Choice, Amy Byer, and Amy Too. The Santa Clara and Milpitas outlets are posh compared to the San Francisco store and have a nicer selection and more current fashions. No returns or exchanges are allowed in San Francisco; 30-day exchange in Santa Clara and Milpitas.

Christine Foley (Factory Outlet)

430 Ninth Street, San Francisco. (415) 621-8126. M–Sat 10–4.
MC, VISA. Parking: street.
Christine Foley's hand-loomed 100% cotton sweaters are very special, offering whimsical designs, bold colors, and real originality. Most styles can be worn by girls or boys, women or men. They're not cheap, and you're likely to find them in elegant department stores or boutiques. This colorful little outlet disposes of discontinued styles, color imperfections, and seconds. Prepare for the prices. Wholesale prices on children's sweaters (sizes 2–12) range from $42 to $72; adult sweaters

(S, M, L) range from $60 to $135. Retail prices are at least double. Seconds are reduced the most, up to 70% off retail; stickers reveal the defects.

Clothing Market at Mason

944 Market Street (at Mason), San Francisco. (415) 362-SAVE. M-Sat 10-6. MC, VISA, AE, DIS, ATM (no checks).
Parking: pay lots.
A worthy destination for women who are part of the briefcase brigade. The owner has contracts with factories in Asia and South America to buy first-quality factory overruns and samples. These foreign contractors make garments for Liz Claiborne, Jones New York, Kaspar (suits), Anne Klein, Dana Buchman, Albert Nipon, Le Coq Sportif, Head Sportswear (tennis), Ixspa, and private-label goods for famous stores like Bloomingdale's and Lord & Taylor. Because these are "left-overs," many fashion lines are from previous seasons, although some are very current. You may not find a complete size range in any particular line, or all the pieces in a group of related separates (just like at Loehmann's, T.J. Maxx, or Burlington). To avoid problems with other retailers that carry these lines, labels are cut in half. Prices are about 60% less than original retail and often more ($275 suits priced $49–$99). Sizes 2–16 (occasionally 18–20s). The emphasis is on career, with many suits and related separates, but there are also blouses, dresses, and active sportswear for both women and men. The store is quite lovely, an amazing transformation from a former bank, but I worry about its just-off-the-mainstream business location. I hope enough savvy shoppers find their way in to ensure its survival. Located one block from the Powell Street BART station and San Francisco Center.

Contemporary Career Outlet (Factory Outlet)

2565 Third Street, Room 309, San Francisco. (415) 285-7177. Occasional Sats (in spring and fall), 10–1. Cash/Check.
Parking: street.
This company's related separates, a very appealing line for mature women, are noteworthy for their soft, feminine look. Rayon and flax blends, rayon crepe, and 100% cotton fabrics result in styles that drape beautifully. Each season, new groups offer unstructured jackets, tops, skirts, jumpsuits, and pants. Their palette of colors ensures that you'll always find something to suit your color harmony or season. Sizes range from

Petite through Large. You can buy past-season seconds, samples, and closeouts for about wholesale. Prices on the separates typically range from $20 to $60. Since the outlet is closed during winter and summer, call first, and once in the building, take a look around for other outlets that may be open.

Cut Loose Factory Outlet (Factory Outlet)
690 Third Street, San Francisco. (415) 495-4581.
M–Sat 10–5:30. MC, VISA. Parking: street.
(Factory warehouse sales first weekend each month:
1780 Armstrong Avenue, San Francisco.)
You can have it two ways here: shop at the main outlet for 50% savings and more on past- and current-season overruns, or wait for its factory warehouse sales, when seconds are sold at truly skinflint prices. Cut Loose offers upscale designs for weekday and weekend wear, garment-dyed separates in distinctive fabrics—textured cottons, crinkled rayons, washed linens, corduroys—and a wonderful variety of solid colors. Prices range from $3 to $65 on separates: pleated pants, leggings, tights, assorted blouse and top styles, skirts (straight, full, short, long), and dramatic oversized jackets. The cut is generous on most styles—perfect for less-than-perfect bodies. Keep it simple and basic, or show your fashion savvy by choosing from sophisticated separates. Sizes: S–XL; Plus sizes 1X–3X. If you're on its mailing list, you won't miss out on any sale opportunity at either site. Note: Cash only at factory sales.

Deja Vu A Paris (Factory Outlet)
400 Brannan Street, 2nd Floor, San Francisco. (415) 541-9177.
F–Sat 11–5, M–Th by appt. MC, VISA, AE. Parking: street.
City women may shop at its sophisticated retail boutique for unique contemporary career apparel with European flair. These fashions, many in specially woven Italian fabrics, work beautifully anytime you want to look stylish. The outlet usually offers full-pleated pants with tapered legs to minimize a body's imperfections, and feminine, sophisticated, and softly tailored career suits originally priced at retail for about $450 (about half in the outlet). Prices overall are steep (even at wholesale), but this reflects the loftier retail prices. Expect to spend $55–$175 on related separates. This outlet is not large but offers airy lighting and personal service. Sizes (with a full cut) 4–14.

Designer Co-Op

625 Third Street, San Francisco. (415) 777-3570.
M–Sat 10–6, Sun 11–5. MC, VISA, AE. Parking: lot.
A perfect place for tandem shopping sprees for women and
men. Men will appreciate the sportswear and sweaters from
makers like Z. Cavaricci, Winston Woods, and Axis. Women will
love the alluring fashions from Nina K and won't hesitate to
pick up a luxurious handknit sweater from Margaret O'Leary.
Each visit to this outlet yields a new cache of stylish merchandise from a manufacturer disposing of overruns and closeouts.
The store is a collection of miniboutiques with women's fashions, children's dresses and play clothes, shoes (Sam & Libby),
tasteful giftware, a consignment corner, and lots of fashion
accessories and fashion jewelry. Prices always discounted
50–70% off retail. Down a cup of your favorite coffee blend
from the espresso bar in front.

Designer's Outlet (Factory Outlet)

300 Brannan Street, #102, San Francisco. (415) 957-5978.
M–Sat 10–5. MC, VISA. Parking: lot.
If you feel most comfortable in soft two- or three-piece sets
(combinations of pants, skirts, tops and tunics, jackets, etc.),
then this outlet deserves your attention. Le Cathay, the owner,
imports specialty sweaters and embellished tops designed for
the Misses market, and designs and manufactures the Caribe
or After All dresses and sportswear. The Caribe line of two- and
three-piece ensembles is very appealing; most are made from
rayons or rayon blends in crepes, crinkles, soft sheers, linen, or
natural cottonlike fabrics. They are usually priced from $40
to $50, work well as daytime outfits, and are elegant enough
for slightly dressier evening occasions. The dresses are more
contemporary—long skimmers or slip dresses—some reflecting
the 1920s and '30s. Young women are bound to favor the
dress collection, while more mature women will find the sim-
plicity and sophistication of the ensembles appropriate for
their lifestyles. Sizes: S, M, L (fits 6–14). The current-season
overruns on Kris Michele or Alyssa Michele sweaters (in cotton,
ramie-cotton blends, and lambswool angora) and embellished
T-shirt tops are always sold at wholesale ranging from $5 to
$29. The store also has a nice selection of men's silk sportshirts
priced at $12 and silk bomber-style jackets at $29.

Dress Market

660 Third Street, Six Sixty Center, San Francisco. (415) 495-6768.
M-Sat 10-5:30. MC, VISA. Parking: private lot.

There's enough variety in this outlet's selection to satisfy
women with diverse fashion tastes—in fact, it has a split personality of sorts. One half could easily be called the cruise,
resort, or vacation outlet, since it presents soft, comfortable
ethnic fashions: wonderful loose-flowing separates and
dresses in gauze, chiffon, and natural fibers with exotic prints,
often made in Indonesia or India. You'll also find a small
mainstream collection of daytime and social occasion dresses,
samples in sizes 8–12 from Phoebe and Wild Rose (dresses,
sets, and jumpsuits) at 50% off retail. The second half of the
outlet is devoted to weekend wear: shorts, fancy T-shirts,
Rene Hauer sweaters, leisure sets, jeans, and fleece tops—
first-quality overruns, samples, and sometimes past-season
goods. Spumoni women's and girls' fleece tops are always in
good supply. Prices are nicely discounted all the time. Sizes
4–16. Exchanges within fourteen days.

Esprit Factory Outlet (Factory Outlet)

499 Illinois Street (at 16th Street), San Francisco. (415) 957-2550.
M-F 10-8, Sat 10-7, Sun 11-5. Hours subject to change
during special sales and holiday season. MC, VISA, AE, DIS.
Parking: free lot.
(Other outlets: Gilroy, Napa centers.)

The Esprit Outlet is more than an outlet, it's a major tourist
attraction. Whatever your age, Esprit can cover you from
head to toe. The outlet sells seasonal overruns, returns, and
samples. Its shoe department is very popular. If you find the
outlet prices still too steep, your best strategy is to wait for
the fabulous sales, when prices may be reduced an additional
30–40% off the lowest marked price. Otherwise, check the
bargain bins in the back. You'll find everything Esprit, including the Susie Tompkins upscale line and the new Ecollection.
Sizes range from Infant 12mos to Toddler 36mos (boys, too)
up to Junior 13/14 and Women's. Exchanges with receipt,
within fourteen days of purchase, for merchandise credit good
for one year. Call for special sales and directions.

Fritzi Factory Outlet (Factory Outlet)

218 Fremont Street (bet. Howard and Folsom), San Francisco.
(415) 979-1394; recording for directions (415) 979-1399. M–Th
9–5, F–Sat 8–5. MC, VISA, DIS, checks over $10. Parking: street.
The fun at Fritzi is buying the latest look for a price that
causes you no remorse if you don't want to wear the garment
next year. Savvy shoppers line up for special sales every Friday
morning from 8 to 10, when selected items are marked down
an additional 20–75%. You'll have to fight traffic to get there,
but it's worth the hassle! Fritzi is a reliable source for those
who have to consider price first and foremost: dresses for $20;
sets (coordinating tops and skirts) for $22; tops, blouses, pants,
sweaters, and skirts for $5–$17. Even better, women will find
larger sizes; styles that appeal to grownup taste; dresses and
sportswear for girls and preteens; even maternity fashions.
Fritzi labels: You Babes (juniors), FR Sport, My Michelle, Fritzi
Woman, You Babes Girls & Teens, and You Babes Kids.
Sizes: Large tops 36–44 (fits 16–24); Large bottoms 30–38
(fits 16–24); Girls S, M, L (7–14); Toddlers 2–4T, Kids 4X–6X;
and Junior and Misses 3/4–15/16. The outlet is crowded
on Saturdays, so if you can shop during the week, you'll only
have to worry about a parking place. All sales final.

Georgiou Factory Outlet (Factory Outlet)

925 Bryant Street (bet. Seventh and Eighth streets),
San Francisco. (415) 554-0150. M–Sat 10–5. MC, VISA, AE, DIS.
Parking: private rear lot, enter on Langston (alley next to store).
(Other outlets: 579 Bridgeway, Sausalito; Milpitas,
Vacaville centers.)
If you're dazzled by Georgiou's fashions, you'll be thrilled with
its outlet's past-season overruns, overstocks, and missed shipments, yet baffled by stuff that's so old you'll wonder if it will
ever be sold. All Georgiou's fashions are made of natural fibers:
wool, cashmere blends, silk, linen, rayon, and cotton, with
each new color and print designed to coordinate with existing
colors in its line. You can build a wardrobe of career separates
piece by piece. Styles are so classic, yet contemporary, they'll
remain au courant for seasons to come. The colorful and fun
cruise, leisure, and resort lines made from 100% cotton are
equally timeless. Misses sizes 4–16. Prices are 50–80% off
retail. Georgiou accessories at discount prices are just what you
need to pull your outfit together. The outlet has a high-tech
look, wonderful lighting, and an accommodating staff.

Go Silk Outlet (Factory Outlet)

625 Second Street (bet. Brannan and Townsend), San Francisco.
(415) 957-1983. M–Sat 10–5. MC, VISA, AE. Parking: street.
(Other outlet: St. Helena center.)

Go Silk "washable silk" apparel is sold in upscale department stores and boutiques; it's beautifully made, soft, and lovely in relaxed and classic styles. At the outlet you'll save 50–75% off retail on past-season merchandise, but you'll still be paying about $100 for long-sleeve shirts and skirts (retail $200–$250); $150 for jackets (retail to $500); $100 for sweaters (retail $200); about $90–$100 for pants (retail over $200). They can be dressed up or down for wardrobe versatility. Since these are overruns, you won't find all styles, colors, or sizes. The separates are easy to wash and they travel well. Sizes are marked 0–3 and will fit women in the 2/4–10/12 range and larger, since some styles are cut oversize and feature elastic waists. If top quality matters, this just might be your place. All sales final.

Gunne Sax/Jessica McClintock Outlets (Factory Outlet)

35 Stanford Street (bet. Second and Third streets, enter from Brannan or Townsend), San Francisco. (415) 495-3326. M–Sat 9–5:30, Sun 11–5. MC, VISA, AE. Parking: very limited street. (Other outlet: 494 Forbes, South San Francisco, (415) 737-2500.)

The Gunne Sax outlets are supermarket-sized! They are two of the Bay Area's few resources for prom and party dresses, which is wonderful if you're enchanted with the feminine, romantic Jessica McClintock look or excited by the more contemporary Scott McClintock line. Suits, skirts, dresses, and blouses come in a wide variety of fabrics for daytime or evening occasions. Many brides and bridesmaids have found beautiful dresses here that would have been off-limits at full retail prices. There are also infant christening gowns and First Communion dresses. Except for a few samples and irregulars, most of the inventory is well past season, maybe more than a year old. Discounts are 50–80% off retail. The prices are tempting, but take care to scrutinize for flaws, which are easily acquired on delicate fabrics. Sizes: Junior, 3–13; Women's 4–16, Plus 14W–24W (Scott McClintock only); Girls dresses in 2–4T (very limited), 4–6X, 7–14; Preteen 6–14. All sales are final. Warning: Don't park in the alley in front of the SOMA outlet! This is prime meter maid territory. Shopping is much easier at the South San Francisco location: more focused merchandising and ample parking (however, no bridal, bridesmaid, or Jessica McClintock collections in 1995).

Heat

660 Third Street, Six Sixty Center, San Francisco. (415) 541-9398. M–Sat 10–5:30. MC, VISA. Parking: lot.

Heat is an outlet for an importer of silk fashions for women and men. Prices are very reasonable, ranging from $9 to $39.99 on silk camisoles, blouses, skirts, baseball jackets, men's shirts, etc. The quality is just fine for the price. Good place to pick up some inexpensive silk shell blouses to extend your wardrobe. Other racks offer chiffon pleated skirts, soft peasant dresses, and denim sportswear ($9.99–$29.99).

Isda & Co. Outlet (Factory Outlet)

29 S. Park (bet. Bryant and Brannan, Second and Third streets), San Francisco. (415) 512-1610. M–Sat 10–5:30. MC, VISA. Parking: street.
(Other outlet: Gilroy center.)

Isda & Co. offers something that is often difficult to find when shopping South of Market: better quality and sophisticated styles for upscale shoppers. It merited a 1993 Golden Shears Award and many articles in the fashion press with its clean, chic, well-tailored designs for women who have grown up and want high-quality clothes at affordable prices. If you admire the Donna Karan line, you'll surely love Isda's designs. You can create your own ensemble from related separates: combine a skirt (short or long), walking shorts, or pants with vest tops or hip-length, slimming jackets. You'll find elegant mercerized cotton knit T-shirts and fine-gauge mercerized sweater knits and vests. These tops are soft and lustrous and look very expensive. The fabrics are the best: quality rayon suitings, tropical weight wool, 100% cotton (in sophisticated white blouses), and rayon/linen blends. At the outlet, past-season groups are at least 50% off retail. That translates to about $146 for a jacket, about $70 for pants, or about $56 for a skirt, with even greater markdowns on way-past-season styles. It may become more difficult to create ensembles as the season progresses and styles sell out. Note: The outlet in Gilroy is much larger with more inventory. Sizes: 2–14 or S, M, L.

Jeanne Marc Factory Outlet (Factory Outlet)

508 Third Street (bet. Bryant and Brannan), San Francisco.
(415) 243-4396. M–Sat 11–5. MC, VISA. Parking: street.
Cab drivers know the way to Jeanne Marc; they tote tourists
from downtown hotels excited by the prospects of saving $$$
on this elegant line. Women buy Jeanne Marc outfits to make
a statement and then wear them for years. The designs are
noted for unique pattern play, shirring, quilting, and bias cuts.
Many prints are exclusive designs created in-house using
the finest cotton, rayon, and rayon-cotton blends from Japan's
leading textile mills. Of course, deeply discounted lovelies—
40–70% off retail—don't last long. More typically, you'll spend
$200 plus for a coordinating skirt, blouse, and jacket. These
bargains are past-season overruns (some way-past-season),
but if you're a Jeanne Marc customer you'll be in heaven.
For the best markdowns and freshest merchandise, get on the
preferred customer mailing list. Sizes: Petite to Large (fits
2–18). All sales final.

Magnolia's Sweater Samples (Factory Outlet)

601 Indiana Street (off Mariposa), San Francisco.
(415) 826-3898. M–F 10–4. MC, VISA. Parking: street.
A bit removed from most outlets, this outlet is almost an after-
thought with this company. Yet, if you're not uncomfortable
exploring on your own, stop by, and someone will let you in
and lead you to the elegant sample showroom on the second
floor. The company designs and makes its sweaters in Hong
Kong—its Magnolia label and others under private label for
major stores. The samples are nicely displayed to impress the
buyers. This is a one-of-a-kind selection with some very special,
better-quality sweaters. Magnolia's own label is associated
with "fashion" sweaters—few basics or sweaters with traditional
styling. Each season's collection reveals new styles of fancy
sweaters with beading, embroidery, ribbons, or other razzma-
tazz (perfect for parties or cruises). There are also handloomed,
handknit, and computer-knit collections, and printed merino.
I prefer the more classic styles in merino wool (classy cardigans,
vests, and mock turtles), but the soft jersey knits and some
silk fabrications produced some oohs and aahs. Prices generally
range from $35 to $60 (coat styles). Sizes S, M, L.

Marguerite Rubel Raincoats/Jackets (Factory Outlet)

543 Howard Street, 2nd Floor, San Francisco. (415) 362-2626.
M–F 8–4, Sat 8–11:30. MC, VISA. Parking: street.

Marguerite Rubel can be unnerving for first-time shoppers;
she is refreshingly honest, painfully direct at times, and altogether something of a character. Once you get past her gruff
demeanor, you'll end up firm friends. Her World Map jackets
made for George Bush and Bill Clinton have garnered exceptional publicity. She enjoys a good reputation for the classic
and innovative styling of her raincoats, blazers, jackets, coats,
and sportswear. Velvets have always been a part of her line,
and she keeps up-to-date by including poplins, silklike polyesters, and other fabrics. Recently, her bestselling styles have
included updated quilted baseball or weekend jackets, some
with appliqués or patchwork utilizing 200 squares in each
jacket. Some of the inventory appears to have been around
since the beginning of time, but retro-fashion buyers love it.
You'll find many one-of-a-kind jackets, coats, and overruns
from her sportswear. It's a grab bag of fashions with some
real treasures; if you've ever wanted a dramatic velvet cape
or wrap, this is your place. You can expect 40–50% savings,
but not Nordstrom's service, and you're in for a scold if you
don't handle the fashions with care. Quilters note: Velvet
scraps are sold in dozens of colors at $3/pound, with a
25-pound minimum.

New West

426 Brannan Street (bet. Third and Fourth streets),
San Francisco. (415) 882-4929. M–Sat 10–5, Sun Noon–5.
MC, VISA, AE. Parking: street.
(Other store: 2967 College Avenue, Berkeley.)

New West buys popular lines of women's and men's contemporary sportswear from status stores in New York. The labels
will leave you agog! Some of these fashions are slightly
irregular, some have been repaired (broken zippers, popped
seams, missing buttons), but no one seems to mind. The men's
department serves guys who want good deals on casual weekend separates, great ties, Saturday night out-to-dinner clothes,
and trendier sportcoats and suits. The women's lines appeal
to ladies who frequent contemporary sportswear departments
of major stores or specialty shops. There's usually a collection

or two that's just right for the partying crowd. Prices are generally 40–60% off original retail and often more (I spotted one status designer men's suit marked down from $1,800 to $425). Women's sizes 4–14. The College Avenue location is classier yet, to fit in with the Elmwood shopping district. Finally, New West now allows exchanges for store credit.

Rock Express (Factory Outlet)

350 Spear Street (bet. Folsom and Harrison), San Francisco. (415) 597-9799. W–F Noon–6, Sat 10–4. MC, VISA, AE, DIS. Parking: street (limited).

Rock Express grew out of concert merchandising for Bill Graham's Winterland Productions, which produces the licensed merchandise of more than seventy-five entertainers, sells rock-and-roll commodities to retail outlets, and prints T-shirts for major corporations and fundraising events. It prints T-shirts, tote bags, and other items for many well-known designers. Rock Express sells "leftovers" from all of its various enterprises, leading to some very nice surprises at the outlet. T-shirts get the most rack space; you'll also find jackets and sweatshirts in a variety of sizes, styles, and colors. Collectors may discover memorabilia that ends up in the outlet from time to time. Sizes for the whole family, but little in the popular XL or XXL.

Secret Oasis

230 Townsend Street (bet. Third and Fourth streets), San Francisco. (415) 442-4840. M–F 11–6. MC, VISA. Parking: street.

This store is so new that I worry whether it will be around for the long haul. Certainly, the prices at 60% off retail will guarantee return visits once women discover its existence. Joan Walters' sets, jumpsuits, and dresses take up the most rack space. Other lines of sportswear were new to me. Everything falls in the moderate price range at retail (which is another way of saying that this is not a resource for upscale shoppers). With dresses and sets priced well under $40 and sportswear separates generally priced at $8–$14, customers seemed more than satisfied with the quality/value/price equation. The displays, decor, and general ambiance are a cut above most discount operations. All sales final.

Susan Lawrence

119 Sacramento Street, San Francisco. (415) 399-0222.
M–F 10–6, Sat 11–5. MC, VISA, AE. Parking: pay lots.
Executive women from the Financial District come here for
the suits, dresses, and blouses that their jobs require, finding
premium lines that are sold concurrently in status downtown
stores. An "investment dressing," better-quality suit from
Susan Lawrence is likely to cost $280–$400 at retail. Dresses
geared for the boardroom are $125–$200. Susan Lawrence
offers discounts ranging from a modest 20% up to 35%
(average about 25%). Mailing-list customers watch for end-of-
season sale announcements featuring even greater discounts.
Everything is upscale and current season from topflight manufacturers. Sizes 4–14. Referrals for alterations are provided,
and the service is professional and personal.

Also See

Under Men's Sportswear:
N. E. Wear

Under Men's Suits:
Kutler Clothiers; Spaccio

Under Active Sportswear:
San Francisco City Lights

Other Bay Area Factory Outlets/Factory Stores

Many factory outlets are conveniently close to the companies' main offices and warehouses in the Bay Area outside the South of Market area in San Francisco. To reach the backstreet locations of some outlets, you may need maps of the area. The following outlets and factory stores are in no way secondary to or less important than the factory outlets and off-price stores listed in other sections. In addition to these, you'll find other factory outlets listed throughout the apparel chapters.

Factory stores: This is a designation I've given to stores owned by companies that have created a thriving and profitable side business by operating not just one, but dozens of factory-owned stores throughout the country. Major brands like Liz Claiborne, Jones New York, Aileen, and Van Heusen go this route. This strategy makes sense in today's retail environment. In this way, they are not entirely dependent on department stores or subject to market forces over which they have little control. Factory stores usually offer more of a manufacturer's products or lines than any one retail or department store. And the prices and discounts at factory stores can range from very modest (and disappointing) to quite impressive. To keep stores well stocked, many companies manufacture or buy merchandise specifically for their outlet divisions. I feel that often this "special" merchandise does not offer the same quality or value as the company's regular merchandise manufactured for full price retailers. Modest discounts (25–30%) most often apply to current, first-quality merchandise.

Factory stores owned by major manufacturers are usually found in the outlet centers on the perimeter of the Bay Area. At times it seems like everyone is participating in an ongoing game of musical chairs as they hopscotch from one space to another, or move from one outlet center to another as leases come up for renewal.

In the following listings, very well-known designers or brand names are afforded minimal space. I'm assuming the name will define the merchandise. However, the locations of the outlets and range of discounts are important in determining whether a trip is worthwhile. Many outlets offer extra-special promotions and discounts during national holidays—e.g., Martin Luther King's Birthday, President's Weekend, Labor Day, etc. These holidays are an especially good time to plan a visit to an outlet center.

For daily hours, see the Appendix.

Adolfo II

Pacific West Outlet Center, Gilroy. (408) 848-6313. Daily.
MC, VISA, DIS. Parking: lot.
Adolfo Sport, Adolfo II, and other labels emphasize leisure and lifestyle clothing for women who want to add a little pizazz to their wardrobes. Shoppers here can find any number of styles when looking for leisure sets; fancy, dress-up T-shirt tops; very casual dresses or sets; and colorful and fun jackets (some casual and some more sophisticated styles including leathers). There is very little serious career clothing. Each spring features styles with a nautical look—great for cruises and Delta Gamma alumnae. Adolfo is a more affordable resource than some other high-profile designers. Sizes S–XL and 1X–3X. All sales final.

Adrienne Vittadini Direct

Petaluma Village Factory Outlets, Petaluma. (707) 763-2250.
Daily. MC, VISA, AE. Parking: lot.
(Other outlet: Napa center.)
This is a beautiful outlet offering liberating discounts on a selection that's very current—just 8–10 weeks behind major stores. If you're familiar with the line, all you need to know is that discounts start at 40% off retail and often reach 60% on sale racks. All collections are represented: sport, career, sweaters, outerwear, better dresses, some dressier pieces for

evening (before and following the holidays), plus other assets including accessories (scarves, shoes, gloves, travel bags, jewelry). No doubt you'll get favorable reviews after shopping here. Sizes are accommodating. Misses 2–16 with smaller groups of Petites and Large sizes. Exchanges allowed within 14 days, but no cash refunds.

Aileen Stores Inc.

Factory Stores of America, Vacaville. (707) 449-3650. Daily. MC, VISA. Parking: lot.
(Other outlets: Folsom, Gilroy, Lathrop, Pacific Grove centers.)
Aileen's prices and all-encompassing size selection make it a department store favorite, appealing to mature women with its understated and trend-proof image. Every season the related separates in 100% cotton are reintroduced in new colors and prints with modest style innovations. You can buy separates from any section. Prices on in-season styles are reduced about 35% off retail, but watch for racks with additional markdowns. Sizes: Misses 8–20; Petite 8–18; Plus 18W–28W. Exchanges allowed with receipt and hang tags.

American Eagle

Outlets at Gilroy, Gilroy. (408) 842-3377. Daily. MC, VISA, AE, DIS. Parking: lot.
(Other outlet: Vacaville center.)
East Coast transplants will be familiar with this company— it has 200 retail stores and nearly 60 company outlet stores. It's a casual clothing headquarters for women and men with mainstream and traditional leanings. Sweaters, jackets, pants (denim and twills always at $19.99), turtle necks (2/$20), winter flannels (2/$35), polo shirts, shirts, skirts, etc. are very affordable. Women's sizes 1/2–18; Men's S–XL or 28–40 (waists). Look for "best buys" on weekly special promotions. Some merchandise purchased just for its outlet division.

Ann Marie Designs

7 East Sixth Street, Antioch. (510) 757-7066. Usually M–F 9–2 (extended hours and Sats during frequent sales). MC, VISA. Parking: street.
The lines: 100% cotton, garment-dyed, preshrunk, and hand-painted active sportswear; some maternity groups sold primarily to specialty stores. It's a little pricey, with shorts, pants and tops, oversize tops, jumpsuits, and cardigan-style

long jackets selling for 50–75% off retail (past-season styles). Prices start at $15 for each piece and may be as much as $48. The line is wonderful! Whimsical handpainting that's not overdone, sometimes ornamented with studs or rhinestones, creates perfect, casual party, resort, or dining-out clothes. Ladies looking for an understated look can grab the "naked" and unadorned styles. The outlet's downside? You may not find matching coordinates in all color groups, especially on way-past-season merchandise. Sizes: S, M, L (fits 6/8–14/16); one-size-fits-all jackets; some styles in XS or XL. Sign up to get advance notice of special sales. Call for directions. Note: Due to a road extension planned for late 1995, the factory and outlet will be relocated to another site in Antioch. Call for new address.

Ann Taylor

Outlets at Gilroy, Gilroy. (408) 848-1188. Daily. MC, VISA, AE. Parking: lot.
(Other outlet: Petaluma center.)

These outlets are real crowd pleasers. In part clearance outlet for its retail stores, the company has also created a "store program" just for its outlets. It chooses proven style winners from its retail division and manufacturers' knock-offs for the outlets. I spotted my timeless black wool worsted suit purchased from one of its stores two years ago on the racks in a nearly identical fabrication at half the original price. Wool blazers in tweeds, plaids, and solids at $99 were an excellent value and the quality was very good. Capture a professional look with a nice silk blouse—many styles priced at $39–$49 on average. Add panache to your outfit with a vest, or if you've got the legs, go for a short pleated skirt. The selection is always up-to-date. Count on an extensive sportswear category with lots of denims, knit tops, etc., a respectable shoe department, and, best of all, an extensive petite department. Sizes: Petite 2–12; Misses 2–14. Returns and refunds.

Anne Klein

Pacific West Outlet Center, Gilroy. (408) 842-7660. Daily. MC, VISA. Parking: lot.
(Other outlets: Pacific Grove, Tracy centers.)

Anne Klein is one of the best outlets for upscale fashions and really delivers on price, quality, and selection. Some style groups are from previous seasons, while the rest are current.

Anne Klein II collections are the big attraction. Prices at the outlet are guaranteed to satisfy the savviest shopper. Solid 40% discounts are the norm on most groups, but look for extra specials. You'll also find modestly discounted Anne Klein accessories, including handbags, scarves, hats, fashion jewelry, and watches. Sizes: Petite 2–14; Misses 4–16. Exchanges accepted within seven days for store credit only.

Bebe Outlet

Great Mall of the Bay Area, Milpitas. (408) 263-BEBE. Daily. MC, VISA. Parking: lot.

Bebe's retail stores are popular with younger career women. The collections of chic and updated career suits and separates in distinct fabrics, with elegant European tailoring and subtle shaping, are stylish enough to go straight from the office to a dinner date. Retail may not accommodate the just-getting-started career woman; at the outlet at 30–70% off, past-season fashions are within reach. (At retail most Fall jackets range from $169 to $189; at the outlet they sell from $80 to $132. Most pants retail from $78 to $124; they sell from $62 to $87 at the outlet.) Women who don't have the legs for the 17-inch skirts may opt for pants to coordinate with the jackets. Love the weekend collections, too! Sizes 2–12.

Cape Isle Knitters

Factory Stores of America, Vacaville. (707) 449-4093. Daily. MC, VISA. Parking: lot.
(Other outlets: Folsom, Lathrop, Napa, Petaluma, Pacific Grove, Tracy centers.)

The largest sweater mill in the country makes sweaters for many companies and designers in a wide range of styles and prices. Cape Isle Knitters is its retail division, selling directly to consumers. The stores display sweaters in basics, classics, and more stylish pieces with novelty patterns or weaves. Many sweaters and tops resemble the styles in the Lands' End and L.L. Bean catalogs: comfortable, appealing, middle-of-the-road. The quality/price/value ratio is solid. Cardigans, vests, pullovers , et al. for men and women (many unisex) sizes S–XL.

Carole Little Outlet

Pacific West Outlet Center, Gilroy. (408) 847-4411. Daily.
MC, VISA, AE. Parking: lot.
(Other outlets: Napa, Pacific Grove centers.)

Carole Little stays very up-to-date by sending new inventory
to its outlets eight weeks after the styles have gone on display
at major stores, and sells this selection for 40% off original
retail. Each season's line of color-themed styles offers tremendous versatility for building an outfit. The related separates
are dramatic and make a statement, and on their own they
have so much character. Dresses and sweaters are staples.
Carole Little is noted for "easy" clothing: mainstream yet chic,
with contemporary and classic career and weekend apparel.
Sizes 4–16. Plus gals love the attention from the company's
Carole Little II Collection, sizes 14–24. Store exchanges only
within five days.

Chaus Factory Outlet

Pacific West Outlet Center, Gilroy. (408) 847-1396. Daily.
MC, VISA, AE, DIS. Parking: lot.
(Other outlet: Folsom center.)

Chaus is strictly for ladies who appreciate its styles in easy-
care synthetics, washable rayons and blends; comfort design
(many elastic waists and over-blouses to hide the tummy);
avoidance of trendiness in its related separates and dresses.
However, that doesn't mean the line is dull—anything but! It's
ideally suited to retirement and traveling, while popular with
working women as well. The outlets are well stocked and the
selection of sizes is guaranteed to please: Petite 4–16; Misses
6–18; Chaus Women 16–24 and 1X–3X. Markdowns 30–60%
off retail, with frequent promotions and special sale racks.
Get on the mailing list for special coupon offers.

Chico's Factory Store

Factory Stores of America, Vacaville. (707) 453-1336. Daily.
MC, VISA. Parking: lot.

I love leftovers! Especially Chico's distinctive color-coordinated
in-house-designed casual clothing in 100% cotton, silk, and
rayon. Loose fitting and designed for easy care, these creative
designs feature attractive, bold colors in contemporary Southwest, Latin American, and Middle Eastern motifs. Combine
pieces from the related separates for a knockout ensemble!
Save 25–50% off every day; look for 50%-off promotions on

discontinued color groups. Sizes: 1, 2, 3 for women 7/8–14/16. You can't possibly leave without adding a piece of dramatic ethnic jewelry. Inquire about Chico's frequent-shopper card.

The Cotton Outlet

2322 Fifth Street (bet. Channing and Bancroft), Berkeley. (510) 849-0492. W–Sat 11–5. MC, VISA. Parking: street.
Ideas for Cotton showcases its line at its three small boutiques in the East Bay. The Cotton Outlet is where you'll find its past-season collections, closeouts, and leftovers. The line is versatile, with many styles just for women, plus some unisex tops that men wear comfortably. There's a children's collection as well. Everything seems very familiar: pleated pants, vests, oversize cardigan-style tops, pullover tops, shorts, split skirts, and a few loose-fitting dresses. There are also a few sweatsuit collections. At retail, the separates range from $27 to $45; at the outlet, prices range from $5 to $25. Most styles are priced under $20.

Donna Karan Company Store

Village Outlets of Napa Valley, 3111 North St. Helena Highway, St. Helena. (707) 963-8755. M–F 10–6:30, Sat 10–7, Sun 11–6. MC, VISA, AE. Parking: lot.
Donna Karan's elegant, upscale outlet is equal to her reputation. Noted for her remarkable sense of style and signature collections, her company store is absolutely posh and beautifully merchandised with recent overruns as well as past-season inventory. The 50% discounts off retail on most everything make the trip worthwhile for a Donna Karan or DKNY customer, but apparel is still somewhat pricey. Retail prices on many pieces are often over $1,000. The expensive New York collections dominate the first floor. The second floor showcases the DKNY and sportswear collections, which approach affordability for most women. Lots of denim, classy and elegant career silk blouses (many body-suit styles), related separates, coats, handbags, belts, sunglasses, fashion jewelry, scarves, et al. A small men's boutique on the first floor has sportshirts, suits, sweaters, etc., all priced about 50% off retail. The company offers a fourteen-day period for exchanges or merchandise credits. Full range of sizes (some 2s–14), including Petites.

Ellen Tracy Outlet

Napa Factory Stores, Napa. (707) 226-2994. Daily. MC, VISA, AE.
Parking: lot.

From day one, this outlet has been drawing hordes of women
from all over the Bay Area. Do yourself a favor and shop
during the week to avoid the long lines for dressing rooms on
weekends. This is a four-star outlet offering Ellen Tracy's
sophisticated apparel from career, sportswear, and after-five
collections. From the company's perspective, the collections
sold in its outlet are well past season, past the point when local
stores may still be selling the merchandise. Yet, since manufacturers and stores work so far ahead of a season, almost
everything in the outlet is timely from a shopper's point of view.
Initially, new merchandise hits the outlet with prices reduced
35% off original retail; progressive markdowns take place as
needed. February and August are set aside for major end-of-
season sales; however, savvy shoppers make sure they're on
the mailing list so that they'll get invitations to other events
when an additional 30–50% is deducted from the lowest
ticketed price. (I still get a thrill when I recall the $112 I spent
on three pieces originally priced at $700 at one unadvertised
sale.) Sizes: Petite 0–12; Misses; 2–16; Plus sizes (expected
soon). Exchanges only within seven days.

Emeryville Outlet

4090 Horton Street, Emeryville. (510) 655-9578.
Spring and summer M–F 10–4; winter M, T, F 10–4. Cash/Check.
Parking: street.

You can call these fashions shifts, floats, dresses, sun dresses,
caftans, patio wear, cruise wear, or casual wear—anything but
muumuus! The comfortable, loose garments combine fabrics,
ribbon, and corded trims, use of patchwork, insets, bands, and
borders in 100% cotton and better cotton blends. Some
are dressy enough for entertaining, some casual and chic for
sunning on the deck of a cruise ship, while others are perfect
for around the house. Sizes: Petite through X-Large (4–20).
Prices at $14–$49 reflect an average of 50% or more off retail.
Sew-it-yourselfers will love the selection of leftover fabrics
in prints, stripes, and solids, in 45- and 60-inch widths, priced
at $2–$5/yard. Directions: Take the Powell Street Exit east from
I-80, turn right at Hollis Street. Follow Hollis to Park Street,
turn right, then turn left on Horton.

Evan Picone

Petaluma Village Factory Outlets, Petaluma.
(707) 769-1803. Daily. MC, VISA, AE. Parking: lot.

The scenario: You have a job interview and need a stylish but classic suit with a knee-length skirt or longer. An easy-to-maintain fabric that won't look haggard at the end of the day, plus a coordinating blouse in washable silk or polyester would be nice, too. You'll find it all and more at Evan Picone (the line has been a great favorite for many years with working women). The outlet is separated into miniboutiques to showcase its collections of career coordinates, suits, casual sportswear, dresses, coats, and fashion accessories. The current, first-quality fashions are introduced at 30% discounts, progressive markdowns follow. Add your name to the mailing list so that you won't miss any special sales. Beautiful store with accommodating size range! Sizes: Petite 2–14; Misses 4–16; Women's 14W–24W.

Executive Suite—Jones New York

Pacific West Outlet Center, Gilroy. (408) 842-2555. Daily.
MC, VISA, AE. Parking: lot.

Whether women or men walk in the door, they can walk out with a new suit. Women's suits start at $210 (retail about $370). Women can also pick up an ensemble (dress and jacket). There's always a few rounds of classy career dresses. The men's side has suits at $225 or two for $400, tuxedos for $250, more contemporary suits for $325, and blazers at $179. The quality, selection, and values make these suits a solid blue-chip investment. Sizes: Women's 4–16, Petite 2–14; Men's 38S–48L.

Group B

Great Mall of the Bay Area, Milpitas. (408) 946-2114. MC, VISA.
Parking: lot.

Recognize these labels?: Bonnie Strauss, Democracy, Freedom to Change, CPX by Mimi. Then you're probably twentysomething or thirtysomething and set on standing out from the crowd. You'll love this cache of trendy, sophisticated clothing that's worlds removed from the boring and blah. Each label has its particular look and addresses a particular need: daytime or weekend casual (many denim groups), daywear that can be worn into the evening, sophisticated dresses with feminine styling, jumpers, overalls, etc. I love the designers' use of interesting fabrics. Prepare to pay a little more for the pricier Bonnie Strauss line. Discounts average 35–50% off. Sizes 2–14.

Guess? Factory Outlet

*Outlets at Gilroy, Gilroy. (408) 847-3400. Daily. MC, VISA.
Parking: lot.*

A little of everything Guess? for teens and adults: discontinued,
seconds, and irregulars, resulting in 30–70% discounts. You'll
find great buys on Guess? shoes designed to complement
its apparel: Western boots, clogs, and clunky street shoes for
women and men. Large store, lots of energy: Guess? heaven
for the faithful.

harvé benard

*Pacific West Outlet Center, Gilroy. (408) 848-5152. Daily.
MC, VISA. Parking: pay lots.*

harvé benard is stocked with women's suits, coats, dresses,
sportswear, scarves, handbags, jewelry, and hosiery. Fashions
are always appropriately in-season, targeting upscale executive women ranging in age from early twenties to early sixties.
Prices (even at discount) are not inexpensive on the career-
oriented dresses, related separates, suits, and coats. Fabrics
are very nice on these updated classics. Discounts are 30-60%
off retail.

Hi Studio Outlet/Jonathan Martin

*Great Mall of the Bay Area, Milpitas. (408) 934-1550. Daily.
MC, VISA, AE. Parking: lot.*
(Other outlet: Pacific Grove center.)

Jonathan Martin makes clothes that are fashion-forward, yet
functional and well priced. They're a great favorite with
younger women, but any woman with the right mindset can
appreciate the styling. (Wardrobe designers from TV's *Melrose
Place* select these clothes for their stars.) You'll be lured by
all the possibilities—sets with palazzo pants or crinkle skirts,
special blouses, chic sweaters, slip dresses, stylish vests—and
styles that range from classy to sassy. Some groups handle
nine-to-five requirements with panache, others are perfect for
weekend parties and dates. Lots of rayons and silks. Discounts
are 30–50% off. Sizes: 3–13. Refunds and exchanges.

J. Crew

Outlets at Gilroy, Gilroy. (408) 848-1633. Daily.
MC, VISA, AE. Parking: lot.
(Other outlet: Napa center.)
A mixed bag of bargains, with some discounts so chintzy you'll
wonder if the company realizes that consumers expect savings,
other pricing and markdowns so good that they prompt a
grab-it-and-go response. All the merchandise at these outlets
is from J. Crew's catalog division, lagging behind by about two
catalog cycles. Discounts 20–70% off original catalog retails.
The women's and men's selections are equally balanced, with a
little of everything originally offered in the catalog. Attentive
staff and beautiful merchandising makes shopping a pleasure.
You've got ten days for exchanges or cash refunds.

J.H. Collectibles Outlet

Pacific West Outlet Center, Gilroy. (408) 847-4420. MC, VISA,
AE. Daily. Parking: lot.
The J.H. Collectibles factory store is beautiful, to fit its dress-
for-success offerings. The line is popular with many women
who appreciate quality and classic styling. Each year's additions
offer neutrals that relate to collections from previous seasons,
so it's easy to keep adding to one's J.H. wardrobe. Even though
each season's assortments look current, they are actually excess
from the year before. Discounts on most groups are about
33–40% off retail, to make the single- and double-breasted
blazers, executive coat-style dresses, suits, related separates,
sweaters, and silk blouses more affordable. While much of the
line is geared to career women, there's a solid inventory of
weekend-related separates. Sizes: Petite 2–14; Misses 4–16. No
cash refunds; exchanges within fourteen days (sale merchandise excluded).

Joan Walters Outlet

5886 Mowry School Road, Newark. (510) 623-7440.
M–F 10–7, Sat 10–6, Sun 11–5. MC, VISA, DIS, AE. Parking: lot.
Joan Walters sportswear and jumpsuits for women in all sizes
sell in mainstream department stores. The line is versatile,
but the quality on some groups may not measure up to the
standards of all shoppers. Although the company makes some
fairly nice apparel, the better stuff occupies less rack space at
the outlet. Most fashions are various blends of polyester, rayon,
and cotton. Prices likely result in many satisfied customers:

$14 on most styles of pants/slacks; poly/silk career blouses for $13–$15; jumpsuits at $15, $29, and $39; unlined jackets/blazers in a linen or shantung look for $12–$15; skirts at $13. Many pant and skirt styles are designed with elastic gussets at the waist for a more accommodating fit. Sizes: Petite 2–20; Women's 14–24 or 1X–4X; Misses 6–16. Directions: From 880, take Stevenson Exit west to Cedar and Duffel Plaza.

Jones New York Factory Store
Pacific West Outlet Center, Gilroy. (408) 848-1411. Daily. MC, VISA. Parking: lot.
(Other outlets: Jones N.Y. Factory Finale, Natoma Station; Folsom, Napa, and Petaluma centers.)
Career women need no introduction to Jones New York: beautifully made, simply designed career apparel, a staple in department stores. Discounts at its factory store are 25–35% off retail, not much better than a good department store sale, but the styles are all current, first quality, and top of the line. Get ready for your 9 to 5 routine or your weekend unwind with the Jones N.Y. Sport, JNY, and J.A.G. sport collection. For best buys catch the end-of-season sales. A very lovely store! Sizes: Petite 2–14, Misses 4–16. Exchanges allowed with receipt within ten days. Sacramento and North Bay women can shop conveniently at Factory Finale, the liquidation stores for the other factory stores around the country. Discounts here are an additional 40% on past-season merchandise—some way-past-season. Even so, the fashions fly out the door, many selected to complete ensembles started the year before. All sales final at these stores.

Koret of California Factory Store
Outlets at Gilroy, Gilroy. (408) 842-3900. Daily. MC, VISA, DIS. Parking: lot.
The Koret faithful will find 30–40% savings on current-season overruns, resulting in a $30–$50 price range. You can put together a nice ensemble from the collections of related separates in mainstream styles. Many fabrics are washable, even the wool jackets/blazers. Collections are geared for the office and weekend, but some are fancy enough for dressy occasions. At the other end of the spectrum, Koret offers very appealing

and more contemporary sportswear groups that teens and younger women will want to wear. The size range is most accommodating: Petite 4–16; Women's 16–26/28; and Misses 6–18. Exchanges only within 30 days.

L. Bates

Outlets at Gilroy, Gilroy. (408) 848-1311. Daily. MC, VISA. Parking: lot.
The accent is on contemporary—a melange of sleek, functional, body-conscious daywear that can be worn into the evening and weekend, beautifully made and simply designed. L. Bates has pegged the 25- to 35-year-old woman for its target market, and it's right on! A great resource for the Generation X shopper, with clothes you're likely to associate with TV's *Melrose Place* and *Friends*. A better line, usually sold through specialty boutiques or through the company's S.U.O. retail stores in Southern California. These are beautifully made, soft, unstructured styles in fabulous fabrics: rayons, silks, panne and stretch velvets, crepes, etc. Prices and discounts at 30–70% off retail will delight the budget-pressured, younger working woman. Great date and party fashions! Some chic career clothing, too. Sizes 2–14.

La Chine

Pacific West Outlet Center at Gilroy, Gilroy. (408) 842-1821. Daily. MC, VISA, AE, DIS. Parking: lot.
It's not easy to find a good selection of wonderful blouses— blouses that stand alone, that are flattering and essential for a working woman's career wardrobe. La Chine specializes in blouses and makes them under private label for department stores and for many well-known designer lines. The line is noted for its detailing (cuffs, pleats, stampings, buttons, etc.) and for its better-quality washable fabrics (prewashed silks, polyesters, and rayons in solids and prints). At the outlet most blouses are $24–$40, although holiday blouses may be higher. La Chine also makes career separates and some sportswear groups. The rayon/linen blazers ($79), skirts, and pants are just as classy as other well-known brands at half the price. Summer sportswear groups reflect the same attention to detail and style, offering mainstream customers many options for mixing and matching. Sizes: Misses 4–16; Plus 14–24. Exchanges and refunds within fourteen days.

Laura Ashley

Outlets at Gilroy, Gilroy. (408) 848-5470. MC, VISA. Parking: lot.
The Laura Ashley outlet is sure to please the fans of this
company. It's everything you would expect—lots of apparel
for women and children (dresses, hats, shoes, some wedding
fashions, etc.). These are past-season closeouts, some fairly
recent, and discontinued inventory from its home furnishings
and accessories division. It's a lovely store with discounts
ranging from 20–60% off retail. I particularly appreciate the
fabric, wallpaper, and trim selection priced at 50% off retail.
Buy all you need at one time, since whatever you buy may not
be there the next time you visit.

Leslie Fay Factory Store

Pacific West Outlet Center, Gilroy. (408) 848-4373. Daily.
MC, VISA, AE, DIS. Parking: lot.
(Other outlets: Folsom, Gilroy, Lathrop, Milpitas,
Vacaville centers.)
The Leslie Fay dress line is directed toward the mainstream
moderate- to better-price shopper. The company also produces
lines of related separates and career suits. Basic proportioned
pants and matching blazers are available for petites in sizes
6–16, Large sizes to 26. The career suit department is always
well stocked and very attractive. Look for top-of-the-line
Kaspar ASL suits and the more modestly priced Lc Suit label.
Lots of Leslie Fay dresses and feminine two-piece sets start
at $39 (past-season racks) and go up to about $79. Working
women should consider this a "best bet" resource for attractive career apparel at reasonable prices. Leslie Fay is a solid
resource for Petite, Large, and Misses sizes. Sizes: Petite 2–16;
Misses 6–16; Large 16–26; Women's 14W–24W. Returns within
fourteen days for merchandise credit only.

Liz Claiborne Outlet

Pacific West Outlet Center, Gilroy. (408) 847-3883. Daily.
MC, VISA, AE. Parking: lot.
(Other outlets: Napa, Tracy centers)
Everything Liz and more. A few other labels are taking up
space: Russ Togs, Russ Sport, Crazy Horse, Villager, and First
Choice (a Liz private label). About 60% of the inventory sold
in the outlet is marked down 30% off retail, the rest 40-50%
off. It's at least one season behind department stores and
has already gone through one markdown cycle. In-season

merchandise is usually excess from the year before; however, the stores are large and well stocked with Liz fashions for women and men. The handbag, hosiery, shoe, fragrance, and fashion jewelry departments are reasons to stop in if the apparel is not your preferred line. Petites are bound to be very pleased with their choices! I think the discounts are a little chintzy considering the status of the merchandise. Sizes: Petite 2–14; Women's 4–14; Large 14–22 (Elizabeth by Liz Claiborne).

Lucia
Factory Stores of America, Vacaville. (707) 451-2676. Daily. MC, VISA. Parking: Lot.
(Other outlet: Gilroy center.)
This line resembles Villager, Country Suburban, Pendleton, and other somewhat conservative lines; it's sold through major stores under private label. Lots of nice suits, blazers, sweaters, pretty blouses, skirts, pants, etc., all very feminine in lovely colors combined with nice prints. These are mostly career clothes, along with festive and fancy sets for dressier needs and nice collections of sportswear for the weekend. Posted signs note each week's discount, usually 40–50% off the tagged price. Prices range from $20 to $50. Sizes: Petite 4–16; Misses 4–16; Junior 3/4–15/16.

M.A.C. Sport Outlet
7049 Redwood Boulevard, #104, Novato. (415) 898-1622.
M–F 10–6, Sat 10–5, Sun Noon–5. MC, VISA, DIS, AE. Parking: lot.
M.A.C. Sport's line consists of preshrunk custom-dyed apparel, most in 100% cotton knits and wovens. Past-season styles are reduced about 50% below normal retail, with added discounts on seconds. These are California casual, related components designed for teens and for women seeking weekend or updated business wear. If you're comfortable in loose, drapey clothes, or want something with a little cinching to flatter the figure, you have options. Many styles are designed and made just for the outlet; others are seconds and overruns. At any one time, you'll have about eight different exciting colors to work with. You can mix and match from its one-size-fits-all in most tops, or S, M, L in other styles. You may not find every element of a complete ensemble. Fashions are priced $5–$55. Bring your daughters size Girls 4 through Preteen for good buys on the girls' collection. Directions: From 101 North, take the Rowland Avenue Exit, go west across overpass, turn right at first set of

stoplights onto Redwood Road. Turn left at Lamont (look for Redwood Chevrolet) and left again onto the frontage road. Drive to the end of cul-de-sac.

MCM Company Store
American Tin Cannery, Pacific Grove. (408) 648-8901. Daily. MC, VISA. Parking: lot.
This may be the smallest outlet at ATC, but it's also the best for upscale shoppers. MCM (a Germany-based company) has more than 250 boutiques in major cities around the world. MCM's leather goods—handbags and luggage—are sold here for 30% off retail (50% and more off on discontinued styles). The classic Signature Collection, that made MCM famous, features very functional coated linen-canvas with brass and leather details. It's a pricey line with many bags priced $400–$700 at retail and luggage pieces to $1,000. The best discounts are found on MCM's exclusive line of clothing bearing the label FCF (Florence Cromer Fashion). MCM defines the line as: "Designed for active, sophisticated women. Fashionable, yet practical clothing that could be worn for a variety of occasions, suiting diverse lifestyles that vary from casual to the most luxurious." It's a knock-out collection with beautiful fabrics, superb tailoring, and good construction as its hallmarks. Closeouts from its boutiques are reduced at least 50% off retail, but are often as much as 70% off original retail. Sizes 2–12. Tres chic!

Max Studio Outlet
Pacific West Outlet Center, Gilroy. (408) 842-3636. Daily. MC, VISA, AE. Parking: lot.
(Other outlet: Napa center.)
The Max Studio Outlet is for those who don't conform or play it safe and want to stand out from the boring and blah. You'll find contemporary sportswear, sometimes avant-garde and updated groups of career, casual, and day-to-evening fashions. The fabrics make the difference: Lycra blends in body-hugging groups with short, short skirts or shorts, stirrup pants, and sassy jackets or tops; soft crepes or double knits resulting in figure-flattering styles. The career groups stand out. Some groups have flowing pants or longer skirts, but each group usually features a short skirt for the woman with great legs. At the other end of the spectrum are the Max Studio Basics with baggy peasant dresses in rayon prints. Special Editions

of its most popular styles are made for the outlet. Prices are reduced about half on all past-season styles, but look around for extra specials and additional 30% discounts. Sizes 0–3 (fits 2–14). Exchanges within ten days on non-sale merchandise for store credit only.

Mishi

801 Delaware Street, Berkeley. (510) 525-1075.
M–Sat 10–5:30, Sun 11–5. MC, VISA. Parking: lot.
(Other outlet: 201 Western Avenue, Petaluma.)
Mishi is known for its contemporary, natural-fiber, garment-dyed sportswear line: "lifestyle" clothing that escapes being trendy without being dull. It's popular with sophisticated women who appreciate styles that camouflage midlife figure imperfections. The colors in the line change every season, providing the faithful with an excuse to buy something up-to-date. Mishi's stores devote half their space to showcasing current and recent styles at full retail prices, while the outlet half offers past-season closeouts and samples. Some very tempting fashions are sold from other popular ethnic and lifestyle casual clothing manufacturers—unfortunately at full price (although on sale from time to time). Outlet inventory at 50% off is priced at $15 to $45. The moderately priced fashion accessories sold here are not discounted but are carefully selected to go with the apparel. Sizes: S, M, L (4–14) and some XL (16).

Omai

1006 First Street (at Main), Napa. (707) 224-2100.
M–Sat 10–5:30, Sun 11–4. MC, VISA. Parking: street.
Omai is Napa's only locally manufactured line of apparel. However, bargains are not that easy to define since Omai has dropped its wholesale division and sells only through its studio outlet. The line is versatile, with carefree separates including leggings, palazzo pants, big shirts, long and short skirts, vests, dresses, and dusters priced from $5 to $50. The line is fun and appeals to a wide variety of women, from young mothers to gals with a few gray hairs. Some oversized styles serve as maternity wear, and many moms leave with something new for their infants and toddlers—the Omai kids' collection is made in sizes 6mos to 6X. Omai uses only natural-fiber fabrics, including 100% cotton interlock knits and jerseys, washable rayon challis, cotton denim, and chambray. Check closeout racks, where prices may be as much as 75% lower. Sizes S, M, L (fits 6–16).

Outback

2517 Sacramento, Berkeley. (510) 548-4183.
M–F 11–6, Sat 10–6, Sun noon–5. MC, VISA, DIS, AE. Parking: lot.
Outback manufactures fashion-forward, contemporary clothing whose most loyal customers are inventive women typically
30 to 50, although younger women are just as inclined
to embrace the look, which is achieved with original prints,
unusual fabrics (many knits), and design details. If you're
interested in an up-to-date, new image, explore the Outback!
You'll find seasonal overruns, discontinued styles, and samples
at 20–50% off original retail. (Some current fashions are not
discounted.) You'll also find funky costume jewelry as well as
children's clothing at good discounts. Check the racks of attire
from small manufacturers in the same fashion-forward out-
look, selling at modest discounts. Sizes S–XL (fits 4–14); some
Large 1X–3X.

Rampage Outlet

Great Mall of the Bay Area, Milpitas. (408) 934-0195. Daily.
MC, VISA. Parking: lot.
This is a place for very trendy buyers. Usually this means the
young, but in this case not necessarily. Rampage says its
customer is defined more by a state of mind rather than age.
Today's junior can be a girl in her teens or a woman in her
thirties. Rampage collections have grown into the essence of a
fast-moving, youth-oriented society, and they are bestsellers
in major department stores and in Judy's specialty stores. This
is the company's only outlet, and it's well stocked with very
recent and past-season collections—sportswear, accessories,
party clothes, lingerie, and dresses at 40–60% discounts. Other
labels add spice to the inventory (this is clearance from the
company's Judy's stores). Don't expect bargain prices on the
few racks in the front of the store that showcase the season's
new styles. Exchanges for store credit. Sizes: Girls 4–14; Junior
3–13. Note: There's killer music, so if you're thirtysomething
or more, don't go in without your earplugs.

Robert Scott & David Brooks

Outlets at Gilroy, Gilroy. (408) 847-3434.
Daily. MC, VISA. Parking: lot.
(Other outlet: Napa center.)

This company sells many groups under private label to national catalog companies and upscale specialty stores around the country, including Talbots. Most of the clothing is current season, sold at 30% discount (end-of-season closeouts usually 60% off on final markdowns). The look is classic, tasteful, and updated. The quality of fabrics and manufacture is first rate, accounting for the slightly higher prices than at many other factory stores. Spring blazers may be about $114, shorts about $42, and blouses $36. I love the career groups, casual coordinates, and extensive sweater collection. Soft and luxurious cotton cashmere sweaters come in classic styles. Other cottons in very appealing cardigan and pullover styles have designs and contrasting trims to coordinate with sportswear groups. Limited dress selection. Sizes: 2–18 or S–XL (few Petites). This store rates high for its beautiful, timely fashions and immaculate merchandising.

Spa Gear

Outlets at Gilroy, Gilroy. (408) 847-1033. Daily.
MC, VISA, AE, DIS. Parking: lot.

Before you take off for a cruise or warm-weather adventures at your favorite resort, allow time for a "get set" shopping haul at Spa Gear. This is an outlet for the La Costa Spa Catalog. The pages are filled with a glorious pastiche of style-charged fashions for the poolside, beach, decks, links, courts, and club rooms. You'll find action-oriented apparel that's geared for the toughest workout or the most leisurely activity; sets and ensembles that add sparkle to vacation days and nights; bathing suits for the svelte as well as suits designed with skirts and wraps to hide one's imperfections; plus shoes, sunglasses, caps, hats, and other goodies to pull a look together. Check the displays for some new goo—personal care products from its Spa line. Discounts 30–70% off retail. Sizes: Misses 6–3X. A real winner!

Swan & Swan Factory Sales

409 First Street, Petaluma. (707) 778-1133.
Occasional F and Sat sales 10-4. Cash/Check. Parking: street.
This Petaluma company manufactures women's T-shirts to be
worn as a fashion top rather than something to knock around
in. They are hand-embroidered in Mexico with clever, whimsical, or just-plain-pretty patterns. Some designs are romantic,
others have themes—resorts, animals, flowers, Western, etc.
Prices at retail are fairly steep ($40–$60), considering that
these are T-shirts, after all. At warehouse sales that occur three
to four times a year, all the T-shirts sold are seconds—most
with minute flaws that will not deter those bent on buying
gifts. Prices typically range from $16 to $20 for short- or
long-sleeved styles. Two sizes: S/M and M/L. Call or write to
have your name added to the mailing list.

Tom Tom Factory Outlet

5890 Christie Avenue, Emeryville. (510) 596-8288.
M–Sat 10–5:30. MC, VISA, DIS. Parking: street.
Tom Tom makes garment-dyed clothing in rayon, linen, and
100% cotton knits and jacquards. Some can go off to the office,
but most are casual, somewhat contemporary, and appealing
to younger women and their young-at-heart moms. At its
factory outlet, you can buy the irregulars off the $1.95 and
$3.95 racks and first-quality past-season overruns at 50% below
wholesale. The challenge is to find all the separates that can be
coordinated; otherwise you can combine colors and groups to
create your own look. Stock up on active or casual sportswear:
leggings, a short or long skirt, an oversized knit top, dresses,
and a one-size-fits-all duster. I also like the jackets and jumpsuits. Big T-shirts, some with collars, have unisex appeal. This
is a fun place for funky weekend clothes, more sophisticated
avant-garde styles for work, or everyday duds for teens. Some
bicycle shorts and tops for men. Sizes S, M, L. All sales final.

TSE Cashmere

Napa Factory Outlets, Napa. Phone: Pending. Daily.
MC, VISA, AE. Parking: lot.
This outlet is scheduled to open in late spring 1995. Expect to
find TSE's ultraluxurious classic and fashion-oriented cashmere
sweaters and sportswear for women and men at end-of-season
prices. Some cashmere silk and linen blends, plus very delicate,
superfine knits distinguish the summer collections. Note: TSE
is pronounced "say."

We Be Bop

1380 Tenth Street, Berkeley. (510) 528-0761.
M–F 10–5, Sat 10–6, Sun Noon–5. MC, VISA. Parking: street.
We Be Bop fashions have pizazz! They're made from natural fibers, usually cotton or rayon. The batik fabrics are distinctive, an interplay of prints and patterns combined in most garments using unique colors. The owners develop the designs in collaboration with Balinese craftspeople. Some garments are straightforward, others so clever you almost need a manual to figure out how to tie or wrap them. In any case, women with an individualistic sense of style embrace the look. Large-sized women are not overlooked and can wear the styles with great panache. We Be Bop also offers an extensive collection for juniors and girls; the free-spirited women who buy the adult line will probably love outfitting their daughters in these original fashions. Prices are discounted about 30% off retail (ranging from $20 to $80), sometimes more on way-past-season closeouts. As offbeat as this line may sound, it shows up in some pretty mainstream stores. Sizes: S, M, L; one-size-fits-all; Large sizes to 4X; Toddler to Preteen.

Weavers Factory Outlet

2570 Bancroft Way, Berkeley. (510) 540-5901.
M–Sat 10–7, Sun 11–7. MC, VISA, AE. Parking: street.
(Other outlet: 587 Castro Street, San Francisco.)
Cal students cross the street to grab budget-priced "leftovers" at Weavers. The line is 100% cotton, garment-dyed, preshrunk sportswear. At the outlet, almost everything is marked down 40–60% since this is where you'll find discontinued styles and colors (thirty-eight new colors each season). Teens and women can find separates in skinny, tight leggings, short tube skirts, roomy coverup tops, jumpsuits, and dresses. Colorful basic T-shirts at $5 (seconds) are popular with women and men, and fellas can find active sportswear (bike shorts, unitards, drawstring pants, etc.). Most prices $5–$30. Overcut sizing fits S–XL.

Also See

Under San Francisco's Factory Outlets and Off-Price Stores:
Byer Factory Outlet; Esprit Factory Outlet; Georgiou Factory Outlet; Go Silk Outlet; Isda & Co. Outlet

Under Chain Discount Stores:
Casual Corner Outlets

Under Men's Sportswear:
Boston Traders Outlet; Izod/Gant Factory Store; N.E. Wear

Under Leather Apparel:
Snyder Leather Outlet

Under General Clothing:
B.U.M. Equipment/Coliseum; Eddie Bauer Outlet Store; Geoffrey Beene; Jordache Factory Store; Levi's Outlet; Polo/Ralph Lauren Outlet Factory Store; Royal Robbins Factory Outlet; Woolrich

Under Shoes:
Joan & David/A Step Forward; Timberland

Other Bay Area Off-Price Stores

These are good to excellent local resources for fashion discounts; circle those in areas where you frequently shop. Their size and selection vary greatly, indicated by the space I give to each listing. Before visiting a store for the first time, call to make sure it's still in business at the same address with the same hours.

Bali Dreams Outlet

595 Bridgeway, Sausalito. (415) 332-3537. Daily 10–6 (some seasonal variations). MC, VISA. Parking: street.
A reliable resource for resort and vacation fashions. Approximately 98% of its merchandise comes from Bali, which means fashions a little different, with unique fabrics and fabrications (batiks, ikats, rayons, cut work). It sells importers' excess inventory at nice discounts. Why Not, Surya, Satyuga, Papillon, Kulit, Dunia, and Synergy are some of the labels you'll find on jammed racks. These styles, once exotic, are now so mainstream that almost everyone finds them appealing. Sizes: Petite to XXXL.

Designers' Club

3899 24th Street, San Francisco. (415) 648-1057. Daily 11–6:30 (closed Mon in January). MC, VISA, AE, DIS. Parking: street.
This unique discount outlet is run by local designers: Audrey Daniels sells updated fashion jewelry, handknit sweaters, and leather belts; Prisca Bonati imports trendy Italian purses, belts, handknit sweaters, and sportswear with flair; Cia Van Orden offers casual elegance in sportswear and career fashions made

of natural fibers. Other treats: fashions and accessories from Pappillon, Bila, What's in Store, Pilot, Michael Alexander, Kohli, Chava, Barganza, and Gado-Gado. Modest 20–30% discounts are better than none at all.

Inga's

3195 Danville Boulevard, Alamo. (510) 837-1123. M–F 9:30–5:30, Sat 9:30–4:30. MC, VISA, AE. Parking: lot.
Inga, a former model who knows the fashion biz inside and out, buys all her fashions in New York—from showrooms, manufacturers, and reps. Dealing with smaller designers and companies with names you may or may not know, she chooses styles that are up-to-date without being trendy, styles that appeal to sophisticated women with multifaceted lifestyles and that address the relaxed side of glamour. This is a great place to shop for a sophisticated cruise wardrobe. Quality combined with value are Inga's goals. There's a little of everything: after-five (some mother-of-the-bride dresses), elegant daytime, some weekend and casual sportswear, star-status sweaters, and a few career suits. Buying right allows her to pass on savings that average 40% off retail on current-season merchandise. Most suits or two- or three-piece ensembles range from $159 to $279. I coveted the silk blazers marked down to $245 from $395. Inga's can't be all things to all people, but the woman who resists being a department store clone will love this place. Inga's service—akin to that of a personal shopper—is thrown in for free. Sizes 4–14 (some 16s). Directions: From 680, take Alamo Exit west. Turn left at Danville Boulevard, go about half a block to The Courtyard; store is located behind the popular Courtyard Cafe.

Madelle's

Diablo Plaza Shopping Center, 2415 San Ramon Valley Boulevard, San Ramon. (510) 820-7751.
M–Sat 10–6, Th until 8. MC, VISA. Parking: lot.
Madelle's produces every season! A pleasing mix of women's sportswear, sweaters, occasional soft sets for dressier daytime needs, and hanging-out-on-the-patio clothing, at 20–40% off. Sizes 4–14.

Marika

1797 Solano Avenue, Berkeley. (510) 524-0500.
M–Sat 10–6, Sun Noon–5. MC, VISA, AE. Parking: street/pay lots.
This jammed off-price boutique offers an eclectic selection
from Action Wear, Rated R, Freewear, Melrose, Rialto, Leon Max,
Johnny WAS, and other contemporary sportswear makers, with
silk blouses for Saturday nights, related separates for the office,
and casual fashions for campus. The samples of in-season
merchandise deserve the closest scrutiny for the chic-minded,
and end-of-season closeouts and special markdowns fit student
budgets. Marika enjoys a loyal following of East Bay women.
Save 30–50% on sizes 4–14.

Raffia

2175 N. California Boulevard, #205-A, Tishman Center,
Walnut Creek. (510) 937-0232. M–F 9–5; Xmas season:
call for Sat hours. MC, VISA. Parking: lot (validated).
Raffia is located on the mezzanine of an office building in
Walnut Creek's "golden triangle" next to BART. It's convenient
for all the office workers in the area and is a source of discount
prices on well-known sportswear lines. You'll find women's
sportswear and sweaters, men's active and casual sportswear,
plus a small selection of fashion and sport shoes, handbags,
watches, even some tennis equipment. It's "roulette" shopping
at its best!

Ragsmatazz

622 Clement Street, San Francisco. (415) 221-2854.
M–Sat 10–6, Sun Noon–5. MC, VISA. Parking: street.
(Other stores: Malson's Ragmatazz, 2021 Broadway, Oakland;
899 Howard, San Francisco.)
Ragsmatazz provides a fun, colorful, fairly current selection of
junior-oriented and contemporary fashions (including some
surprising labels). Discounts are 40–60% off retail. If you love
trendy junior styles, you'll want to check out the new shipments frequently. Moms and sisters can buy clever and cute
sportswear for younger girls (sizes 12mos to Girls 14—best
selection at Clement Street store). Sizes: Junior 1–13; Women's
4–16. Exchanges are allowed up to seven days after purchase
with receipt.

Sandy's—The Unique Boutique

3569 Mt. Diablo Boulevard, Lafayette. (510) 284-2653.
M–F 10–6, Sat 10–5:30. MC, VISA. Parking: lot.

Sandy's gets a high rating. Sandy has the magic touch at selecting upscale, intriguing women's apparel for discriminating customers. This has been a secret source for many local women. The store is so beautiful, you'll feel that you're shopping in a very special boutique and, once initiated, you'll return again and again. Although Sandy's caters to the up-to-date mature woman, younger women will find fancier dresses for parties, proms, and weddings. Regulars grab the Dennis Goldsmith, Arthur Max, Wild Rose, MZM, Laundry, Componix, CPX, Jonathan Martin, Nina Picalino, Bonnie Marx, Barbara Barbara, and other lines of dresses, related separates, sportswear, and jumpsuits. Sandy buys lots of wonderful fashion jewelry, hats, handbags, and watches. You'll see discounts of 30–50% off retail, and everything is current. Sizes 2–18 (a few 20s). If you're willing to go a little out of your way to seek out Sandy's (next to the chic Tourelle Restaurant), you won't be disappointed.

Chain Discount Stores

Many of these stores have been around so long and are so familiar that Bay Area shoppers hardly need any introduction to them. They consistently offer a good product mix for consumers who appreciate shopping close to home.

Casual Corner Outlets
Great Mall of the Bay Area, Milpitas. (408) 956-9640. Daily. MC, VISA, AE, DIS. Parking: lot.
(Other outlets: Petaluma, Tracy, Vacaville centers.)
Stores from the new outlet division of Casual Corner have been popping up all over like mushrooms on a wet lawn. Business is good, too! The "outlets" (seventy-three around the country) carry the same categories of merchandise that one might find at its full-priced mall stores, but there is a difference. The outlet division has its own buyers committed to finding merchandise that conveys the "Casual Corner" image, but at a more affordable price. You won't find anything originally sold through its regular stores. Even so, the values were very good on all the casual weekend apparel groups, career and soft dresses, related separates, suits, blouses, outerwear and some very special fashion sweaters. Everything is first quality, in-season, and priced at 20–60% off comparable retail. In spring '95, linen blazers at $50 and linen-rayon blend pants at $34 were great buys. Sizes: 4–16.

Clothestime

2026 El Camino Real, Mervyn's Plaza, Santa Clara.
(408) 984-7863. M–F 10–9, Sat 10–6, Sun 11–5.
MC, VISA. Parking: lot.
(There are fifty-three stores in Northern California.
Call (800) 775-8000 for locations.)
Teens and college students love the inventory and the fun and
lively ambience of this chain, while its diversity also appeals to
the 24- to 34-year-old career woman. It's a good source of teen
styles at very low prices. Returns, exchanges, or cash refunds.

Dress Barn

1670 S. Bascom Avenue, Hamilton Plaza, Campbell.
(408) 377-7544. M–F 10–9, Sat 10–6, Sun Noon–5.
MC, VISA. Parking: lot.
(Other stores: fourteen in greater Bay Area —
refer to Geographical Index for location nearest you.)
The selection here is dedicated to a clearly defined target
customer (career women aged 18–40). Besides career apparel,
you'll find a very nice dress line and activewear department:
coats, bathing suits, and accessories. Sizes 3/4–16. Dress Barn
tries to maintain a small inventory of petite suits. Most
discounts are approximately 25–35%; clearances and special
promotions up to 50% off.

Hit or Miss

2226 Shattuck Avenue, Berkeley. (510) 644-3888.
M–F 10–8, Sat 10–6, Sun Noon–6. MC, VISA, AE, DIS.
Parking: pay garage.
(Other stores: twenty-one in greater Bay Area —
refer to Geographical Index for location nearest you.)
Hit or Miss sells stylish work and weekend apparel at value
prices. You'll find an in-depth selection of dresses, weekend
sportswear, related separates, all-weather and wool coats,
suits, dresses, blouses, jackets, and fashion accessories. Savings
usually 20–50% off retail; sizes 3/4–13/14 (rarely 16s). Good
service, good savings, tasteful merchandising, and convenience—
a winning combination. Refunds and exchanges.

Loehmann's

75 Westlake Mall, Daly City. (415) 755-2424.
M–F 10–9, Sat 10–7, Sun Noon–6. MC, VISA. Parking: lot.
(Other stores: Sacramento; 222 Sutter, San Francisco;
San Ramon; Sunnyvale.)

Loehmann's is the original off-price fashion store, with a solid reputation for designer and couture lines at discount prices, covering all the basics and then some: cocktail, dressy, in-between, career apparel, coats, swimsuits, activewear, sportswear, shoes, and accessories. If you can spot designer clothes without a label, you'll recognize fashions from many status designers. Prices are guaranteed at least 33% off retail, and there is a reliable quantity always priced at 50% off. The Sutter Street store excels in its selection of career apparel. Exchanges for store credit within seven days. Sizes 4–16 with a few racks of Plus sizes and a fair selection of Petites.

Studio Five

1247 Marina Boulevard, Marina Square, San Leandro.
(510) 483-9245. M–F 10–9, Sat 10–7, Sun 11–6. MC, VISA, DIS.
Parking: lot.
(Other stores: eleven in greater Bay Area —
refer to Geographical Index for location nearest you.)

I love these stores for what they are! Any preteen, teenager, or young woman can come in with $25 and leave with a new outfit. While many separates are priced about $8, nothing is over $25! I'm impressed by such cute styles at such low prices. They aren't the best made, but they're not junk. Occasionally you'll see name brands (closeouts from mall stores). Sizes S, M, L (fits 3–14). Exchanges only.

Westport Ltd.

Factory Stores of America, Vacaville. (707) 449-0833. Daily.
MC, VISA, AE, DIS. Parking: lot.
(Other outlets: Anderson/Shasta, Folsom, Lathrop, Milpitas,
Pacific Grove centers.)

Westport Ltd. offers a well-rounded, always-current selection: ascending in quality and price, you'll find career suits, lovely daytime go-to-lunch-or-meeting dresses, sophisticated career dresses, and separates. Discounts are 20–50% off, maybe more on frequent in-store unadvertised specials. Sizes 4–16. Returns, exchanges, and refunds.

Women's Accessories

Charisma (Mail Order)

115 112th Avenue North, Suite 614, St. Petersburg, FL 33716. (800) TRY-HOSE. MC, VISA, C.O.D.

If you're fed up with spending too much money replacing pantyhose, call Charisma, the U.S. distributor of a Canadian line. Though the difference between the U.S. 15-denier standard and Charisma's 20-denier hose may seem negligible, it makes a world of difference in terms of wear. Washing: Just throw the hosiery in a mesh bag and run it through your washing machine and dryer. Charisma's prices are an extra incentive. You must buy its one-size Regular (90–155 pounds) sandal foot by the dozen—select any combination of twenty colors. Price (March 1995): $33/dozen. Other sizes available by the dozen and individually: Tall (140–190 pounds); control-top Regular or Tall; Princess (180–210 pounds); and Queen (225+ pounds). More expensive special groups of opaque and maxi-support hosiery can be ordered individually, knee-highs by the dozen. Your pantyhose by the dozen will arrive in a plain plastic bag to keep prices down. Charisma also has a network of sales representatives around the country who buy at lower-than-mail-order prices and make a few bucks on each pair sold. Get details or place orders using Charisma's 800 number.

Designer Brands/Accessories

Factory Stores of America, Vacaville. (707) 449-8106. Daily.
MC, VISA. Parking: lot.
(Other outlets: Anderson/Shasta, Folsom, Gilroy,
Pacific Grove centers.)

Stop in for the "extras" to fill the spaces in your jewelry chest
and dresser drawers. You'll save a minimum of 40–50% every
day on costume jewelry from the 1928 Jewelry Co., Kenneth
Jay Lane, Catherine Stein, Jody Coyote, and Roman. Look for
famous-maker handbags and small leather goods; Fossil and
Seiko watches at 50% off; sunglasses; Buxton wallets; men's
jewelry; scarves; hair accessories; jewelry boxes; picture frames;
and more. Solid discounts on gold chain, Italian Sterling silver,
and Langstrom's Black Hills gold.

Icing Outlet

Outlets at Gilroy, Gilroy. (408) 847-1212. Daily.
MC, VISA, AE, DIS. Parking: lot.

With 100 stores nationwide, surely you've shopped at one
of The Icing stores. At the outlet, you can signal your fashion
savvy by picking up a new accessory to set off your outfit.
Belts, fashion jewelry, scarves, handbags, hair accessories, and
apparel collections are all priced at least 25% off retail. Look
carefully for each week's red-line special for an additional
35–50% off discounts. The apparel is out of the ordinary and
can add an element of the exotic to your wardrobe. Party
clothes with extra dazzle and glitz are available all year round.
Contemporary styling and distinctive fabrics and prints prevail
on the sets, blazers, sweaters, and resort collections. Fun store!

Socks Galore & More

Factory Stores of America, Vacaville. (707) 448-2420. Daily.
MC, VISA, DIS. Parking: lot.
(Other outlet: Folsom center)

You want socks, you got socks! You'll find socks for everyone
in the family. Over 60,000 pairs of designer brand socks (with
and without labels) are sold for 20–80% off retail. Whatever
your size or needs, you've got options. Money back guarantee.

Successories

152 Reina Del Mar (on Highway 1), Pacifica. (415) 359-0260.
Daily 11–5. Cash/Check. Parking: street.

This eclectic selection of fashion jewelry, belts, hats, handbags, hair accessories, clothing, scarves, and other fancies show-cased by a sales rep for Bay Area designers is worth the trip. Most jewelry pieces are contemporary, collectible, and qualify as artwork. The prices are surprisingly affordable ($6–$150), especially at the 30–60% discount offered by the rep. The artists/designers include Famous Melissa (jewelry made from computer chips and components), Dessini (rubber handbags), Paula Lerner's (pearls), Spinoso (scarves), and several others. It's artistic and unusual. Look for the little red caboose that houses this gem.

Sunglass City

568 San Anselmo Avenue, San Anselmo. (415) 456-7297.
M–Sat 10–5:30, Sun 10–5. MC, VISA, AE. Parking: street.

If you're serious about sunglasses, Sunglass City is the place to go. The folks here are specialists who can give you all the technical information you need to make an intelligent choice. You'll find top brands like Ray-Ban, Vuarnet, Revo, Serengeti, Armani, Persol, Hobie, Ski Optiks, and Suncloud 15–40% off retail. Ray-Bans are always 30% off list. Vuarnets are dis-counted 15–20%. If you're like me and only buy glasses you can afford to lose, check the inexpensive lines, $3.95–$20.

Totes Factory Store

Factory Stores of America, Vacaville. (707) 449-8707. Daily.
MC, VISA. Parking: lot.
(Other outlets: Anderson/Shasta, Pacific Grove centers.)

Women and men can poke around here and come up with treasures so inventive, clever, and practical that it's hard to leave without a tote of some kind. Check the selection of rain-wear for women, children and men, ranging from lightweight to heavyweight. Plus, there are umbrellas in all configurations, duffel bags, lightweight luggage, sunglasses, portfolios, note-books, and more goodies to solve many gift-giving occasions. A universally popular store!

Also See

Under Women's Apparel/Fashion:
Most sections

Under Cosmetics and Fragrances:
Most listings

Under Handbags and Luggage:
Most listings

Under Shoes:
Most listings

Women's Accessories

Petites

Many stores in all clothing categories may have a small
selection of Petite sizes; you can find them at Loehmann's,
Marshall's, Dress Barn, Aileen, Anne Klein, Donna Karan, Joan
Walters, Adrienne Vittadinni, Koret Factory Stores, Lucia, Liz
Claiborne, J.H. Collectibles, Leslie Fay, Chaus, Lilli Ann Outlet,
Jones New York, Westport Ltd., Carole Little, Robert Scott &
David Brooks, Ross Dress for Less, T.J. Maxx, Burlington Coat
Outlet, Nordstrom Rack, and Emporium Capwell Clearance
Center. The selections range from two to three racks to whole
sections of a store or outlet specifically devoted to Petite
customers. Check the Store Index for the page numbers of
these stores.

Petite Sophisticate Outlet
Petaluma Village Factory Outlets, Petaluma. (707) 763-8097.
Daily. MC, VISA, AE, DIS. Parking: lot.
(Other outlet: Great Mall, Milpitas.)
At last! At last! Petites are likely to go absolutely wild when
they spot all the great buys at this outlet. There's a slew of
terrific fashions to cover all a Petite needs. Career suits, active
wear (or spectator) casual weekend collections, dresses, related
separates, sweaters, and accessories. A division of Casual Corner,
the company has won a loyal following of diminutive women
with its specialty stores. While the merchandise in the outlets
does not come from its full-price retail division, the same image
is conveyed. Discounts are from 20–50% off retail on comparable merchandise, averaging about 40%. Fashions are in
season and first quality. Make a splash with less cash if you're
5'4" or under and wear sizes 2–16. Refunds and exchanges.

Large Sizes

All the More to Love (Consignment)
2325 Alameda Avenue, Alameda. (510) 521-6206.
M–Sat 10–5. Cash/Check. Parking: street.
A tiny consignment shop where a few better-quality like-new dresses or ensembles show up. Otherwise, it's a fairly middling collection. Good prospects for women in transition up or down the scale.

Casual Corner Woman
Great Mall of the Bay Area, Milpitas. Phone: (408) 934-9788.
Daily. MC, VISA, AE, DIS. Parking: lot.
Just like the petites who shop Casual Corner's Petite Sophisti-cate Outlets or the misses size women who shop Casual Corner Outlets, women sized 14–24 can find well-priced collections of casual sportswear and career apparel at Casual Corner Woman. The company does a very nice job of selecting stylish, main-stream fashions that are appropriately in season. Ensembles, related separates, sweaters, some dresses, and small groups of extra-fancy special-occasion fashions are ready for the taking.

Dress Barn Woman/Westport Woman
1660 S. Bascom Avenue, Hamilton Plaza, Campbell.
(408) 371-7730. M–F 10–9, Sat 10–8, Sun 11–6.
MC, VISA, AE, DIS. Parking: lot.
(Other Westport Woman outlets: Folsom, Gilroy,
Milpitas, Vacaville centers.)
Dress Barn Woman and Westport Woman are worthwhile destinations for all large size ladies. Their selection of depart-

ment store brands in large-sized fashions at 20–50% off retail
is impressive. In December, you'll find dazzling holiday dresses;
in summer, vacation wear. Everything—coats, jackets, swimwear,
sweaters, casual weekend garb, active wear, and accessories—
appears very current. Sizes: 14–24 (a few 26s), or 1X–3X.
Exchanges and cash refunds are available within fourteen days.
How nice!

French Vanilla Factory Sales

101 Townsend Street, Suite 230, San Francisco. No phone.
Seasonal sales. Cash/Check. Parking: street.
These are very nice contemporary related separates, career
apparel, and some spiffy coats. Three to four times a year,
French Vanilla gathers up all its past-season overruns and
holds a Saturday sale where prices fall well below wholesale
($15–$200), since the only goal is to get rid of the leftovers.
Send a postcard addressed to the above address for your sale
announcement.

Full Size Fashions

Factory Stores of America, Vacaville. (707) 447-9505. Daily.
MC, VISA, DIS. Parking: lot.
(Other outlet: Anderson/Redding center.)
Since Full Size Fashions is dedicated to addressing the "whole
woman," you'll find lingerie (panties, bras, girdles), sleepwear,
bathing suits, coordinated groups of sportswear and career
fashions, dresses, separates (jeans, sweaters, tops, et al.), and
cover-ups, all discounted 30–50% off original retail. This isn't
a resource for expensive designer label apparel at discount;
its lines are moderately priced at retail. Young women, career
women, and even silver-haired senior ladies can find fashions
for their lifestyles. Sizes: dresses (full and half sizes) 16–32;
tops 36–60; bottoms 30–54. Exchanges only within two weeks.

Harper Greer

580 Fourth Street, San Francisco. (415) 543-4066.
M–Sat 10–6, Sun Noon–5. MC, VISA, AE, DIS. Parking: street.
Large size career women will find better quality and good
design at Harper Greer. Since 1989 it has sold all its designs
exclusively through its company store; it delivers sophisticated
clothing in silk, wool, cotton, and better synthetics in chic and
updated styles. Career coordinates, dresses, and a tempting
selection of separates for workdays and weekends will keep

you going in and out of the dressing rooms. Dresses range in price from $69 to $249 (executive boardroom dress); jackets in several lengths and career blazers range from $96 to $229. Obviously, the higher prices are equal to fine-quality wool, silk, or linen. Sizes 14–26 (depending on style or cut many fit larger sizes). Tailor on premises for quick alterations.

Making It Big

9595 Main Street, Penngrove. (707) 795-6861.
M–Sat 10–5:30, Sun Noon–5. MC, VISA, AE, DIS. Parking: lot.
Catalog requests to: 501 Aaron Street, Cotati, CA 94931.
This company fills a special niche in the large size marketplace. It manufactures garment-dyed, 100% cotton dresses, and sportswear in sizes 32–72. Catalog prices usually range from $30 to $60 on its sportswear separates. It's a crossover line, going from work to weekend wear. At its large store it sells current-season fashions at retail prices, plus a small selection of seconds and past-season merchandise discounted 20–40% off retail. Get on the mailing list for its semiannual blowout sales. Directions: Take the Penngrove Exit off 101 (just past Petaluma), turn right, and go about 1½ miles.

Seams to Fit

6527 Telegraph Avenue, Oakland. (510) 428-9463.
M–F 11–6, Sat 10–6, Sun Noon–4. MC, VISA, DIS. Parking: street.
Seams to Fit is in part the clearance center for Says Who, a large size specialty store. It also connects with manufacturers to buy seconds and overruns, which it sells for discount prices alongside consigned merchandise. If you're planning a career change but can't afford a new wardrobe, if your body size has changed, or if you just want to buy clothing at affordable prices, you'll want to pick through the racks. The consigned clothing may have a bit of history, but they're still pretty fresh, or they would not have been accepted for resale. You'll find seconds and overruns in new fashions from Chez, Synchronicity, Red's Threads, August Silk, We Be Bop, and Says Who private label fashions plus any and all major brands on consignment. Located between Alcatraz and Ashby.

Sizes Unlimited
1809 Willow Pass Road (Park and Shop Center), Concord.
(510) 825-2022. M–F 10–9, Sat 10–7, Sun Noon–5. MC, VISA, AE.
Parking: lot.
(More than twenty Northern California stores.)
Sizes Unlimited has updated and improved all its full size fashions. Women of all ages find attractive sportswear, career apparel, lingerie, sleepwear, and outerwear at pleasing prices. Weekly promotions keep bargain hunters happy and "card holders" get special discount coupons. Sizes 14–32. Returns and refunds allowed.

Also See

Under San Francisco's Factory Outlets and Off-Price Stores:
Byer Factory Outlet; Cut Loose Factory Outlet; Fritzi Factory Outlet; Gunne Sax/Jessica McClintock Outlet

Under Other Bay Area Factory Outlets/Factory Stores:
Adrienne Vittadini Direct; Aileen Stores, Inc.; Chaus Factory Outlet; Evan Piccone; Joan Walters Outlet; Koret of California Factory Store; Leslie Fay Factory Store; Liz Claiborne Outlet; Lucia; We Be Bop

Under Lingerie, Sleepwear, and Robes:
San Francisco Mercantile

Under General Clothing:
Burlington; Marshall's; Ross; T.J. Maxx

Under Clearance Centers:
Emporium Capwell Clearance Store

Lingerie, Sleepwear, and Robes

Barbizon Factory Outlet

Factory Stores of America, Vacaville. (707) 447-0482. Daily. MC, VISA, DIS. Parking: lot.
(Other outlets: Folsom, Gilroy, Lathrop centers.)

For sheer savings, embark on what will be the first of many pilgrimages to any of the beautiful Barbizon Outlet stores. You'll find truly sweet discounts on this fresh and lovely selection of current, first-quality sleepwear and lingerie: batiste gowns, matching peignoirs, featherweight flannels, and cuddle-skin nightgowns and pajamas. The supporting cast includes bras, panties, teddies, camisoles, terry robes, tap pants, and slips. Discounts are 50% off original retail, even greater on special promotions and end-of-season clearances. Each spring brings Jantzen bathing suits, and Vanity Fair robes grace the racks before the holidays. Sizes range from Petite to XL, although the biggest selection is in S, M, L. Bras range from 32 to 42DDD. Occasionally, you'll find Lady Barbizon in sizes 1X–3X. Exchanges or refunds anytime.

Bernard Bernard & Co.

1525 Tennessee Street (at 26th), San Francisco. (415) 550-1188. M–F 9–4. Occas. Sats 9–3. Cash/Check. Parking: street.

Stay in any posh hotel and chances are you'll be wrapping up in a Bernard robe. You know the kind: plush, heavy, usually white, in thirsty terry cloth, maybe with a logo—the kind you're tempted to steal. They're typically one-size-fits-all, although Bernard also makes oversized robes, hooded robes, and some in vibrant colors. You can buy irregulars (very minor flaws) for wholesale prices (about $25); first-quality oversized robes are about $33 or $50. Bernard is usually open weekdays all year round; call for Saturday hours.

Farr*West Factory Outlet

294 Anna Street, Watsonville. (408) 728-0880, (800) 848-7891. M–F 10–4. MC, VISA. Parking: lot.

It may be a drive, but once there you'll find 66–75% reductions on briefs, half slips, full slips, camisoles, wraps, panties, garter belts, and chemises. These are samples, discontinued styles, and irregulars priced $4–$23 at 60–75% off retail. Farr*West produces fine lingerie collections in woven goods: polyester "taffe-crepe," stretch charmeuse, crepe georgette, cotton batiste, and a very high quality noncling woven polyester charmeuse. Sizes: P–XL, slips 32–40. Directions: Take the Airport Exit from Highway 1. The first street is Westgate, turn right, then left on Anna.

Josef Robe Outlet

510 Third Street, #550, San Francisco. (415) 546-5722. M–Sat 10–4. MC, VISA. Parking: street.

This is for those who have no qualms about spending a little more for quality. Josef Robes makes luxury robes for hotels and for the general public. Retail robes are sized by height and circumference to insure a proper fit for all body types. There are numerous styles, including both wrap robes and pullover robes in 100% cotton in basic white or fashion colors. These are expensive for velour or terry cloth robes, often selling at retail for $100 and up. First-quality robes are sold for a 20% discount, but pick up a second and you'll save at least 50%— that means as little as $30 on a short white kimono-style terry robe, or about $45 on a logo robe from the Ventana Resort or The Inn at Spanish Bay. Many seconds priced $40–$80. Note: In February 1996, the company will be moving to a new location in the same area.

L'Eggs, Hanes & Bali

Factory Stores of America, Vacaville. (707) 449-4243. Daily. MC, VISA. Parking: lot.
(Other outlets: Folsom, Gilroy, Lathrop, Milpitas, Petaluma, Pacific Grove centers.)

From the name you can assume that you'll find pantyhose, knee highs, lingerie, men's underwear, Isotoner gloves, thermal underwear, socks, and children's underwear and socks. These are closeouts or slightly imperfect goods (usually nonconforming colors). Sizes to 50DD bras for women and undershirts in XXL and Tall for men. The variety in Bali lingerie is gratifying. Larger gals will be particularly pleased with the panty selection that goes to size 13. Savings 20–60% off original pricing. Returns and refunds.

Lily of France

Outlets at Gilroy, Gilroy. (408) 847-4044. Daily.
MC, VISA, AE, DIS. Parking: lot.
(Other outlet: Milpitas center.)
Lily of France, Christian Dior, Sara Beth, and Carol Hochman labels can be found on the lingerie, foundations, designer sleepwear, robes, and lounge wear here. You'll be enticed by the sheer savings on the beautiful gowns, peignoirs, teddies, etc. These feminine, delicate, saucy, and sexy bras and panties may bare a lot, but the savings are far from skimpy. Savings are 30–70% off retail, although Lily and Dior bras and panties are always 50% off. Of course, the submarine discounts are only found on irregulars. Exchanges possible on some garments. Sizes: Petite to Large; bras, Teen size to 44DD; gowns and robes for big women.

Lingerie Factory

Great Mall of the Bay Area, Milpitas. (408) 262-5755. Daily.
MC, VISA, AE, DIS. Parking: lot.
This East Coast chain with more than 30 stores sells name-brand lingerie and sleepwear for everyday discounts of 20–60%. Lily of France, Lilyette, Warner, Christian Dior, St. Eve., and Olga are some of the brands that should strike a responsive chord with women. Bra sizes 32AA–42DD.

Maidenform Outlet

Factory Stores of America, Vacaville. (707) 451-1211. Daily.
MC, VISA, ATM. Parking: lot.
(Other outlets: Gilroy, Pacific Grove, Tracy centers.)
At Maidenform you'll find bras (32–42DD, also full-figure), camisoles, tap pants, full slips, bustiers, half slips, garter belts, sleepwear, and lounge wear in Regular and Queen sizes. The lingerie ranges from basic to elegant in fashion colors and dependable neutrals; also sleepwear and robes designed for good-looking comfort. Discounts are 25–70% off.

Nap Outlet

Petaluma Village Factory Outlets, Petaluma. (707) 766-8081.
Daily. MC, VISA, AE. Parking: lot.

This is truly a manufacturer's outlet—you'll love it, I promise. Lovely fabrics, interesting textures, great prints and colors, and wonderful styling all add up to a collection of sleepwear, robes, and lingerie that's exceptional in every way. This is a great place to choose your next "reward." The line, which is sold in upscale stores, is quite a departure from the frilly, filmy, and fancy (often chilly and impractical, too) sleepwear that's been around for ages. Instead, there's a contemporary, comfortable, and cozy look and feel to most sleepwear groups. (You may never quite make it out of some of the thermal knit groups and into your daywear if you're having a day at home.) Loved the terry velour robes, pajama and robe sets, sleepshirts, and gowns—in fact, everything designed for slumber. The men's corner is equally impressive, with silk or polyester boxers, flannel or cotton kimonos in great paisleys or masculine prints and colors. The lingerie collection goes off in another direction with alluring bodysuits and camisoles in panne velvet, lace blouses and camisoles, everything designed for a sophisticated woman in mind. Almost everything is 100% cotton. Prices are nicely discounted (about 30% off) to take the sting out of this pricier line. Additional discounts on occasional irregulars and featured specials. Sizes: S–L, 1X–3X.

Olga/Warner's Outlets

798 Blossom Hill Road, #7–8, Kings Court Shopping Center,
Los Gatos. (408) 356-9047. M–F 10–6, Sat 10–5, Sun 11–4.
MC, VISA. Parking: lot.
(Other outlets: Vacaville, Folsom, Gilroy centers.)

The selection of Olga's discontinued and irregular styles in nightgowns (sizes Petite–38), panty girdles, pajamas, panties (sizes 4–10), bras (sizes 30A–44DDD), slips, camisoles, bodysuits, and lovely peignoir sets designed for the bride is very impressive. The discounts range from very modest to sensational. The staff is always ready to assist with measurements and fitting if requested.

San Francisco Mercantile

2915 Sacramento Street (off Divisadero), San Francisco.
(415) 563-0113. M–Sat 10-6, Sun Noon–5. MC, VISA.
Parking: street.

This is a boutique-style outlet for San Francisco's most famous sleepwear manufacturer; its four different lines start with the most expensive Queen Anne's Lace, made from imported fabrics. Next, Eileen West's better sleepwear, primarily in cotton in Misses sizes and a separate collection for Large sizes. Eileen West S.F. is the modestly priced line. Everything here is irrepressibly feminine whether it's old-fashioned and romantic or contemporary. Your savings start at about 30% off retail, but you save about 50% and up to 80% during quarterly blowout sales. Nightgowns, robes (velvets, terrys, cottons), and pajamas can be found year-round. Sizes: Petite to Large; Large sizes to 3X. Look for a few racks of Eileen West dresses—romantic, updated, and sometimes sensual—in sizes 4–14. Occasionally, you'll find bed linens and other accessory items. Very nice outlet; the parking isn't. You'll circle and circle!

Also See

Under Clearance Centers:
All listings

Under Fabrics:
Thai Silks

Under General Clothing:
Burlington Coat Factory; Marshall's; Ross; T.J. Maxx

Under Late Additions:
Off Fifth

Maternity

Coming Attractions

1435 Santa Rosa Avenue, Santa Rosa Center, Santa Rosa.
(707) 573-9779. M–Sat 10–6, Sun Noon–5. MC, VISA, AE, DIS.
Parking: lot.
This little boutique-type outlet must make North Bay shoppers very happy. The owner sells end-of-season closeouts and over-runs on sportswear, dresses, jumpsuits, sleepwear, jeans, etc. at nice discounts (30–40% off retail) from sixteen major mater-nity lines. These are moderately priced brands for the most part; some better lines, too. You'll find nice discounts on Fit for 2, a locally made line with no elastic waists, and modest discounts on bras and accessories. Sizes: Petite to XXL, or 4–18.

Dax & Coe Maternity Factory Outlet

935 El Camino Real, Menlo Park. (415) 327-4371.
M–F 10–6, Sat–Sun Noon–5. MC, VISA. Parking: street.
This line has been worn by the Duchess of York and Melanie Griffith. Its success is easy to understand, since it's fabricated in 100% cotton knits and includes a wonderful sweater group that will still be wearable after the baby comes. The outlet is wonderful, with samples, prior-season merchandise, and sec-onds in groups of coordinates, some career and casual dresses ($15–$50), tops ($10–$50), shorts, pants, skirts ($10–$35), and nonmaternity sleepwear designed by Jane Tise ($15–$40). Prices are 40–75% off original retail. Sizes: 4–14 or S, M, L.

Fashion After Passion (Consignment)

1335 Park Street, Alameda. (510) 769-MOMS.
M–Sat 10–6, Sun Noon–4. MC, VISA, AE, DIS. Parking: street.
To add a few pieces to your temporary maternity wardrobe,
Fashion After Passion offers good buys; it's packed with sportswear and separates. Better dresses and career apparel are
in short supply and don't last long. All sizes in lines that were
originally moderately priced. The full line of undergarments
and bras to 46H are in good supply but not discounted.

Maternity Works

Outlets at Gilroy, Gilroy. (408) 847-7560. Daily. MC, VISA, AE.
Parking: lot.
(Other outlet: Petaluma center.)
If you're set on maintaining a professional image and putting
on the ritz through the ninth month, or you just want to
look your best when your waist grows to 44 inches, then make
the trek to Maternity Works. Owned by The Mothers Work
(including Mimi specialty retail chain and Maternité catalog),
this is the best maternity outlet I've found yet, with satisfying
discounts and markdowns (30–75% off), a stylish selection
of apparel for all occasions, and quality that should meet the
requirements of the most discriminating shopper. About 50%
of the merchandise is past-season closeout inventory from
its regular stores, and the remaining selection is a collection
designed for its outlet division offered at special value pricing.
The private label outlet merchandise measures up in every way
to the regular lines. The company designs and manufacturers
almost everything in the United States, but a few outside
lines are carried (bras, panties, pantyhose, etc.). This is a great
resource for professional women! I loved the inventory of past-
season holiday fashions, the many styles of jumpsuits and long
split-skirt dresses, the one-piece slip skirt (top with any jacket),
the denim collection, cotton cashmere knit tops and pants,
and many nursing style fashions. Overall, a nice mix of traditional and contemporary fashions (under the Mimi label).
Sizes: Petite to XL.

MOM (Maternity Center of Marin)
874 Fourth Street, San Rafael. (415) 457-4955. M–Sat 10:30–5.
MC, VISA, DIS. Parking: street.
You'll want to hit the racks here for consignment clothing that
encompasses all categories of maternity apparel. Don't miss
the new apparel (past-season overruns) at nicely discounted
prices. Good selection of necessities for the nursing mom.
Directory of baby furniture and equipment for sale, too. Sleep
well after picking up a Prego pillow. Consignments accepted
anytime!

Motherhood Maternity Outlet
Factory Stores of America, Vacaville. (707) 446-4792. Daily.
MC, VISA, AE, DIS. Parking: lot.
Motherhood Maternity's leftover and surplus inventory from
its 200 stores is very current and beautifully displayed. The
modest 20% discounts on very current fashions are better
than none at all, but you'll have to watch for end-of-season
markdowns to get gratifying 50% discounts. The selection
reflects the complete "cover" Motherhood offers for expectant
moms: lingerie, sleepwear, swimsuits, sweaters, sportswear,
dresses (career and dressy), jumpsuits, pantyhose, etc. Sizes:
S, M, L (occasionally some XS and XL). Exchanges or store
credit within thirty days, but no refunds.

Natural Resources
4081 24th Street, San Francisco. (415) 550-2611.
M–F 10:30–6, Sat 10–5. MC, VISA. Parking: street.
As a resource center for pregnant women and new families,
Natural Resources offers classes, a reference library, health-
care products, breastfeeding supplies and more. You'll also
find closeouts and overruns of new maternity fashions and
consignment maternity apparel. Nice discounts on the new
merchandise; consignment prices for shoestring budgets.

Also See

Under General Clothing:
Burlington Coat Factory; Marshall's; Ross; T.J. Maxx

Bridal, Wedding, and Formal Wear

Bridal Outlet

4409 Piedmont Avenue, Oakland. (510) 653-2877.
T–Sat Noon–5 (appointments preferred). Cash/Check, AE.
Parking: street.
You can buy right off the rack at the Bridal Outlet. The owner
buys sample gowns, closeout inventories from other salons,
and liquidated inventories from stores that have gone out of
business. These gowns are priced about half off original retail,
with the average price at $350, but generally ranging from
$199 to $600 (representing moderately priced lines). Occasionally, a few high-end gowns in silk show up on the racks, but
most gowns are made from synthetics with elegant beading
and lace adornments. You can also rent a gown for half the
sale price—even have it altered. About a third of the selection
is devoted to previously worn or vintage gowns priced at
$99–$499. Many of these are from the 1940s, '50s, and '60s.
Occasionally, a sample gown may be a little tired from many
try-ons, but it's priced accordingly. Restoration is another service offered for brides who need to have Mom's gown updated
or altered. Best size range in 8–12, but dresses available in
sizes 4–20.

Bridal Veil Outlet

124 Spear Street (2nd Floor—rear), San Francisco.
(415) 777-9531. M–Sat 10–4. Cash/Check. Parking: pay lots.
Here you'll save at least 20–50% off retail on samples and
discontinued headpieces and veils for brides and bridesmaids.
Prices range from $45 to $145, while retail prices would be

more like from $150 to $300. You'll find veils in informal to cathedral lengths, and headpieces in tiara, crown, bandeau, juliet, wreath, pillbox, and other styles. Many have exquisite beading and appliqués on fabrics that include silk shantung and satin. You'll find accessories like ring bearer pillows, gloves, guest books, etc. Special orders and custom designs are available, but at strictly "custom" prices.

Bridal Warehouse

625 Second Street, #218 (bet. Brannan and Townsend), San Francisco. (415) 882-4696. M–Sun 10–5, Closed Wed. MC, VISA. Parking: street.

The Bridal Warehouse is a new type of bridal store, stocking gowns in a complete size range for purchase off the rack. Some gowns are made overseas and imported by companies advertising in bridal magazines. In spring 1995, most gowns were in shiny synthetic fabrics, heavily beaded, and very ornate. Prices ranged from $300 to $600 on average (some lower, some higher priced). Two racks held higher-quality samples of special-order gowns (prices reduced about 15–20% off retail). Before shopping at a "warehouse" store, visit a few bridal shops first to get a feel for quality and price. Sizes 2–20 in stock. Bridesmaid dresses are 15% off when at least three are ordered. Check the racks for prom dresses and good values on beaded mother-of-the-bride dresses. You can special order many gowns shown in Modern Bride or Bride's magazine at a discount price (unlikely for gowns priced $1,200 and more).

Cheryl T's

3215 Stevens Creek Boulevard, San Jose. (408) 244-5158. M–Th Noon–8, Fri Noon–6, Sat 10–5, Sun Noon–4. MC, VISA. Parking: lot.
(Other store: 1148 San Carlos, San Carlos.)

At Cheryl T's sample sizes range from 8 to 12, and when these gowns are discontinued they are sold for 50% off the original price. Closeout racks have really low prices on discontinued sample bridesmaid and mother-of-the-bride dresses. Most of these dresses are a little tired! New bridal gowns can be special ordered from samples—tagged with manufacturer's name, retail price, discount price of 10% if ordered with a 50% deposit, and 20% discount price if ordered, and paid for in full, five months in advance. These gowns, currently advertised in bridal magazines, include Demetrios, Ilissa, Alfred Angelo,

Bill Levkoff, Watters & Watters, Jordan, Princess, Jasmine, Bianchi, Joelle, and Jim Hjelm. You may not find all these brands' styles, but you can special order. Samples of bridesmaid dresses offer the same applied discount rate. And bring the fellas along for new tuxedos sold or rented at discount prices.

Clarissa II

1821 Mt. Diablo Boulevard, Walnut Creek. (510) 256-0450.
W, F, Sat 10–5, T, Th 10–8. MC, VISA. Parking: street.
Brides-to-be in sample sizes (6–12) will have a happy time at this clearance backroom for the upscale Clarissa Bridal Salon. Since Clarissa specializes in high-end gowns from Priscilla, Galina, Bianchi, Diamond Collection, Fink, Ilissa, and others, discount prices of 25–70% off original retail may still elude some budgets. At retail the collection is priced from $800 to $3,600; at clearance prices, from $350 up. The more expensive gowns use elegant silk fabrics and extraordinary laces and beading. The discounts vary according to how long the gown has been on the rack and its condition. Finally, headpieces and bridal veils are available in the outlet at 25–50% off original retail. Alterations done for a fee.

Discount Bridal Outlet

300 Brannan Street (bet. Second and Third streets),
San Francisco. (415) 495-7922. M–Sat 10–5, Sun 11–5.
MC, VISA. Parking: street.
You won't find the elegant salon feeling of most bridal shops here; its no-frills, no-glamour, close-to-tacky decor keeps prices down. But if you covet gowns in the $250–$1,000 range at retail, you're a good candidate for the selection. Of course, dresses at more modest prices are available, too. Discounts are about 20% off retail, but may be more since many salons take a higher markup. You can buy right off the rack for a wedding on Saturday. Other dresses may be ordered for delivery in a week or two, or at most two to four months. Discontinued styles may be discounted as much as 50% off retail, while fluffy petticoats are 20–30% less than salon prices. I spotted a few dogs, but in order to get the best styles, the owner sometimes has to take a loser. The same discounts apply to gowns for bridesmaids and flower girls, or a dress for a prom or a quinciñera. Large selection of gowns in sizes 4–42 (off the rack or special order).

Elan

5890 Mowry School Road, Newark. (510) 623-7440.
M–F 10–7, Sat 10–6, Sun 11–5. MC, VISA, AE. Parking: lot.
A very nice discount store connected to the Joan Walters
Outlet, Elan stocks many dresses for daytime and social occasions. You can count on an attractive selection of mother-of-
the-bride dresses, beaded dresses (also beaded two- or three-
piece sets), dressy suits, and some bridal fashions (for second
weddings) in velvets, crepes, chiffons, brocades, shantungs,
silks, etc. at 25–50% off retail, priced at $70–$130. Also prom
dresses all the time at parent-pleasing prices! Petites (2–14)
and Large sizes (16–24) get a fair shake, too. The quality on
most of these dresses is very satisfying—a good quality/price/
value ratio. Directions: From 880, take Stevenson Exit west
to Cedar and Duffel Plaza.

He-Ro Outlet

Great Mall of the Bay Area, Milpitas. Phone: (408) 934-9582.
Daily. MC, VISA, AE. Parking: lot.
The main attraction here is the glittering selection of scene-
stealing after-five fashions from Black Tie, Oleg Cassini, Nite-
line, and Roufogali. Elegant beaded and sequined dresses,
evening suits with beaded trim, party pants, full-length and
street-length heavily beaded gowns, and little strapless dresses
with jackets are always on hand. Mothers of the bride or
groom may even find a knockout dress or suit. Prices are discounted 30–70% off retail (averaging about 40%). At that,
a dazzling full-length heavily beaded dress may range from
$300 to $650, a shorter version from $225 to $400. If you find
a dress you love, but it's not available in your size, it can be
special ordered for delivery in five to seven days. Note: Protect
your investment. Don't leave without obtaining a referral to a
nationwide cleaning service that specializes in beaded formal
wear and wedding gowns. The service is easy to use with an
800 number and UPS shipping.

Another facet of this store is the section (about 20%) devoted
to classy sportswear and sophisticated daytime wear: Kenar,
Regina Porter, Terry Jon (suits), Halsey (vest, sweaters, and
blouses), and Carryback (linen blouses). European-inspired
dresses and suits set you apart from the conventional Talbots'
customer while Schraeder Sport offers traditional dresses for
the more conservative woman. Sizes 4–18.

New Things Rack

410 Town & Country Village (Stevens Creek and Winchester),
San Jose. (408) 241-8136. M–F 11–7:30, Sat 10–6, Sun 1–5.
MC, VISA, DIS, AE. Parking: lot.

New Things Rack has two different aspects. First, sample
bridal, prom, and formal wear from its main store, at modest
to maximum discounts. Bridesmaid dresses start at $19.99,
bridal gowns from $99, and prom dresses generally from $29–
$59. Clearance racks of formal wear (some mother-of-the-
bride and cocktail dresses) are always reduced a minimum of
60%, many 80%. Naturally, you'll find some forlorn fashions
on the racks, but also some real beauties. Second, New Things
West, its main store across the parking lot, isn't a bargain
resource but offers the most extensive and exciting selection
of prom and party dresses anywhere. If you have a prom or
formal occasion upcoming, this store will save you endless
shopping. The selection includes a very nice selection of
mother-of-the-bride dresses and will solve most women's
after-five requirements. The "new" bridal department at New
Things covers the spectrum, with gowns priced for every
budget, including some very elegant and expensive gowns.
There are gowns available off the rack in sizes 6–26. Any
sample is available as a special order. Note: The more expensive sample closeouts of bridal gowns are sold from the main
store instead of The Rack.

Wedding Trunk

3084 Claremont Avenue, Berkeley. (510) 547-7343.
W–F Noon–6, Sat, Sun by appt. MC, VISA. Parking: street.

If you don't have your mother's dress to wear, then wear
someone else's mother's dress. The Wedding Trunk sells a very
intriguing collection of wedding gowns from every decade of
this century. The oldest gowns are really special, even though
they are often in very small sizes. The selection changes
almost weekly and may be quite lean at times. To keep the
racks filled, new sample gowns are carried—some discounted,
some at full retail. This is a small boutique-style shop but
worth a visit if you're looking for something a little different.
Some special styles for mothers of the bride, second-time
brides, and informal weddings.

Rental and Previously Worn

Formal Rendezvous

118 South Boulevard (south end of B Street), San Mateo. (415) 345-4302. By appt. T–F Noon–6:30, Sat 10–5. MC, VISA, AE. Parking: street.

At this boutique-style salon crammed with beautiful fashions, those needing a wedding, cocktail party, formal, or semiformal dress have a good chance of finding a real dazzler. It may be a showstopping beaded and sequined formal, tea-length lovely or cocktail dress, even a basic black cocktail dress. The selection provides options for women of varying ages and style orientations, in sizes 4–20. Most designer dresses and bridal gowns come with status labels like Bob Mackie, Sho Max, Oleg Cassini, Demetrios, and Victor Costa. To allow the staff time to give you the personal service and attention you may require, appointments are preferred.

Once Worn Gowns

901-A Irwin Street (corner of Third Street), San Rafael. (415) 485-5550. M–Sat Noon–6 (closed Mon in Nov/Dec). MC, VISA, Lay-aways. Parking: private lot off Third Street.

If you have a hard time justifying the cost of a new bridal gown or the money just isn't there to buy one, then consider the alternative offered by Once Worn Gowns. This upstairs boutique specializes in selling once-worn gowns placed on consignment by women in the area. In the selection of approximately 200 wedding gowns, there are many styles and no single look. You may find a gown you've admired in a bridal magazine, a custom-made gown, or a gown originally sold off the rack.

The goal is to satisfy the needs of a diverse clientele. The largest selection is found in the $200–$500 range, which represents a savings of at least half off retail. The more expensive designer gowns, originally priced $1000–$3000 at retail (many in beautiful silk fabrics), come in frequently but usually sell quickly. Another plus—there's no guesswork involved. What you see is what you get. When selecting a gown from a bridal salon, often the sample you try on is much too big or too small, requiring you to "guess" that it will be perfection when delivered in the right size. I particularly liked the selection of bridal veils and headpieces priced $30–$150. Also, shoes, petticoats, bras, a good selection of bridesmaid dresses (occasionally even four or five matching gowns), some mother-of-the-bride dresses, junior bridesmaid dresses and flower girl dresses. Sizes 2–30. Alterations can be handled by a resident seamstress and bridal designer. This woman is also available to make custom wedding gowns of your own design or using one of her original sample designs as inspiration (these were very nice). The other side of this business may appeal to any recent bride (or member of the wedding) who may want to turn her dress into cash. Consignees receive 50% of the selling price.

Also See

Under San Francisco's Factory Outlets and Off-Price Stores:
Gunne Sax/Jessica McClintock Outlets

Under Chain Discount Stores:
Loehmann's

Under General Clothing:
Burlington Coat Factory

Under Late Additions:
Off Fifth

Men's
Sportswear

Arrow Factory Store
Factory Stores of America, Vacaville. (707) 451-3720. Daily.
MC, VISA. Parking: lot.
(Other outlets: Folsom, Lathrop, South Lake Tahoe centers.)
Arrow shirts come in these labels: Fairfield, Kent, Dover,
Brigade, and Bradstreet. Neck sizes 14½–18½, sleeves
32/33–36/37. Great prices! Frequent promo racks at $7.99,
$9.99, and $12.99; others $16–$22. Also a very nice casual
and mainstream selection of sportswear, especially Arrow's
River Brand. Fill in with belts, ties, socks, briefs.

Boston Traders Outlet
Outlets at Gilroy, Gilroy. (408) 842-3454. Daily.
MC, VISA, DIS, AE. Parking: lot.
Boston Traders' beautiful handknit sweaters are distinctive
and relatively expensive, bestsellers in status stores. Recent
and current styles of in-season merchandise with discounts of
30–40% off retail add up to a winning combination of price,
value, and selection. Men will like the sportswear: long-sleeved
shirts, and casual pants in cotton, linen, or wool. Everything
here reflects a commitment to quality. Women can spend
equally on classic sportswear collections. Sizes: Men's S–XL,
waists 30–40; Big and Tall sizes too!

California Big & Tall

822 Mission Street (bet. Fourth and Fifth streets), San Francisco.
(415) 495-4484. M–Sat 10–6, Th until 7, Sun Noon–5.
MC, VISA. Parking: Fifth and Mission Garage (pay).

Everything sent to California Big & Tall is initially marked down at least 20–40% off retail; some racks add up to 60% and more. The bargains are usually past-season styles and include suits, sportcoats, sweaters, wool and poly/wool slacks for workday and weekend clothing. Some basics like underwear and belts are not discounted. Sizes: suits 46–60 Reg, Long, and Extra Long; shirts to 20-inch neck, 38-inch sleeve. A small shoe selection to 16 Medium, 15 Wide. As at most clearance centers, not everything is wonderful, but there are many good-quality buys. Alterations extra; all sales final.

Champs Sports

Great Mall of the Bay Area, Milpitas. (408) 956-0771.
MC, VISA. Parking: lot.

Whether you're a fan of the NBA, NFL, or NHL, or you want to sport your favorite university or college logo, you have a good chance of finding something to broadcast your loyalty at Champs Sports. However, 49er and Raider logos are seldom found. Save 50% on past-season styles of apparel (tanks, tops, sweats, outerwear, wind or jog suits, shorts, etc.) and about 20–50% off on discontinued styles of athletic shoes. Current merchandise is regular retail price, although there are always promotional racks and specials posted around the store.

Colours by Alexander Julian

Factory Stores of America, Vacaville. (707) 448-8396. Daily.
MC, VISA, AE, DIS. Parking: lot.
(Other outlet: Pacific Grove center.)

Men can go upscale and high style here with this discriminating selection of sportswear, pants, sweaters, socks, and ties, etc. in beautiful colors and patterns. Love the quality and the discounts that start at 30% off retail on most current-season groups and reach 60% off retail on end-of-season closeouts. Sizes: S–XL; 30–40 waists. Refunds and exchanges within ten days.

Izod/Gant Factory Store

Outlets at Gilroy, Gilroy. (408) 847-1448. Daily. MC, VISA, AE, DIS. Parking: lot.
(Other outlets: Anderson/Shasta, Truckee, Vacaville centers.)
It's been years since the Izod logo set you apart, but the line is still appealing and much desired. Golfers in particular love the Izod Factory Store, where I spotted the classic "links" cardigan and many styles of pullovers, twill and cotton/linen slacks, shorts, shirts for any weather or season, and accessories, all at 20–50% discounts. Izod's smaller sportswear collection for women particularly appeals to a more mature and mainstream customer. Sizes: S–XXL, some Big and Tall sizes. Refunds and exchanges within sixty days.

John Henry & Friends

Pacific West Outlet Center, Gilroy. (408) 848-1777.
MC, VISA, DIS. Parking: lot.
(Other outlet: Monterey center.)
Naturally you'll find John Henry shirts (a popular department store label), but also Thomson slacks, several collections from Nino Cerruti, and a colorful selection of ties from Perry Ellis and Liberty of London. Men can break out of the executive mode with a whimsical "theme tie." This is another excellent resource for men with merchandise nicely presented and prices nicely discounted. Sizes: shirts 14½–17½, sleeves to 34/35; pants to 42. Exchanges and cash refunds.

N. E. Wear

96 Townsend Street (off Second Street), San Francisco.
(415) 357-1002. M–Sat 10–6. MC, VISA, AE. Parking: street.
What happens when two former professional football players, both savvy and enthusiastic, join forces with a former fabric designer of the Polo/Ralph Lauren home collection? An innovative, classy, and irresistible line of casual and active sportswear called N. E. Wear. It's a line with a European attitude, an outdoor feel, and an American appeal. The fabrics are the stand-out factor in this line: sherpa fleece with great textural interest; soft, cotton, flat-back rib knits; double-sided polar fleeces; sanded twills and interlock knits; and wide-wale corduroys. One cruise through the racks and women will start thinking gifts—gifts their fellas will actually wear. Along with the wonderful fabrics, the quality is evident in the construction, which is why the line is sold at better men's specialty

stores and most upscale department stores (including Barney's N.Y.). Also, it shows up in classy resorts like La Costa, Pebble Beach, Grand Teton Ranch, and the Sonoma Mission Inn, as well as the Sundance catalog. Plan on spending $27–$35 and you can pick up a cozy and comfortable top in several styles— a simple crew neck pullover, a five-button pullover, a shirt jacket, or a mock turtle just for starters. A range or stadium coat in sherpa fleece may set you back about $60—a real bargain, everything considered. Action pants with gathered and button cuff at $30 (good for biking or climbing), sport-shirts, lightweight jackets, shorts, fleece caps, polo-style shirts, and hooded tops are some of your other style options. Prices on these past-season styles, overruns, samples, and occasional irregulars are 35–50% off original retail. Sizes: Men's S–XL.

N. E. Wear's new line, designed expressly for women, is accentuated by great buttons, accent stitching, soft sanded or brushed fabrics (great knits and rayons), and prewashed linen. Related separates offering fashion with function include short boxy jackets, longer stadium-style coats, vests, body-conscious tops and body suits, palazzo pants with pockets, leggings, and other styles. Some dresses are loose and drapey like the printed rayon peasant styles, while the svelte, body-skimming knit dresses suit the contemporary dress code. Sizes: Women's XS–L. All sales final. This outlet gets a high rating.

Nautica Outlet
Napa Factory Stores, Napa. (707) 252-3992. Daily.
MC, VISA, AE, DIS. Parking: lot.
This is the consummate headquarters for the sailing crowd. It's true that some men may find Nautica's prices steep at retail, but that's directly related to the quality of its well-made line and the quality of its fabrics. You'll get some price relief with discounts that average about 35% off retail. A $76 sweat-shirt that looks as good a year later as the day you bought it will set you back about $48; a casual $300 jacket (perfect for cold days out on the Bay) may be reduced to $200 or $149 on special end-of-season racks. The store is done up with taste and style, the better to showcase the classic, clean lines of Nautica's first-quality pants, shorts, shirts, sweaters, jackets, sweats, and all the other bits and pieces. Sizes: S–XL (with accommodating athletic cut).

Robert Talbott Factory Outlet

The Village Center, Carmel Valley. (408) 659-4540.
M–Sat 10–5:30, Sun Noon–5. MC, VISA, AE. Parking: lot.
The next time you're visiting Carmel, take a ride out to the
Robert Talbott Factory Outlet. You'll save at least 50% on fine
ties that typically retail for $42–$80. Many have minute to
major flaws like slubs in the fabric, wrinkles, and pulled threads.
Prices are discounted accordingly. Frequent in-store specials
feature ties as low as $5. Also, fabulous buys on elegant dis-
continued fabrics such as silks (all types), wool challis, and
fine cottons. The shirt selection has been expanded. Both the
shirts and shirt fabrics are in demand because of the superior
quality of the cotton fabric and the high thread count. Don't
overlook the good deals on cotton shirts, bow ties, cummer-
bunds, and pocket squares. Directions: From Highway 1, take
Carmel Valley Road 13 miles to the Village Center; turn right
at the Texaco station.

Van Heusen Factory Stores

601 Mission Street, San Francisco. (415) 243-0750.
M–F 8–8, Sat 9–6. MC, VISA, DIS. Parking: street.
(Other outlets: Folsom, Gilroy, Lathrop, Milpitas,
Napa, Petaluma, Vacaville centers.)
The Van Heusen Factory Group comprises over 400 off-price
stores selling Van Heusen and other labels directly to the
consumer. You can always find dress shirts in dozens of fabri-
cations in regular and European (slim) fits, sizes 14½–17.
You'll also want to browse through racks of casual sportswear
for both men and women, geared for traditional tastes.

Windsor Shirt Company

Factory Stores of America, Vacaville. (707) 453-0146.
MC, VISA, AE, DIS. Parking: lot.
(Other outlet: Gilroy, Napa, Petaluma, Tracy centers.)
The focus is on men's dress shirts. Stick with the basics (pin-
point cottons at $29.99) or for "Friday wear," break loose
with patterns, stripes, casual fabrics, and bold colors oriented
toward a contemporary look. Casual sportswear groups of
shirts and pants are mainstream. Better than most at sizes:
necks to 18½; sleeves to 36/37. Nice selection in shirts and
ties for that big and tall guy (lots of XXL in sportswear).

Also See

Under San Francisco's Factory Outlets and Off-Price Stores:
Designer Co-Op; New West Design; Bill's Sweater Outlet

Under Other Bay Area Factory Outlets/Factory Stores:
Cape Isle; Executive Suite; Guess?; Evan Picone; Donna Karan; J. Crew; American Eagle

Under Other Bay Area Off-Price Stores:
Raffia

Under General Clothing:
Big Dogs Sportswear; B.U.M. Equipment; Burlington Coat Factory; Eddie Bauer; Geoffrey Beene; Jordache; Levi's Factory Store; London Fog; Pacific Trail; Pangea Outlet; Polo/Ralph Lauren Factory Store; Royal Robbins Factory Outlet; Woolrich

Under Children's Clothing:
Bugle Boy Outlet

Under Shoes:
Timberland

Under Appliances, Electronics, and Home Entertainment:
Whole Earth Access

Under Sporting Goods:
All listings

Under Late Additions:
Off Fifth

Men's Suits

Afterwards

1137 El Camino Real (at Santa Cruz), Menlo Park. (415) 324-2377.
M–Sat 10–6, Th until 8. MC, VISA. Parking: street.

Afterwards is a consignment store offering an intriguing selection of new and used men's suits from upscale stores: every day some Polo by Ralph Lauren and occasionally status labels like Brioni, Mani, or Armani. Since the owners have good industry connections, men will find new "samples" from Robert Talbott and Ferrell Reed (ties), Alexander Julian, Trafalgar (belts), J. Aboud (sweaters), and others. Afterwards also takes new excess inventory on consignment. New merchandise is marked at about 50% off retail; consignment inventory is about 75% off original retail. Prices are $100–$400 plus. The women's half of the store is equally impressive, with better labels. These folks obviously refuse more than they accept for consignment.

Ballerini Italian Clothing

3680 Northgate Drive, Northgate Mall, San Rafael.
(415) 499-8812. M–F 10–8, Sat 11–7, Sun Noon–5.
MC, VISA, AE. Parking: lot.

Beware, not all suits sold as "Italian" are actually made in Italy. The real thing, Ballerini's suits range in price from $398 to $550, sportcoats from $95 to $225. These ~~[CLOSED]~~ well-known Italian makers: Zanetti, Luigi ~~[CLOSED]~~ gone, and others. Very nice quality in li~~[CLOSED]~~ wool slacks and silk blends ranging in price from ~~[CLOSED]~~ to $128. Ballerini also imports stylish men's wool-blend sweaters with novelty prints and designs. Sizes: 36–56 (Short, Regular, and Long) in suits; 28–40 in pants; 14½–17½ in shirts; and S–XL in sweaters.

Brooks Brothers Factory Stores

Outlets at Gilroy, Gilroy. (408) 847-3440. Daily. MC, VISA, AE. Parking: lot.

(Other outlets: Petaluma, St. Helena centers.)

Brooks Brothers career clothing appeals equally to men and women, with dependable basics and fine quality. Prices are discounted about 30% on average, with extra point-of-purchase markdowns to 50% off on selected groups every day. The company has expanded its sportswear: casual slacks, shirts, and sweaters. Pick up some essentials—ties, pajamas, socks, belts, and more. Sizes for men: 36 Short to 48 Long and Extra Long; dress shirts from 14 (32-inch sleeve) to 17½ (36-inch sleeve). I loved the women's career clothing—suits, separates, and silk sets and dresses. Returns within thirty days with receipt. No alterations.

Clothing Broker

5327 Jacuzzi Street, Richmond. (510) 528-2196.

F 10–7, Sat 10–6, Sun 11–5. MC, VISA. Parking: lot.

(Other stores: 3280 Victor Street, Santa Clara, (408) 748-7637; Sacramento.)

The Clothing Broker stores are located in industrial parks, are open only three days a week, and use minimal advertising: a successful formula for very low pricing. Each store is well stocked with suits and sportcoats in sizes 36S to 60 Regular. In Spring 1995 navy blue blazers were $109; most suits ranged from $99 to $179 (international collections from Begair, Lebus, and others to $269). All-wool tuxedos were $169. The company buys directly from manufacturers or manufacturers' reps and occasionally buys closeouts. There is an extensive selection in Big and Tall from 40 Portly to 60 Long; to 22-inch neck in shirts. Dress shirts were priced from $12.99 to $24.99. Ties from $7.99 to $14.99. A separate vendor maintains a very nice shoe department with styles from Johnston & Murphy, Florsheim, Stuart James, Bally, and others for $54–$119. Most slacks were priced $39–$44. This is a pipe-rack operation but nicely presented; all in all, I think Clothing Broker does a very nice job, satisfying all but the most elitist shoppers. Alterations done on site for a fee. Returns, exchanges, and refunds. Call for directions.

Designer Forum

Outlets at Gilroy, Gilroy. (408) 842-2700. Daily.
MC, VISA, AE, DIS. Parking: lot.

Silicon Valley executives have an advantage over most Bay
Area men—they have a relatively short jaunt to Gilroy when it
comes time to update their wardrobes. J. Schoeneman, Inc. is
the second largest manufacturer of tailored clothing for men
in the United States. Labels under its corporate umbrella are
impressive: Burberrys, Halston, Christian Dior, Evan Picone,
Palm Beach, and Southbrook (its house brand). You'll find all
these labels and more in its factory store selling for 20–60%
off retail. The up-to-date, first-quality selection of suits is
priced $99–$400 in wool and wool blends (some cotton
poplin and blends during summer); sportcoats in cashmere,
cashmere blends, camel hair, wool, wood blends, linen, raw
silk, and other exotic natural fibers are priced $99–$329; slacks
$49–$99 (Burberrys); topcoats to $299; and ties from Nicole
Miller and Bill Robinson $13–$25. The precision-fit program is
one that athletes appreciate: a suit can be selected by choosing the individual jacket and waist measurements. It may be
possible to special order a suit if your size is not available. The
company makes savings apparent with its reference retail
pricing and percentage-off calculations listed on every tag.
Sizes: 36 Short to 60 XXL. Alterations done on site for an
additional charge. A very upscale shopping ambiance, a good
range of apparel (including some fine-quality labels), and
excellent prices justify the trip from just about anywhere.
With Brooks Bros. and Executive Suite also located in the
complex, men can do some serious shopping for their nine-
to-five wardrobes in Gilroy.

European Menswear Outlet

Great Mall of the Bay Area, Milpitas. (408) 956-1098. Daily.
MC, VISA, AE. Parking: lot.

This specialty retailer of contemporary European men's fashions
puts his connections to work, combing factories around Europe
for good deals on men's suits, sportcoats, slacks, shirts, ties,
and sweaters. His good buys result in extra special pricing on
everything sold. Expect apparel to reflect European and contemporary styling. Sizes: 36–50L.

Men's Suits

Good Byes

3464 Sacramento, San Francisco. (415) 346-6388.
M–Sat 10–6, Th until 8, Sun 11–5. MC, VISA. Parking: street.
Good Byes offers cut-above consignment men's apparel. You'll
find prices starting at $50, averaging about $125, and top-
ping out at about $300. Sizes usually 36–46. Good selection
of slacks, new dress shirts ($18), ties (many new), belts, and
shoes. The owner has a pipeline to an upscale line of men's
sportswear, resulting in new merchandise (mostly samples)
in all categories of men's apparel. Go to the women's side for
tempting buys.

Kutler Clothiers

625 Howard Street, San Francisco. (415) 543-7770.
M–F 9–5:30, Sat 9–4. MC, VISA, DIS, AE. Parking: lot.
Kutler Clothiers has the Bay Area's most impressive selection
of fine-quality men's clothing at discount prices (25–50% off).
It stocks suits, sportcoats, slacks, and raincoats, along with
dress shirts, sportshirts, sweaters, ties, belts, tuxedos, and
formal wear accessories usually sold in the best men's stores
or departments. Some labels: suits and sportcoats from Gieves
& Hawkes, Aquascutum, Burberrys, Charles Jourdan, and
Chaps by Ralph Lauren; shoes from Bally, Johnston & Murphy,
Cole Haan, and Allen Edmonds. A large part of its inventory
may seem expensive even at discount; a $475–$1,200 suit, a
bargain for one customer at $319–$800, is out of reach for
the next, who will choose among the more modestly priced
lines. The size range is extensive and includes the hard-to-fit in
any dimension. Alterations are done at a minimal charge on
the premises. The shoe department offers a full range of styles
in fine brands at 25% discounts; shoe sizes 7–13, mostly
Medium, some B–EEE. Its business is restricted to a clientele
based on personal referrals, or employees of large companies
that have had entry arrangements made for them. Check to
see if your company has customer privileges. If not, use my
name as a referral.

Planteen Men's Clothing Loft

17 Drumm Street, Third Floor (across from the Hyatt Regency),
San Francisco. (415) 788-8927.
M–F 11–7, Sat 11–4. MC, VISA, AE. Parking: pay lots.
Financial District fellas can shop conveniently here for a new
suit, sportcoat, or pair of slacks; low overhead leads to its

everyday low-price policy. The overall style orientation leans toward updated European, but the classics are represented as well. Sportcoats and suits range from $99 to $350. The owners are always present, working hard and committed to providing good service. An on-site tailor is available for alterations. Sizes: 38 Short to 54XL. Special orders on Big and Tall sizes a nice accommodation.

President Tuxedo Outlet

1933 Davis, #190, Westgate Shopping Center, San Leandro.
(510) 562-9551. M–Sat 10–6, Th until 8, F until 7.
MC, VISA. Parking: lot.

If you've added up the cost of renting a tuxedo and accessories, you'll find that buying used equals about two rental charges, maybe less, and the tux will be in the closet for future use. Most used wool-blend jackets at the President Tuxedo Outlet are priced at about $110; pants range from $40 to $50. You can buy used or new shirts and accessories. The rental inventory reflects the selection found at its twenty-six regular stores. You'll find a few new tuxedos (all wool or wool blend) that are priced reasonably. Alterations are extra. Sizes for everyone, including a few boys' sizes.

Spaccio

645 Howard Street (at New Montgomery), San Francisco.
(415) 777-2221. M–Sat 9–6. MC, VISA, AE, DIS.
Parking: free garage on side of building.
(Other store: 1840 Union Street, San Francisco.)

This major Italian manufacturer sells direct at consumer-friendly prices. Bottom line: savings of 35–40% off other store retails. Spaccio makes Italian suits in four different cuts, including one that comes close to the American traditional fit. Italian suits use very fine fabrics like lighter weight Merino wool or wool gabardine (rather than the worsted wool used by most American manufacturers). You'll find somber and dignified fabric suitings along with standout bold colors appealing to a younger fashion-liberated customer. Sizes 34S to 50XL. Alterations can be done on the premises for a modest fee. Completing the selection: sportcoats, full-length topcoats, lightweight contemporary fashion sweaters, well-made and elegant slacks, Italian ties, and dress shirts of fine 100% cotton.

Suits & Shoes

Factory Stores of America, Vacaville. (707) 452-8982.
MC, VISA, AE, DIS. Parking: lot.

The industry conglomerate that owns this outfit has several desirable labels and makers in its family. The "suits" part of the store refers to a selection provided by Grieff, a company that makes suits and sportcoats for Ralph Lauren and Perry Ellis and many suits sold by major stores under private label. First-quality suit overruns are sold for $129–$199 in sizes 36S to 56XL, while sportcoats in sizes 38S to 54XL are priced at $99. The selection is pretty good—mainstream and traditional. I didn't see any obvious "uglies" on the racks. The "shoes" refers to shoes made by Johnston & Murphy and others with labels from Dockers, Kid's University, Toddler University, and Mitre (great soccer shoes). These are mostly athletic and casual dress styles. Prices are always 50% off original retail. This is a prototype store for the company. I hope it will prove successful so that it will be around for a while.

Also See

Under Other Bay Area Factory Outlets/Factory Stores:
Donna Karan Company Store;
Executive Suite—Jones New York

Under General Clothing:
Burlington Coat Factory; Polo/Ralph Lauren Factory Store

General Clothing

The Big Four:

Ross, Marshall's, T.J. Maxx, Burlington Coat Factory

Think of these stores as your "four best friends": Ross, Marshall's, T.J. Maxx, and Burlington Coat Factory do an admirable job of providing solid discounts and a head-to-toe selection of apparel, accessories, and shoes for each family member. Each store has its own personality and slight differences in merchandising. In my comparison surveys, I've often found that prices on many brand names at these four stores are significantly lower than those found at the factory stores or outlets.

Highlights: Burlington Coat Factory has the best selection of coats and outerwear (some skiwear) in all sizes and styles for adults and children of any Bay Area store. Its men's and young men's departments are the best of the four—Big and Tall sizes, too! Also great home and kitchen accessories, shoes, linens, and, at some stores, baby furniture. T.J. Maxx comes up with surprising status labels in women's apparel and has a discriminating selection of giftware, a satisfying shoe department, linens, and good Petite and Plus size selections. Ross offers moderately priced fashions (selected stores receive upscale labels), plus shoes, fragrances, picture frames, handbags, and body and bath products. Marshall's captures occasional groups of better women's apparel. Check in for fragrances, jewelry, giftware, and linens.

Women's Petite and Plus fashions get respectable rack space at all four stores, and men's and children's selections are generally excellent. Each company's stores are stocked according to the customer base of their area. If you feel your store doesn't have enough "good stuff," try another location. These stores are consumer-friendly, allowing returns, exchanges, and refunds. For the Marshall's nearest you, call (800) MARSHALL (627-7425); for Ross (800) 945-ROSS (945-7677).

Other Stores

Ashworth

Factory Stores of America, Vacaville. (707) 447-0237. Daily. MC, VISA, AE, DIS. Parking: lot.
Ashworth sportswear, designed as a golf collection, goes just about anywhere. At pro shops, prices are a lot higher; here they're just about right. PGA tour star Freddy Couples endorses Ashworth. Men shop on one side of the store, women on the other. Sweaters, slacks, shorts, tops, and jackets from about $15 to $39.

B.U.M. Equipment/Coliseum

Factory Stores of America, Vacaville. (707) 448-5050. Daily. MC, VISA, DIS, AE. Parking: lot.
(Other B.U.M. outlets: Gilroy, Petaluma centers; Coliseum: Great Mall, Milpitas.)
B.U.M. Equipment now crosses over all age and gender boundaries. Clothing with the B.U.M. label is generally unisex, many styles oversized, baggy, and comfortable, in 100% preshrunk cotton. Great fabrics, high quality, great colors, distinctive logos—a winning combination! Prices about 25–40% off retail. Sizes for the whole family, from infants to Unisex XL.

Coliseum, the B.U.M. Equipment superstore at the Great Mall in Milpitas, has expanded departments for children (preschool to college), teens, women, and men. Styles are up-to-the-minute, capturing all the trends that teens must have, while providing stylish options for everyone else in the family. Lots of denim, dresses, sportswear, sweaters, jackets, and basics in addition to everything B.U.M. Some great fashions for guys—sportcoats and slacks with just the right look for Saturday nightclub rounds and parties. Other labels in evidence: Eber,

Paris Blues, Big Star, Ivy Wear, Zodiac (shoes), Re-Union, and Tribeca. Great resource for back-to-school shopping expeditions.

Big Dog Sportswear

Factory Stores of America, Vacaville. (707) 446-6852. Daily.
MC, VISA, AE. Parking: lot.
(Other outlets: Gilroy, Pacific Grove, Petaluma centers.)
Reflecting the Southern California lifestyle and a sense of whimsy with its St. Bernard logos, Big Dog sportswear for men, women, and kids is great fun. Savings are about 25–40% off on sweats, T-shirts, graphic ties, shorts, pants, shirts, jackets, and beach towels. Sizes from 12mos to adult 4X (big and tall). Great for lighthearted gifts. For a "warm and fuzzy" gift, pick up an adorable stuffed "big dog" with ageless appeal.

Crazy Shirts Factory Store

Great Mall of the Bay Area, Milpitas. (408) 934-9425.
MC, VISA. Parking: lot.
Visit many tourist locations around the country, or go down to Fisherman's Wharf, and you're likely to cruise through one of Crazy Shirts' twenty-seven stores selling specialty active wear. The company is proud that all its apparel is made in America of 100% cotton. At the outlet you'll find that most tops sport a colorful tourist logo, although there are occasional blank tops. These are usually first-quality, discontinued colors or designs or past-season overruns. The tourist logos are very well done, the colors crisp, and the quality superior to most tourist-oriented merchandise. Almost everything is reduced 50%. Good source for T-shirts and fleece or sweat tops. Sizes S–XL (a few XXLs).

Eddie Bauer Outlet Store

1295 Marina Boulevard, Marina Square, San Leandro.
(510) 895-1484. M–F 10–9, Sat 10–6, Sun Noon–5.
MC, VISA, AE. Parking: lot.
(Other stores/outlets: Sunrise Shopping Center, Citrus Heights;
Hilltop Mall, Richmond; Gilroy center.)
Eddie Bauer's outlets emphasize its casual apparel and outer-wear for men and women: pants, shirts, dresses, sweaters, and jackets. You'll also find some shoes, socks, backpacks, and small accessory items. Catalog overstocks, discontinued products, and some apparel made specifically for its outlet stores make up the selection. Prices are reduced 40–70% off original. Exchanges but no cash refunds.

Galt Sand

Pacific West Outlet Center, Gilroy. (408) 848-4343. Daily.
MC, VISA, DIS. Parking: lot.
(Other outlet: South Lake Tahoe center.)
For casual class—really great, high-quality sweats and T-shirts—
you can't do better than the Galt Sand outlets. Upscale
department stores carry this line. Themes abound, including
countries, colleges and universities, states, flags, sports, and
wildlife. Pricey at retail, 30% discount on average; you'll spend
about $22–$26 on sweatshirts or about $9–$15 on T-shirts
in adult sizes. Sizes: S–XXL for adults; S–XL for kids. The line
is oversized. Beautiful stores and inventory.

Geoffrey Beene

Factory Stores of America, Vacaville. (707) 452-0603. Daily.
MC, VISA. Parking: lot.
(Other outlets: Folsom, Gilroy, Pacific Grove, Napa,
Petaluma centers.)
Geoffrey Beene factory stores are stocked with an impressive
array of men's fashions. Everything is very current and stylish,
and priced an average 25–50% off. A versatile array of sport-
shirts, occasional sportcoats, slacks, lots of denim pants and
shirts, active wear, robes, gorgeous ties, and a posh stock of
dress shirts make it possible for a fella to build a wardrobe that
everyone will admire. Most stores have a split personality—
devoting about half the space to a well-designed collection of
women's sportswear. Refunds and exchanges allowed.

Jockey

Factory Stores of America, Vacaville. (707) 451-8119. Daily.
MC, VISA, AE, DIS. Parking: lot.
(Other outlets: Folsom, Gilroy, Lathrop centers.)
There's a lot more to Jockey than men's briefs: you'll find
underwear for women and children, casual shirts, pantyhose,
tank tops, etc. Sizes for all dimensions. All first-quality goods
at average 30% off retail.

Jordache Factory Store

Pacific West Outlet Center, Gilroy. (408) 842-1037. Daily.
MC, VISA, AE, DIS. Parking: lot.
With forty-nine domestic licensees making apparel, there's a
lot more to Jordache than jeans. Even so, everywhere you look,
you see blue: denim, cottons, chambrays, and other fabrics in

clothing for the entire family. Everyday discounts are 20–40% off retail, with special markdown racks offering up to 50%. Men, women, and children can buy jeans, jackets, shirts, shorts, and sweaters. A decent Petite size section for the ladies. The merchandise is a mixture of current- and prior-season goods and irregulars.

Levi's Outlet
Factory Stores of America, Vacaville. (707) 451-0155. Daily. MC, VISA, DIS, AE. Parking: lot.
(Other outlets: Anderson/Redding, Folsom, Gilroy, Milpitas, Petaluma, Tracy centers.)
This company sells Levi's irregulars and closeouts. In some instances the flaws were obvious to me, like small spots from sewing machine oil or unequal fading on stonewashed jeans, but most of the time I was at a loss to find anything wrong with the apparel. You'll find all the Levi's labels: Dockers for women and men (men's pants usually at $19.99–$29.99); popular pants styles from the 501, 540, 550, and 560 collections; many styles for students, girls and boys (all sizes covered), all at about 50% discounts! Plus shirts in an endless selection, casual tops, belts, socks, and a little bit of everything Levi's. Children's wear discounts are modest—about 25% off original retail. Great store, great selection, great bargains!

London Fog Factory Stores
Factory Stores of America, Vacaville. (707) 447-1196. Daily. MC, VISA. Parking: lot.
(Other outlets: Anderson/Redding, St. Helena, South Lake Tahoe centers.)
London Fog has two different aspects to its factory stores. You'll find traditional collections of sportswear for men and women in wonderful fabrics, comparable to Lands' End and L.L. Bean in style, quality, value and price. It's possible to assemble a versatile vacation or weekend wardrobe here. This is headquarters for outerwear and rainwear for men and women. It's all quite nice, and nicely discounted. The factory stores primarily showcase men's and women's raincoats, all-weather coats (many with zip-out linings), jackets, and heavyweight down jackets (for the slopes), all with water-repellent fabrics, at 50% discounts. Sizes: Petite 2–20; Misses 2–26½; Men's 36–52 in short, regular, and long. Some children's outerwear, too! If you think you might need to exchange an item, don't cut off the tags.

Miller Stockman Western Wear Outlet

Vintage Oaks Shopping Center, Novato. (415) 898-4154.
M–F 10–9, Sat 10–9, Sun 11–6. MC, VISA, AE, DIS. Parking: lot.
Urban cowboys or cowgirls and those who really ride the
range will want to check out the bargains here. The store's
inventory, from the Rocky Mountain Clothing company, Miller
Stockman retail stores, and Miller Stockman's catalog division,
offers Western fashions and accessories head to toe. There's a
variety of brand names: irregulars in pants from Wrangler and
Rocky Mountain; overruns from Australian Outback (dusters);
factory blems in Nocona, Larry Mahan, Tony Lama and Justin
boots. The boot selection takes up one wall, with over 3,000
pairs for women and men. Shoe sizes: Men's sizes 6½–13 (all
widths); Women's 5–10. Most boot prices reduced about 40%
off retail. Rocky Mountain pant sizes: Men's 28–40 (cowboy
and slim fit); Women's 00 (tiny) to 20. Note: Hats are not
discounted.

Pacific Trail

Factory Stores at Nut Tree, Vacaville. (707) 446-4196.
MC, VISA. Parking: lot.
The place to go when you need to bundle up! Pacific Trail
offers its line of familiar, no-nonsense traditional outerwear
and weekend jackets along with some fairly high-tech fabrications utilizing space-age fabrics, insulated linings, and a
fashion orientation. Bring the family along, because there are
jackets for kids, women, and men. Wonderful pricing, too!
Discounts are 20–60% off retail (many coats at 40–60% off
retail). When ski season approaches, stop in to try on the
skiwear, including snowboard styles.

Pangea Outlet

110 Howard Street, Petaluma. (707) 778-0110. Sat only 9–4
(May–Dec), 10–2 (Jan–Apr). Cash/Check. Parking: street.
Pangea screenprints messages on T-shirts, jackets, sweatshirts,
and other garments customers may want their message or
logo on. Flawed merchandise and test prints are tossed into
the reject box, where you can hunt for T-shirts, all for $2.
About 70% of the merchandise is first-quality, the remaining
irregulars have minor flaws. Seconds in T-shirts are priced
$3–$4, firsts $6–$9; seconds in sweatshirts $5–$12, firsts
$8–$12. Sizes for the whole family.

Polo/Ralph Lauren Factory Store

3300 Broadway Road, Bayshore Mall, Eureka. (707) 444-3075. M–Sat 10–9, Sun 11–6. MC, VISA, AE, DC. (Other stores: Anderson/Shasta, Barstow, Mammoth Lakes centers.)

The Polo/Ralph Lauren Factory Stores are in remote sites for a very good reason—they're safely removed from important retail accounts. Discounts are 30–50% off original retail; 30% on current-season overruns, while greater discounts apply to merchandise that may be one or two years old or irregular. About 95% of the merchandise is first-quality; the remaining irregulars have minor flaws. If you time your visit right, you'll catch additional markdowns on the already well-priced merchandise (get on the mailing list!). Polo's "designer collections" aren't stocked, but you'll find just about everything else in its extensive line, including men's and women's apparel from the classic collection, boy's clothing, and homewares (towels, duvets, comforters, sheets, bed skirts, and rugs). Refunds (usually a MC, VISA, or AE credit) on merchandise returned within seven days in person or by mail. Exchanges for credit are accepted up to thirty days after purchase.

Royal Robbins Factory Outlet

841-A Gilman, Berkeley. (510) 527-1961. M–F 10–6, Sat 10–5, Sun 11–5 (extended summer hours). MC, VISA, DIS. Parking: lot. (Other store: 1508 Tenth Street, Modesto.)

Royal Robbins classic clothing for outdoor—and indoor—living is sold nationally through well-known mail-order companies and stores specializing in men's and women's outdoor wear. At the outlets you'll find seconds (very small flaws) on current collections and overruns from preceding seasons. The clothing is transitional for year-round use. Most is made from 100% cotton or other natural fibers in many distinctive patterns and weaves. Many styles are unisex. Prices at the outlets are 35–70% off retail. The line includes sweaters, belts, hats, skirts, pants, shorts, dresses, shirts, and tops. The outlets are nicely stocked and a pleasure to shop. Exchanges and credits are allowed, but no cash refunds.

Shirtique

Great Mall of the Bay Area, Milpitas. (408) 934-9164.
MC, VISA. Parking: lot.

If you've shopped its mall stores, you'll know what to expect: T-shirts, sweats, jackets, etc. with team logos, funny and irreverent messages, and wild, whimsical, and cute graphics. Everything is discounted—a little to a lot. Styles and sizes for everyone in the family.

The Sweatshirt Company

Factory Stores of America, Vacaville. (707) 451-0307. Daily.
MC, VISA. Parking: lot.
(Other outlets: Anderson/Redding, Folsom, Gilroy centers.)

The Sweatshirt Company sells crewneck sweatshirts, track pants, and hooded sweatshirt jackets in sizes ranging from Infant to Adult XXXL and some Talls. All its first-quality goods are sold for 30% off full retail. Also, sweatshirts with college logos or unique pocket treatments and printed T-shirts. Prices range from $6.99 to $25.

VF Factory Outlet

Factory Stores of America, Vacaville. (707) 451-1990. Daily.
MC, VISA. Parking: lot.
(Other outlet: Gilroy center.)

The VF Factory Outlet offers a wealth of merchandise and good values for the whole family. You'll find fashions sporting labels from Health Tex (newborn to teenagers), Jantzen and Jan Sport (sportswear and swimsuits), Vanity Fair (intimate, daywear, and sleepwear), Wrangler and Lee (men's, women's, and youth fashions—jeans, shirts, shorts, and jackets). These are first-quality fashions, plus irregulars and way-past-season merchandise marked down substantially. Overall discounts are 30–70% off every day. Sizes for everyone: women's fashions from Junior size 1 to Women's 26; Men's pants to waist sizes 44, lengths to 36. If you need Boys Husky sizes they can be ordered, along with just about anything else in these brands. Returns and refunds okay.

Woolrich

American Tin Cannery, Pacific Grove. (408) 644-9218. Daily.
MC, VISA, DIS. Parking: lot.

One glance at the apparel at Woolrich and you'll think of
weekends in the country. The store showcases far more of its
sportswear and outerwear collections for men and women
than you'll ever see in any one store. Rugged, warm, and
weather-proof outerwear (jackets, coats, windbreakers, parkas),
fishing vests with dozens of pockets, warm bulky sweaters,
plus pants, skirts, shirts, hats, caps, packs, slippers, etc. prove
there's lots more to the line than you might have imagined.
There are the enduring classic Woolrich styles and some groups
designed with more fashion. The women's groups offer some
surprises—charming prints, novelty fabrics, and chic jackets
and coats. Woolrich blankets (often tagged as seconds) are good
buys, too. Expect to save 30–50% off retail on past-season
overruns and seconds. A very nice store for traditionalists.

Also See

Under San Francisco's Factory Outlets and Off-Price Stores:
Rock Express

Under Clearance Centers:
All listings

Under Appliances, Electronics, and Home Entertainment:
Whole Earth Access

Active Sportswear

Aerobics, Camping, Dance, Exercise, Golf, Skiing, Tennis, etc.

Body Body
224 Greenfield Avenue, San Anselmo. (415) 459-2336.
M–Th 9–7:30, F 9–6, Sat–Sun 9–5. MC, VISA. Parking: street.
(Other store: 19-E Blythedale, Mill Valley.)
Body Body offers a collection of bodywear at modest discounts: past-season apparel 20–40% off and some current styles at minimal 10% discounts. Racks are jammed with brand-name apparel devoted to the workout crowd, plus a nice collection of active sportswear. Sizes 4–14, small selection of XL to fit up to size 18. Leotards and tights for kids at 20–33% off retail.

Champion/Hanes
Factory Stores of America, Vacaville. (707) 448-5081. Daily.
MC, VISA. Parking: lot.
(Other outlets: Folsom, Lathrop, Pacific Grove centers.)
Hanes Activewear's store is filled with activewear for women, men, and children. Most separates are cotton or cotton-blend interlock knits in regular and heavy weights. Sizes: X–XXL (fits 50–52); youth sweats 6–8 to 14–16.

Columbia Sportswear Co. Factory Outlet
Outlets at Gilroy, Gilroy. (408) 848-3740. Daily.
MC, VISA, AE, DIS. Parking: lot.
Columbia Sportswear is your destination for bargains in women's and men's skiwear and outerwear in high-tech fabrics, plus apparel for hunters and fishers (vests, parkas, caps, shirts, and pants), and an expanded line of sportswear for women,

men, and children. Closeouts average 30% discount, seconds
are usually 50% off original retail. The company does not
warranty the outlet's goods for waterproofing or construction.
Sizes: Women's S–XL (4–18); Men's: S–XXXL; Children's 2T–16.

Danskin

Factory Stores of America, Vacaville. (707) 448-9313. Daily.
MC, VISA. Parking: lot.
(Other outlets: Folsom, Gilroy, Pacific Grove centers.)
Whatever your size, Danskin has got you covered. Dance wear,
aerobic wear, Dance France (Petite sizing), Danskin Plus (sizes
14–24), and Danskin Pro (for heavy use by serious athletes
involved in daily training) are reduced 30–50%. Great colors,
prints, and styles add up to a sizzling selection. Girls can get
ready for the gym or dance studio with Danskin's collection in
sizes 2T–14.

Fila Factory Store

Pacific West Outlet Center, Gilroy. (408) 848-3452. Daily.
MC, VISA, AE. Parking: lot.
(Other outlet: Tracy center.)
If wearing expensive tennis clothes might improve your game,
consider the togs at the Fila Factory Store. It sells past-season
merchandise, samples, and overruns. Fila uses quality fabric,
resulting in clothes that are made well to wear well. Prices
are reduced approximately 40%, more affordable but still not
inexpensive. Current merchandise is discounted a minimum of
40%. Although limited in style and size, the selection of tennis
skirts, golf/warm-up suits, ski vests, sweaters, bathing suits,
shorts, shoes, etc. changes frequently. Sizes: Women's 4–14,
Women's shoes 5½–10; Men's 44½–56, Men's shoes 6½–13.
Exchanges only within thirty days.

Marika

Factory Stores of America, Vacaville. (707) 446-6460.
MC, VISA, DIS, AE. Parking: lot.
The merchandise may be old to the manufacturer, but it looks
fresh and new and it's reduced 20–50% off retail. (Goods are
shipped to the outlet two months after close of delivery to
major accounts.) The racks are filled with everything you need
for your health club, even weekend sportswear to wear before
and after your workout. All first quality. Sizes: S–XL; girls and
preteens get rack space, too!

Mont-Bell Company Store

940 41st Avenue, Santa Cruz. (408) 479-5424.
M–Sat 10–6, Sun Noon–5. MC, VISA. Parking: street.
Reading the Mont-Bell dealer workbook is like perusing a technical manual for a NASA project. It uses the most technologically advanced fabrics in its apparel, which includes rainwear, Alpine wear, fleece, cycling apparel, kayaking clothes, and lightweight sportswear. At the company store you'll find samples, closeouts, irregulars, and first-quality goods discounted 20–70% off original retail. This stuff is relatively expensive. Current-season merchandise sells at full retail prices. Most styles sizes: Unisex S–XXL. Also a few sleeping bags, backpacks, and other accessories. Returns and exchanges with receipt.

One Step Ahead

Great Mall of the Bay Area, Milpitas. (408) 956-1244. Daily.
MC, VISA. Parking: lot.
This line in 100% cotton in sizes 5/6 to 16/18 will inspire you to work up a sweat at aerobic classes or on gym equipment. Top off your leotards, tights, bra tops, etc. with a stylish cover-up, fleece, or French terry top from its line of supercomfy sportswear. Past-season fashions discounted 25–50% off retail.

San Francisco City Lights Factory Outlet

333 Ninth Street (bet. Folsom and Harrison), San Francisco.
(415) 861-6063. M–Sat 10–6. MC, VISA. Parking: street.
San Francisco City Lights is an innovative manufacturer of body- and aerobic wear. Aerobics buffs beat a path here for wholesale prices or better on discontinued styles, seconds (usually dye imperfections), and overruns. The basics: leggings in five different lengths, leotards, unitards, briefs, several styles of bra tops, body belts, crop tops, plus a selection of sweats in soft fleece. You'll find the hottest new colors in fabrics made from comfortable 90% cotton and 10% lycra. Many of the fashions (particularly the coordinating sportswear) are perfect for casual weekend activities. Loved the washed linens, nubby knits, and other innovative textured fabrics! Its new children's collection of playwear will win the heart of moms. Sizes: Children's 2T–14; Women's S, M, L (some Petite), fits 4–12 (to 14 in some styles). All sales final. Communal dressing room, so don your best underwear.

Sideout Sport

Outlets at Gilroy, Gilroy. (408) 848-8040. Daily.
MC, VISA. Parking: lot.

If you know the name Sinjin Smith, you'll know what this outlet is all about. He's the all-time champion volleyball player who wears and promotes this line. Sideout should be de rigueur for the volleyball crowd. An average 25% is discounted on Sideout's slightly past-season shorts, shirts, sweats, and tank tops. Expect greater discounts on occasional seconds and it's-got-to-go sale racks. Carry the image to the fullest extent with bags, hats, watches, balls, and nets. The newer sportswear—Polo-style shirts and casual shirts (in handprinted fabrics from Bali)—are perfect for standing or sitting on the sidelines.

Sierra Designs

Outlets at Gilroy, Gilroy. (408) 842-6544. Daily.
MC, VISA, AE. Parking: lot.
(Other store: 1255 Powell Street, Emeryville.)

Sierra Designs makes mistakes, too! Seconds are reduced a minimum of 40% off retail at the outlet. Bargains may be found in trail, snow, and hiking boots; down sleeping bags and tents; and occasionally, packs and other related backpacking, cross-country skiing, and mountaineering equipment. Bigger discounts are usually found on monthly specials and on the complete selection of outdoor apparel. Overstock or discontinued goods are marked down 20%. Get on the mailing list so you won't miss the spring and fall supersales. Bargains at the Emeryville retail store are stashed in the outlet "corner." Sizes: Women's 6–14; Men's XS–XL.

Starter Sportswear

Outlets at Gilroy, Gilroy. (408) 847-1147. Daily.
MC, VISA, DIS. Parking: lot.

Starter manufactures apparel for some names you may have heard of: NFL, AFL, NBA, NCAA, etc. and colleges and universities around the country. Not only sportswear, but the actual team uniforms! You can tell the world the name of your game or team with Starter's logo jackets, jerseys, warm-up suits, sweats, shorts, T-shirts, and outerwear. Discounts are 20–60% (average 40%) off retail on past-season merchandise and some seconds. Sizes: from small tots to XXXXL. A popular store with sports fans!

T.L. Broderick Co.

2605 Lafayette Street, Santa Clara. (408) 748-0880.
M–F 10–8, Sat 10–6, Sun Noon–5; closed April 1–Sept 1.
MC, VISA. Parking: lot.

If price rather than jet-set appearance is your criterion in family skiwear, stop off at T.L. Broderick Co. for discounts on brand-name apparel, goggles, gloves, socks, caps, sweaters, turtlenecks, and thermals. It sells its in-house lines of well-made, moderately priced down or polyester jackets and ski bibs for men, women and children, and snowboard clothing and accessories. Prices are reduced 30–60% on the first-quality selection. Sizes: Toddler (12–24mos) and smaller Children's 2–16; Women's 6–16 or XS, M, XL (some Talls in stretch pants); Men's 28–38, or XS–XXL (to XXXL in ski bibs); some items in Tall sizes. The store is easy to miss; call for directions.

Tight End

434 Ninth Street, San Francisco. (415) 255-8881. M–F 8–4,
Call for Sat hours. Cash/Check. Parking: street.

Tight End first received attention for its leggings, made in sophisticated and colorful prints, paired with solid T-shirt tops in screenprinted designs that capture the look of the print. The more recent groups are made from organic fabrics or prewashed and shrunk thermal knits. These are comfortable weekend separates for when comfort is key, and they're priced from $5 to $24 (wholesale prices on samples, discontinued patterns, and overruns). Sizes: S, M, L (fits 4–14). All sales are final.

Vigorelli Monthly Sales

1933 Davis Street, Suite 277, San Leandro. (510) 635-4115.
Sales first Sat every month 10–5. MC, VISA. Parking: lot.

Vigorelli manufactures cycling and fitness activewear for women and men using fine-quality fabrics and offering aerodynamically designed comfort features, so whether you're hunkered down over the handlebars or stretching toward the ceiling, you won't be hindered by uncomfortable bands or binding crotches. These monthly sales feature first-quality overruns, samples, and seconds priced at 40–50% discounts. Watch for several styles of tops, including T-shirts, halters, sweatshirts, road shirts, jerseys and jackets, tights, shorts, helmet covers, and other odds and ends. Everything is pretty much unisex in style. Prices $5–$45. Sizes S–XL. All sales are final. Drive around the back of Price/Costco to reach entry.

Also See

Under Other Bay Area Outlets:
J. Crew; Spa Gear

Under Chain Discount Stores:
Loehmann's

Under Men's Sportswear:
Champs Sports; N.E. Wear

Under General Clothing:
Most listings

Under Shoes:
Nike Factory Store; Reebok Factory Store

Under Sporting Goods:
All listings

Children's
Clothing

Aunt Duck's/Saratoga Sport Outlet

979 Moraga Road, Lafayette. (510) 284-3711. T–Sat 10–5.
MC, VISA. Parking: lot.

Aunt Duck's makes comfortable, colorful, sturdy play clothes for boys and girls. Sizes range from 6mos to 14 (biggest selection from 2T to 7). Each season the company produces a collection of basics: gathered-waist pull-on pants and skirts, related T-shirts and tops (often with whimsical graphics), jackets, jum~~~~ant and toddler one-piece suits. The st~~~~~~itional, and the fabrics (corduroy, fleece, cotton knits, and twills) are preshrunk. Most prices on its fresh selection of first-quality, past-season styles are 30–70% off retail. Saratoga Sport (about half of the store) is a ladies' line of moderately priced sportswear priced for buyers with 50% savings on past-season overruns.

CLOSED

Baby Guess? Guess Kids?

Outlets at Gilroy, Gilroy. (408) 847-6333. Daily.
MC, VISA. Parking: lot.

I always thought that parents who paid premium dollars for the Baby Guess? line had rocks in their heads, but I'm reconsidering after seeing the cute line at Baby Guess? and Guess Kids? Best buys are captured on the irregulars with red tags, usually priced at 50% off original retail. Overstock and seasonal merchandise is always at least 35% less than full-price boutiques. Everything's more affordable, with shortalls at $17, denim jackets at $25. Sizes: Infant 3mos to 14.

Biobottoms Retail Outlet

1253 Marina Boulevard, Marina Square, San Leandro.
(510) 352-9401. M–F 10–9, Sat 10–7, Sun 11–6.
MC, VISA. AE, DIS. Parking: lot.
(Other store: 620-H Petaluma Boulevard North, Petaluma.)

Biobottoms sends out a catalog with appealing fashions for infants through preteens, including coveralls, longjohns, dresses, pants, tops, shorts, and bathing suits, all in 100% cotton. At its retail stores you'll find overruns and discontinued goods from previous catalogs, samples, and a large selection of seconds at 30–70% off; additionally, some styles from the current catalog are often available at a 10% discount. Diapering with cloth is a specialty, and there's a complete supply of Biobottoms, diaper covers, and diapering needs in the stores at full price. Write for catalog to P.O. Box 6009, Petaluma, CA 94953.

Bo Bo Kidz

180 Townsend Street, San Francisco. (415) 495-7365.
M–Sat 11–5. MC, VISA. Parking: street.

The hats made by this catalog company are darling! The reversible polar fleece hat with ear flaps and chin strap offers maximum protection for tots taking the air in strollers or digging in sand lots. Strike a fashion note with other styles: berets, beanies, jester caps in whimsical prints and solids in cotton, flannel velour, or polar fleece. All the hats are priced $2–$9 (about half off). This store is also the final resting place for many manufacturers' leftovers—some way past season. The roster of names covers budget to best. Buy fancy dresses, playwear, accessories, and outerwear. The store is a bit of a jumble, understandable with so many different shipments frequently arriving. Sizes: Newborn to 14 for girls, to size 10 for boys.

Bugle Boy Outlet

Factory Stores of America, Vacaville. (707) 446-9297. Daily.
MC, VISA, AE. Parking: lot.
(Other outlets: Anderson/Redding, Folsom, Milpitas centers.)

Boys, teens, and young men can have it any way they want at Bugle Boy. Racks are jammed with pants and shorts in all sizes. Generally, the discounts are 22–30% on current-season merchandise and get better during the frequent in-store promotions. Girls, teens, and women get a little rack space, too. Sizes: Girls 4 to Women's 16/18; Boys 4 to Men's 40; decent selection of Boys Huskies 8–16. No cash or credit card refunds. Exchanges only within thirty days.

Carter's Childrenswear

Factory Stores of America, Vacaville. (707) 447-7440. Daily.
MC, VISA. Parking: lot.
(Other outlets: Folsom, Gilroy, Pacific Grove centers.)
Carter's is well stocked with everything Carter's makes, as well as other national brands. Good selection of playwear, sleepwear, and layettes; some dress duds, too, for the under–size 7 crowd. Everyday discounts are 30% off retail. There are always some irregulars in the layette and sleepwear selection, but they're clearly marked and in no way less desirable. Carter's also makes clothing exclusively for its own stores, and prices are quite pleasing. Sizes to 14 for girls; to 10 for boys.

Cary's Factory Outlet

2390 Fourth Street, Berkeley. (510) 841-5700.
M–Sat 10–4:30. MC, VISA. Parking: private lot.
Cary makes a versatile collection of absolutely charming children's clothing: precious dresses, wool coats, and velvet capes. The lines: Cary—beautiful dresses, rompers, and coats for girls in sizes 9mos to Preteen; Baby Cary—baby dresses and rompers 9mos to 4T for girls (to 6 for boys); Tini Kini—fun, playful swimwear 9mos to 16; Cary Sport—coordinating separates 2T–7 for boys and 2T–16 for girls. Little boys' tailored shorts, fun striped overalls, separates, and coordinating sets match the girls' dresses. The line is better priced at retail, but the outlet offers parents welcome price relief with discounts of 30–70% off samples, irregulars, and end-of-season merchandise. Cary's mails out a postcard every month spotlighting sales and special promotions. For those who sew their own clothes, there are always a few bolts of delightful trims and fabrics priced $1.50–$3/yard stashed in a large barrel.

Chicken Noodle Outlet

605 Addison Street, Berkeley. (510) 848-8880. M–F 10–5.
MC, VISA. Parking: lot.
Chicken Noodle children's playwear is every bit as cute as the name would imply—wonderful prints and practicality along with clever and engaging design details. The 100% cotton fabrics in wovens or knits predominate. Deck out your boys in

Infant sizes to 7; your girls in Infant to 10. Prices are reduced 40–60% off retail on past-season overruns, ranging from $5 to $35 (special dresses); seconds (very small quantities) are marked way down. The accessories caught my eye: hair bows, suspenders, and hats. Bundled remnants of fabric are priced $3–$4/yard. Directions: From 80 take the University Exit east, turn right at Sixth Street. Go one block to Addison, turn right, and drive to end of street (toward Aquatic Park). Building and parking on right.

Daisy Adriana

1712 Lincoln Avenue, Alameda. (510) 522-2601.
MC, VISA. T–Sat 10–5. Parking: street.
This outlet has such an out-of-the-way location that I worry that many mothers and grandmothers will miss the action. Daisy Adriana is a new line just starting to show up in upscale department stores. The precious dresses and rompers are made from beautiful 100% cotton prints and solids, many with wonderful detailing and trims. The look? Traditional and pretty! Toddler styles often have diaper covers to go along with the dresses—really cute! Sizes 9mos to 14. At retail, the 4–6X dresses and rompers range from $50 to $60 (an elegant holiday dress may be $70 to $100 plus). At the outlet everyday prices on overruns are about 40% off retail, but end-of-season progressive markdowns go down to sublime levels. Best buys? Check the $10–$12 rack, the fabric remnant bin ($3–$4), and bins of excess trims. An extra bonus? The racks of Queen Anne's Lace sleepwear and Eileen West dresses. Located about seven blocks North of Park Street. Directions: From 880, take 23rd Street bridge to Alameda. Turn right on Lincoln. From Oakland/Berkeley, take the Broadway Exit and Webster Street tunnel to Alameda, turn left on Lincoln.

Esse Pink

2325 Third Street (at 20th), Room 209, San Francisco.
(415) 255-6855. Most Fris 10–3 (call first). Cash/Check.
Parking: street.
It's almost a miracle! An outlet with an excellent selection for boys. The styles are comfortable and stylish without being too cutesy—and wear like iron. The line uses imaginative patterns and colors and inventive styling on hooded T-shirts, reversible pants, jackets, and overalls. Sizes 6mos to 7. Discontinued styles, samples, and some basics are 40–50% off with prices

at $10–$36. The new girls' collection offers the same innovative styling and original prints. Match-up sister-and-brother
outfits with several styles of women's gardening apparel in
the same cheerful and original prints—overalls, jackets, vests,
aprons, tops, etc. Esse Pink also makes a new line of gifts
that includes table linens, mitts, and chef's hats and jackets
(worn by the staff in some of San Francisco's trendier restaurants). Get on the mailing list for occasional Saturday sales.
The outlet is located near the elevator in the huge American
Industrial Building.

Genuine Kids

Factory Stores of America, Vacaville. (707) 453-0114. Daily.
MC, VISA. Parking: lot.
(Other outlets: Gilroy, Petaluma, Tracy centers.)
Genuine Kids is now owned by OshKosh, reflected in its spirited
and colorful play and school clothes. Boys get their fair share
of shopping choices in sizes 12mos to 18. Girls can buy just
about everything to size 16. For perfect picture taking, outfit
your sons and daughters in coordinated outfits. Parents with
boys in private schools love the khaki and navy pants for $20.
Clothes are 20–40% off department store prices on a very
current, first-quality selection.

Golden Rainbow

435-A Brannan Street, San Francisco. (415) 543-5191.
Seasonal warehouse sales. MC, VISA. Parking: street/pay lots.
Don't miss Golden Rainbow's sale of leftovers at the end of
each season; precious playsuits, sportswear, and baby sacks
made from fine-quality 100% cotton stretch terry, velour,
cotton flannel, and denim in charming prints are available
at 50–70% discounts. Golden Rainbow stands out with its
appealing use of bright colors and practical styles for active
wear. The line (with many unisex styles) is available in sizes
Infant 3mos–24mos, Toddler 2T–4T, Girls and Boys 4–6X. Each
season features innovative fabric choices for related separates,
playsuits, fetching caps, reversible jackets, and darling sweaters
(included in some fall groups). Most overruns, discontinued
styles, and samples in playsuits are $5–$36. Get your name on
the mailing list for special invitations to warehouse, fabric,
end-of-season blowouts!

Hi Studio II

Great Mall of the Bay Area, Milpitas. (408) 934-1550. Daily.
MC, VISA, AE. Parking: lot.

The same contemporary look that distinguishes the Jonathan
Martin/Hi Studio lines has been interpreted for the company's
girls' dress and sportswear collections. Girls from 7–16 (Preteen)
can emulate their sisters and moms with layered sets (vests,
T-shirts, and palazzo pants), jumpers with matching tops,
dresses that are sophisticated but still sweet, and denim groups
with just a little extra pizazz. Some pretty party dresses are
just right for girls who resist looking too traditional and fussy.
Altogether, a delightful collection—conveniently located next
to the grown-ups' outlet. Exchanges, but no cash refunds.

In Cahoots

5214-B Diamond Heights Boulevard, San Francisco.
(415) 824-8599. M–Sat 10–6. Sun 11–4. MC, VISA. Parking: lot.

Bring a camera along. When you see the breathtaking view of
downtown San Francisco from Diamond Heights, you'll want
to capture a picture for your album. Then prepare to see some
of the most innovative and prestigious children's wear made
in the Bay Area. American Widgeon gets the most rack space,
with its colorful line of kids' outerwear (perfect for biking,
hiking, skiing, sailing, or just being outdoors). Current-season
duds are 20% off, so penny pinchers look for the seconds at
40–60% off. Great fabrics and bold and bright colors on the
slickers, snow suits and bibs, fleece jackets, and polar coats
make it easy to pick your kid out of a crowd and distinguish
the line. Other lines that will get your attention: Mousefeathers
(dresses); Caspi Kids (innerwear); South Park Designs (sportswear); Monster Wear (boys' playwear), and others. Sizes fit
wee babies to preteens. From downtown, head west on Market
to the top of the hill, turn left.

Kids R Us

220 Walnut Street, Mervyn's Plaza, Redwood City.
(415) 367-6005. M–Sat 10–9, Sun 11–6.
MC, VISA, AE, DIS. Parking: lot.
(Other stores: Citrus Heights; Colma; Newark;
Sacramento; Sunnyvale.)

Kudos to Kids R Us for providing a one-stop resource for busy parents seeking solid values, name brands, good selection, and maximum convenience when shopping for their children (ages newborn to about 13). From no-nonsense basics to accommodating a child with a penchant for trendy styles, you'll shop with success! And everyday discounts average about 30% off retail, even more on end-of-season specials or promotions.

Mousefeathers Factory Store

1005 Camelia Street, Berkeley. (510) 526-0261. T–Sat 10–5.
MC, VISA. Parking: street.

Mousefeathers' line is European-inspired with an American interpretation and very expensive at retail! Even at the outlet, dresses may be as high as $58 for end-of-season overruns. That's why the faithful get on the mailing list so as not to miss its three major sales during the year. You can also stop in anytime to buy charming girls' dresses, jumpsuits, and sportswear. My favorite styles are the wonderful unique prints in 100% cotton, suitable for portrait sittings. Its Rococo sportswear line in wonderful knits is very fashion-forward in sizes 12mos to 14. The outlet has a boutique ambience, but the racks are filled with seconds, past-season clothes and samples in sizes 2T–4T, 4–6X, and 7–14 at 40–50% off retail.

Multiple Choices

899 Howard Street, Yerba Buena Center, San Francisco.
(415) 495-2628. M–Sat 9:30–6, Sun 11:30–5. MC, VISA, AE.
Parking: street.
(Other stores: Andy's Dad's Place, Greenbrae and Novato.)

Multiple Choices is aptly named! You've got choices whether you're shopping for infants, toddlers, school-age kids 6 to 18 (including the "surf" brands that boys have to have) or men's fun sportswear. Look for racks of cute Spumoni girls' fleece and sweat fashions. Expect 30–70% discounts on top-selling department store brands: Stussy, Mossimo, Quiksilver, Guess Kids, OshKosh, Billa Bong, O'Neill, Buster Brown, Rusty, Red Sand, Gotcha, and more. Parochial school uniforms are always on hand at discount prices. Exchanges any time!

OshKosh B'Gosh

Outlets at Gilroy, Gilroy. (408) 842-3280. Daily. MC, VISA.
Parking: lot.
(Other outlets: Milpitas, Petaluma, Vacaville centers.)
For the best deals at these large and colorful factory stores,
look for the yellow tags that say, "No one's perfect, though we
try, so when we're not, it's your best buy." Otherwise, discounts
are modest—averaging about 25% off retail. Sizes: Girls to 6X;
Boys to 7; plus a few rounds of adult-sized overalls for men.

Pattycakes Outlet

2669 Santa Rosa Avenue, Santa Rosa. (707) 575-5020.
M-Sat 10-6, Sun 11-5. MC, VISA. Parking: street.
If you're in the area, or you're willing to drive to Santa Rosa,
the rewards are great at the Pattycakes Outlet. The Pattycakes
line is bright, clever, and colorful for infants, toddlers, and
children, whether as special birthday gifts or everyday clothing. High retail prices reflect the use of screenprinted quality
cottons, fleece, and knits, plus extraordinary detailing. The
Wollypogs label by Pattycakes is just for boys in sizes 12mos
to 7. The outlet has overruns, past-season inventory, and
seconds at an average 40% discount. Sizes: Girls to 10 (occasionally to 14); Boys to 6X. Exchanges only.

Petals Factory Outlet

Great Mall of the Bay Area, Milpitas. (408) 934-9717. Daily.
MC, VISA. Parking: lot.
Intricate designs and detailing plus better-quality, unusual
fabrics and prints make up the charming Petals line of dresses
and jumpsuits for little girls (sizes 12mos to 14). Retail prices
go as high as $95. Overruns are sold on most Fridays; at the
factory, prepare to pay $10-$44 (40-50% off retail). Petals'
dresses are perfect for dressing up and looking pretty, and they
can do double duty as school clothes. The new Rapscallions
line of coordinated playwear in Lycra and knits displays whimsical styling. I doubt anyone will be able to resist the adorable
hats, headbands, hair bows, and purses designed to accessorize
the dresses. All sales final.

Rebecca Rags Outlet

10200 Imperial Avenue, Cupertino. (408) 257-7884.
M–F 9–5:30 (Some Sats, call first). MC, VISA. Parking: lot.
Rebecca Rags makes a charming line of children's clothing!
Many of its styles are made from lovely velours in vibrant
colors, others in soft flannels or cotton knits. Rebecca Rags
designs are appealing, with unique appliqués on the dresses,
jumpers, and warm-up suits in sizes 6mos to 14. The quality is
excellent. Ruff! Raggs is a boys' line that moms will love. The
outlet is jammed with end-of-season overruns, seconds, and
production samples. Prices are 20% above wholesale, much
less if the item is damaged or way past season.

Rose Cage

10 Cleveland Street (off Seventh Street), San Francisco.
(415) 431-8562. M–Sat 10–5. Cash/Check. Parking: street.
This small outlet yields fetching girls' fashions in sizes Infant
and 2T–14. Rose Cage has made a name for itself with clever
and distinctive appliqués on its tops; its related separates are
made from 100% cotton knits (some fleece in fall collections)
in whimsical prints and solids, and sell in the outlet as overruns at 25–50% off original retail. Prices range from $5 for
tank tops to $16 for dresses. The skirts, bike and regular shorts,
skorts, T-shirts, peplum tops, etc. are priced $7–$12. You can
also find items useful for craft projects: rosettes, bows, embel-
lishments, printed appliqués and lace. If the outlet is locked,
someone will let you in to shop. Parking is easier on Saturdays.

The Sample Room

699 Eighth Street (in the Fashion Center), San Francisco.
(415) 621-9945; on Sat (415) 391-1768. F 1–5, by appointment
only. Occasional Sat hours by appointment as well. Cash/Check.
Parking: garages.
If "going behind closed doors" to shop wholesale appeals to
you, you'll love your jaunts to the Sample Room. This children's
rep sells popular brands usually found in major stores at
wholesale prices or less. You'll often find adorable velvet suits
at holiday time, special-occasion dresses, little sportcoat-
and-pants sets for toddlers, bathing suits, sweaters and jackets,
and jog sets and playwear for everyday rough and tumble.
The selection is typically greater for girls than boys. Sizes range
from Newborn up to 14/16 for girls and boys. All sales final.

Sara's Prints (Factory Outlet)

3018-A Alvarado Street, San Leandro. (510) 352-6060.
M–F 10–4. MC, VISA. Parking: lot.

Sara's Prints are made in Israel from fine Egyptian or Israeli cotton, the softest fabric imaginable. The colorful and whimsical prints are highlighted against the fresh white background of all garments. The line consists of full layette sets, caps and booties, rompers, diaper sets, coveralls, playsuits, polo-style shirts, dresses, turtlenecks, boys' undershirt and brief sets, girls' panties and camisole sets, long underwear sets, and playsets for boys and girls. ECotton, a new line, is made from unprocessed pure cotton in an assortment of styles for newborns and infants (available in long underwear, too). The Mother and Daughter sleepwear collection ranges from oversized T-shirts to nightgowns. Retail prices are moderate depending on your budget. The well-stocked outlet offers 30–50% off retail on seconds and past-season overruns.

2nd Street Kids

625 Second Street, #102, San Francisco. (415) 495-6659;
(800) 350-5437. M–Sat 10–5. MC, VISA. Parking: street.

2nd Street Kids is where the original and unique Bizzy Gear, Inc. line is sold. Much is designed to be reversible, especially the outerwear. Leftovers (jackets, jumpers/overalls, bubble suits) are available in vibrant colors in polar fleece lined with bold prints (fall collections); spring/summer styles feature print/solid terry robes and shorts; wonderful prints on 100% cotton varsity jackets and shorts, baseball shirts and pants, and ruffled jumpers. Naturally, such originality does not come cheap at retail; it's even expensive at half off. Overall prices range from $6 to $40. In Spring 1995, overalls, jumpsuits, dresses, and barncoats hit the outlet priced from $10 to $20. Leftover fabric is $5.50/yard. The owners help other small designers unload merchandise: charming layette gifts, diaper bags, imported shoes, precious party dresses, baby blankets, etc. Sizes: Newborn to 14 (best selection to size 6X).

Storybook Heirlooms

Outlets at Gilroy, Gilroy. (408) 842-3880. Daily.
MC, VISA, AE, DIS. Parking: lot.

Storybook Heirlooms, an upscale catalog company of "timeless clothing for girls," sends its catalog surplus inventory here: a wonderful selection of girls' clothing and accessories in sizes

Infant through 16. You'll find top-quality merchandise bearing the Storybook Heirlooms label and fashions from other recognized manufacturers. Since the lines are moderately to very expensive at retail, prices may still seem high even at discount. Discounts start at 20% off on recent merchandise and go to 30–60% on the older stuff. You can find dresses, casual sportswear, special occasion wear, darling footwear, First Communion dresses, bouffant petticoats and slips, and a few dress styles in mother-daughter coordinates. Join the mailing list for invitations to the occasional major blowout sales at its Hayward warehouse. Call (800) 825-6565 for a complimentary catalog.

Sweet Potatoes Factory Outlet
1716 Fourth Street, Berkeley. (510) 527-7633.
M-Sat 10-6, Sun 11-6. MC, VISA. Parking: lot.
Sweet Potatoes active sportswear features bright colors, prints, plaids, and fun details. Dresses, overalls, shirts, jog sets, jumpsuits, tights, leggings, socks, skirts, hats, suspenders, and turtlenecks add up to many options when outfitting the kids. You'll love the whimsical Yazoo line for girls in sizes 4–14; Spuds for boys in sizes 12mos–7; Sweet Potatoes for Infants to 10; and New Potato and Marimekko Layette to Toddler. The seconds, overruns, samples, and past-season styles are discounted 30–60%, which doesn't make them cheap by any means since they are boutique-priced at retail. For your projects, you can often pick up leftover fabrics, trims, and patches (10¢ to $4). Note: Some very petite women find the preteen sportswear just right for their tiny proportions.

We Be Bop for Kids
1380 Tenth Street, Berkeley. (510) 527-7256.
M-Sat 10-5, Sun Noon-5. MC, VISA, AE. Parking: street.
We Be Bop for Kids is a smaller version of the adult line. The same playful styles are made in Bali from rayon and cotton in sometimes wild batiks and print combinations. Some styles for boys. As much as I like the merchandise, I'm lukewarm about the 30% discounts on overruns and past-season goods. Sizes 4–14, with an excellent selection of sizes in 7–14 and Preteen styles. Size 7/8 girls are lucky, they can often find el cheapo prices on samples—like dresses at $5.

Wee Clancy Factory Sales

2682-F Middlefield Road, Redwood City. (415) 366-5597.
F 10-4, Sat 9-1. Cash/Check. Parking: lot.

On Fridays and Saturdays, Peninsula moms can cruise through Wee Clancy's racks finding new booty for their girls, especially wonderful European-styled dresses and playwear made from 100% cotton. Many dresses and fancy jumpsuits are perfect for V.I.P. occasions. The detailing, fabrics, and intricate designs justify the prices—expensive for some even when greatly discounted. Frequent specials where additional discounts are taken at the register make these dresses more affordable for everyone. These dresses are guaranteed to make any little girl feel very pretty and special. The outlet sells seasonal overruns, samples (size 4), and sometimes slightly imperfect merchandise. Sizes: Infant to 14. Get on the mailing list!

Also See

Under San Francisco's Factory Outlets and Off-Price Stores:
Christine Foley; Designer Co-Op

Under General Clothing:
Most listings

Under Clearance Centers:
All listings

Under Furniture and Home Accessories—Baby and Juvenile:
All listings

Under General Merchandise—Membership Warehouse Clubs:
Price/Costco Club

Clearance Centers

For Major Department Stores and Retail Chains

Clearinghouse by Saks
If all goes as planned this clearance center should be open
by August 1995 at the Great Mall of the Bay Area in Milpitas.
See Off Fifth in Late Additions for details.

Contempo Casuals Outlet
Vintage Oaks Shopping Center, Novato. (415) 892-6966.
M–Sat 10–9, Sun 11–6. MC, VISA, AE, DIS. Parking: lot.
(Other store: 148 Woodside Place Center, Redwood City.)
Heads up! This is one for young women, and they're really
gonna love it. Contempo Casuals, mall headquarters for teen
trendsetters, has two Bay Area clearance centers, the Novato
store and its smaller counterpart in Redwood City. At both,
everything is priced at least 50% off retail. However, prices on
many groups or categories of merchandise are marked down
to 70–80% off retail: some jeans and pants at $2, $4, or $9.
You'll find every category of apparel that it sells: coats, active
wear, bathing suits, dresses, pants, sweaters, skirts, blouses and
tops, even prom dresses. I spotted some "uglies" in the selection, but 14- to 17-year-old girls may think they're totally
awesome! Sizes 1–13 in the Contempo line designed for the
17- to 25-year-old market. The prices and selection are so
enticing that teens and younger women are in for a shopping
bonanza!

Emporium Capwell Clearance Store

Broadway at 20th Street, Oakland. (510) 891-5000.
M–F 10–8, Sat 10–6, Sun 11–6. MC, VISA, AE, Emporium Charge
Card. Parking: lot.

The survivors of sales and markdowns at other Emporium stores
end up in the basement here. There's a bit of everything: some
men's, some kids', and gobs of misses and junior apparel.
Prices are reduced 50–80% off retail. Some pieces are a little
worse for wear; fine fashions are almost nonexistent. You'll
need time and patience to liberate the better pieces from the
endless rows of racks. Check the color codes for additional
25–60% discounts off the lowest ticketed price on each tag.

Nordstrom Rack

81 Colma Boulevard, 280 Metro Center, Colma. (415) 755-1444.
M–Sat 10–9, Sun 11–6. Nordstrom Card, MC, VISA, AE.
Parking: lot.
(Other store: Marina Square, San Leandro, (510) 614-1742.)

The Rack's inventory consists of clearance and out-of-season
fashions from the main Nordstrom stores, as well as special
purchases from regular Nordstrom manufacturers (easy to spot
since some of this stuff would never be selected for the stores).
Expect to save 30–70% off Nordstrom's original retail, and
30–50% on special purchases. I think some of the best buys
and quality are found in the men's department. The emphasis
at The Rack is on apparel and shoes for the entire family.
Exchanges, refunds, and Nordstrom's unconditional guarantee.

Spin-Off

3506 Mt. Diablo Road (behind Guy's Drug Store), Lafayette
Square, Lafayette. (510) 283-4084. M–Sat 10–6, Sun 11–5.
MC, VISA. Parking: lot.

Spin-Off carries in-season clearance inventory at minimum
50% discounts off retail. I spotted these labels: Koret, Aileen,
Liz Sport, Jones New York, Calvin Klein Sport, Vittadini, Chaus,
Jessica McClintock, and others. Some groups were discounted
65% off retail. The emphasis is on sportswear, but you may
find holiday fashions at 50% off before Christmas. The store
only carries fashions from the women's departments. Sizes
4–16 (you won't find all sizes in all groups). Returns and
refunds with receipt.

Talbots Outlet

1235 Marina Boulevard, Marina Square, San Leandro.
(510) 614-1090. M–F 10–9, Sat 10–7, Sun 11–6. MC, VISA, AE.
Parking: lot.

Talbots really comes through with quality goods and solid discounts (30–60% off). It's a great favorite—drawing women from all over Northern California. Year-round, you're likely to find "nice" dresses for special occasions, some with extra dazzle for the holidays. There's a small children's department with worth-the-trip bargains. Occasional extras include career and casual shoes, bathing suits, and fashion accessories. I liked the career and dress departments best of all. Savvy shoppers, don't ignore the postcards announcing special sale events. Talbots rewards petite ladies with a very extensive selection of fashions and has a better-than-average inventory of clothing for that often-neglected 14–20 size woman. Kudos to the staff for their gracious service. Sizes: Petite 2–16; Misses 4–20. Refunds and exchanges.

Leather Apparel

J.L. Leathers

60 E. Third Street, San Mateo. (415) 342-4266.
M–Sat 10–5. MC, VISA. Parking: street.
Women and men shop here for sophisticated styling, better quality, and good prices on apparel made from butter-soft lambskin, nubuck, and suede with European styling (some knockoffs of high-style designs). Women can find jackets in short or three-quarter lengths to match pants, vests, or skirts, or they can turn heads with a chic leather dress. Men can go contemporary, weekend casual, or classic in jackets priced from $199 to $650. Women's prices range from $139 to $800 (full-length coats). Sizes: Women's 4–14 (a few 16s); Men's: 38–46. Nice selection of handbags and accessories at discount prices.

Leather Outlet/Down Under Imports

950 Detroit Avenue, #14, Concord. (510) 687-8883.
F–Sun Noon–5. MC, VISA. Parking: lot.
The Leather Outlet sells leather fashions (lamb, deer, wild boar) from Australia and New Zealand, but most come from better U.S. companies. The outlet is small but offers a very versatile selection. Men can opt for bomber styles, motorcycle jackets (with requisite zippers and snaps), blazers, flight jackets, and long fingertip jackets, some with zip-out inserts for warmth. Women will find racks of elegant and chic butter-soft jackets in vibrant colors and some Western-style fringed jackets. Prices are around wholesale. Most men's jackets are $59–$229 in sizes 36–64; women's $99–$259 in sizes XS–XL (5/6–18).

Leather to Go

200 Potrero Avenue, San Francisco. (415) 863-6171.
M–F 9–4, Sat 10–2. MC, VISA. Parking: street.
Maybe you've seen President Clinton in his casual mode sporting his favorite brown cowhide jacket. The jacket came from
this local company—a source of much pride and satisfaction.
Buy this jacket and others at Leather to Go's factory showroom,
where samples, imperfects, closeouts, and first-quality overruns are 40% off retail. If approximately $80–$300 sounds like
a good price range for better-quality leather jackets in bomber,
Western, and blazer styles, or suede and shearling outerwear,
you'll be right at home here. The company sells through fine
stores, specialty shops, and catalogs in the United States, Europe,
and Asia. It also makes jackets for law-enforcement agencies,
athletic teams, etc. Sizes: Men's 36–46; Women's 6–16.

Leathermode

Outlets at Gilroy, Gilroy. (408) 848-4114. Daily.
MC, VISA, AE, DIS. Parking: lot.
(Other outlet: Great Mall, Milpitas.)
Leathermode is well known in Southern California with its
thirteen retail stores. Excess inventory, past-season styles,
and closeouts on apparel, casual luggage, handbags, executive
cases, and accessories keep this outlet well stocked. First-
quality fashions are reduced in price 20–60% off original retail.
Couples can find cowhide or brushed-leather bombers, motorcycle jackets, men's full-length coats, or three-quarters-
length lambskin ladies' jackets. Leather portfolios, attachés,
and similar goods are all very nicely priced. Men's jackets
range from $89 to $299; women's from $79 to $299. Sizes:
Men's to XXL; women's to XL. Very good leather source!

New Territory Leathers

Village Outlets of Napa Valley, St. Helena. (707) 963-8660.
Daily 10–6, Sun 11–6. MC, VISA, AE. Parking: lot.
Most of the upscale leather jackets here wear the Sawyer of
Napa label; however, this is a separate enterprise. What counts
are prices 40–60% off original retail on first-quality overruns,
past-season styles, and canceled orders from Sawyer of Napa
and other wholesalers including Marc Buchanan, Andrew
Marc, and others. Men's and women's selections are about
50/50. Women who are not into rustic and rugged wear will
appreciate the new fashion collections. Sawyer's signature

shearling jackets range from $399 to $999 in a variety of styles. Status shoppers will find sublime prices on Marc Buchanan's colorful jackets (worn by Michael Jordan and others). New Territory's private label collection of bombers, barn jackets, and suedes with fringe are excellent values priced at $99 to $229. Don't miss the small selection of sweaters including nice cashmeres and the popular Mondo line. Sizes: Men's S–XXL; Women's S–L. Returns and refunds.

Sawyer of Napa Outlet

68 Coombs, Napa. (707) 253-1000. Seasonal hours: Oct–Nov W–Sun 10–5; Dec open daily. MC, VISA, AE. Parking: lot.

A word of warning: This outlet is unpredictable. It may or may not be open, but if it is, it's usually only on a seasonal basis (October through December, sometimes January, too). Call first! Sawyer of Napa sells its seconds here at 30–70% below regular retail. The selection changes, but there's usually a little of everything made by the company, from its basic lamb-skin shearling jackets to innovative fashion jackets for women. Prices during 1995: jackets ranging from $89 to $279; coats from $299 to $1299. Sizes: S–XXL (size selection can be very limited in many styles). Slippers, lambskins, and large lambskin quad rugs are outlet priced. Cashmere sweaters at wonderful prices have been part of the selection during the past few seasons. All sales are final.

Snyder Leather Outlet

Great Mall of the Bay Area, Milpitas. (408) 934-9095. Daily. MC, VISA, AE, DIS. Parking: street.

Whatever your leather fantasy, you'll find it at Snyder. Owned by Wilson's, they've got the right pipeline to the goods. Men and women can buy jackets, coats, pants, vests, hats, whatever! Basics, classics, and some real high-fashion contemporary styles are in the mix. Prices reduced 20–40%.

Also See

Under Other Bay Area Factory Outlets/Factory Stores:
Adrienne Vittadini Direct; Anne Klein; Ellen Tracy Outlet; Donna Karan Company Store; J. Crew

Under General Clothing:
Burlington Coat Factory; London Fog Factory Stores; Marshall's; Polo/Ralph Lauren Factory Store; Ross; T.J. Maxx; Woolrich

Under Late Additions:
Off Fifth

Under Chain Discount Stores:
Loehmann's

Under Clearance Centers:
All listings

Recycled Apparel

Consignment, Resale, and Thrift Shops

In today's politically correct environment there's a certain cachet to buying resale. Consumers from all income and education levels enjoy the pursuit and pleasure of finding great buys from resale, consignment, and thrift shops. A consignment shop is where one is likely to find the best quality. Usually their prices are higher than thrift shops. The affluent use these shops as a discreet way to recycle their clothing and recoup some of the original cost. Most resale shops operate on a consignment basis. Usually the potential seller brings in any items she wants to dispose of, and the store agrees to try to sell them for her for a certain percentage of the price. Other stores agree on the price the item will go for (the amount depending on the item's condition and age), and this is split fifty-fifty with the shop owner. Strictly resale shops buy outright. Either way, it's a winning proposition for everyone involved: the original owner makes a profit, the store owner makes a profit, and customers are able to buy clothes that might otherwise be out of reach. Expect to save 50–70% buying this way; when you pay $40 for a dress, it probably cost about $200 new.

At many shops, you'll find some very sophisticated clothes with designer labels. Often clothing may be as good as new—an indication that the original owner may never have worn the item. Even the best of us make mistakes with our purchases: we buy a garment that's a tad too tight and then never quite get our weight down to wearable size, or the color or style seems all wrong after consideration (and returning the merchandise to the store is no longer an option). Finding these shops is not difficult. Many advertise in community newspapers, while a quick perusal of the Yellow Pages of your phone book under "Clothing: Used" will provide a list of shops closest to you. Some shoppers "follow the money" by choosing shops in areas that are obviously supplied by an affluent clientele.

There are hundreds of resale shops around the Bay Area, and it may take time to find the one(s) that suits your fashion personality. Stores do vary, particularly in the standards applied to the merchandise they accept. The most discerning resale shops accept only recent fashions, in like-new condition, with recognized labels that denote quality. Some feature vintage or retro clothing, and prices may be based more on the collectible status of the goods. Always ask if there's more to see, since some shops keep the best merchandise in the back room for their regulars. As you begin your explorations, be prepared to see some stores that will leave you cold, with merchandise that's out-of-date, too tired, and presented in such a hodge-podge fashion that you can't generate any enthusiasm for shopping. If the store smells like old clothes and sweat, just leave and keep on trekking, there's a store somewhere that's perfect for you.

Resale stores specializing in children's clothing are a boon to budget-pressed parents. Fortunately, there are several free publications that focus on the services, concerns, and interests of parents and their children. *Parents' Press, Bay Parent, Valley Parent, Peninsula Parent* and others are widely distributed at places where children and parents congregate: preschools, clinics, doctor's offices, supermarkets, and children's toy, apparel, and specialty stores. These publications are filled with advertising from children's resale and consignment stores. Many of these children's shops are also very good sources for used shoes, toys, baby equipment, books, and maternity clothing.

Cosmetics and Fragrances

In almost every shopping center around the Bay Area you'll find a beauty supply store that offers more than what you'll see in most drugstores and supermarkets. Even though the selections of hair-care, nail, and sometimes skin-care, and beauty aids are extensive, prices all around are pretty competitive. Often these stores offer incentives for return visits, such as a card to tote up cumulative totals in purchases leading to rebates or extra discounts. It pays to stick with one store if this is the case.

Bare Escentuals Outlet and Refill Center

2516 Bancroft Way, Berkeley. (510) 845-2272.
M–Sat 10–7, Sun 11–6. MC, VISA. Parking: lot.
Bare Escentuals' natural line is made without animal ingredients, nor is it tested on animals. The cosmetics are free of mineral oil, talc, perfume, alcohol, and artificial dyes that may cause allergic reactions. The basic product groups—skin care, shampoos, bath, aromatherapy oils, fragrances and essential oils, and cosmetics—come in classy yet simple packaging. Discontinued products or packaging, damaged goods, and overruns are sent to this store/outlet next to the University of California. Prices are reduced 50–75% off retail. Bins of special $1, $2, and $3 values should get a thorough going-over. The complete Bare Escentuals line is also sold here at regular prices.

California Theatrical Supply

132 Ninth Street, Second Floor, San Francisco. (415) 863-9684.
M–F 10–4, Sat 11–4. MC, VISA. Parking: street (until 4 p.m.).
This company deals mainly with local and national television personalities, theater and opera stars, and performing troupes. The shelves offer a rainbow collection of cosmetics that fill the requirements of stage and studio. Geared for the pros, the staff is not equipped to spend time giving makeup lessons or helping you make decisions. Kryolan, Dermacolor, Mehron, Ben Nye, and Bob Kelly are the professional lines offered, along with some generic products in lipsticks, eyeshadows, foundations, pancakes, powders, blushes, mascaras, pencils, and a baffling array of brushes. Professionals buy nose putty, eyelashes, moustaches, wigs, feathers, and other tricks of the theatrical trade. Plastic surgeons refer patients for its line of camouflage makeup. Planning a face-painting party for kids or fundraisers? This is where to buy the makeup/paints that are guaranteed to wash off. Prices, while not discounted, are substantially lower than on comparable lines in department stores. You'll also see many products no longer found in department store selections.

Colours & Scents

Outlets at Gilroy, Gilroy. (408) 842-3575. MC, VISA. Parking: lot.
(Other outlets: Milpitas, Pacific Grove, St. Helena centers.)
If Elizabeth Arden is your preferred brand, you'll like what you see here. The discounts are modest at best: $5–$10 off on most products. You'll save a few dollars on Ceramide Time Capsules, or about 18% on Visible Difference. Borghese makeup, moisture treatments, and body creams are well stocked. Ultima II comes through with some of the best discounts—almost half off. A nice discount fragrance selection balances out the inventory of these elegant stores. Look around for extra specials—your best buys. Order by phone if you don't like to drive.

New York Cosmetics and Fragrances

318 Brannan Street, San Francisco. (415) 543-3880.
M–F 11–5, Sat 10–5. MC, VISA, DIS. Parking: limited street.
(Other store: Vintage Oaks Center, Novato.)
If you're trying to trim your budget, consider buying your makeup here. This company does some of its business on a wholesale basis with hair and beauty salons, selling cosmetics under its own salon label. At the outlet, you can buy the unbranded, naked product at a minimal markup. Lipsticks,

foundations, nail polish, eyeshadow, blush, and mascara cover the basics. Whenever it can get a good buy on brand-name cosmetics like Calvin Klein, Estée Lauder, Clinique, or Lancôme, it passes on the discounts. Brand-name fragrances are 10–70% off retail. Request a catalog for easy ordering by phone or mail.

Perfumania
359 Grant Avenue, San Francisco. (415) 956-1229.
M–Sat 10–7, Sun 11–6. MC, VISA, DIS. Parking: pay lots.
(Other stores/outlets: Anderson/Redding, Concord, Daly City, Folsom, Gilroy, Lathrop, Milpitas, Petaluma, Pleasanton, Richmond, Tracy, Vacaville.)
The first thing to do when stopping in is to pick up the monthly flyer that highlights selected fragrance specials: great savings on promotional merchandise, unboxed products, miniatures, testers, and other brand-name products. Your best bet? Special boxed gift sets. Overall, 20–60% off on your favorite fragrances for women or men. No cosmetics.

Prestige Fragrance and Cosmetics
Factory Stores of America, Vacaville. (707) 449-8067. Daily.
MC, VISA. Parking: lot.
(Other stores/outlets: Lake Tahoe, Lathrop, Milpitas, Pacific Grove, Petaluma, Tracy.)
PFC stores are owned by one of the biggest cosmetic companies in the country. You can get nationally advertised lines formulated for specific skin types, or products to minimize aging. Waiting for you: cosmetics and skin-care lines at 30–70% off retail. Also, discontinued products and leftovers from special promotional campaigns that are super buys with the additional discount at PFC. The same conditions apply to the fragrances and fragrance-based products (body powders, lotions, and soaps). Suntan products, men's fragrances, nail-care needs, and other beauty-related items round out the selection. Check the "annex" for the best buys going.

Also See

Under General Clothing:
Ross

Under Other Bay Area Factory Outlets/Factory Stores:
Spa Gear

Handbags and Luggage

AAA Luggage Repair Depot

585 Howard Street (near Second Street), San Francisco.
(415) 781-5007. M–F 8–5, Sat 9–3. MC, VISA, AE.
Parking: street/pay lots.

AAA is the Bay Area's largest authorized repair station for most national brands of luggage; it also sells luggage, attaché cases, portfolios, travel accessories, etc. It features samples, factory closeouts, and unclaimed repaired items. In stock, luggage from Skyway, Samsonite, Halliburton, Atlas, Schlesinger, and the complete Travelpro collection are stashed around the showroom. The attaché cases range from very inexpensive to top quality. When your suitcase's wheels go berserk, bring it in. AAA handles the claims from twenty-nine airlines. Savings 20–70% off.

American Tourister

Factory Stores of America, Vacaville. (707) 446-1595. Daily.
MC, VISA, AE, DIS. Parking: lot.
(Other outlets: Folsom, Gilroy, Napa, Tracy centers.)

American Tourister's factory store is well stocked with molded and soft-sided luggage, along with sport bags, backpacks, handbags, Buxton wallets, travel accessories, and business cases. These are closeouts and irregulars with minor cosmetic flaws. You'll also find a fair amount of first-quality merchandise. Discounts overall are 40–70% off retail.

Borsa Fine Leathers

Great Mall of the Bay Area, Milpitas. (408) 263-9867. Daily.
MC, VISA, AE, DIS. Parking: lot.

Borsa was created by this Italian manufacturer as a store name
since it was reluctant to draw too much attention to the label
on its leather goods, which are well known in Europe and
Japan. In the United States much of what it makes is sold under
private label by other well-known companies or designers. The
label Castello may not be a household word, but that takes
nothing away from the very fine quality of all its leather handbags, wallets, and professional cases. Made to the company's
specifications in China from all Italian top-grain leathers, the
line is very European in style and definitely classy. Prices on
its handbags generally range from $100 to $200 at discount;
small leather goods and wallets from $9 to $50; and document
cases/totes from $200 to $300. You can find lower prices at
other leather companies in this mall, but not the quality. All
the most recognized handbag styles are carried in the line.
Many have detachable straps. (Some two-tone bags bring to
mind Dooney & Bourke handbags.) Prices are reduced every
day about 30% off retail, but look around for designated weekly
specials of extra 20% discounts. Each bag comes with a cloth
bag for careful storage. The clasps or fastenings may be gold-
plated or solid brass. A lifetime maintenance policy on Borsa's
handbags allows you to return at any time for repairs or cleaning (they'll even refurbish edges that may get a little worn
with use). Returns and refunds up to five days, returns up to
fourteen days. Close to Airplane Court entrance at the mall.

Bruce Alan Bags, Etc.

Outlets at Gilroy, Gilroy. (408) 848-4104. Daily. MC, VISA.
Parking: lot.

The handbags range from low-priced to quite pricey, but all
are discounted 20–40% off retail. Career basics and many
special fashion bags in leather, fabric, and novelty fabrications
sport famous and less-known labels. Also: totes, executive
cases, luggage, sport bags, duffels, travel accessories, security
pouches, and other goodies. Nice selection overall.

California Luggage Outlet

Outlets at Gilroy, Gilroy. (408) 847-4181. Daily.
MC, VISA, AE, DIS. Parking: lot.
(Other outlet: Vacaville center.)

You have to wonder if anyone buys luggage at retail anymore. This store is owned by El Portal Luggage & Leather Goods, usually found in shopping malls. It's capturing some business from bargain hunters by offering 20–50% discounts on major brands: Tumi, Samsonite, Delsey, Skyway, Travelpro, and Lark. All types of luggage, plus backpacks, soft weekend bags, travel accessories, games, and even Mont Blanc and Waterman pens (special orders at 20% off) and in-stock Cross pens.

Choice Luggage

1742 El Camino Real, Mountain View. (415) 968-3479.
M–Sat 10–6. MC, VISA. Parking: lot.

Choice offers bargain prices on an extensive inventory of brand-name garment bags, carry-on luggage and tote bags from moderate to top-of-the-line companies. You'll find Lark, Skyway, Samsonite, Atlantic, Atlas of Boston, Halliburton, East Pak, and others. It also stocks small travel accessories, men's over-the-shoulder pouches, fine leather wallets, and attachés. Exchanges allowed only within thirty days of purchase.

The Coach Store

Village Outlets of Napa Valley, St. Helena. (707) 963-7272.
Daily 10–6. MC, VISA, AE. Parking: street.
(Other store: Carmel.)

At Coach Stores, everything is "value priced," 20–50% off retail. The leathers may have surface flaws, but usually the merchandise is simply discontinued. Travelers might consider its leather duffels, carry-ons, and totes. Men should stop in for an executive case, belt, wallet, or travel kit, and examine its handsome line of ties. Ladies will naturally zero in on the handbags that constitute about 75% of the store's overall selection. Anything made by Coach might be available, including pocket diaries or organizers. Prices average 26% off original retail; 50% discounts can be found on the special sale tables. All merchandise bears a discreet mark inside noting that the item was purchased from a Coach value-priced store. This should not deter you from buying any item as a gift.

Edwards Adventures in Travel

Great Mall of the Bay Area, Milpitas. (408) 934-9559. Daily.
MC, VISA, AE, DIS. Parking: lot.

Edwards puts on a new personality with this clearance outlet, a fun, high-energy store in keeping with the Great Mall's orientation. Customers love the mock airline cabin with seats and overhead bins. The focus is on travel everything: a variety of luggage, attachés, travel aids (security, passport cases, personal accessories, etc.), games, maps, and books. Discontinued inventory from its posh full-price stores—agendas, business cases, computer bags, and women's small leather goods—are sold at 20–50% off original retail. Better brands of luggage like Hartmann, Tumi, Lark, and Samsonite are 30–50% off retail on seconds, overruns, and discontinued colors.

Ganson Handbag Outlet

Pacific West Outlet Center, Gilroy. (408) 847-4433. Daily.
MC, VISA. Parking: lot.

Ganson has been a source of classic tailored styles in handbags for many years, carried in major department stores. You'll capture 30–60% discounts on first-quality discontinued styles and colors, plus closeouts. At retail the line sells for $80–$130; at the outlet, prices start at $29 and top out with a few priced at $89 (leather briefcases originally $220). Buy carefully; all sales are final. Lovely outlet store!

Glaser Designs

32 Otis Street (at S. Van Ness and Mission), San Francisco.
(415) 552-3188. M–F 9:30–5:30, Sat Noon–5. MC, VISA.
Parking: street/pay lot off Brady Alley.

The emphasis here is on long-lasting handmade travel gear that costs a lot, but less than comparable lines sold in status stores. Glaser's handsome travel and custom-finished leather garment and stadium bags cost $500–$600, and in the $400 range for packing cases. Customers have inspired innovations like the "insiders"—stretch-proof nylon mesh containers to organize travel goods. Business travelers also appreciate its Traveler's briefcases, which double as computer bags ($500–$800), totes, soft briefcases, and ladies' lightweight leather handbags priced $175–$400. Garment bags are designed to "stand" when folded so that they won't collapse on your garments. You'll find a few seconds year-round, but most customers are willing to pay premium prices for the regular merchandise and feel the quality/price/value ratio is reasonable.

Graffeo Leather & Handbag Outlet

1232 Burlingame Avenue, Burlingame. (415) 342-6276,
(800) 472-3336. M–Sat 10–5. MC, VISA, AE. Parking: street.
Graffeo sells under private label through a fascinating list of
stores. All its handbags, leather goods, and luggage are very
versatile, encompassing an attractive selection (generally in
black, brown, or natural) of ladies' handbags, totes, backpacks,
executive attachés, portfolios, specialty bags (camcorder,
cellular phones, shave kits, etc.), garment bags, carry-ons, and
a luggage line. These pieces feature clever compartments,
organizing aspects, pockets, and detachable straps. The handbags are soft and casual, while making the grade as an "executive" accessory. At the outlet these leather goods are sold at
wholesale prices. Some guidelines: handbags $10–$39; totes
and backpacks $44–$69; carry-ons $79–$99; garment bags
$199; executive cases $49–$99. The leathers are typically black,
brown, or natural. Nylon sport bags, duffels, and carry-ons
are well priced at $10–$20.

Griffco Handbag Co.

204 Martin Luther King Way (at Second Street), Oakland.
(510) 444-3800. M–F 9–5, Sat 9–4:30. MC, VISA.
Parking: side lot.
Griffco manufactures more than forty styles of soft, casual,
genuine leather handbags in a wide array of colors. They aren't
for elegant dressing, but rather for everyday use. Factory
prices are $10–$36 on the handbags. Small backpacks, men's
bags, and shaving bags are well priced, with soft-sided briefcases at $39–$65. Leather book bags are $53.50, while luggage
carry-ons are an exceptional value at $76. If you need repairs
later on your purchase, no problem. All bags guaranteed!

Handbag Factory Outlet

2100 Fifth Street, Berkeley. (510) 843-6022.
M–F 8:30–4:30, Sat 10–4:30. MC, VISA. Parking: lot.
You'll bag some great buys here, even though its prices are not
cheap. This anonymous outfit manufactures a moderate- to
high-priced line (retail $36–$200). You'll find discontinued
items, samples, and seconds with minor flaws for 30–60% off
retail. All its bags are made from superior-grade leathers. You'll
have your choice of style with compartments and pockets.
Expect to spend about $80 for a midsized bag. The color range
is very good, with all the basics and some fashion hues. Fanny

packs and wallets are also popular here; the wallets and belts at discount are from other manufacturers.

Harband's Luggage

46 Kentucky Street, Petaluma. (707) 769-0610. M–F 10–6, Sat 10–3. MC, VISA, AE, DIS. Parking: street/lot.
Harband's portfolios and attaché cases are a very good gift resource. Fine leather is its specialty, although vinyls and hard cases are also available. Samsonite, Briggs & Riley, Florentine, Schlesinger, Korchmar, Leathermill, Remin Kart-a-Bags, and many more are some of its lines. The discounts are typically a modest 20% off manufacturers' list prices; special sales take prices down to 50% off. Little leathers—wallets, passport cases, travel accessories—are also discounted.

Leather Loft

Factory Stores of America, Vacaville. (707) 446-7262. Daily. MC, VISA, DIS, AE. Parking: lot.
(Other outlets: Folsom, Gilroy, Lathrop, Milpitas, Petaluma, Pacific Grove centers.)
Leather Loft stocks its 125-plus factory stores with handbags, belts, wallets, briefcases, travel and desk accessories, gifts, designer accessories, and a small array of leather jackets. The selection includes timeless classic styles as well as the latest color or design. You'll find first-quality merchandise, seconds, irregulars, and closeouts. Discounts are 25–60% off retail. Handbags for every budget from $25 to $150. The leather jackets deserve a close look!

Luggage Center

828 Mission Street (across from Fifth and Mission Garage), San Francisco. (415) 543-3771.
M–F 8:30–6, Sat 10–5, Sun 11:30–5. Parking: street/pay lots.
(Other stores: See Geographical Index.)
The Luggage Center offers solid discounts to first-class as well as economy-minded travelers. The luggage is first-line merchandise, open stock, and special purchases from companies like Skyway, Samsonite, Eagle Creek, Delsey, Travelpro, Atlantic, High Sierra, Halliburton, and others. There are no seconds. Savings are 20–50%. The inventory includes all types of luggage, and a wide variety of travel accessories, totes, attachés, and wallets. Exchanges and refunds within thirty days with receipt.

Luggage to Go

75 Bellam Boulevard, Marin Square, San Rafael. (415) 459-5167.
M-Sat 10-6, Sun Noon-5. MC, VISA, AE. Parking: lot.
This store's discounts are 20-60% off retail on luggage (many
current styles and fabrications), plus bonus pricing on special
manufacturers' promotions, factory purchases, and leftovers
from the owner's Beverly Hills store. Attachés, luggage, and
almost anything required for carrying goodies on a trip are
stocked. The selection is particularly choice for those wanting
better lines not often found at discount. You'll like these labels:
Samsonite, Lark, Delsey, Halliburton, Travelpro, Hartmann, The
French Co., and more. The beautiful Italian leather collection
is for the very chic. Monogramming is free—how nice!

Malm Warehouse & Repair

1429 Burlingame Avenue, Burlingame. (415) 343-0990.
M-F 9-6, Sat 10-6. MC, VISA, AE, DIS. Parking: street.
Malm offers new suitcases, carry-ons, garment bags, and more
from its inventory of discontinued and slightly irregular luggage.
Hartmann, Tumi, Lark, Delsey, and Samsonite are some of the
brands you'll find at 25-50% markdowns. Take care of details
with a discounted portfolio, attaché, toiletry kit, business case,
agenda, or small leather good. Repairs, too—a complete service
for luggage and attachés. Free monogramming.

Rockridge Luggage

5816 College Avenue, Oakland. (510) 428-2247. MC, VISA, AE.
M-F 10-7, Sat 10-6. Parking: street.
This company manages to cram an extensive selection of
luggage from many recognized companies into its small space:
Tumi, Boyt, Lark, Samsonite, Travelpro, Andiamo, Hartmann,
and others. Discounts everyday are 20-40% off retail. Students
will have any number of choices when it comes to choosing
a pack to tote heavy textbooks, while executives can find a
leather attaché, portfolio, or briefcase in just the right configuration and size. Travel carts, small leather goods, gift items,
and pens are the right price for gift givers.

Sven Design

2301 Fourth Street, Berkeley. (510) 848-7836.
M–F 9–5, Sat 11–5. MC, VISA. Parking: street.
Sven's outlet showcases its line, which it sells primarily through craft shows and boutiques, although selected styles show up in status department stores. About 75% of the selection here is current season offered at 20% discount. Handbag prices are $22–$100; you'll find deeper discounts (40–50% off retail) only on closeouts and discontinued styles. Its drum-dyed leather requires skilled artisanry (which means higher prices). Fine-quality construction features suit the most exacting requirements. Handbags come in neutrals and fashion colors, plus a few styles in exotic leathers or tapestry fabrics, serving traditional and contemporary tastes. You'll also find totes, book bags, fanny packs, and minibags/wallets with detachable straps. The handbags here are not inexpensive, but if quality is your concern and you feel that a little saving is better than none, you'll be very pleased.

The Wallet Works

Pacific West Outlet Center, Gilroy. (408) 842-7488. Daily.
MC, VISA. Parking: street/pay lots.
(Other outlets: Folsom, Napa, Petaluma, Pacific Grove centers.)
The Wallet Works is perhaps known best for its wallets, available in department stores around the country. Think of a leather item in any configuration made to hold money, credit cards, or passports, and it'll be here, plus portfolios, soft luggage, fanny packs, daily organizers, tote bags, and portable coolers. The handbag selection is tempting, too. The few seconds are clearly marked, with extra discounts as the trade-off. Discounts range from a modest 20% to 60% off retail.

Also See

Under General Clothing:
B.U.M. Equipment/Coliseum; Burlington Coat Factory; Eddie Bauer; Marshall's; Ross; T.J. Maxx

Under Shoes:
Bass Shoe Outlet; Cole-Haan; Etienne Aigner; Timberland

Under San Francisco's Factory Outlets and Off-Price Stores:
Esprit Factory Outlet

Under Other Bay Area Factory Outlets/Factory Stores:
**Ann Taylor; Anne Klein; Liz Claiborne Outlet;
MCM Company Store; Rampage Outlet**

Under Women's Accessories:
Designer Brands/Accessories; Icing Outlet

Under Appliances, Electronics, and Home Entertainment:
Whole Earth Access

Under General Merchandise:
All listings

Jewelry and Watches

Fine and Costume Jewelry, Diamonds, and Watches

Some ABCs on Buying Fine Jewelry

If you're buying fine jewelry for the first time, you're probably quite wary, because diamonds, gemstones, and gold don't come with labels and brands that make comparison shopping easy. You may feel ill-equipped to determine quality and value, to be sure that you're buying at a fair price, or know if you're paying more than you have to. Armed with some basics about buying jewelry, using common sense, taking time, asking questions, and above all comparison shopping, you need not hesitate to venture out of malls or high-profile jewelers to make your purchase.

A word about diamonds: Two diamonds that look alike at first may be very different, and two diamonds of equal size can have very unequal values. Since no two diamonds are alike, experts use four criteria to determine a diamond's value, the "Four Cs"—carat, color, clarity, and cut. The different combinations of all these characteristics determine the quality and value of a diamond.

Azevedo Jewelers & Gemologists, Inc.

210 Post Street, Third Floor, Suite 321, San Francisco.
(415) 781-0063. T–Sat 10–5. MC, VISA. Parking: pay lots.
Azevedo offers a beautiful selection of diamonds, colored stones, gold jewelry, and cultured pearls at substantial savings; its success is due to low overhead, careful buying, and referrals

from satisfied customers. Appraisals are done by graduate gemologists. Its showroom is very classy, but most of the jewels are kept under wraps for obvious security reasons. Azevedo features jewelry designed by Oscar Heyman & Bros. at the lowest prices you'll find in the Bay Area. This is one of six American Gem Society stores in San Francisco.

Bead Brain Outlet

2700 18th Street (at York bet. Bryant and Potrero),
San Francisco. (415) 621-8815. T–Sat 10–6. MC, VISA.
Parking: street.

Bead Brain is an outlet for Jan Michaels, whose fashion jewelry always looks more expensive than it is. It is made from primary materials like brass chain and stampings, acrylic components, and glass stones and beads. Antique brass and antique silver plating characterize the basic finishes of both the contemporary women's and men's accessories. The finished jewelry selection ranges from the conventional to Baroque to contemporary styles—accents that really make the outfit. Also, necklaces, pins, hair accessories for women; cuff links, tie clips, money clips, and suspenders for men. Closeouts go for at least 50% off retail. Aspiring jewelry designers can find all the components (beads, findings, stones, stampings) to make one-of-a-kind jewelry pieces at el cheapo prices. Women have been known to lose all track of time when poking through the leftovers. Regular workshops are offered in jewelry making and wirework household designs.

Beadco/Small Things Company

760 Market Street (Phelan Building), Suite 860, San Francisco.
(415) 397-0110. M–F 10–4; other hours and Sat by appt.
Cash/Check, VISA. Parking: pay lots.

This company's talent lies in finding maximum value for the best price, using connections developed over the years. If you're interested in a special gift—pearls, lapis, jade, diamonds, precious gemstones, gold, or silver—Beadco probably has it in stock, or can find it, usually at a price 30–60% lower than conventional retailers. Contact Beadco if you need pearls restrung, plating, jewelry repaired (including sterling silver and costume jewelry) or remodeled, a custom design, or an appraisal. Creating innovative wedding rings is the store's special pleasure. Unless you're coming in for repairs, it's essential to call for an appointment.

Broder Jewelry Company

210 Post Street, Room 611, San Francisco. (415) 421-9313.
M–F 9–3:30, Sat by appt. Cash/Check. Parking: pay lots.
Mr. Broder does custom design, appraisals, and repair work for
many of San Francisco's finest jewelry stores and works closely
with a private clientele, creating special pieces like rings,
pendants, and bracelets. However, he does not sell watches or
other items usually found in jewelry stores. His closet-sized
office has no stock on hand, so this is definitely not a store for
casual browsing. If you have a picture of a design, bring it in,
or Mr. Broder can create one. His low overhead accounts for
the low prices on diamonds and colored stones. Naturally, if
you need a ring sized, repaired, or reset, his talents are at your
disposal. One of the few jewelers who works in platinum.
A 50% deposit is required before custom orders are started.

Cresalia Jewelers Diamond Expertise

111 Sutter Street (at Montgomery), San Francisco. (415) 781-7371
or (800) 781-7371. M–Sat 9:30–5:30. AE, MC, VISA, DIS.
Parking: validated parking in garage next door.
Cresalia displays an extensive selection of diamond rings,
fine jewels, and watches. It designs and manufactures its own
rings and carries well-known brands as well. You'll recognize
the companies in its selection: Artcarved, Italiano gold,
Kobe pearls, Krementz, Concord, Movado, Seiko, 18K Concord
Collection, Gorham, Reed & Barton, Lunt, Wallace, Ballou,
Sheffield, Kirk, and Cross pens just for starters. Prices are
guaranteed to be 25–50% below the regular retail at other
jewelry stores. Cresalia has a staff of graduate gemologists
from the Gemological Institute of America to help you choose
a diamond or gem, and to grade and appraise jewelry you
own. If you're shopping for elegant gifts, you'll appreciate
the extensive array of silverware, crystal, clocks, hollowware,
china, and dinner accessories that can be wrapped and
shipped UPS if requested.

Evanton Niederholzer Jewelers

503 Magnolia Avenue, Larkspur. (415) 924-7885.
T–Th and Sat 10–5, F 10–6, Sun 11–4. MC, VISA. Parking: street.
This is where "people in the know" go for quality jewelry at
lower prices: gold and silver accessories, jewelry, diamond
rings (also Lazare Kaplan ideal-cut diamonds), wedding sets,
and precious stones. There are substantial savings on prestige

watches from companies like Seiko, Lassale, and Omega; sterling silver flatware and hollowware from Gorham, Reed & Barton, and others; Cross pens; Colle crystal. You can have your jewelry repaired on the premises (watches are sent out), or utilize its custom jewelry design services.

The Fenton Company

210 Post Street, Suite 502, San Francisco. (415) 563-0258.
By appt. Cash/Check. Parking: pay lots.
Joan Fenton serves as a personal jewelry shopper. In her twelve and a half years in business, Joan has helped many brides, professional women, and "awfully smart men." She keeps no inventory, and her low overhead lets her pass on good prices to her discriminating clientele. She knows how to get things done and brings a sense of style and charm along with her expertise to her business. Call for an appointment to assess your needs. When Joan knows what you want, she can present choices that meet the specifications of size and price that you've requested. Using her trade resources, she'll either find it for you or have it custom-designed at wholesale prices plus a slight markup, generally 10–20%.

Guardian International

150 Bellam Boulevard, San Rafael. (415) 258-0601.
M–F 9–5, Sat by appt. MC, VISA. Parking: street.
Guardian International has solid credentials. It manufactures and supplies large inventories of fine jewelry to PX stores on military installations and many major stores. When buying directly from this source, you'll save about 35% off the "major store price." If you need something fast, you'll be able to find something that's just right. Guardian provides extraordinary quality in original custom designs, special orders its forte. It keeps a good inventory of diamonds up to one carat, and can readily provide larger sizes upon request. If you're in the market for a status watch (most priced over $1,000 at retail) such as Bertolucci, Omega, Cartier, Rolex, and many more, you can pick a style from a notebook full of catalogs, and on most lines you'll pay just 10% over Guardian's cost. Don't come in expecting to see several cases of fine jewelry. It's more of an office serving its private clientele (the public) on an appointment basis; this keeps wholesale buyers and the public from doing business at the same time.

Hockerman & Son Jewelers

760 Market Street, Suites 346–348, San Francisco.
(415) 986-4066. M–F 8:30–4:30 by appt. MC, VISA.
Parking: pay garages.

"Bargain" is a relative term; if you haven't had to adjust your spending because of the recession, Hockerman may be the perfect resource when you're contemplating fine jewelry purchases. It's not set up for casual browsing, since most of its work is done on a custom design basis. Many couples come here seeking unusual settings (true works of art) for wedding rings and will spend $6,000–$8,000 for a ring that would cost $12,000–$14,000 at a Union Square jeweler. Of course, other customers spend much less, especially on wedding bands, gemstone jewelry or pearls, or jewelry resetting. If you'd like estate jewelry reset or want to rework original wedding sets into something more up-to-date, consider this resource. The company keeps an extensive selection of loose diamonds and gemstones on hand, and works with you to develop a design for your jewelry piece. There are modest charges for designing the model and renderings, and work proceeds with a 50% deposit.

K-Gold Co.

2229 Bunker Hill Drive (off 280), San Mateo. (415) 349-2912.
M–Sat by appt. Cash/Check. Parking: street.

If you have old jewelry tucked away and you'd like to have it updated, reset, or repaired, this company can do the job. For years K-Gold has worked with prominent jewelry stores creating custom designs and repairing gold, platinum, and precious stones. It has also created replacement jewelry for insurance claims. You can bring in stones for setting, or stones can be purchased for you if you know what you want. No inventory is kept on the premises. If you want a wedding set, ring, or piece designed, you can browse through wholesale catalogs, or you can bring in a picture. When updating jewelry, the gold or platinum in your jewelry can be reused. Note: No work is done with sterling silver jewelry. Although this small studio is not a conventional retail setting, I think customers will feel very comfortable here. However, it's important to schedule an appointment, since K-Gold is not set up for walk-in business. I think you'll find the savings very worthwhile, and the work is done to the highest standards.

Movado

Village Outlets of Napa Valley, St. Helena. (707) 967-0738.
Daily. MC, VISA, AE, Movado Card. Parking: lot.
Upscale buyers are very impressed by the watches they see
under lock and key at Movado. Many are classified as seconds,
although they're really samples. Others are discontinued styles.
You don't have to be rich to shop here, since you can find
many styles priced $100–$300. On the other hand, you can
buy a handmade Piaget 18K solid-gold watch with sapphire
crystal for $4,000 (retail originally $14,000). Movado's 14K
solid-gold watches are priced at $375 and up, while its sportier
Esquire line goes for $35–$136. Overall discounts are 20–70%
off original retail. Buy with care since there are no refunds;
exchanges only within ten days for an item of equal or higher
value. This elegant store hardly seems to fit the term "bargain,"
but you will be surprised.

Peter Jacobs Jewelry Resources

369-C Third Street, Montecito Plaza Square, San Rafael.
(415) 459-4300. M–Sat 10–6, MC, VISA, DIS. Parking: lot.
Peter Jacobs was a distributor of fine jewelry to department
stores; he's kept the resources to buy direct and sell to consumers, who now pay him what department stores paid. He
keeps a notebook filled with ads from local department stores
and mall jewelers to compare their prices with his for the
same items. The difference is impressive. You'll find cases of
gold jewelry (bracelets, chains, necklaces, earrings, charms,
and pins), gemstones, diamonds, pearls, and sterling silver
jewelry. I was very impressed with his selection of wedding
sets and bands (most are tucked away in the safe). After
receiving an education on diamond buying, you'll be able to
select a diamond that suits the ring and your budget. Better
watches can be purchased on a special order basis with
savings of about 30%. Whenever possible, Jacobs tries to
accommodate special needs and requests.

A Piece of the Rainbow

1015 Camelia Street (one block south of Gilman), Berkeley.
(510) 527-2431. M–F 10–4. Cash/Check. Parking: street.
This company manufactures (to my mind) a somewhat esoteric line of funky, novelty, whimsical, and appealing rhinestone jewelry. Prices are half off wholesale. Most pins are $7.50–$30; earrings $10–$40. Some themes: sports, wildlife, domestic pets, Christmas, patriotic symbols, flowers, recreational activities, and many more. These are all discontinued, prototypes, samples, mistakes, and occasional seconds. A popular store for collectors of rhinestone jewelry.

Taylor & Jacobson

1475 N. Broadway (Lincoln Broadway Building), Suite 490,
Walnut Creek. (510) 937-9570. M–F 9–6 by appt. MC, VISA.
Parking: garage across street.
The best values are often found in the least likely locations. This company does most of its business with stores that use its custom fabricating, diamond-setting, and repair service. Essentially a wholesaler, it also works directly with local consumers. It doesn't claim to sell at wholesale prices (how refreshing!), but it certainly offers substantial savings. It has a display case with many dazzling rings; however, most of its available settings are kept in trays or are represented in wax patterns that you can try on. Services include repair, remounts, sizing, repronging, reshanking, and polishing. You can choose from loose stones including diamonds, jade, lapis lazuli, pearls, and other precious and semiprecious beauties. Appointments are essential to get through the locked doors.

Zwillinger & Co.

760 Market Street (Phelan Building), Suite 800, San Francisco.
(415) 392-4086. T–Sat 9:30–5. MC, VISA, AE, DIS.
Parking: downtown pay garages.
You'll feel more comfortable if you wear your Sunday best before entering the vaultlike security doors of this firm, which has been in the same location for the past forty years. For those great occasions in life—engagements, anniversaries and graduations—when you desire a very special memento, a piece of fine jewelry can be purchased here at considerable savings (20–50% off retail). Prices on 14K gold jewelry, watches, and diamond rings are very impressive. You can create your own wedding set by selecting a mounting with or without stone,

and then pick a center diamond of the size and quality to fit your budget. The selection of loose diamonds is breathtaking! Discriminating women and men appreciate the large array of fashion jewelry from such noted designers as Steven Kretchmen, Charles Garnier, Bagley & Hotchkiss, and others usually seen advertised in *Architectural Digest, Connoisseur, Town & Country*, et al. If Zwillinger doesn't have a particular piece in stock, bring in a picture; chances are the piece can be ordered or custom-made for you. Watches from Omega, Movado, Seiko, Tag Heuer, and other status brands ($3,000-plus range) are available. Graduates from the Gemological Institute of America are on staff. Appraisals and full jewelry repairs are done. Zwillinger buys diamonds and replacement jewelry for several large insurance companies. First-time jewelry buyers will be in good hands.

Also See

Under Women's Accessories:
Icing Outlet; Successories

Under Giftware and Home Decor:
All listings

Under General Merchandise:
All sections

Shoes

Athlete's Foot Outlet

1237 Marina Boulevard, Marina Square (next to Talbots),
San Leandro. (510) 895-9738. M–F 10–9, Sat 10–7, Sun 11–6.
MC, VISA, AE, DIS. Parking: lot.
(Other outlets: Milpitas, Novato centers.)

Most parents cringe at the prospect of outfitting their children
with new shoes, especially the Nike, Reebok, and Adidas types.
Athlete's Foot Outlets carry the major high-profile brands
of shoes for crosstraining, tennis, soccer, football, basketball,
aerobics, running, track, and all-around everyday wear. Prices
at this self-service store are reduced 15–60% off retail, averaging about 30% off retail, plus occasional super markdowns.
Sizes for the whole family start with Infant 0–8, children's
1½–6, Youth 10½–13, Women's 5½–11, Men's 6½–15. Also,
T-shirts, shorts, sweats, and warm-ups. Refunds or exchanges
within thirty days with receipt.

Bass Shoe Outlet

Pacific West Outlet Center, Gilroy. (408) 842-3632. Daily.
MC, VISA, DIS. Parking: lot.
(Other outlets: Lake Tahoe, Lathrop, Pacific Grove, Petaluma,
Truckee, Vacaville centers.)

Finding the perfect vacation walking shoe is difficult, especially
if you're trying to find a style that won't get you arrested by
the fashion police. Bass provides the comfort and style to take
you through hours of museums and miles of city streets. You'll
find the original Bass Weejuns, Sunjuns, and Saddles, as well
as the latest fashion footwear. Prices reflect 16–30% discounts

on most styles and up to 50% discounts on some seconds. Also, belts, wallets, shoelaces, mink oil, and more at discount prices. A few stores showcase Bass's new sportswear line.

Boot Factory

Factory Stores of America, Vacaville. (707) 449-6429. Daily.
MC, VISA, DIS, AE. Parking: lot.
(Other outlet: Gilroy center.)

Take the whole family up to the Boot Factory for rompin', stompin' Western-style boots. You'll find cosmetic irregulars or discontinued styles from a famous Texas-based maker of traditional boots and its Western-inspired more contemporary label. Prices $60–$400; most average $75–$100. About 30% of the shelf space is devoted to sturdy and heavy casual boots; insulated, waterproof, and leather hiking boots; and some steel-toe work boots for men. Kids love the cowboy/cowgirl boots! Shoe sizes: Women's 5–11; Men's: 7–13, some wide widths for men. Most boots appear discounted about 35–40% off original retail (extra specials to 60% off).

Brown Bros. Shoe Warehouse

848 Lincoln Avenue (at Ninth Street), Alameda. (510) 865-3701.
M–Sat 9:30–6. Cash/Check. Parking: street.

Brown Bros.' shoes are all first quality, in up-to-date styles from Florsheim, Stacy Adams, Dexter, Sperry Topsiders, and Rockport. It's strictly a men's shoe store with sizes 6–15 to EEE widths. It sells athletic shoes for solid discount prices and has some of the lowest-priced work boots that I've found, which is why so many hard-working fellas come here from miles around. You'll always find a good shoe at a reasonable price, usually 25–35% off retail. Exchanges and refunds allowed.

Carlin's Shoe World

880 El Portal Center, San Pablo. (510) 236-8121.
M–F 10–8, Sat 10–6, Sun Noon–5. MC, VISA, DIS. Parking: lot.
(Other store: Children's Shoe World, Pleasant Hill.)

Good values for the whole family! Many dependable brand-names are available at 25–75% off retail, purchased from volume lots, short lots, make-up orders, and overstocks. Shoe World is also a clearance center for the Carlin's chain. You'll find an in-depth selection of Jumping Jacks from tots to teens. Hard-to-find sizes (EE for women and EEEE for men) as well as a complete selection of styles suit every taste and need. Most are very recent in middle-of-the-road styles, including many "comfort shoes." If you've got a mind of your own and seek comfort above all else, you can find comfortable, classic styles. All sizes for infants, toddlers, children, teens, men, and women.

Carole's Shoe Warehouse
665 Third Street, San Francisco. (415) 543-5151.
M–Sat 10–5:30, Sun Noon–5. MC, VISA, DIS, AE. Parking: street.
Carole's is a self-service operation displaying an intriguing selection of shoes warehouse-style. There are funky, fashion, conventional, and sporty styles—occasionally including a few dogs. Buying liquidations, overruns, and clearance inventories yields an extensive variety of dress heels (including chic imports from Italy and Spain), boots, and casuals. Fellas can buy nice Italian dress and casual shoes (average price $40–$80). I found the quality to be very good, more like the shoes found in upscale stores. Savings 30–60% off retail (average discount 40–50% off). Shoe sizes: Women's 5½–12; Men's, a few 5s to 13. Best shoe resource in the SOMA area!

Cole-Haan
Napa Factory Stores, Napa. Phone: (707) 258-0898. Daily.
MC, VISA, AE, DIS. Parking: lot.
If you love Cole-Haan shoes but hate the price tags, you'll find a measure of savings at its elegant factory store. Collections of shoes for women and men are about one season behind and priced 20–50% off retail. In addition to its signature shoe styles, Cole-Haan stocks nicely executed luggage, handbags, belts, and small leather goods. Those seeking shoes in narrow or wide widths, small or extra-large sizes, will want to splurge when they find these shoes available—an unpredictable occurrence. Those wearing medium or narrow widths have the most options when shopping. Shoe sizes: Women's 5–11 AAAA–W; Men's 7–15 B–D (a few Es).

Converse
Factory Stores of America, Vacaville. (707) 447-7657. Daily.
MC, VISA, DIS, AE. Parking: lot.
Converse needs no introduction to anyone who's shopped for athletic or sport shoes; men and women, even infants and toddlers, can find shoes for active lifestyles. Since Converse is sold throughout the Bay Area and the country, all shoes are

marked as "irregulars" (wink wink) to avoid alienating full-price retailers. Savings 30–50% off retail. Shoe sizes: Infant 1–13½; Girls and Boys 1–6; Women's 4–11; Men's 6–14 (some styles to 17). If you've got a hard-to-find size, talk with the staff to see if a special order is possible.

Enzo Angiolini

Great Mall of the Bay Area, Milpitas. (408) 934-1349. Daily. MC, VISA, AE, DIS. Parking: lot.

This label is made by 9-West. It's a more expensive line for women, European-inspired, featuring Italian leathers in a more tailored collection of shoe styles. Retail prices range from $68 to $150, at this outlet you'll save 20–40% every day. The shoe styles convey classic silhouettes with contemporary fluidity and they're destined to outlast the season. Casual boots, booties, flats and loafers, daytime heels (in beautiful leathers and nubuck), fabric shoes (for evening), and a few metallics define the collection. The store is pretty posh—complementing nicely this quality selection. Shoe sizes: Women's Medium width 5–11, Narrow and Wide 7–10. Returns and refunds.

Etienne Aigner

Factory Stores of America, Vacaville. (707) 452-1385. Daily. MC, VISA, AE. Parking: lot.
(Other outlet: opening Gilroy center, fall 1995.)

This is a real winner for women's shoes, an elegant factory store beautifully merchandised with upscale-quality shoes, handbags, leather accessories, gloves, and leather jackets. Those familiar with this line will not be disappointed with the extensive selection of classic, tailored, and dress shoes. Shoe sizes: Women's 5½–10 (a few 5s and 11s); widths: Narrow to Wide. Prices on handbags (all leather) varied from $39 to $110, with the average price nesting at $63. Discounts are 33% off retail across the board. During special sale promotions many groups are posted with additional 20% markdowns. Add your name to the mailing list; it's your only pipeline to special sale promotions and discount coupons. Exchanges only allowed within fourteen days with receipt.

Famous Footwear/Factory Brand Shoes

1600 Saratoga Avenue, Westgate Mall, San Jose.
(408) 378-5064. M–F 10–9, Sat 10–7, Sun 11–6. MC, VISA.
Parking: lot.
(Other stores: Anderson/Redding; Carmichael; Fremont; Gilroy;
Lathrop; Milpitas; Roseville; Sacramento; San Jose; Stockton;
Vacaville.)

Famous Footwear and Factory Brand Shoes offer a full selection of moderately priced brand-name shoes, discounted a
minimum of 10% to a maximum of 40% off retail. Its strength
lies in the selection of what I call family basics and "sensible"
shoes for women. Expect a complete range of sizes and styles
for the whole family.

Florsheim Factory Outlet

Factory Stores of America, Vacaville. (707) 453-1552. Daily.
MC, VISA, AE. DIS. Parking: lot.
(Other outlets: Anderson/Redding, Gilroy, Lathrop,
Petaluma centers.)

It's high time they opened an outlet! This well-known company
now offers 20–50% discounts on overruns, closeouts, and
slightly blemished (surfaces only) shoes. Men can revel in the
selection of everything Florsheim: dress shoes and boots
(including the top-of-the-line Royal Imperial group), casual
street and outdoor shoes, Comfortech styles, tennis shoes, and
slippers during the holidays. Shoe sizes: Men's 6–15, A–EEE.
Refunds or exchange on unworn shoes.

Footwear First Warehouse Outlet

2301 Fourth Street (south of University off 80), Berkeley.
(510) 848-8585. Th, F, and Sun 11–5, Sat 11–6. MC, VISA.
Parking: street.

If you need shoes to complement your contemporary dress code,
then stop in just to check the trendy shoes from Footwear
First's retail stores. These are overstocks and closeouts from its
four stores. You'll find shoes on the cutting edge of fashion—
clunky, funky, chic, and elegant. Occasionally, the company
still manages to stock a small selection of boots, including
some Western styles. Shoe sizes: Women's 5½–10, some Men's
in Western boots. All sales final.

Joan & David/A Step Forward

2010 Mountain Boulevard, Montclair Village, Oakland.
(510) 339-0500. M–Sat 10–6, Sun 11–5. MC, VISA. Parking: lot.
(Other outlets: Gilroy, Pacific Grove, St. Helena centers.)
Most Joan & David loyalists buy these shoes as an investment.
The line's popularity is due in part to its classic styling, even
though each season "the classics" reflect a new interpretation
of fashion trends and colors. The prices are higher than other
outlet stores that focus on American brands. You'll usually
save 40–50% off original retail. Expect to pay at least $69–
$89, up to $159 (original retail $325). Boots are $129–$269
(original retail to $450). Shoe sizes: Women's 5–10 (occasionally
larger sizes and some Narrows are available). Handbags and
belts are an extra plus. At outlet center stores, discriminating
shoppers appreciate the exquisitely made updated sportswear
collection from Joan & David. Beautiful fabrics and quality
construction justify the high prices on this line.

Johnston & Murphy Factory Store

Factory Stores of America, Vacaville. (707) 446-4652. Daily.
MC, VISA, AE, DIS. Parking: lot.
A 25% discount off a $10 item isn't much, but 25% off $200
is $50, an entirely different prospect. So I'm satisfied with the
20–40% discounts here. You'll find discontinued styles, past-
season shoes, and occasional slight imperfects, plus markdowns
on current-season men's shoes. Johnston & Murphy's quality
is a given in its lines of classic dress, dress casuals, comfort
dress, modern classic (more Italian), or athletic casuals. Expect
classic wingtips retail priced at $195 to be about $129, or golf
shoes at $170 to be $139. Shoe sizes: Men's 7–15 A–EEE. Sign
up for mailing list specials. No-hassle refunds or exchanges.

Kenneth Cole

Outlets at Gilroy, Gilroy. (408) 848-2026. Daily.
MC, VISA, AE. (No checks). Parking: lot.
(Other outlet: Napa center.)
I love this line of footwear for men and women. Its best customers are 20- to 30-year-olds who seek comfort, plus some
flash, glamour, and sexiness in their lives. Kenneth Cole's line
is a forerunner of fashion and trends—the line is trendy without
being extreme. The quality is great. Many women's shoes
are menswear influenced (oxfords, chukka boots, ghillie-laced
shoes, and kiltie shoes) yet, there are more feminine styles

and some styles just perfect for brides. At retail the shoes are usually priced from $89 to $160. Good selection of men's shoes. I wish the company would be more aggressive with its discounts. Discounts of 18–30% are unlikely to increase the pulse rate of seasoned bargain hunters. Men's ties, hosiery, luggage, briefcases, small leather goods, eyeglasses, and handbags add spice to the shoe collection. Shoe sizes: Women's 5½–12; Men's 7–13 (some Wide).

L.A. Gear Factory Store
Outlets at Gilroy, Gilroy. (408) 848-2623. Daily. MC, VISA, AE. Parking: lot.
L.A. Gear—if you know the label, you know you can expect shoes for active families. Sizes range from Infant 1 to Men's 13 in standard widths. Savings rack up to about 30–70% off retail, with big discounts along the back wall. Most shoes are first-quality discontinued styles. No blems. Some active wear for the family, too!

Leeds Outlet
Great Mall of the Bay Area, Milpitas. (408) 945-8386. Daily. MC, VISA, AE, DIS. Parking: lot.
Leeds shoppers will be delighted with the last-chance buys on past-season women's shoes here. Shoes may be promotionally priced at $3.77–$9.77 with boots often at $12.77. More current shoes are discounted at least 20%. Shoe sizes: Women's 5–11.

Mark's Shoes
805 Marina Village Parkway, Alameda. (510) 769-9240. M–F 10:30–7, Sat 10–6, Sun 11–5. MC, VISA, AE, DIS. Parking: lot.
Mark's Shoes carries canceled orders, excess inventory, reconditioned store returns, and past-season styles for women and men. The selection covers the spectrum from modestly priced labels to a few upscale status brands. The men's collection is much smaller but worthwhile nonetheless. Savings can be as much as 70% off, or as little as 20% off if you choose a simple budget-brand flat. Shoe sizes: Women's 5½–11 in all widths (mostly Medium); Men's 7–13.

Mephisto Outlet

Great Mall of the Bay Area, Milpitas. (408) 262-5105. Daily.
MC, VISA, AE, DIS. Parking: lot.

Be kind to your feet. Before going on vacation stop by this outlet, which is owned by a chain of specialty "walking shoe" stores (eighteen retail stores). The Mephisto brand is the headliner here, with discount prices (30–50% off) on men's and women's discontinued styles and surplus inventory. These shoes are noted for their durability, comfort, support, and breathability of the natural materials used in each hand-made pair of shoes. Other popular brands of walking shoes are carried: Rockport, Teva, Easy Spirit, Clark's, Soft Spots, and Timberland at closeout prices. Shoe sizes: Women's 5–11½; Men's 5½–13½.

Naturalizer Outlet

Factory Stores of America, Vacaville. (707) 452-1083. Daily.
MC, VISA, DIS. Parking: lot.

If Naturalizer, Life Stride, Connie, or Natural Sport are your brands, then stop in for 30–50% discounts on a wide selection for women of all ages. Lots of no-nonsense comfort shoes! Very good choices of in-season styles; great markdowns on slightly past-season goods. Shoe sizes: Women's 5–11 (some 4s and 12s); widths: Slim (AAA) to Wide (WW) in some styles.

Nike Factory Store

Pacific West Outlet Center, Gilroy. (408) 847-4300. Daily.
MC, VISA, AE. Parking: lot.
(Other outlet: Folsom center.)

You won't find the latest, hippest, or hottest styles from Nike. However, you may find fairly recent popular styles priced about 30% off retail as blems. The selection of blems, close-outs, and discontinued styles covers just about all of Nike's sport shoes. Sizes: Infant 2–8; Preschool 8½–13; Girls 1–6; Boys 1–6; Women's 5–12; Men's 6–15. Discounts are 20–40% off retail. Half of the store is devoted to many styles of first-quality discontinued apparel for active sports or simple leisure for men, women, and children. Discounts average 30% off retail. Exchanges only; no cash refunds.

9-West Factory Store

1251 Marina Boulevard, Marina Square, San Leandro.
(510) 614-0758. M–F 10–9, Sat 10–7, Sun 11–6. (510) 614-0758.
MC, VISA. Parking: lot.
(Other outlets: Folsom, Gilroy, Milpitas, Napa, Petaluma,
Vacaville centers.)

9-West offers a mixed bag of bargains, from hardly worth
noting to dazzling. You'll save just $5 on some current women's
styles, but more like 30–60% on last season's regular prices.
The selection covers a little of everything 9-West. Look for
two-for-one price offers on absolutely going, going, gone
past-season styles! Shoe sizes: Women's 5½–10 (a few 5s and
11s). The outlets accept returns and give refunds within twenty-
one days on unworn shoes with receipt.

Reebok Factory Store

Factory Stores of America, Vacaville. (707) 452-0235. Daily.
MC, VISA, AE. Parking: lot.
(Other outlets: Pacific Grove, Petaluma, Tracy centers)

The Reebok stores are upbeat and energizing, but for me that
doesn't make up for the fact that the discounts are often
downright chintzy. However, you may find a shoe that addresses
your needs on the more deeply discounted closeout tables.
The stores also carry Reebok active wear for the whole family.
Shoes in sizes for tiny tots, kids, teens, women, and up to
great big lugs (men's size 15–16).

Rockport Outlet

Tracy Outlet Center, Tracy. (209) 835-0482. Daily. MC, VISA, AE.
Parking: lot.

If this is your label, then this is the place to shop. Connected
to the Reebok Outlet at this center, you'll find a combination
of discontinued styles, current overruns, and some blems
(cosmetic only) sold at average 30% discounts. Not all sizes
available in each style. Note: Vacaville's Reebok Outlet has a
respectable Rockport selection. Shoe sizes: Women's 5–11;
Men's 7–15.

Sam & Libby Factory Store

Factory Stores of America, Vacaville. (707) 451-0456. MC, VISA, AE. Daily. Parking: lot.

Sam & Libby is stocked with a trendy collection of women's and children's shoes, discounted 20–50% off retail. There's a strong emphasis on color, and the styles are flirty and fun. Some fairly current models have minimal discounts, maybe 15%, but often you'll find two-for-one offers or other special promotions that allow a babysitter's earnings to go a long way. Sizes: Toddler 5–8½; Girls 9–4; Women's 5½–10.

Shoe Depot

280 Metro Center, 43 Colma Boulevard, Colma. (415) 755-0556. M–F 9–9, Sat 9–7, Sun 10–6. MC, VISA. Parking: lot.

When a steel-toe boot or heavy work shoe is necessary for OSHA's safety requirements on the job, Shoe Depot makes it easy to find the appropriate footgear; it has more work shoes than I've seen anywhere, starting at hard-to-find small sizes (6) and going up to 14, in widths D–EEE. The discounts are decent. You'll also find athletic-style, casual, dress comfort, and traditional dress shoes. Some famous brands: Nunn Bush, Stacy Adams, Florsheim, Sperry, Rockport, Dexter, Gorilla, Wolverine, and Georgia.

The Shoe Loft/Shoe Palace

225 Front Street (off California), San Francisco. (415) 956-4648. M–F 10–6, Sat 11–5. MC, VISA, AE. Parking: pay lots.
(Other store: Shoe Palace, 123 Second Street, bet. Howard and Mission, San Francisco.)

A dedicated following of the Financial District's lunchtime women shoppers comes to The Shoe Loft for its better brands and size selection. It buys "after sale" stock from posh retail shoe stores. Of course, the standard sizes and widths are prevalent (Women's 4–12), but the hard-to-fit may find odd sizes as well (a few triple and quad widths). Prices are generally $25–$70. If you shop below Market, then stop at the Shoe Palace for a men's selection of dress and casual shoes and more women's shoes at moderate prices.

Shoe Pavilion

899 Howard Street, Yerba Buena Square (at Fifth Street),
San Francisco. (415) 974-1821. Daily. MC, VISA, AE, DIS.
Parking: street/pay lots.
(Other stores/outlet centers: Corte Madera; Daly City;
Emeryville; Gilroy; Millbrae; Milpitas; Pittsburg; Sacramento;
Santa Cruz; San Jose; San Ramon; Sunnyvale; Vacaville,
Walnut Creek.)

Shoe Pavilion describes itself as the "leading off-price retailer
of quality brand-name footwear on the West Coast," offering
women's shoes with 30–70% discounts daily on major brands.
Although I feel the rapid expansion of this company has
led to a decrease in the selection of "better" shoe brands, for
the most part, the styles are very current and service is very
accommodating. Prices range from $10 to $89 for shoes and
$10 to $60 for handbags. Most discounts on current styles are
in the 35% range. Check the displays that highlight the latest
arrivals in full size ranges. Even shoes on the self-serve racks
are often backed by additional sizes in the stock room, so
don't hesitate to ask for your size. Good selection of men's
shoes, too!

Stride-Rite

Outlets at Gilroy, Gilroy. (408) 842-1011. Daily. MC, VISA.
Parking: lot.

Closeouts, slight irregulars, and past-season styles from
Stride-Rite's shoe divisions are offered at 30% off every day.
Specials on the "dump" tables take discounts down to 50–60%
off retail. Sperry Top-Siders, Keds, and Stride-Rite shoes
come in all sizes for everyone in the family.

Timberland

Napa Factory Outlets, Napa. (707) 259-1191. Daily. MC, VISA,
AE. Parking: lot.
(Other outlets: Gilroy center.)

Timberland has been a rising star in the shoe industry. Its
rugged outdoor shoes have become fashionable as everyday
streetwear. With success comes excess, and that leads to outlet
stores. Discontinued styles and factory blems (cosmetic flaws)
are discounted 30–50% off retail. There's a little of everything
made by Timberland in the selection and it's all guaranteed.
Shoe sizes: Women's 5–10; Men's 7–13. About half the space
at Timberland's outlets is devoted to its apparel (sportswear

and outerwear) and accessory divisions for men and women. You can pick up a short-sleeve sweater for $24 or a leather field coat reduced to $499 from $900. Just like the shoes, many styles of its weathergear are waterproof. Handbags, backpacks, duffel bags, gloves, and caps provide customers with head-to-toe cover options.

Unisa Factory Store

Pacific West Outlet Center, Gilroy. (408) 848-2424. Daily.
MC, VISA. Parking: lot.
If you feel most comfortable walking close to the ground, Unisa's fashion flats and sandals for women are what you're looking for. This factory store is one of the best for bargain prices and good selection. Regular discount prices are 30–50% off retail, further reduced by weekly in-store specials. Unisa offers a shoe for every occasion, from picnics to soirees. Women's shoe sizes: a few 5s to 10 (some styles to 12), Narrow and Medium widths. Exchanges for store credit within ten days.

Vans

Factory Stores of America, Vacaville. (707) 447-8368. Daily.
MC, VISA. Parking: lot.
(Other outlets: Gilroy, Petaluma centers.)
Vans updates the classic canvas boat shoe with bold colors and prints. Entire families can choose comfortable fun shoes at this outlet; irregulars and discontinued styles keep the racks well stocked. Both lace-up and slip-on styles available, plus some in suede. Vans fills a special niche with its snowboard and skateboarding shoes. Since the styles are more or less unisex, you can purchase by fit, or stick to Toddler 5–10½; Boys 2½–6; Youth 11–2; Women's 4–10; Men's 6½–13. Discounts 30–65% off original retail.

Also See

Under Other Bay Area Factory Outlets/Factory Stores:
Ann Taylor; Guess? Factory Outlet; J. Crew

Under Chain Discount Stores:
Loehmann's

Under Other Bay Area Off-Price Stores:
Raffia

Under Men's Suits:
Kutler Clothiers; Suits & Shoes

Under General Clothing:
Burlington Coat Factory; Marshall's; Ross; T.J. Maxx

Under Children's Clothing:
Kids R Us

Under Clearance Centers:
Nordstrom Rack

Under Appliances, Electronics, and Home Entertainment:
Whole Earth Access

Shoes

4

Appliances, Electronics, and Home Entertainment

The superchains dominate the Bay Area appliance and home electronics market. Their volume purchasing power gives them a price advantage, but if you read the want ads, you'll see that they pay their sales "counselors" hefty commissions. These stores are careful to avoid blatant bait-and-switch tactics, but you can be sure that a salesperson is motivated to trade you up to models or brands that offer a larger commission and/or greater profits. In my opinion, most chains offer a "price guarantee" that is almost worthless. Each store appears to carry many exclusive models (known as "derivatives"). Typically the only difference between models at competing stores are in exterior color, finish, or other minor cosmetic or technical features. Good luck comparison shopping on the basis of model numbers! Since the numbers differ, it's very hard to meet the requirements for the price guarantee. Instead, you must note the features in detail to get a feel for comparative pricing. And when the salesperson starts pushing an extended service warranty, remember that stores consider such a warranty the best way to increase profits in times of intense competition for market share, which otherwise keeps profit margins low. These stores have driven many smaller operations out of business, but independents survive who operate with small margins, no commissions, and without the high overhead of the super chains. Shop smart! Take careful measurements of the existing space or cavity for a replacement appliance so you don't spin your wheels selecting something that doesn't fit. Standard sizes of twenty years ago are not the standard anymore.

ABC Appliance Service

2050 Taraval Street (at 31st Avenue), San Francisco.
(415) 564-8166, (800) 942-1242. M–Sat 9–4, Sun 10–2.
MC, VISA, DIS. Parking: street.
ABC's modest store lacks razzle-dazzle merchandising glamour.
Its secret for low prices on major brands of kitchen and laundry
appliances is volume purchasing. Most built-in appliances
on display are connected to gas, water, or electricity, allowing
for working demonstrations. That's convenient! Check out
the new displays of imported kitchen sinks and faucets. ABC
can provide immediate delivery on most of the lines it carries.
Phone quotes are given (sometimes grudgingly when busy).
Delivery charges vary with the size of your order and distance
involved.

Airport Appliances

20286 Hesperian Boulevard, Hayward. (510) 783-3494.
M–F 9–8, Sat–Sun 10–6. MC, VISA, DIS. Parking: lot.
To survive competition from superstores, Airport Appliances
offers an inventive pricing policy; its prices on appliances
include a package of several extras. The prices don't seem that
sharp until you get rid of the frills, so ask for the lowest,
no-package price. The selection of major brands in laundry
and kitchen appliances includes high-tech lines like Creda,
Bosch, Caloric, Asko, Best Hoods, and Wolf (by catalog only),
which are popular with remodelers. Designer faucets, sinks,
and custom-made countertops in Corian or Swanstone can be
special ordered at solid discounts from catalogs. Its kitchen
remodeling center offers European-style kitchen cabinets.
Airport feels that its prices on custom cabinets provide a good
quality/price/value ratio. Prices are just competitive on
Mitsubishi TVs and VCRs. Delivery to almost anywhere (evening
delivery and installation), extra charges for installations and
hook-ups.

Appliance Sales & Service

655 Mission Street, San Francisco. (415) 362-7195, M–F
8:30–5:30, Sat 9–5. MC, VISA, AE, DIS. Parking: street/pay lot.
Bargain hunters will really appreciate the selection of as-is
blems and factory seconds on many brands of small appliances
here. These were once display models, samples, discontinued
styles, or closeouts; all pieces are mechanically perfect and
carry a manufacturer's warranty. All accessories and parts are

carried for these lines, which include air purifiers, espresso makers, water filtration units, pressure cookers, and electric shavers. There are also hard-to-find appliances such as egg cookers, large juicers, and meat grinders. Brands include Braun, Cuisinart, Rowenta, Oster, Sunbeam, Krups, Bionaire, West Bend, and Kitchen Aid, all at competitive prices. The store will special order any new item and can provide or order any replacement part or accessory for small appliances. And it ships anywhere via UPS.

California Discount

9550 Main Street, Penngrove. (707) 795-9065, (800) 866-1222.
M–F 10–7, Sat 10–6. MC, VISA, AE. Parking: lot.
You'll feel right at home here with the wide range of audio and video products. VCRs, TVs, stereo components, car stereos, telephones, answering machines, video cameras, and most other high-tech gadgets can be ordered if not in stock. Lines represented include JVC, Panasonic, Zenith, Hitachi, Quasar, Magnavox, Harmon Kardon, Aiwa, Onkyo, JBL, Polk, Denon, Carver, Nakamichi, NHI, Infinity, Yamaha, Bogen, and Pioneer. California Discount's prices are very good every day and it tries to beat any advertised special sale price. The folks who work here do their best to provide all the attention and help you need, especially if you've driven a distance to do business with them. You'll get a sound perspective when buying a fine audio/video system after spending time in the comfortable environment of the home theater room. You can get phone quotes over the free 800 number and have articles shipped anywhere. Directions: Take 101 to the Penngrove exit, go right on Old Redwood Highway one and a half miles, right on Main.

Cherin's

727 Valencia Street, San Francisco. (415) 864-2111.
M–F 9:30–5:30, Sat 10–5. Cash/Check.
Parking: private lot at 18th and Valencia.
They must be doing something right—they've been in business since 1892 (decor hasn't changed much since then). This is a great source for home appliances: refrigerators, freezers, washers, dryers, ranges, and microwave ovens. Remodelers can find esoteric brands like Wolf, Viking Range, Caloric, Asko, Miele, Sub-Zero, U.S. Range, Gaggenau, and Traulsen. If you're updating or upgrading and covet European-style appliances, you'll have plenty of options here. Cherin's also sells mainstream

brands like GE, Maytag, Amana, Thermador, Dacor, and Kitchen Aid. It specializes in built-in appliances. Contractor prices prevail for everyone. Its business is mostly referral since it rarely advertises, and its low prices reflect a minimal markup. No price quotes over the phone. Delivery is free within the Bay Area.

Famous Brand Electronics

Factory Stores of America, Vacaville. (707) 447-7085. Daily. MC, VISA, AE, DIS. Parking: lot.
(Other store: Milpitas Center.)
Tandy Corporation, the largest electronics retailer, has a big umbrella covering stores like Radio Shack, Computer City, and the Incredible Universe Chain. With its industry connections and many stores it generates a fair amount of overstocks and closeouts, makes special purchases from the many vendors it deals with, and refurbishes many returned high-end products that failed initially after purchase. This creates an interesting mix of everything electronic at its company-owned clearance stores. Browse around and you'll find CB radios, electronic organs, CD players, TVs, VCRs, boom boxes, compact stereo systems, telephones, and household electronics like bread makers, vacuums, indoor grills, juicers, battery-operated toys, and many more things to plug in. Brands include Krups, Norelco, Radio Shack, Sanyo, Seiko, Panasonic, Sanyo, JVC, Waring, Jensen, and others. Prices are reduced 30–70% off every day, and products come complete with full warranties.

Filco

1433 Fulton Avenue, Filco Plaza, Sacramento. (916) 483-4526, (800) 223-4526. M–F 10–7, Sat 10–6, Sun 11–5. MC, VISA, DIS. Parking: lot.
(Other stores: Chico; Citrus Heights; Folsom; Lodi.)
Filco offers an extensive selection in cameras, appliances, home entertainment, and electronics at minimal markup. Prices on cellular phones keep competitors steaming, but consumers have no complaints. Most major brands of 35mm cameras, accessories, and instant cameras are in stock at terrific prices. Kodak film is sold at cost. Filco's on-site processing is its loss leader. JennAir, Kitchen Aid, Panasonic, Whirlpool, Amana, Sony, GE, Sub-Zero, Mitsubishi, Hitachi, Quasar, RCA, Onkyo, and Bose are a few of the major brands found in appliances and home entertainment.

Friedman's Appliances

1923 San Pablo Avenue (behind Capwell's), Oakland.
(510) 444-0544. M–Sat 9–5. MC, VISA. Parking: street.
Freidman's Appliances is located in an area that has seen better days, and its showroom isn't deluxe. Family members own the building and run the store, meaning low overhead and low markup. There is a very good floor selection, and immediate delivery is available on a wide variety of major kitchen and laundry appliances. The best-known brands are in stock: GE, Maytag, Amana, et al., plus Creda, Baron, U-Line, Best Hoods, Caloric, Garland, Wolf, and Bocuse ranges favored by upscale remodelers. Only "built-in" microwave ovens are carried. Inquire about special reductions on scratched and dented GE and Hotpoint products. Expect extra-special discounts on freight-damaged and contractor's missed orders. Call for a phone quote before making the trip. Installation is available, and old appliances are removed for a modest charge.

Friedman's Microwave

2301 Broadway, Oakland. (510) 444-1119.
M–F 10–5:30, Sat 10–5. VISA, AE, DIS. Parking: street.
(Other stores: Dublin; Hayward; Palo Alto; Pleasant Hill;
San Francisco; San Mateo; San Rafael.)
I approach the purchase of a new appliance as if I were planning the invasion of Normandy. Enter Friedman's Microwave. It sells a full range of microwaves from the most basic and inexpensive models up to top-of-the-line types. The prices are competitive with superstores. Thanks to a price guarantee, weekly free classes in microwave cooking, trade-in allowance, and 20% discounts on accessories (including carts) bought with the microwave (10% thereafter), you come out the winner. Most of all, you'll appreciate the information provided by the staff in a sane, no-pressure atmosphere. The Oakland store is also an "as-is" center for GE microwaves.

Fry's Electronics

1177 Kern Avenue, Sunnyvale. (408) 733-1770.
M–F 8–9, Sat 9–8, Sun 9–7. MC, VISA. Parking: lot.
(Other stores: Campbell; Milpitas; Palo Alto.)
Fry's is well established with tech types for computers and related products. Also, home and office electronics, high-tech toys and gadgets, TVs, boom boxes, cordless phones, speakers, CD players, cassette players, and fax machines—enough to keep you wandering the aisles for hours. Very competitive prices!

House of Louie

1045 Bryant Street (at Ninth Street), San Francisco.
(415) 621-7100. M–Sat 9–6, Sun Noon–5. MC, VISA, DIS.
Parking: small side lot; street.

House of Louie offers aggressive pricing on kitchen and laundry appliances, televisions, VCRs, and bedding. Its bilingual staff is appreciated by many consumers. It's also very sharp on prices! It can't always beat loss-leader "door buster" prices, but what you want usually isn't the "door buster" anyway. House of Louie offers an everyday and upscale selection of brands, including Wolf ranges and cooktops, Bosch and ASKO dishwashers, Kitchen Aid, Amana, GE, Whirlpool, Sub-Zero, JennAir, Dacor, etc. You'll see Sony and Panasonic TVs from small "spare room" sets up to huge 53-inch Videoscope units; the more expensive the model, the greater the savings are likely to be. You can also resort to catalogs. Upstairs is a room full of mattress sets from Simmons, Sealy, and Serta at solid discounts. The furniture selection is rather ho-hum, definitely not for upscale buyers.

L. Z. Premiums

1162 Saratoga Avenue, San Jose. (408) 985-9718. T–Sat 10–6.
MC, VISA, and financing. Parking: lot.

L.Z. Premiums carries major appliances, electronics (TVs, VCRs, faxes, beepers, home and car stereos), cameras (new and used), camera gear, and cellular phones, and their extensive catalog library extends your options. Prices reflect a modest markup, and delivery charges are reasonable. Forget hype and hustle; the staff is knowledgeable and low-pressure. L.Z. has a loyal shutterbug following for its prices on cameras, accessories, and developing equipment. Kodak film is sold at dealer's cost; Kodak processing is 30% off. No phone quotes.

OEMI Inc.

102 Grand Avenue (corner of Airport Boulevard),
South San Francisco. (415) 872-6668. M–F 9–5, Sat 11–3.
MC, VISA. Parking: lot.

If you're in the market for a typewriter of any configuration, basic to computerized, you'll find an in-depth selection at OEMI. Its prices are just about the lowest around because it often skips U.S. distributors to buy directly from manufacturers. Many repairs and some warranty work done on the premises. There are also some used manual machines. You'll find just about every brand on the market. OEMI's prices on computer printers, office copiers, fax machines, calculators, and cash registers are competitive with deep-discount chains. Many used, demo, discontinued, or closeout items available at extra discounts. All sales final!

Orion Telescope Center

2450 17th Avenue, Santa Cruz. (408) 464-0465; catalog requests (800) 447-1001. M–Sat 10–5:30. MC, VISA. Parking: lot. (Other stores: Cupertino; San Francisco.)

Orion is the largest telescope firm in North America; its catalog is very helpful to consumers in the prepurchase stage. Get set to view celestial wonders by doing your homework, then contact the Orion Telescope Center. If you know what you want, you can order over the phone by credit card. Or you can stop by and pick the brains of the pros on the staff. You can gaze through models from Celestron, Pentax, Edmund Scientific, Orion, and Televue. Naturally, all the esoteric accessories you haven't even thought of buying, but will eventually, are available. Orion also sells binoculars, spotting scopes, photographic accessories, and telescope-making parts. And you're going to save 10–30% on anything you buy!

Reed Supply

1328 Fruitvale Avenue, Oakland. (510) 436-7171. M–Sat 9:30–5. Cash/Check. Parking: lot.

You'll be surprised at the selection of kitchen and laundry appliances that can be crammed into this relatively small space. Major brands, including status lines popular with architects and kitchen planners, are sold at very good prices. If you have special installation problems, you'll be referred to someone who can do the job. Reed also sells kitchen cabinets (Omega, Westwood, Mid Continent), bathroom vanities, custom countertops (including Corian, marble, and maple), greenhouse windows, water heaters, shower doors, wall heaters, Cadillac lines of faucets, and more. Something really esoteric on your list? You can special order from catalogs. Working on a low markup, Reed essentially sells to everyone at contractors' prices. Beware: At times the staff is stretched too thin for prompt service. Delivery charges relate to distance involved.

Remington

Factory Stores of America, Vacaville. (707) 447-6548. Daily.
MC, VISA, AE, DIS. Parking: Lot.
(Other stores/outlets: 84 Second Street, San Francisco; Gilroy.)
At the Remington store you'll obviously find shavers and trim-
mers of all description for men and women (face, leg, nose,
ear, mustache, etc.), as well as parts and accessories. But that's
not all. There are knives for every use: Swiss Army knives, cutlery sets and kitchen knives from Gerber and Henckels, Buck
knives, and other knives I'm not sure how to describe except
that some looked fairly menacing (the Fury Scimitar, for
example). A good selection of flashlights, some Pentax binoculars, knife sharpeners and whetstones, manicure sets, scissors
(all uses), and travel aids complete the inventory. Discounts
from minimal to fairly good.

San Jose Honda/Sony

1610 S. First Street, San Jose. (408) 294-6632, (800) 297-6692.
M–F 10–7, T and Th 10–8, Sat 9–5:30, Sun Noon–5.
MC, VISA, DIS. Parking: lot.
San Jose Honda/Sony is hard to beat with Sony devotees.
An authorized dealer, its focus is on volume sales at discount
prices, and it monitors the competition closely to make sure
it beats everyone. TVs in all configurations and sizes including
big screen. VCRs, 8mm camcorders, laser disc players, telephones, minirack stereo systems, and audio components at
good prices, too. The showroom is filled with boxed units
ready for your car trunk. The store can provide setup and
delivery for a reasonable price.

Sharper Image Outlet

120 Vintage Way, Vintage Oaks Shopping Center, Novato.
(415) 898-3387. M–Sat 10–8, Sun 11–5. MC, VISA, AE, DIS, DC.
Parking: lot.
Merchandise in The Sharper Image catalog is high-tech and
usually expensive. At its clearance center you'll save 20–50%
on overstocks, one-of-a-kind products, samples, closeouts,
returns, and slightly damaged items from its stores. Pick up
executive toys and more eclectic and esoteric items like novelty
phones, security gadgets, exercise equipment, jewelry, luggage,
executive cases, golf and ski products, and just about anything
else in its catalog. About 20–30% of the inventory is current
at straight retail pricing. All sales final.

Telecenter

1830 S. Delaware Street, San Mateo. (415) 341-5804. M, W, F 9–6, T, Th 9–8, Sat 9–5, Sun Noon–5. MC, VISA, DIS. Parking: lot.
After surveying Telecenter's prices, I concluded that it's very competitive with other stores and superstores. It carries brand names in kitchen and laundry appliances (popular new high-end appliances for remodeling projects), plus TVs, video equipment, stereos, and more. There's no aggressive sales bafflegab here. If you're working with a contractor, you'll get a contractor's discount if you can provide their name and license number. Modest delivery charges.

Whole Earth Access

2990 Seventh Street (at Ashby), Berkeley. (510) 845-3000. M–Sun 10–6, Th–F 10–8 (hours may vary from store to store). MC, VISA. Parking: lot.
(Other stores: Concord; San Francisco; San Jose; San Rafael.)
Not only are the values and selection so appealing, Whole Earth Access is a neat place to shop. There's a special emphasis on major home appliances, power and hand tools, cameras, binoculars, and sunglasses, plus an extensive consumer electronics department with stereo systems, radios, VCRs, camcorders, TVs, and a complete computer and software department. Competitive pricing is a top priority. You'll find leading brands in kitchen, housewares, and home accessories departments, plus mattress sets, lighting, home storage, and appealing lifestyle furniture including popular pine bedroom furniture for adults and children. Also, look to Whole Earth for modestly discounted natural-fiber sportswear and shoes.

Also See

Under Cameras and Photography:
San Jose Camera & Video

Under Furniture and Home Accessories—Catalog Discounters:
David Morris Co.; Deovlet & Sons; Giorgi Bros.; Millbrae Furniture Company

Under Linens:
Home Express

Under General Merchandise:
Membership Warehouse Clubs

Cameras and Photography

If you're looking for a camera that requires no fancy accessories or particular savvy, you're probably in the market for something under $100—a basic point-and-shoot, no-hassle model. Your best bet is to rely on local superstores, which frequently offer promotional pricing on these cameras. Check ads for K-Mart, Target, Service Merchandise, Best Products, Wal-Mart, and Circuit City, or visit Price/Costco or Sam's Club. On the other hand, if you're serious about your photography and investing in esoteric camera equipment, look in on the local resources listed below or consider the many mail-order companies that advertise extensively in publications like Popular Photography. Ordering by mail, especially when dealing with brand-name products, can be a time- and money-saving option if you've done your homework and follow sensible consumer guidelines. The trade-off for mail-order savings? You forego the personal service and technical support that local camera shops offer. I've listed three mail-order companies that my shutterbug friends consistently recommend for price and reliability. One other essential is required before tackling the advertisements, which can cover many pages—a magnifying glass!

Alpha Photo Products
985 Third Street, Oakland. (510) 893-1436. M–Sat 9–5:30. MC, VISA. Parking: lot.
Alpha Photo offers a lot to professionals: photographic supplies, graphic arts, presentation equipment, materials, and more. I suspect many consumers will focus on the albums,

particularly wedding albums, those not often found in retail stores (fancy leather, premium-priced wedding albums sold in wedding-photo packages by most photographers). If you're willing to do the work of assembling an album, you can order all the components from a professional photographer's line carried at this distribution center. Several styles and configurations are available. You choose the cover set, the leaves (pages), mats, etc. Some minimums are involved on the leaves and mats (packages of six or twelve), but the prices are so reasonable you won't mind ending up with a few extras. Some components may have to be special ordered (like leather cover sets). Stop by and pick up a catalog. Located in a warehouse district north of Jack London Square.

B & H Photo-Video (Mail Order)
119 W. 17th Street, New York, NY 10011.
Orders: (800) 947-9970. MC, VISA, DIS.
Orders and information: (212) 444-6670; fax (800) 947-7008.
Camcorders, VCRs, video monitors, videotape, printers, microphones, editing equipment, and other essentials for professionals fill its ad pages. Ordinary folks will zero in on binoculars, cameras, lenses, film, and accessories.

Cambridge Camera Exchange, Inc. (Mail Order)
Seventh Avenue and 13th Street, New York, NY 10011.
Order desk: (800) 221-2253.
24-hour fax order line: (212) 463-0093.
Information: (212) 675-8600.
Customer relations: (212) 255-3744. MC, VISA, DIS, C.O.D.
A good resource for amateurs and professionals—you could set up your own studio and darkroom by ordering from Cambridge. Some video cameras, camcorders, telephones, radios; accessories for all categories, too. Used department to sell and trade. Write for free Cambridge Camera Catalog.

The Camera Swap
2540 Santa Clara Avenue, Alameda. (510) 522-3336.
Sun 8–1. Cash/Check. Parking: street.
The Alameda Camera Swap is held each Sunday in the Gold Ballroom at the corner of Santa Clara and Broadway. At this indoor flea market there's a good selection of cameras, accessories, books, images, lenses, darkroom gear, paper prints, and other merchandise for photographer and collector. There are

usually about fifteen dealers of new merchandise, but no stores are represented. This is a very legitimate operation—many dealers have been coming regularly for years and enjoy a reputation for reliability. Most will guarantee their equipment. Be sure to ask for a guarantee and a receipt for your purchase. To sell equipment, go to the swap on Sunday morning between 7:30 and 8:30 to reserve your table; the charge is $20–$30. There is a $2.50 admission charge to the public; children under twelve are free.

47th Street Photo (Mail Order)

67 W. 47th Street, New York, NY 10003.
Orders: (800) 234-4747; Video: (800) 221-3513.
Fax: (718) 722-3510; Customer service: (800) 847-4191.
MC, VISA, DIS. Catalog: $2.

If you know what you want, call the 800 number for a price quote. If not, order the catalog and you'll be impressed with the brand names in cameras, watches, audio, video, binoculars, telescopes, computers, faxes, copiers, answering machines, microwaves, typewriters, cordless phones, and almost everything else in the way of high-tech electronics. The reputation is well established for low prices and reliable service. A thirty-day money-back guarantee is offered.

Photographers Lighting

436 Bryant Street, San Francisco. (415) 882-9380,
(800) 833-0060. M–F 8–6:30, Sat 10–5. MC, VISA, DIS.
Parking: garage at 435 Bryant.

Professionals spend hours browsing through the inventory here. There are two angles to this operation: This company rents lighting equipment, grips, and medium format cameras, and sells flashes, strobes, adapters, grip equipment, background paper, and other professional stuff. It claims to have the lowest prices on seamless paper in the country. Local pros wait for the first Saturday each December, when rental equipment with a lot of usefulness left is sold off.

Photographers Studio Supply

432 Bryant Street, San Francisco. (415) 495-5145,
(800) 447-5888. M–F 9–5, Sat 10–5. MC, VISA, DIS.
Parking: garage at 435 Bryant.

This company serves the professional photographers and graphic arts firms that are concentrated in the SOMA area.

The emphasis is on supplying products for mounting, storage, and presentation—allowing for direct purchase of many items that must often be bought through mail-order companies. Except for some very esoteric items, everything is discounted. Photography students, hobbyists, and other consumers seek out this resource to purchase albums, mount board, foam core, and archival papers for mats. All too often when one needs mat board for mounting, it can only be purchased in large sheets. Sizes here start at 8 by 10 inches. Many appreciate the use of its dry mount press and mat cutter for a small fee. Check the bargain tables for "whatever." Don't hassle with street parking, pull into the garage across the street for Photographers Lighting.

Photographers Supply
576 Folsom Street, San Francisco. (415) 495-8640. M–F 9-5:30, Sat 9:30–5, Sun 11–4. Cash/Check. Parking: spaces provided.
If you're a novice, bring a knowledgeable friend. This is for serious photographers who buy film, paper, and chemicals in quantity and relinquish seminars at the cash register in favor of 25% discount on Kodak film. Everything for the darkroom, a nice array of background paper, and equipment for the professional studio. Feel secure with its roster of brands: Kodak, Fuji, Agfa, and Ilford films and papers for starters.

San Jose Camera & Video
1600 Winchester Boulevard, Campbell. (408) 374-1880. M–Sat 10-6, Th 10–8, Sun Noon–5. MC, VISA, DIS. Parking: lot.
Photo buffs looking for sophisticated and usually expensive cameras and accessories will feel right at home here. Most major brands are on hand: Canon, Nikon, Olympus, Vivitar, Minolta, Pentax, Hasselblad, Mamiya, Leica, Bogen, Kodak, Metz and Beseler enlargers, Kodak carousel projectors, and Gossen exposure meters. It aggressively discounts video cameras from Canon, Nikon, Quasar, and Minolta, ruffling the feathers of other dealers by not playing ball and offering products at higher prices as they do. It's a hero to consumers. For a close-up look at the world, check out the binocular department. The staff doesn't have time for lengthy seminars, but if you know what you want, you'll probably get the lowest price in the Bay Area. Save gas if you're out of the area; order by phone and have it shipped UPS.

Under Appliances, Electronics, and Home Entertainment:
Filco; L.Z. Premiums; Whole Earth Access

Under General Merchandise:
Membership Warehouse Clubs

Computers

The Bay Area abounds with computer stores. Trying to pick just a few and applying the label "bargain" is extremely difficult. Prices, products, locations, and the marketing direction of various stores tend to change so often I'm wary about making recommendations. There are so many variables to this market—whether you're buying a branded product or a clone, which system you're buying, whether you're trying to build one yourself, etc.—that it can hardly be covered with a few recommendations. Choosing a store on the basis of price alone may lead to nothing but frustration if the service and support you need is not part of the price. When canvassing other computer users I find that their advice is most often based on a special relationship they have developed with a particular store or dealer, while some choose stores based on price rather than support. Some hard cases think the best way to spend a day off is perusing the esoterica of the computer market at someplace like Fry's Electronics or Comp USA, while novices will undoubtedly end up on sensory overload and feel like their brains have been scrambled. Price buyers tend to be folks who can whip off the top of their system unit, pull a screwdriver out of the pocket, and add new chips, cards, drives, or other hardware without any apprehension at all.

I suggest networking with high-tech friends or user groups to lead you to businesses with a reputation for good prices and support. Your local user group is hands down your best resource for all kinds of information, shopping recommendations, and cheap public domain software. Finding a dealer in the Bay Area is not difficult. After you've passed the novice stage, you'll find bargain-priced resources for software and add-on hardware (memory, modems, boards, et al.) located all over the Bay Area, particularly in Silicon Valley.

Two valuable Bay Area publications for information on micro-computers are *Computer Currents* and *MicroTimes*. They provide practical computer information for businesses, professionals, serious home users, and absolute novices. They have question-and-answer columns, let you know what's available in the Bay Area, and list services and products, events and classes to attend, and organizations and user groups to join. *Computer Currents* and *MicroTimes* are distributed from hundreds of locations in seven counties around the Bay. You're most likely to find them in local libraries, colleges, adult education facilities, record stores, video and electronic stores, and anyplace where high-tech people are likely to hang out. If you can't find one, call their offices 9–5. Another useful publication for the beginner is *PC Novice*.

Computer Currents
(510) 547-6800 to find local distribution points or for subscription information.

Microtimes
(510) 934-3700 to find local distributors or for subscription information.

PC Novice
(800) 848-1478 for information.

Art, Craft, and Hobby Supplies

Amsterdam Art

1013 University Avenue, Berkeley. (510) 649-4800.
M–Sat 9:30–6, Th 9:30–8, Sun 11–6. MC, VISA. Parking: lot.
(Other Stores: Oakland; San Francisco; Walnut Creek.)
Here's an excellent resource with virtually everything for
drafting, graphics, and fine arts. Its second floor is chock full
of graphic, architectural, and engineering resources. Discounts
are from 20–40% on all major brands of art supplies and fine
arts tools. You'll delight in the complete selection of fixings
that makes it a cinch to prepare a flyer or notice for printing,
even for the absolute novice. Amsterdam's fine paper department offers over 700 types of papers. Fine writing instruments
from Mont Blanc, Parker, Cross, Waterman, Sheaffer, Yafa, and
Lamy are all sold at 10–20% discounts. It has a good selection
of prefab frames at solid discount prices; precut mats, glass,
and framing sections for the do-it-yourselfer are discounted;
custom frame orders done in-house are competitively priced
with other frame shops. Pay attention to special promotions
and closeouts for super savings.

Art Exchange

77 Geary Boulevard (Second Floor), San Francisco.
(415) 956-5750. T–Sat 11:30–5:30. MC, VISA. Parking: street.
The Art Exchange is a wonderful resource for those who
have art that no longer fits their lifestyles. Perhaps they've
moved, gone through a divorce, inherited art that doesn't suit
their decor or taste, or they've redecorated. The gallery
resells artwork, including paintings, sculpture, prints, and other

objets d'art. The only requirement is that it be original: no reproductions like posters or photographs. The emphasis is on contemporary art. There are watercolors, monoprints, wood-cuts, sculptures, carvings, etchings, oils, and more at prices ranging from $300 to $3,000 (some works to $25,000) and including the works of famous artists like Henrietta Berk, Gary Bukovnik, Richard Diebenkorn, David Hockney, Roy Lichtenstein, Joan Miró, and Robert Motherwell alongside those of lesser-known talents. Before you bring your art in, call the owner to discuss what you'd like to place on consignment, and its price. When the work is sold, the gallery gets one-third of the selling price. Documentation about the artist or the work is especially desirable.

Arts & Craft Supplies Outlet

41 14th Street, San Francisco. (415) 431-7122. M–F 9–4. MC, VISA. Parking: street. (Other store: Annex, 50 13th Street, San Francisco. Sat only 10–5.)

Arts & Craft Supplies is an outlet for an importer and dis-tributor of many of the categories of merchandise you find in major arts and crafts supply stores: painting supplies, acrylic paints, pens, X-acto knives, glues, lace, transfer type, paper goods, beads (lots and lots!), macrame, inks, canvas, brushes, basketry, doll parts and accessories, craft patterns and magazines, jewelry findings, jute, oil paints, stuffed animals, floral supplies, wedding and shower party favors, and more. Organization may not be the outlet's strong suit, but keeping such a convoluted inventory in order would defy all but the pathologically organized. Most folks like the mess—it seems more in keeping with one's expectation of an outlet. Pick up a shopping basket, I guarantee you'll find goodies you didn't know you wanted when strolling along the long wall with merchandise dangling off pegboards and stashed on the shelves. Discontinued or surplus merchandise is usually discounted at least 50% off original retail. (Expect some surprises—the company picks up some very interesting inven-tory buying up entire booths at trade shows.) Small craft manufacturers or anyone else interested in volume purchases may have access to additional discounts. Inquire! Shop on Saturdays at the company's annex, located a block away.

Beeswax Candl'Art Outlet

5743-D Landregan, Emeryville. (510) 547-8469.
W only 11–5:30. Cash/Check. Parking: street.

Make sure it's Wednesday (or call for an appointment) before setting out to replenish your candle stock. This outlet sells two different lines of candles: one for special Jewish occasions, the other perfect for any time lovely candles are appropriate. They're made from honeycomb beeswax, giving them a distinctive finish. Most candles are sold in boxes or in pairs and priced 30–50% below retail as seconds or overruns. A 12-inch pair of dinner candles at retail runs about $9; for overruns you'll pay about $6. Pillars, fluted tapers, chime, and birthday candles in gorgeous colors add beauty to entertaining and special holiday occasions. The Shabbat, Hanukkah, and Havdalah candles are dripless, virtually smokeless, and emit a fresh honey scent. Make your own candles after buying sheets of honeycomb beeswax and the candlemaking kits that are sold here. Beeswax candles in all shapes and sizes work especially well with rustic accessories and decorations that are popular now—the new "natural" look sweeping the home accessories industry. Add your name to the mailing list for invitations to special sales prior to Hanukkah and Christmas.

The Candle Factory

21 Duffy Place (at Irwin Street), San Rafael. (415) 457-3610.
M–F 9–5, Sat 11–4. MC, VISA. Parking: lot.

Candles not only add atmosphere, but actually tend to slow down life to a more relaxed pace. We need to use them more often instead of reserving them just for special occasions. Increase your stash by stopping by The Candle Factory, where you'll find your senses overpowered with the combined fragrances of the thirty-one scents used in candlemaking here. Because the candles are made on the premises, you can buy at factory prices. These dripless and smokeless candles are made of organic domestic ingredients, and it's claimed they outburn imported ones. Occasionally you'll find specials when a wheel runs off color or a tint proves unpopular. Seeking wellness? Then you'll appreciate the line of holistic healing candles.

Cheap Pete's Frame Factory Outlet

4720 Geary Boulevard, San Francisco. (415) 221-4720.
M–Sat 10–6, except W–Th 10–8, Sun Noon–5. MC, VISA, DIS.
Parking: street.
(Other stores: Montecito Plaza, San Rafael;
1666 Locust Street, Walnut Creek.)

If you have travel posters, prints, and family photos languishing in your closets and drawers because the cost of framing far exceeds the price of the picture, Cheap Pete's comes to the rescue, with over 10,000 ready-made frames in sizes ranging from 3 by 5 inches to 30 by 40 inches, including hard-to-find 4 by 6 and 5 by 5. The frames, available in metal, Plexiglas, and wood (styles for all decors), are wonderfully discounted. Also table-top, collage, and frames for gift giving. You'll achieve maximum savings (20–60% off) if you select a ready-made frame; on custom framing expect savings of 20–40% off pricey frame shops. Labor costs and overhead are kept down by doing custom work on a production-line basis. Also, volume purchasing of frames and using leftover materials result in the discount prices.

Collector's Corner Art Gallery

2441 San Ramon Valley Boulevard, #4, Diablo Plaza,
San Ramon. (510) 829-3428. M–Sat 10–6, Sun Noon–5.
MC, VISA. Parking: lot.

Collector's Corner sells original art—numbered and limited editions—at nicely discounted prices. Its inventory is quite eclectic, ranging from very modest prints to more expensive (investment) pieces priced in the hundreds and even thousands. By far the largest part of the selection is in the middle range of framed pieces selling for $195–$350. Markdowns on designated pieces can reach 30–40% off comparable prices at other galleries. Those able to spend big bucks (thousands) might be able to order a piece of art that they have seen in another fine art gallery and save 20–40% on the framed piece. The selection will appeal to the sophisticated connoisseur as well as those who simply want an affordable lithograph. Written certification on everything guarantees authenticity. Artists in their collection include Thomas Kinkade, Pradzynski, Behrens, Rockwell, Eidenberger, Mark King, Hatfield, Susan Rios, Buckles, Barbara Wood, Jack Terry, G. Gordon Harvey, and many others. Framing prices are about 20–30% below typical frame shops.

Dharma Trading Co.

1604 Fourth Street (corner of F Street), San Rafael.
(415) 456-1211. M–Sat 10–6. MC, VISA, DIS. Parking: lot.
If the textile artist in you needs an avenue for expression,
Dharma Trading can provide the essentials for you to "paint
your wardrobe." It carries dyes and coloring agents for fabric
painting, silkscreening, batiking, etc. The company provides
excellent information and how-to advice. It also offers a wide
range of cotton and silk fabrics ready for dyeing. Even better,
its extensive inventory of ready-made clothing for babies,
children, and adults in "naked white" cotton and silk needs
only a dip in the dye or a brushstroke before it's transformed
into an original creation. Apparel includes baby sets, basic
T-shirts, bodywear, dresses, jumpers, scarf blanks, rompers, and
other styles. Their yarn brings in many women, who carefully
check for special markdowns on this out-of-the ordinary
selection. Dharma satisfies the needs of "cottage industry"
apparel manufacturers as well as just plain folks. To get the
full picture, write or call for a catalog. Requests to: P.O. Box
150916, San Rafael, CA 94915, or (800) 542-5227.

Elite Picture Frames (Mail Order)

9775 Marconi Drive, Suite D, Otay Mesa, 92173. (800) 854-6606.
M–Sat 7–3:30. MC, VISA.
This mail-order company specializes in preassembled frames
and wood sectionals for assembling your own frames at home.
Many preassembled frames come complete with linen liners
(some with gold or wood lips) in many different finishes:
antique white, Renaissance gold, walnut, driftwood, cherry, oak,
pewter, etc. Prices are good: a 12-by-16-inch frame ranges
from $12.50 to $29.50. Custom wood sectionals are sold by the
pair. The framing finishes available offer lots of design choices—
traditional, ornate, contemporary, natural, in widths ranging
from $3/4$ to $2\frac{1}{2}$ inches. Order two pairs for a frame and you'll
receive four miter clips for easy joining. No special tools are
needed, although wood glue is recommended for more secure
joining. (Glue and hangers are not included.) To finish the
project you may have to go to a local resource for mats and
glass. Nielsen metal sectionals, linen liners, Fredrix stretched
canvas, and oval stretched canvas are also available. The catalog features color pictures of its frames, but if you're still not
certain about a particular framing finish, you can order samples for a small charge (to cover shipping). Call for a catalog

and join all the corporations, schools, and galleries that have discovered this money-saving option for framing.

Fantastico
559 Sixth Street, San Francisco. (415) 982-0680.
M–F 7–5:30, Sat 8:30–4. Cash/Check. Parking: street/lot.
Fantastico's warehouse has just about everything for craft-oriented people. It stocks an extensive selection of dried and silk flowers (exotic specimens you see beautifully arranged in fancy stores), plus all the makings to put them together: tapes, wires, ribbons, foam, et al. My favorite is florist ribbon in rolls for gift wrapping at one-third the cost of the Hallmark kind. Come here for holiday decorations and ideas. It also has baskets, plastic flowers and fruits, dollhouses, ceramics, garden statuary, and many accessory items. Prices to the general public are usually 10–30% lower than stores closer to home except for paper party supplies, which are competitive with all the other party discount stores. Nice wedding department and 10% off on wedding and party invitations from several books.

Flax's Primary Values
1699 Market Street (at Valencia), San Francisco.
(415) 552-2355. Bargain basement T–Sat 11–4.
Store: M–Sat 9:30–6. MC, VISA. Parking: lot.
Flax's Art & Design, a wonderful art supply store, has a new wrinkle—Primary Values, a bargain basement. The main store has a very upscale appearance with a wide range of merchandise that appeals even to customers who have no inclination to paint or craft. It's a major resource for decorative papers, stationery, picture frames, desk accessories and pens, in addition to everything for artists and technical art work. There's a major emphasis on presentation, with many materials and products that allow one to create or buy ready-made tasteful boxes or other decorative containers to use for gifts or home accessories. I would barely characterize these main-floor specialties as bargains. For the real bargains, go down to the basement, where closeouts, overstock, one-of-a-kind, or slightly damaged items are banished and sold for 50–80% discounts. Artist's portfolios, cases, stationery supplies, desk accessories, mats, picture frames, easels, sketch books, drafting tables and lamps, paints, decorative storage boxes, and lots of other goodies create an unpredictable and worthwhile shopping excursion.

Framers Workshop

156 Russ Street, San Francisco. (415) 621-4226.
M–F 9–5:30, Sat 9–2. MC, VISA. Parking: limited street
(two spaces marked Tenant Only).

This is a do-it-yourself frame shop only if you buy all the materials and assemble them at home, an option for artists who find that the $6.39–$13.50 assembly charge adds up when they're framing many pictures for exhibit or sale. Aluminum framing and custom wood frames are available. You can select budget-priced materials to frame an inexpensive picture or print, or go first class with museum-quality materials for conservation mounting of fine artworks. Prices on aluminum frames are often lower than at do-it-yourself frame shops, even when all the work is done for you. Prices on basic conservation matting is also lower, but on the more elaborate fabric and French detail mats, Framers is competitive.

General Bead

637 Minna Street, San Francisco. (415) 621-8187.
T–Sat 10–4, Sun 1–4. VISA, MC. Parking: street.

The General Bead store in San Francisco is both wholesale and retail. Its strength is its high-fashion beads for the style-conscious client. Be warned: I've received several complaints about rude and impatient treatment from the staff. I suppose customers persevere simply because the beads in all varieties (ethnic, glass, bone, shell, pearl, antique, sterling, crystal, ceramic, brass, etc., etc.) from around the world are not readily available anyplace else. With two floors and 18,000 items in inventory, artists can find fabric dyes and paints, metal studs, sequins and rhinestones, plus such "tools and fixin's" as jewelry findings and much more.

Graphik Dimensions Ltd. (Mail Order)

2103 Brentwood Street, High Point, NC 27263.
Catalog requests and orders (800) 221-0262. Daily 24 hours.
MC, VISA, DIS.

Graphik Dimensions Ltd. is a mail-order company that publishes a catalog for consumers and volume frame users including smaller frame shops. Its prices are the result of volume buying of framing materials. Most small frame shops pay a premium price to keep a wide variety of wood molding and aluminum framing on hand. Graphik offers preassembled frames in 5 by 7 inches to 14 by 18 inches (some to 20 by 24 inches), with prices ranging from $9.95 to $38.95. Several styles have linen liners. Sectional metal/aluminum or lacquer-finished frames are easy to assemble with the hardware, hangers, and spring clips provided. Custom-made frames are just that—assembled at the factory and shipped to you. Frames larger than 50 inches are shipped in sections with an easy assembly kit. Turn page after page in the catalog and you'll see that almost every style of frame molding is available, whether you want an ornate gold-finished carved frame, a faux stone finish, burled wood, hand-lacquered, contemporary woods, touches of silver or gold, or a frame with linen liner or antique brass corners. You don't have to buy blind. You can order a free sample of the metal or custom-made wood moldings. Precut acid-free mats, glass, and nonglare plastic in standard sizes are also available. Service is another point of pride for the company. Most orders are shipped within forty-eight hours. Shipping costs in many cases are offset by the fact that no sales tax is charged.

Mitchell's Beeswax Candles

Factory Stores of America, Vacaville. (707) 446-6448. Daily.
MC, VISA. Parking: lot.

Beeswax candles are virtually drip-free, burn smoke-free, and last longer than petroleum-based candles. Mitchell's Beeswax Candles are expensive—some would say extravagant—and are sold in gift stores around the globe. A pair of 10-inch silhouette tapers may be priced $17–$25 at these stores; at the factory store you'll pay about $12. The store offers a complete range of pillars and tapers in a setting that's hard to resist.

The Ornament Collector

5749 Doyle Street (at Powell), Emeryville. (510) 428-1722.
Nov and Dec, M–F 10–5, Sat 10–4, Sun Noon–4.
MC, VISA. Parking: street.

The Ornament Collector is open all year, but prime bargain time is during November and December, when it's filled with overruns, seconds, and samples of Christmas ornaments and giftware. Unique Chinese handmade straw ornaments, decoys, and clever gift boxes come in Christmas and all-occasion themes; straw birds, butterflies, tropical fish, dogs, and additional animals appeal to collectors; others opt for traditional Scandinavian-inspired straw ornaments. Often you'll find Christmas lights, garlands, and artificial trees at markdown prices. Occasionally, clearance inventory from the company's retail store, The Incredible Christmas Store, is sent here. Most items in the outlet are about 50% off the retail of other Christmas stores.

The Ribbon Outlet

Factory Outlet Stores of America, Vacaville. (707) 449-4888.
Daily. MC, VISA. Parking: lot.
(Other outlet: Pacific Grove center.)
The Ribbon Outlet carries 3,000 varieties of ribbons and fabric trims in a multitude of sizes and widths. You'll find woven as well as nonwoven novelty ribbons; lace, floral, and craft ribbons; and luxurious ribbons like satins, velvets, and tone-on-tone jacquards. This company is a major outlet for other ribbon manufacturers and the industry as a whole, and offers factory-direct pricing. Check the bins for "pound goods" (leftovers or end-of-runs in bales), $1–$2 for all you can cram into a ziplock bag. Also, items like craft, floral, and potpourri supplies, plus some handcrafted, finished gift items.

San Francisco Museum of Modern Art Rental Gallery

Building A, Fort Mason Center (at Buchanan and Marina),
San Francisco. (415) 441-4777. T–Sat 11:30–5:30; closed August.
MC, VISA. Parking: lot.
This gallery's goal is to give new artists exposure; you get an excellent chance to take part in the beginning of an artist's career, at very low cost. You can rent a painting, sculpture, or photograph for a two-month period, with the option of renting for another two months. If you decide to buy, half the rental fee applies toward the purchase price. Rental fees vary: an artwork with a purchase price of $300–$399 rents for $40 for two months, while a $800–$900 work would rent for $65. A suggestion: When selling your home, rent a dramatic piece of art to increase the buyer appeal.

Stamp Francisco Factory Outlet Store

466 Eighth Street (bet. Harrison and Bryant), San Francisco.
(415) 252-5975. T–F 10–5, Sat 11–3. Special die sales each
month, second Sat only. MC, VISA. Parking: street.
At Stamp Francisco every second Saturday is a special sale day. Become a stamp maker by buying the essentials. First, buy the rubber dies for 25¢ each. Next, pick up a sheet of self-adhesive backing (cushion) for $8, and finally the blocks for 10¢–25¢ each. Some folks make their own wooden blocks.

Discontinued and/or used stamps 25% off. Parents can create endless hours of fun and quiet activity for their children by collecting stamps and colored pads. Hone your do-it-yourself skills by taking one of its classes held every third Saturday.

Stone Candle Outlet

650 University Avenue, Berkeley. (510) 849-3191.
M–F 8:30–4:30. (Sat hours before Christmas). MC, VISA.
Parking: street.
Stone Candle is innovative. It conceived the "original glowing candle," and more recently the hidden-color concept (as the candle burns, beautiful colors magically appear). At the factory outlet, you can buy seconds with small imperfections, balls priced at $9.95 (retail $18–$25)—maybe even the beautiful ball that duplicates Grace Cathedral's stained glass window in the City. Occasionally, Stone's hand-sculpted wildlife candles show up; they're lifelike, with beautiful detailing, rich lustrous colors, and prices usually associated with collectibles. Chances are you'll promptly clip the wicks to ensure that no one burns them.

Straw Into Gold

3006 San Pablo Avenue (corner of Ashby), Berkeley.
(510) 548-5247. T–F Noon–5:30, Sat 10–5:30. MC, VISA, DIS.
Parking: street.
If your pleasure comes from knitting or crocheting a fine-quality "treasure," you'll want to use a natural fiber commensurate with the time you're going to spend making it. Straw Into Gold's customers approach this store as if making a pilgrimage to a religious shrine. Its attraction? One of the most impressive selections of fibers on the West Coast. This company serves a clientele of weavers, machine knitters, stores, and the retail public. The bargains are in the center aisle's baskets of closeout yarns and in the "cone" selection. It's much cheaper to buy off the cone, priced by the pound. You can save about 30% if you buy a whole cone (unused portions can be returned within six months for a refund). You'll also find notions, supplies, wonderful buttons, and more. Inquire about receiving a catalog and price list for mail orders.

Up Against the Wall

3400-D De La Cruz Boulevard, Santa Clara. (408) 727-1995.
M–F 9–4:30, Sat by appt. only. MC, VISA. Parking: lot.
Catering to artists, galleries, and interior designers, Up
Against the Wall primarily uses aluminum frames as well as
lovely wood framing materials, at prices about 15% below
standard frame shops (higher discounts on quantity orders). If
you have works to frame, you have two options: You can have
the work done here from start to finish; or you can do it
yourself at home, after purchasing the materials. This is a time-
saver of special value to artists who may be framing a number
of pieces at once for a show or fair. Call for directions.

Valley Art Gallery

1661 Botelho Drive, Suite 110, Walnut Creek. (510) 935-4311.
T–Sat 11–5. MC, VISA. Parking: lot.
Valley Art exhibits, sells, and rents the work of established and
emerging artists. Artists submit work to a jury of professionals
for inclusion in its sales and rental program. There's a nice
selection of original canvasses priced $150–$3,000. Over 200
artists are represented. The gallery also sells fine crafts, jewelry,
and sculpture by talented local artisans. Rental periods extend
for three months starting at $10/month.

Also See

Under Food and Drink:
San Francisco Herb Co.

Under General Merchandise—Liquidators:
All Listings

Fabrics

General Fabrics

Alley Kat Fabric Outlet

148 Townsend Street (between Second and Third streets),
San Francisco. (415) 546-7066. M–F 10–5:30, Sat 9–5:30,
Sun 11–5. Cash/Check. Parking: street.
Do you sew? Then you must subscribe to the theory that
"she who dies with the most fabric wins." If so, you must need
more fabric to add to your pile. Alley Kat Fabric Outlet is
worth checking out just to ogle the leftover fabrics the owner
buys from apparel manufacturers. These are fabrics that you
don't find at local fabric stores. That's good. You'll love the
widths—most 60–64 inches. The selection: lots of cotton knits
at $2.50–$3/yard, many in wonderful original prints that are
perfect for children's sportswear; taffetas at $2.50; a few bolts
of heavy tapestry at $5/yard; great selection of fleece; some
woven dress fabrics; corduroy, rayon challis, flannel, Gore-Tex,
and more. Loved the table filled with button boxes selling
at eight for $1 and cards of lace at $1/yard. Saw nothing
over $5/yard.

Bali Fabrications Fabric Sales

47 Paul Drive, Suite 1, San Rafael. (415) 472-4410.
Monthly sales last Th and F 10–5. Parking: street.
Bali Fabrications' fabrics have been used in collections
produced by Ralph Lauren, Bob Mackie, Joan Vass, and many
others. Its vibrant hand-waxed batiks have designs that are
occasionally very mainstream; some are unique, and many

are witty. Only the finest quality rayon or cotton is used in production. Since the material has been prewashed with near-boiling water, the clothes wash very well. While retail prices range from $15 to $25/yard, prices at the company's monthly two-day sales are closer to $5.50–$6/yard on overruns. A few fabrics are sold for as little as $2/yard. There's no minimum. Sales are generally held the last Thursday or Friday of each month (holiday months may vary). Get on Bali's mailing list for bimonthly flyer with details. Call for directions. Note: This company may relocate in the near future. Call to verify.

Bolts End

2743 Castro Valley Boulevard (behind Burger King), Castro Valley. (510) 537-1684. T–Sat 10–5, Th 10–8. Cash/Check. Parking: lot.
Bolts End is overloaded with fabrics, lace, and trims, plus buttons, linings, and other paraphernalia, leftovers from apparel manufacturers. Prices are very good. The selection is always interesting, although somewhat eclectic. Check the bridal department for laces, headpieces, and some fabrics. Discounts are 20–70% off retail. Good resource for buttons.

Britex Fabrics

146 Geary Boulevard; 147 Maiden Lane, San Francisco. (415) 392-2910. M–Sat 9:30–6, Th 9:30–8. MC, VISA, AE. Parking: lot.
Britex is an institution, its four floors stocked to the ceilings with a most distinctive selection of fabrics. It's the place of last resort, where you go when you can't find a particular fabric anyplace else. Now there is a bargain angle: on the third floor, you'll see remnants and end cuts at drastic reductions. Additionally, each floor has a sale table. I won't claim that the trims, tassels, wonderful selection of buttons (about 30,000), bridal, and jewelry findings are bargain priced, but just learning what is available makes most people happy.

Discount Fabrics

501 Third Street (at Bryant), San Francisco. (415) 495-4201. M–F 10:30–5:30, Sat 10:30–3:30. MC, VISA. Parking: street.
The goal at Discount Fabrics' warehouse is to sell fabric by the bolt, but you can buy in any quantity you want. This outfit buys up leftovers, bankruptcies, etc. from a variety of sources. Certain fabrics appeared outdated, and some I found hard to

picture in any application. Yet there are times when one wants cheap fabric of any kind for utility without regard to quality, color, or pattern—to protect plants from frost, cover furniture, provide insulation, to use as drop cloths, whatever. There's a little of everything: merino wool knits, an extensive selection of velvet, felt, drapery yardage, sheers, raw silk, flannel, printed rayon, muslin, Lycra, vinyl, woven prints, knits (jersey and interlock), upholstery yardage, and more. Small craft makers don't have to worry about minimums and can utilize the full library of fabric catalogs from Eastern and New York suppliers to find what they need. Check in for notions: excellent prices on bulk buttons, zippers, etc. Special order bridal fabrics at discount prices, too! Prices seemed very good across the board.

Gunne Sax Fabric Outlet

35 Stanford Street (bet. Second and Third, off Brannan), San Francisco. (415) 495-3326. M–F 10–5, Sat 9–5, Sun 11–5. MC, VISA. Parking: street.

Since Gunne Sax uses thousands of bolts of fabric each year, inevitably there are leftovers. You can get all the fabric, appliqués, trims, and linings you need at the Gunne Sax Fabric Outlet. In addition to prom and wedding-type fabrics (velvet, taffeta, brocade, chiffon, netting, lace, and eyelets) you'll find cotton chintz, lightweight linen, cotton, and fabrics from Gunne Sax and Scott McClintock fashions. Prices are very reasonable—about half of what you'd pay at most fabric stores. Great prices on trims and buttons!

M.I. Discount

2026 Shattuck Avenue (at Addison), Berkeley. (510) 704-8834. M–F 11–7, Sat 10–5, Sun Noon–5. MC, VISA. Parking: street/pay lots.

Fabric fanatics always on the prowl for bargains won't mind the hodgepodge selection of many old, outdated fabrics in all categories, along with some beauties and quality fabrics. M.I. Discount is a fabric liquidator. Initially, the outfit took over the inventory remaining from Kaufman's (former tenant at this site), and has since added fabrics from many other sources. Discounts average 60% off original retail. Some prices by the yard: 65-inch denim at $2.99, 44-inch muslin at $2.49, 54-inch drapery sheers at $2, bolt ends of home-decorating fabric at $2–$6, 54-inch cotton canvas at $3.75, dupioni silks at $10, and many drapery linens and open weaves at $6.

I particularly liked the extensive selection of special buttons (about 500,000 on hand), current and discontinued patterns, and Kirsch drapery hardware, all at 60% off. Polyester products like pillow forms and sheeting for quilts or upholstery uses are usually well stocked.

New Pieces & Chamber Music

1597 Solano Avenue, Berkeley. (510) 527-6779.
M–Sat 10–6, Sun Noon–5. MC, VISA, AE, DIS. Parking: street.
For quilters the quest for good fabric is never ending. At this charming little store, there are about sixty bolts of fabric marked down 40–60% off original retail at any one time. This is older fabric, marked down to make space for fresh fabric. It starts at 40% off; after a month it's discounted an additional 40%. Also, anytime you buy all the fabric remaining on a bolt, sale or nonsale, you get an additional 25% off.

Stonemountain & Daughter

2518 Shattuck Avenue, Berkeley. (510) 845-6106.
M–F 9:30–6:30, Th until 7:30, Sat 10–6, Sun 11–5:30.
MC, VISA, AE. Parking: street.
The owners of this shop have long-established connections with the apparel industries in Los Angeles and New York. They combine quality with modest to maximum discounts in purchasing and pass on savings of 10–60% to their customers. They bring in leftover designer wools and silks from Calvin Klein, Donna Karan, Ellen Tracy, Liz Claiborne, and others. Along with some ordinary fabrics, there's a superior selection of quality, (relatively) bargain-priced wool, silk, cotton, and rayon blends that are really quite special—the fabrics are much more elegant than the store. Love the bridal fabrics and accessories, French reembroidered lace with coordinating trims, the hand-selected bulk buttons to match with fashion fabrics, expanded selection of cotton for quilters, and patterns always discounted 20%. Discriminating customers seeking fabric for sophisticated apparel rarely leave disappointed and look forward to discount coupons sent throughout the year to mailing list customers.

Thai Silks

252 State Street, Los Altos. (415) 948-8611. M–Sat 9–5:30.
MC, VISA, AE. Parking: street.

Thai Silks is the retail division of Exotic Silks, an importer whose materials are used by artists, decorators, designers, yardage shops, quilters, and home sewers. Thai Silks has an extensive inventory of white and natural silks, hand-hemmed scarf blanks, and other items for artists to paint and dye, including ties, Christmas ornaments, and fashion accessories. There are exclusive prints, a dazzling array of fashion and bridal silks, velvets, and cut velvets. The prices are 20–40% off regular retail. La Soie lingerie is also available, in a wide range of styles, fabrics, and prints. The first-quality silk gowns, chemises, kimono robes, teddies, camisole and tap pants sets, nightshirts, and pajamas are the most popular styles sold. Silk boxers for men in sizes 32–44. Women's sizes: P–XL. Prices are well below regular retail of specialty shops.

Home-Decorating Fabrics

Alameda Upholstery Shop

859 W. San Carlos, San Jose. (408) 295-7885. M–F 9–5:30.
MC, VISA, DIS. Parking: street/back lot.

This shop caters to do-it-yourselfers with a huge selection of upholstery fabrics, plus fabrics that can be ordered from most major manufacturers, including Waverly, Schumacher, Pacific Hide & Leather, Barrow Industries, and many others at a 25% discount. Draperies, vertical blinds, pleated shades, and miniblinds are sold for a 25–50% discount when customers measure and hang their own. Foam rubber is cut to order.

Ann's Fabrique

170-C Alamo Plaza, Alamo. (510) 837-8579.
M–F 10–6, Sat 10–5. MC, VISA. Parking: lot.

If you'd like to buy a charming 100% cotton print fabric that usually retails at $25 for $7.99–$11.99, you'll love Ann's Fabrique. That's a fairly typical price range and discount on its lovely selection of factory overruns and first-quality goods. Most can be coordinated with current patterns from well-known wallpaper manufacturers. Sample books are available so that you can do all your matching and even order wallpaper at a 25–30% discount. Fabric discounts are 25–70% off retail. The staff's know-how and referrals to workrooms are helpful to the novice.

Calico Corners

2700 El Camino Real, Redwood City. (415) 364-1610.
M–Sat 10–5:30, Sun Noon–5. MC, VISA. Parking: lot.
(Other stores: Greenbrae; Pacheco; Sacramento; San Jose.)
The real bargains are not actually calico, but beautiful imported
and domestic fabrics for upholstery, draperies, and slipcovers
at 20–50% off regular retail. The emphasis is on first-quality
fabrics, but you will find occasional seconds. Sample books
further extend the selection with discount pricing. Capture
the look of hot new trends with specialty rods, finials, home-
decorating books, and publications. Calico Corners now has
its own workrooms if you can't do it yourself. With low prices,
beautiful displays, and helpful clerks, these stores are an
absolute pleasure to shop in.

Fabrics & More

460 Montgomery Street, The Marketplace, San Ramon.
(510) 277-1783. M–Sat 10–6, Th until 8, Sun Noon–5.
MC, VISA. Parking: lot.
Fabrics & More is beautifully stocked with the latest home-
decorating fabrics: lovely tapestries, chintz, jacquards, velvet,
neutral cotton upholstery, sheers, and more. Overstocks offer
the lowest pricing, starting at $5/yard, while discounts are
20–70% off retail. Special orders at discount pricing are offered
(buy more, save more). You'll find fabric from Schumacher,
Braemore, Cyrus Clark, Waverly, Robert Allen, Harris, Peter
Kaufman, Bloomcraft, Covington, and many others. Need rods?
There's the standard selection in stock, with more choices
available from catalogs, at modest discounts. You can order
elegant trims and tiebacks or pick up a tapestry pillow square.
The staff is very knowledgeable, and advice is freely given.
There is a $50 one-time charge for home visits. Once you have
the fabric, the staff will arrange for labor. Directions: From
680, take Bolinger Canyon Road east to Alcosta. Turn right one
block to Montgomery/The Marketplace.

Furbelows

6050 Johnson Drive, Suite A, Pleasanton. (510) 463-0242.
M–F 10–6, Sat 10–5. MC, VISA. Parking: lot.
Fur·be·low (noun) 1. A ruffle or flounce on a garment;
2. A piece of showy ornamentation. This store is aptly named
with its selection of trims, fabrics, and wallpapers. It offers
an upscale selection at downscale prices. On wallpaper books

from most well-known companies you'll save 30% off papers, 20% off companion fabrics. Other fabrics, about 250, are sold for 50–70% discounts off bolts nicely arrayed around the store. These are home-decorating fabrics geared primarily to contemporary and traditional decors. You can always spend time looking through sample fabric books and special order what you need for a 20% discount; on large quantities, you may save even more. I was very interested in the sample selection of expensive, elegant decorator trims at a 20% discount by special order. Best bargain of all is the free decorating assistance by the talented and enthusiastic owners. They can arrange to have your project made for you. Directions: Take the Hopyard Exit from 580. Located in the Pleasanton Square Shopping Center.

Kay Chesterfield Mfg. Co.
6365 Coliseum Way, Oakland. (510) 533-5565.
M–F 8:30–5, Sat 9–1. MC, VISA. Parking: lot.
The Kay Chesterfield Mfg. Co. specializes in reupholstering furniture for residential and commercial clients around the Bay Area; to serve its clientele, it maintains an extensive in-stock inventory of fabrics. Bargains come into play when the bolts are sold down to a relatively small amount of yardage. Additionally, the owners buy roll balances and discontinued fabrics from mills and often find deals that are too good to pass up. The deepest discounts are on small pieces, one to eight yards. In any case, the minimum you'll save is about 50% off retail. Since fabrics can cost up to $50–$100/yard wholesale, some prices may be unnerving. The greater part of the selection falls in the $10–$30 price range. Many people who come in are making handbags, place mats, teddy bears, art, or craft projects. Very little in the way of drapery or bed-spread materials. Directions: Take 66th Avenue Exit from 880 to first light, turn left (near Coliseum parking lot).

Myung Jin Studio Outlet
10 Liberty Ship Way, #185 (Schoonmaker Building), Sausalito. (415) 331-8011. F–Sat only 10–4 (or by appt.). MC, VISA. Parking: lot.
Myung Jin Studio Outlet is top-notch for beautiful home-decorating fabrics. The owners design them in-house and have them made in India or the United States. These exclusive and expensive fabrics are sold to the design trade, and discontinued

fabrics and mill ends await you at the studio. There are two primary fabric collections. First, the 54-inch heavy cottons in both subtle and crisp colorations (stripes, checks), ikat prints, and solids to be used on leaning-toward-contemporary/ informal furnishings. They'd also make great slipcovers. These are outlet priced at $8–$12/yard. Next, the exquisite rayon chenilles in unique weaves for more elegant and traditional applications priced $35–$45/yard. Some fabrics are available in small quantities, others (mostly cottons) can easily accommodate any yardage requirements. Creative sewers with upscale inclinations will see many possibilities in the luxurious chenilles for making apparel. There's a small selection of beautiful silks. Finally, cones of chenille yarn (discontinued dye lots) are sold by the pound (about $15/pound)—of interest to weavers or knitters. Chenille throws and scarves, pillows, and chef aprons are ready to go for those without time to sew.

Norman S. Bernie Co.

1135 N. Amphlett Boulevard, San Mateo. (415) 342-8586. M–F 8–4:30. Cash/Check. Parking: street.

The founder of this company is a fabric man from way back, selling mill ends to fabric retailers and dyeing and printing "naked" fabrics for manufacturers. Bernie buys leftover current patterns of upholstery fabrics and other home-decorating and special-use fabrics. Often there are only six to nine yards left on a bolt, not enough to cover a sofa, but maybe enough to cover dining room chairs, a small chair, or pillows. The fabrics are well priced, too! You'll also find full bolts of 60-inch denim (many types of stripes plus solids in various weights); muslin (all weights and widths); cotton duck; sheeting; canvas; marine fabrics; drapery fabrics; scrims (gauzelike); occasionally luxury and liner furs by the pound; chintz; raw silk; and lots more. A few fabrics got my yuck response, but for the most part I loved the selection. In the upstairs gallery you'll find full bolts of home-decorating and craft fabrics. Decorators and wanna-bees waste no time in snatching up yards of laundered jacquard for "shabby chic" treatments at $12.50/yard. Elegant damasks don't gather any dust either, with most priced at $22.50. Located between Peninsula Avenue and Broadway exits off 101. Outlet faces freeway.

S. Beressi Fabric Sales

1504 Bryant Street, Second Floor, San Francisco.
(415) 861-5004. M, W, F Noon–2. Sales in fall and spring:
M–Sat 10–5, Sun Noon–5. MC, VISA. Parking: lot.

S. Beressi, a local fabric wholesaler, gives the public a chance
to buy a huge variety of first-quality leftover and discontinued
fabric, thread, polyester fiberfill, and bedspreads from his
upstairs warehouse. Prices are below wholesale to encourage
fast sales and speedy removal. These materials are used not
only for bedspreads, but for draperies, upholstery, slipcovers,
costumes, apparel, and crafts. Fabrics purchased from mills on
buying trips around the world include exquisite velvets, 120-
inch drapery sheers, and silk damasks from Europe. Regulars at
these sales will recognize the almost prehistoric fabrics that
get cheaper and cheaper every year. Call the office for weekday access anytime during the year, when prices are 40%
off marked prices, or for sale dates (50% off wholesale) that
usually start in mid-April and mid-October. Rely on Mr. Beressi
for workroom referrals to suit your pocketbook—budget to
best and priced accordingly. He's been around long enough to
know everyone in the business.

Zoo-Ink Factory Fabric Sales

707 Army Street (near piers), San Francisco. (415) 821-6300.
By appt only. Cash/Check. Parking: street.

You'll find fabric here that has won New York's prestigious
Roscoe Award for printed contemporary textiles; fabric that
hangs in the permanent collection of the Cooper Hewitt
Museum in Manhattan; and fabric sold in one of the most
elegant showrooms at Showplace Square. These fabrics, retailing for $70–$130/yard, can be purchased as one- to four-yard
bolt ends for $4–$15/yard, perfect for small projects. Sometimes you can find several matching bolt ends in the same
pattern to use for a larger project. Zoo-Ink fabrics are noted
for a distinctive, casual appearance that, while reminiscent
of Impressionist painting, is thoroughly contemporary. These
hand-silkscreened fabrics are typically 100% cotton; about
10% are silk. Additionally, there are bargains in leftover goods
from local silkscreen artists, blank white fabric in different
weights useful for craft projects, fabrics classed as seconds, and
some home-sewing materials. Consumers are welcome on an
appointment basis. Say you were referred by *Bargain Hunting in
the Bay Area*; this is a very underground shopping experience!

Also See

Under Other Bay Area Factory Outlets/Factory Stores:
Emeryville Outlet; Laura Ashley

Under Children's Clothing:
**Cary's Factory Outlet; Chicken Noodle Outlet;
Petals Factory Outlet; Sweet Potatoes Factory Outlet;
Storybook Heirlooms**

Under Art, Craft, and Hobby Supplies:
Dharma Trading

Under Draperies and Window Coverings:
Crow's Nest Interiors; The Drapery Outlet; The Yardstick

Under Furniture and Home Accessories—Catalog Discounters:
Most listings

Office Supplies

Two mammoth stores with locations all over the Bay Area dominate the office supply market. OfficeMax and Office Depot are self-service operations selling a complete selection of basic office supplies and necessities. Prices at both chains are very competitive—each claims discounts of 30–70% off retail—and they're usually much lower than at other office supply or stationery stores. Both companies offer special services, including delivery, copying, printing, engraving, rubber stamps, and phone orders. Great resources for home, office, or back-to-school supplies. I shop both equally, according to which has a store closest to wherever I'm shopping on any particular day.

Arvey Paper Co.
2275 Alameda Street (at Potrero), San Francisco.
(415) 863-3664. M–F 8–5:30, Sat 10–4. MC, VISA.
Parking: street/lot.
(Other stores: Oakland; Redwood City; Sacramento; San Jose.)
Arvey offers the best selection of printers' supplies and papers of every description, plus graphic supplies, light printing equipment, etc. It caters to small to midsize businesses; the average consumer gets a fair shake, too! Arvey sells business machines, pens, janitorial needs, and lots more; its office supply section has expanded to keep up with the super office stores. If you're a big user of stationery supplies, get on its mailing list.

Stationery and Party Supplies

Party supply stores have proliferated all around the Bay Area. Here's the general profile that applies to the following stores. Select the store that is closest to you, but note that particular stores may have something extra to offer. Generally, they all have a good selection of paper party products. Paper plates, napkins, plastic utensils, table covers, and paper placemats are typically about 25% less than at well-known specialty stores. You'll frequently find lots of extras: bibs, crystal (plastic) hostess or caterers' trays and punchbowls, regular and helium balloons, party hats, favors, carnival-type toys for children, and more. Most stores have good buys on giftwrap; some also carry craft supplies, silk flowers, and baskets.

Boswell's Discount Party Supplies
1901 Camino Ramon, Danville. (510) 866-1644.
M–Sat 9–6:30, Sun 10–5. MC, VISA, DIS. Parking: lot.
(Other stores: 5759 Pacheco Boulevard, Pacheco; 967 Moraga Road, Lafayette; Rosewood Pavilion Center, Pleasanton.)
Boswell's has wonderful gifts, gags, et al. Great selection of paper products in fabulous colors discounted 30%. Everything for weddings and parties for all ages and occasions. Trophy ribbons, stocking stuffers, jokes, toys, gag gifts, wedding and shower accessories, bandannas, inexpensive hats, and scads more. Depending on the size of your order, you can save up to 25% on wedding invitations. Craft and educational supplies, too!

The Card and Party Discount Outlets

33 S. Capitol Avenue, San Jose. (408) 254-7060.
M–F 9:30–7, Sat–Sun 10–5. MC, VISA. Parking: lot.
(Other stores: 562 E. El Camino Real, Paulina Plaza, Sunnyvale;
545 Meridian Avenue, Suite F, San Jose.)

For help planning for a big event, you've come to the right place. Not only will you find all paper goods at 20–50% off, you'll also scoop up wrappings and ribbons at minimum 20% discount and catering supplies at 30–50% off. Greeting cards are always 50% off retail, while the intriguing collection of closeout giftware (including stuffed animals, ceramics, rubber stamps, stamping accessories, and frames) is also discounted 30–50%. Lots of little goodies for tots, hats for grownups, piñatas, and balloons complete the picture. Also, wedding invitations at modest discounts. Those with resale numbers can shop at its Cash & Carry warehouse at 143 E. Virginia St. in San Jose, (408) 287-3177.

Current Factory Store

Great Mall of the Bay Area, Milpitas. (408) 263-5560. Daily.
MC, VISA. Parking: lot. (Other store: 190 Golf Club Road,
Pleasant Hill.)

Over the years I'd speculate that anyone involved with fundraising efforts has come across the Current company. It has two Bay Area outlets, where overstock and discontinued merchandise are sold at modest to very gratifying markdowns. Stock up on stationery, greeting cards, giftwrap, paper party supplies, stickers, gift items, ribbons, bows, and more. Current keeps everyone in mind, so all occasions, ages, and styles are well represented.

Diddams Discount Party Headquarters

215 Hamilton Avenue, Palo Alto. (415) 327-6204.
M–W 10–7, Th–F 10–8, Sat–Sun 9:30–5. MC, VISA.
Parking: street. (Other store: 10171 South De Anza Boulevard,
Cupertino.)

A great place for children's parties, but also reliable for all adult occasions! Balloon prices are really sharp. Theme parties a specialty; lots of hats, hostess servers, and party accessories. You may save considerably (up to 40%) on wedding invitations, depending on the size of your order and the processing time involved; appointments required and a minimum $50 processing charge for this service.

Gifted Line Outlet

Outlets at Gilroy, Gilroy. (408) 848-2588. Daily.
MC, VISA. Parking: lot.

You've probably seen this line. It's very pretty and distinctive, based on Victorian artwork. First-quality closeouts and some seconds are discounted 20–70% off original retail (average 25% discount). For tasteful gift giving, pick up a stash of cards, stickers, totes, wrapping and tissue paper, basket boxes, stationery, notecards, and more. Even though the discounts are modest, this beautiful line of paper products is hard to resist!

Greetings 'N' More

Factory Stores of America, Vacaville. (707) 449-9551.
MC, VISA. Parking: lot. (Other outlets: Folsom,
Pacific Grove centers.)

Stationery, bows, giftwrap, gift bags, paper party supplies and an extensive selection of greeting cards for all occasions (at 50% off every day), Christmas paper all year round.

Half Price Cards

1212-J El Camino Real, San Bruno Towne Center, San Bruno.
(415) 875-7113. M–Sat 10–6, Sun 11–5. Cash/Check. Parking: lot.

The greeting-card field has become fiercely competitive, which accounts for the increasing number of stores that sell half-price cards. Now a store devoted entirely to this concept has opened, selling mostly current line products that are heavily discounted by the manufacturers to gain market share. Half Price Cards offers a full range of greeting cards, over 3,000 designs, at half the price charged by other stores. In addition to greeting cards, a large range of wrapping paper, gift bags, ribbons, bows, and gift items are priced at 20–75% below prices found at typical Hallmark stores. Gift items include frames, wind chimes, mugs, coloring books, crayons, children's books, and balloons. Note: No paper party goods.

Mad Hatter's Outlet

228 Townsend Street (off Third), San Francisco. (415) 512-8487.
M–Sat 11–5:30. Cash/Check. Parking: street/pay lots.

At the Mad Hatter's Outlet, you'll find the expected and unexpected: greeting cards at 50% off; framed or matted prints; whimsical stickers; mugs; 50% off on rolls of giftwrap; Enesco products (figurines, ceramics, frames, music boxes); small leather goods; gift bags; elegant handmade storage boxes;

candles; potpourri; picture frames; small toys; and Christmas merchandise. These are closeouts, discontinued items, and samples. Loved the elegant G. Lalo stationery from France! Most items are 40–50% off retail.

The Paper Outlet
Factory Stores of America, Vacaville. (707) 449-3442. Daily. MC, VISA, DIS. Parking: lot. (Other outlets: Folsom, Gilroy, Lathrop centers.)
Stop by for giftwrap, gift boxes, ribbons, party goods and decorations, greeting cards, invitations, thank-yous, books, games and puzzles, plus paper products for the home and office at proper savings. These are selected closeouts and seconds. The wonderful stock of giftwrap (appears to be roll ends from giftwrap departments) is hard to resist.

Paper Plus Outlets
1643 and 1659 San Pablo Avenue (north of University Avenue at Virginia), Berkeley. (510) 525-1799.
M–Sat 10–6, Sun Noon–5. MC, VISA. Parking: side lot.
(Other store: 2924 College Avenue, Berkeley.)
The store may be a bit of a mess, but you'll discover satisfying bargains on discontinued and surplus inventory from the well-known Papyrus stores. There's a tantalizing selection of quality cards, giftwrap, and stationery at 50–80% off. Its unique giftwrap is sold in single sheets; greeting cards are always at least 50% off; half off on giftwrap, children's books, small children's toys, and stuffed animals. Also photo albums, stationery in boxes or lovely portfolio packs, diaries, and more. A complete party goods inventory at very competitive prices. You'll even find boxes for your truffles! The store at 1659 San Pablo is devoted to seasonal specials and is merchandised accordingly (some very special Christmas and Hanukkah merchandise). Great source whenever you're planning theme parties around holidays.

Party America
1257 Marina Boulevard, Marina Square, San Leandro. (510) 297-5110. Daily. MC, VISA. Parking: lot. (Other stores: Campbell; Cupertino; Fremont; Pleasant Hill; Redwood City; San Carlos; San Jose; Santa Clara; Union City.)
Party America stores sell paper products for parties, plus balloons, Wilton cake decorating supplies, hostess servers, etc. Giftwrap and cards are discounted 50% every day; wedding

and party invitations from several catalogs at 20% discount. Good overall party resource.

The Party Warehouse

221 Oak Street (at Third Street), Oakland. (510) 893-1951.
M–F 10–6, Sat–Sun 10–5. MC, VISA. Parking: street.
(Other stores: Daly City; San Bruno; San Francisco;
San Leandro; San Mateo.)
The Party Warehouse discounts 20–50% on party necessities: theme party paper products, wedding, juvenile birthday, and baby shower departments are quite impressive. Bargain prices apply on giftwrap, ribbon, classroom decorations, Christmas and other seasonal decorations. Additional discounts are available for caterers, churches, and schools.

Paula Skene Designs

1250 45th Street, Suite 240, Emeryville. (510) 654-3510.
First Sat of every month, 9–3. Bimonthly sales. Checks/VISA.
Parking: street.
Paula Skene is a wonderful resource for premium-quality and elegant stationery, sold in galleries, museums, and fine stationery stores in the United States and Europe. These are cards that people do not throw away. Paula uses heavy, fine quality paper and creates designs of deeply embossed and elegantly foil-stamped images that may require as many as seven passes through the presses. These cards are works of art, most worthy of framing. At the warehouse sales, the stationery is sold for 50% off retail. Occasional cards are about $1.50 each; boxed cards about $12 for 8; boxed stationery (20–30 sheets) for $12; and enclosures about 60¢ each. Not inexpensive (when compared to the discount card and party stores), but a solid value. You'll want to stock up and keep these beauties on hand for classy correspondence. To keep up with sale dates, make sure to have your name added to the mailing list. Note: Corporate designs are a specialty. Look for the City Rock on Doyle Street and you won't get lost.

Sutter Party Sales

6121 San Pablo Avenue, Oakland. (510) 655-0132.
M–F 10–6, Sat 10–5. MC, VISA. Parking: street.
Paper party supplies and props for children's parties: balloons, piñatas, carnival toys, and more. Nice discounts on paper goods for grown-up occasions as well, such as weddings, showers, and other social events.

Wedding Invitations

Many of the stores listed above sell wedding invitations from budget to midpriced books for modest discounts, typically 20–25% off published price lists. There are also many mail-order companies for invitations that advertise prominently in bridal magazines. Most have 800 numbers, special consultation lines, and unconditional guarantees. If you requested information from each company, you could fill a shopping basket with packets that include sample invitations, catalogs, and complete instructions for ordering. Mail-order prices are considerably less than the prices listed in most midpriced books carried locally, but there is a definite difference in the quality of the paper. In other words, for half the price, you'll get half the quality. Depending on how one wants to allocate the money in a wedding budget, and how important the quality or image conveyed by choice of an invitation is, the mail-order option may be an acceptable alternative to local stores. It's a very personal decision. I can guarantee that when it comes to the wording and many esoteric details of invitations, you'll wish you were sitting face-to-face with an experienced stationer.

Also See

Under Art, Craft, and Hobby Supplies:
Amsterdam Art

Under Food and Drink:
Cash and Carry Warehouse; Central Cash 'N Carry

Under General Merchandise:
All listings

6

I don't want to be accused of overlooking any commonsense strategies, so forgive me if you think I'm stating the obvious. What was true thirty years ago is still true today: savvy consumers can easily trim grocery bills by monitoring weekly ads for specials at local supermarkets. When prices are low, buy in quantity. If you have a freezer, stock up. Clip and use coupons, but only on products that suit your family's needs. Often coupons don't bring prices below store brands, or below featured specials on competing brands. Too often, they apply to products that have little nutritional value and "save" on products you wouldn't buy otherwise. Check local papers for announcements of seasonal farmers' markets in your area. The produce, fresh from the farm, is usually—not always—offered at lower than supermarket prices. (Many folks are more concerned about flavor and freshness than price.) If it's convenient, shop warehouse supermarkets like Food 4 Less and Pak N Save. Price/ Costco and Sam's Club are obvious money-saving sources if you can handle the multiple or oversize packaging on most products.

Bakery thrift shops: It's truly worth your while to check the Yellow Pages for the bakery outlets close to you and to include a stop on your way around town. Parisian, Oroweat, Langendorf, Kilpatrick, and many other bakeries maintain thrift stores to sell their day-old bread and freshly baked surplus. Savings range anywhere from 20% to 75% off retail, depending on the category. Buy a lot at one time; you can freeze whatever you don't use right away. My favorite? Oroweat/Entenmann's Boboli pizza breads sold half-price every day. Stock up for great freezer emergency rations.

Beverages, & More

2900 N. Main Street, Walnut Creek. (510) 472-0130. MC, VISA.
M–Fri 10–8, Sat 9–8, Sun 10–7. Parking: lot.
(Other stores: Albany; Oakland; San Francisco; San Jose;
San Rafael.)

When a company like Beverages, & More enters the local
market, its competitors roll up their sleeves to do battle.
Consumers should rejoice—stiff competition results in lower
prices. Along with its competitive pricing Beverages, & More
brings a connoisseur's selection of wines, organized by country
and varietal and accommodating to just about any budget—
box wines to fine vintages. If your dessert or drink recipe calls
for an exotic liquor or liqueur, no problem. It would take
you almost two years to sample a new beer every day if you
worked through the beer selection. Conscientious hosts
who want to provide nonalcoholic drinks, healthy punches,
or fancy waters for their guests have hundreds of choices. In
the "More" category are packaged specialty foods including
mustards, seasoning mixes, candies, snacks, coffees, and teas.
The company's not timid about posting comparison prices of
local competitors. While the stores are spartan, their selection
and prices are excellent—what more could you ask for?

The Candy Jar Factory Outlet

2065 Oakdale Avenue, San Francisco. (415) 550-8846. W–F 8–4.
Before major holidays: M–F 8–4. MC, VISA. Parking: street.

The Candy Jar produces truffles for specialty candy stores and
upscale shops. If you're willing to go off the beaten path to
its plant, you can save a little or a lot depending on what you
buy. Basic and deluxe truffles in more than a dozen flavors sell
for $1 each ($1.25 to $1.50 elsewhere). In addition to truffles,
it also sells oversize turtles (nuts and caramel) and other heav-
enly chocolate candies. The best everyday buys are on seconds
(small surface imperfections), closeouts, and overruns. After
holidays you may find deep discounts on packaged chocolates.
You can stock up. Truffles can stay fresh for five to six weeks,
or even longer if refrigerated. Budget watchers can buy truffles
in any amount for a big event or wedding and handle all the
packaging and wrapping themselves, or take it easy, pay more,
and have them do it.

Cash & Carry Warehouse

452 Dubois Street, San Rafael. (415) 457-1040.
M–Sat 8:30–5, Sat 8:30–3. Cash/Check. Parking: lot.
If you're cooking for a crowd or planning a big party, the
Cash and Carry Warehouse may make your preparations easier
with institutional products used by restaurants, catering services and schools. The paper and party products selection is as
complete as most party supply stores listed in the Stationery
and Party Supplies section of this book, plus there is a good
selection of janitorial products.

Central Cash 'n Carry

190 Keyes Street (at Fifth), San Jose. (408) 975-2485.
M–F 7:30–6, Sat 9–5, Sun 10–4. Cash/Check. Parking: lot.
(Other store: 1131 Elko Drive, Sunnyvale.)
Central Cash 'n Carry is another option for the party planner,
especially its paper and food products. You'll find restaurant-
sized cans and jars of condiments, sauces, salsas and cheese
sauces, as well as ice cream toppings, punches, and syrups.
Also many hostess and catering trays, bowls, and pans. Good
paper party products, piñatas, and favors, too. This is a
no-frills warehouse store with many institutional supplies.
Delivery service available.

Chocolate Factory Outlet

1291 Fremont Boulevard, Seaside. (408) 899-7963.
M–Sat 10–6, Sun 11–5. Cash/Check. Parking: lot.
It's right out of "I Love Lucy"—chocolate tunnels and fast-
moving belts. A tasty detour for visiting tourists. The decor
here is a Willy Wonka fantasy come true. Pick up a plastic
glove and any size box you want and ramble down the 40-
foot chocolate bar. Choose your favorite or a variety of
chocolates: truffles, turtles, peanut butter cups, caramels,
English toffee, nuts, chews, and more. When you're done and
box weighed you'll pay $7.50/pound (close to wholesale).
If you're going to hide in the closet to eat these treats, then
maybe you'll settle for "bloopers" at $5.95/pound. They may
be ugly, misshaped, or stuck together, but they taste just the
same as the firsts. If you shopped at its popular candy store
in Carmel, you'd pay more like $11–$12/pound. Lovely gift
boxes available. Locals and visitors alike can tour the factory
anytime, or arrange for special chocolate-making classes.

Country Cheese

2101 San Pablo Avenue, Berkeley. (510) 841-0752.
M–Sat 9–6, Sun 10–5. Cash/Check. Parking: street.
Domestic and imported cheeses, meat products, dried fruits,
nuts and seeds, grains, spices by the ounce, and health food
items at wonderful prices keep Berkeley residents happy.
Love the old-fashioned country store atmosphere, with bins
for scooping out grains and rice. I've found some pricey ingredients, like dried porcini mushrooms, at decent discounts.
Inquire about discounts for co-ops and volume orders.

Delicieux Fine Desserts

48 Paul Drive, San Rafael. (415) 479-1020.
M, W, Th 10–3 (call first). Cash/Check. Parking: lot.
This company sells its just-like-home-baked pies and cobblers
for about half off. Its excess inventory is usually available
after delivery and sales to farmers' markets, caterers, gourmet
grocers, and restaurants around the area. The baked pies can
be frozen indefinitely; otherwise they'll keep for about four
to seven days. A cobbler (11 by 17 inches) runs about $12
at the outlet. Pies can run from $2 to $6—more than pies
from supermarket frozen food shelves, but there's no comparison. Hand-rolled and -shaped crusts create that homemade
appearance, allowing you to pass off a pie as one of your own
efforts (if you're so inclined). The pie selection may change
according to the season, but you can usually count on some
favorite fruit flavors (love the strawberry rhubarb), nut pies,
etc. Cobblers may be purchased by the piece or sheet.

Eureka Coffee

2747 19th Street (bet. Bryant and York), San Francisco.
(415) 550-0625. M–F 8–4. Cash/Check. Parking: street.
A straightforward proposition. This outfit sells one item: coffee
beans. No cups, no high-tech coffeemakers, not even a fresh
cup of coffee. If you consume quantities of coffee and prefer
fresh-roasted beans to anything sold in cans at the supermarket, then buy a pound or two to sample the blends and
you'll probably become a regular. Eureka roasts fresh coffee
beans on the premises and supplies many restaurants and
other food-service establishments. Six dollars a pound for
French, Italian, Vienna, Columbian, Mocha/Java or the house
roast ($6.50 for decaf), a solid 25–50% less than other high-
profile coffee purveyors charge. I've sampled several of the

blends and found the rich flavors so satisfying that I routinely replenish when I find myself in the area.

Grocery Outlets

2001 Fourth Street, Berkeley. (510) 845-1771.
M–Sat 8–9, Sun 9–7. Cash/Check/Food stamps. Parking: lot.
(Other stores: Antioch; Hayward; Petaluma; Rancho Cordova;
Redwood City; Sacramento; Salinas; San Jose; San Pablo;
Stockton; Vacaville; Woodland.)

Specializing in closeouts, packaging changes, and surplus goods, Grocery Outlets (formerly Canned Foods) offers a constantly changing inventory at up to 40% savings every day. Be prepared to buy whatever the company has captured from the marketplace. Dry groceries, frozen and refrigerated foods, health and beauty aids, wines and beers, housewares, and general merchandise are backed with a 100% money-back guarantee. You may find well-known and unfamiliar brand names, as well as I've-never-seen-that-before products. Some excellent buys on gourmet and diet frozen dinners, gourmet ice creams, seasonal items, juices, and snacks!

Harry and David

Factory Stores of America, Vacaville. (707) 451-6435. Daily.
MC, VISA, AE, DIS. Parking: lot.
(Other outlet centers: Gilroy; Napa; Petaluma; Tracy.)

Harry and David is a catalog company specializing in gourmet treats. Each catalog's tempting selection of gift baskets may include cheeses, candies, fruit (fresh or dried), jams, and more. You'll find products from the catalogs at the outlets, or you can order spiral-sliced hams, smoked turkey, gourmet steaks, snack foods, boxes of candy, baked sweets, very elegant tortes, and luscious cheesecakes, a company specialty. All are sold at the stores for 20–50% off catalog retail. They are every bit as good, wholesome, and fresh as what you'd get by ordering from the catalog; you derive the savings of buying direct. Other catalog items include gifts, home decor, kitchen-oriented products, and garden items from the Jackson & Perkins catalog.

Herman Goelitz Candy Store

2400 N. Watney Way, Fairfield. (707) 428-2838.
M–F 9–5, Sat 10–4. MC, VISA. Parking: lot.

Stop by for a sweet deal on candy. The Herman Goelitz candy factory in Fairfield is the company Ronald Reagan made famous. The factory store mainly sells first-quality, full-priced candies. However, there's always a selection of Belly Flops, Jelly Bellies that may be stuck together or oddly shaped, priced at $4 for a two-pound bag. (Normal Jelly Belly beans are typically $5.50/pound.) The seconds are always fresh, tasty, and, just like first-quality candy, fattening! Finally, factory tours (M–F 9–2) are very popular for groups of all ages. Directions: Going east on 80, take Chadbourne Road right to Courage, turn left to Watney. From 80 West, take the Abernathy Exit, turn left on Chadbourne, left on Courage, and left on Watney.

Hooper's Chocolates

4632 Telegraph Avenue (at 46th Street), Oakland.
(510) 654-3373. M–F 9:30–6, Sat 10–5. MC, VISA. Parking: lot.
Hooper's chocolates retail from $5.95 to $10.50/pound. Its seconds, Hooper's Bloopers (imperfectly formed pieces discovered through Hooper's careful screening), are sweetly priced at $5/pound. Just ask for them and you can buy whatever is on hand from the stockroom. They usually include most varieties of creams, chews, chips, nut rolls, mints, and truffles. You have to buy a 50¢ minimum, but that's not hard when you contemplate all the deeeee-licious sweets!

Joseph Schmidt Confections

3489 16th Street (at Sanchez, one block south of Market),
San Francisco. (415) 861-8682. M–Sat 10–6:30. MC, VISA.
Parking: street.
Joseph Schmidt makes premium chocolates—truffles are its best-known confection—sold at quality department stores. They're very expensive! A single truffle may sell for $1.50 to $2, or $25/pound and more at upscale stores. It's a lot more than mass-produced See's candy, but less than Godiva's and Teuscher's premium candies. This small store serves as an outlet and a test market, and is always stocked with a tempting selection of truffles and other candies, like chocolate-covered nuts and the exceptional candy sculptures (many holiday-themed) that are Joseph Schmidt hallmarks. Depending on whose prices you use for comparison, you may be saving 25–50% off retail. Truffles in a tempting variety of flavors are just $1 each. The store is stocked with many appealing and unique gift-oriented candy assortments, perfect for hostess gifts or special acknowledgments.

Lettieri & Co.

108 Associated Road, South San Francisco. (415) 873-1916.
M–F 10–5. Cash/Check. Parking: lot.

This company imports gourmet brands for delis, supermarkets, and gourmet food outlets. Specialties: olive oils, pastas, fancy treats, desserts, jams, and fruits. There's a smattering of other gourmet items and condiments like capers, pasta sauces, polenta, red chili pepper sauce, and balsamic vinegar. Stock up on assorted bags of pastas for 50¢ or 89¢/pound, 16-ounce jars of jam for 95¢, and cold-pressed olive oil for $5.25 a bottle. You'll pay more than wholesale, but quite a bit below retail. This small outlet is located in front of the office.

Plump Jack

3201 Fillmore Street, San Francisco. (415) 346-9870.
M–F 11–8, Sat–Sun 10–7. MC, VISA, AE. Parking: street.

Plump Jack sells a surprising 150 wines under $10 and is committed to offering good values on all its wines, indicated by its printed "Compare Our Prices" list and price guarantee. The company specializes in California and Italian wines. You'll find familiar labels and vintners, as well as those more easily recognizable to connoisseurs. Stymied for a gift, or need a second wedding gift? Call or stop by and you'll get help putting together a case of wine that should delight wine aficionados. A 10% case discount helps, too! Delivery free anywhere in San Francisco; UPS otherwise.

Price Rite Cheese

1385 N. Main Street, Walnut Creek. (510) 933-2983.
M–Sat 9:30–7. Cash/Check. Parking: lot.

Buy two pounds of cheese, save plenty; buy ten pounds, save even more. You'll find low-priced, high-quality jack, cheddar, and mozzarella and a vast assortment of fancy cheeses, Dutch and Indonesian spices, patés, and specialty meats at discount prices.

San Francisco Herb Co.

250 14th Street (bet. Mission and Folsom), San Francisco.
(800) 227-4530, (415) 861-7174. M–F 10–4. MC, VISA.
Parking: street.

Go to the San Francisco Herb Co. for ingredients! It's a whole-sale distributor of spice blends, culinary herbs and spices, dehydrated veggies, potpourri ingredients, fragrance oils, sprouting seeds, baking and food items, shelled nuts and seeds, wreath ingredients, botanicals, and tasty teas. It does most of its business by mail and requires a $30 minimum to place an order—no such requirement for outlet shoppers. You pay only one price: wholesale, divided into a basic unit price (4 ounce) or quantity price (by the pound). You can request a free price list, which includes a collection of 30 recipes for make-it-yourself fragrant products. Use the 800 number to order its most recent price list (published each spring and fall).

Smart & Final
24601 Mission Boulevard, Hayward. (510) 733-6934.
M–Sat 8–8, Sun 9–5. Cash/Check. Parking: lot.
(Other stores: 17 Bay Area locations—see Geographical Index.)
Smart & Final stores offer a spic-and-span shopping environment along with a fairly complete grocery selection; institutional foods; paper, party, and janitorial supplies; business and office supplies; and extensive frozen food and deli departments. Prices are sometimes higher than warehouse clubs, but there's no membership requirement. Labels in English and Spanish on most products. Also, its convenient and accessible locations are a boon to many underserved neighborhoods and communities.

Stelvio Distributors
1461 Old Bayshore Highway, Burlingame. (415) 343-6642.
M–F 9–4, Sat 10–4. Cash/Check. Parking: lot.
If you're trying out recipes from a new Italian cookbook, you may find essential but hard-to-find ingredients here. Some prices are just sensational, others merely competitive. Dried porcini mushrooms were a steal at $17 for a 7-ounce bag. The catch is you may have to buy more than you'd like if you only need an ounce or two. Reggiano Parmigiano cheese, aged three years, was $7.99/pound. It's fun to buy some of the more exotic dried and fresh pastas (from refrigerator cases), even more so since they're bargain priced. Polenta rolls, mascarpone, pancetta, and imported cheeses are all much lower than supermarket prices. Check the freezer and refrigerator for cheeses, sausage, and fresh pasta.

Sugaripe Farms Country Store

2070 S. Seventh Street, San Jose. (408) 280-2349.
M–F 9:30–5, (Sat hours, Christmas season only).
MC, VISA. Parking: lot.

At Mayfair Packing's warehouse store, you'll find Sugaripe housebrand prunes; dried apricots, peaches, pears, and apples; shelled or unshelled walnuts; also raisins, dates, almonds, cashews, filberts, and Brazil nuts, all selling at below supermarket prices. At holiday times inquire about gift packs, premade to your specifications. Any time of year, stop in with your gourmet recipes for deals on specialties that are sometimes hard to find reasonably priced at your local supermarket. Also mustards, vinegars, olives, fused oils, preserves, candies, and coffee beans. You can order by phone; they ship anywhere.

Trader Joe's

337 Third Street, Montecito Plaza, San Rafael. (415) 454-9530.
Daily 9–9. MC, VISA. Parking: lot.
(Other stores: 17 Bay Area locations—see Geographical Index.)

You can be forgiven for not knowing about Trader Joe's if you're new to the area. Just about everyone else stops by to load up on gourmet foods and condiments, bakery products, cheeses, ready-to-serve wholesome gourmet specialties, wine, beer, health products, etc. There's a wonderful casual and friendly ambience to these stores, and prices are usually excellent on the often exotic offerings highlighted in every Fearless Flyer. Some of the foods will please health-conscious consumers who want products without eggs, salt, sugar, MSG, dairy, or preservatives. The wine selection is so-so to superb; prices are excellent. Caveat: I wouldn't buy a case without first trying a bottle.

Wine Club

953 Harrison Street, San Francisco. (415) 512-9086.
M–Sat 9–7, Sun Noon–5. MC, VISA. Parking: lot.

The wine connoisseurs I know have voted with their dollars! They've put Wine Club on their list of sources thanks to its pricing and selection. Anyone can shop and take advantage of its low markups, about 6–12% above wholesale. Budget shoppers can find a Chardonnay or Cabernet priced under $5 or $10, while serious connoisseurs can trim costs even when buying a world-class Burgundy at $78. Wines come from California, France, Italy, Germany, Spain, Portugal, Australia,

New Zealand, Chile, Madeira, et al. If you're on the mailing list you'll get *For Wine Lovers*, the monthly buyer's guide, which lists most wines in stock followed by a designation of their value and availability. You can follow up with a phone order; UPS delivery or local courier service for a $15 flat fee for up to five cases.

Also See

Under General Merchandise:
All listings

Carpets and Flooring

The carpet industry has been in turmoil for the past few years. On the manufacturing level, companies have merged and consolidated until the greater part of the market is controlled by just two companies. On the dealer level, buying groups have been formed (like Tru Value and Ace Hardware) to gain more leverage in buying. Through these alliances, they've combined advertising and marketing efforts. The major buying groups are recognized through their advertising as Trustmark, Carpet One, and Carpet Max. Many local dealers have joined these alliances. While this is beneficial to the dealers, it does not allow consumers the wide latitude to comparison shop that they have enjoyed in the past. The Trustmark members are able to private label their carpets, while Carpet One dealers sell carpets exclusively to their members. Price guarantees offered by members ensure that dealers are likely to keep pricing in line. Territories are protected to further control competition.

As a consumer, it will be more difficult to rely on brand identification and style names when making comparisons. To determine value, shoppers will have to pay more attention to comparable qualities between carpets: the depth and density of pile, warranties and guarantees, stain-protection finishes, etc. When making comparisons, be sure to note the type of padding and all aspects of installation, including removal and disposal of old carpeting. Make sure the bid is complete and that it includes all extras. Carpeting is often the single biggest investment you'll make in furnishing your home, so buy wisely!

Independent carpet stores and sources still abound, however, and these continue to offer exceptional values and selection. Certain stores specialize in buying overstocks and closeout patterns and colors. Some buy room-sized remnants or pieces in off-color dye lots. Others go in for bankrupt inventories. For these reasons, you can still save on your carpeting dollar. Remember that it's a changing market. Always take your time, comparison shop, and consider all the factors. Be sure to check the listings in this book under Furniture and Home Accessories—Catalog Discounters, General Furnishings, and Clearance Centers. Many companies in these categories come through with exceptional prices on carpeting.

General Carpets and Flooring

Carpet One

1985 San Ramon Valley Boulevard, San Ramon.
(510) 837-3716. M–Sat 9–5, Sun Noon–5. MC, VISA. Parking: lot.
Carpet One's personal service and beautiful gallery displays offer a close-to-home shopping alternative. They're nicely positioned to handle the influx of new home owners into the Danville and San Ramon areas. Prices may be a tad more than those at the City's deep discounters, but convenience is the trade-off. This store is a member of the Carpet One buying group, and the selection is extended to include some designer-oriented high-end lines, which appeal to the upscale residents in the area. You'll find carpets priced from budget to best, including carpets from Masland and Fabrica and a complete Karastan gallery. Prices include padding and installation. There is also a very complete display of vinyl and wood flooring.

Carpet Systems

1515 Bayshore Highway, Burlingame. (415) 692-6300.
M–F 8:30–4, Sun by appt. (closed Sat). Cash/Check.
Parking: street/rear lot.
This off-beat location south of the airport can be attributed to the fact that most of the company's business is done with commercial and property-management companies. However, consumers can cross the freeway for Carpet Systems' excellent pricing. The showroom is neatly organized and well stocked with sample books from major carpet mills. You can go budget or top-of-the-line, or choose a contract carpet for your home

office. Prices quoted include pull-up and disposal of existing carpets, labor, padding, and sales tax. A 30% deposit is requested with your order, the balance paid at installation. Nice, low-key setting and accommodating staff. Directions: From the SF/101 south, take Millbrae Exit east to Old Bayshore, turn right. Going north on 101, take Broadway/Burlingame Exit right to first light. Turn left. Across from Charley Brown's.

Carpets of New Zealand

1940 Olivera Road, Suite C, Concord. (510) 689-9665. M–Sat 10–6. MC, VISA, DIS, AE, financing. Parking: lot.
Most wool carpeting is imported, entailing heavy freight, customs, and distribution costs. Cavalier Carpets, the second biggest carpet manufacturer in New Zealand, bypasses traditional distribution and sells directly to customers. Thus, prices on wool carpets here are competitive with quality nylon carpeting, e.g., Ultron or Antron. You'll pay about half the price of competitors' wool carpeting. To extend your choices, the company sells wool carpeting from other manufacturers, also well priced. Your choices in pads are extensive. All carpets are moth-proofed and naturally resist soiling. Of course, you can borrow samples. You can have area rugs made from simple berbers or from carpets with more elaborate designs. Also, if you're some distance from the store, you can have the carpeting shipped to a local installer.

Hals Carpet & Vinyl

7804 E. 14th Street (at 78th Avenue), Oakland. (510) 632-1228. M–F 9:30–4:30, Sat 9:30–2. MC, VISA. Parking: street.
Hals's location keeps overhead down; he also owns the building, employs no commissioned sales staff, and deals directly with each customer. His main clientele is apartment-building owners. Closeouts, mill drops, some seconds, and short rolls are sold at reduced prices for as much as 50% off original wholesale. You'll find moderate- to better-quality carpets among the mill rejects and special buys. Additionally, he stocks samples from major mills so that you can special order carpeting in just the right color, style, and price range. Custom orders are sold for a minimal markup, and prices may vary with the type of installation and your skill at negotiating the lowest price after you've done some comparison shopping. Prefinished wood flooring from Bruce, Anderson, and Hartco, plus vinyl flooring from Armstrong, Tarkett, Congoleum, and Mannington are well priced. For a one-man operation his volume is impressive!

Lawrence Contract Furnishers

470-B Vandell Way, Campbell. (408) 374-7590.
T, W, F 9–5:30, Th 9–8, Sat 9–3. MC, VISA. Parking: lot.
Lawrence Contract Furnishers is one of the best resources for carpeting, vinyl floor coverings, hardwood flooring, and hardwood flooring kits from more than eighty companies. You'll probably have to arrive first thing in the morning to pat all the samples and if you work fast, maybe you'll be done by closing time. After you've chosen your carpet, you can start again if you're shopping for wallpaper, draperies, or furniture from well-known manufacturers. Display room samples show retail prices, but Lawrence's discount system earns you average savings of 25–35%. Check the catalog library for additional resources. Most wallpaper books are discounted 30%. You're pretty much on your own, since decorator services are not available at these prices. Three times a year Lawrence has clearance sales on showroom samples, with prices 40–70% off retail. To find this out-of-the-way showroom from the San Tomas Expressway, take the Winchester Exit in Campbell, go south to Hacienda, turn left, then right on Dell. Lawrence's is on the corner of Vandell and Dell.

Pioneer Home Supply

657 Mission Street (bet. New Montgomery and Third),
Third Floor, San Francisco. (415) 543-1234, (415) 781-2374.
T–F 10–5. Cash/Check. Parking: street/pay lots.
Taking one of the smallest markups around, Pioneer occupies a special niche in the marketplace with pricing that its competitors are hard-pressed to meet. Amazingly, Pioneer has never spent a penny on advertising, depending instead on the loyal following it's acquired through more than forty years in business. The emphasis at Pioneer is now on carpeting and bedding. The selection of carpeting and floor coverings is extensive. There's no push to trade up for bigger bucks and more profit. Just let Linda know your budget, and she'll point out the appropriate book, whether you're redoing an office with sleek contemporary contract carpeting, or playing it safe with a conventional plush. If you live in the hinterlands, carpeting can be ordered and shipped directly to an installer in your area. I know some busy customers who are so confident of Pioneer's pricing and integrity that when they need a new boxspring and mattress set they just call and say "send a new set." If you're like most people, you'll want to bounce on the

mattresses first. No problem; when you stop in you'll have a variety of major lines in several price ranges to choose from. Delivery and installation are provided. Note: Pioneer is closed Monday, Saturday, and Sunday, and weekday hours may vary since this "new mom" is still fine-tuning her schedule.

Styler's Floor Coverings
664 Rancho Shopping Center (Foothill Boulevard at Magdalena Street), Los Altos. (415) 948-6441. M–Sat 10–5. Cash/Check. Parking: lot.

You can relax here. The service is low-key, in keeping with its easy-to-overlook location in this small shopping center. The focus is on better carpeting (although you can buy budget, too), with some of the best brands coming from smaller mills on the West Coast. Markups are minimal, which leads to very competitive pricing. Major brands of vinyl flooring take care of baths and kitchens, and prices are equally competitive. Large-size carpet samples and books can be borrowed for making sure that the color that looks so great in the store will look equally great at home. The lighting, wall color, and window orientation in your home can produce striking color differences from store lighting. Styler's licensed installers will see that the job is done to the highest standards.

Tradeway Stores Warehouse
350-A Carlson Boulevard, Richmond. (510) 233-0841. M–Sat 10–5:30, Sun Noon–5. MC, VISA. Parking: lot. (Other store [furniture only]: 10860 San Pablo Avenue, El Cerrito.)

If you're looking for good deals on carpeting, this gloomy warehouse for Tradeway Stores offers carpeting that has been written off as an insurance loss. Name-brand mills also dispose of overruns, excess inventories, seconds, and off-color carpeting. Stacked in rolls twenty feet and higher, the carpets will make you feel like you're walking through a mini–Grand Canyon. I'm always impressed at the good buys on commercial carpets, which is why so many savvy architects and contractors make their way here. Prices are usually lower than original wholesale, and on the dogs that have been around too long, substantially lower. This is strictly a case of "what you see is what you get." You'll be impressed by the many fine-quality rolls, yet bewildered by others that seem unlikely to ever find a permanent resting place. There are no special or custom orders.

Padding is sometimes available below wholesale. Tradeway does not install, but will provide you with contractor references. All carpeting is ready for immediate delivery.

Remnants

Carpet Connection

390 Bayshore Boulevard, San Francisco. (415) 550-7125.
M–Th 8–7, F 8–6, Sat–Sun 9–4. MC, VISA, AE, DIS.
Parking: street.
Carpet Connection has a particularly choice selection of remnants, including many that are very effective in contemporary decors. You'll find stain-resistant carpets plus 100% wool and woolex blends. In many instances the remnant prices are below manufacturers' listed wholesale prices. Along with remnants, rolls of discontinued carpets are priced with bargain hunters in mind. There is a minimum installation charge of $75, and binding is $1.25/linear foot.

Dick's Wholesale Carpet Warehouse

444 Lesser Street, Oakland. (510) 534-2100.
M–Sat 9–5:30, Sun Noon–5. MC, VISA. Parking: lot.
Dick's has one of the biggest selections of remnant carpets in the Bay Area, from absolutely tacky to superb, and of course prices vary accordingly. What's nice about Dick's is that the remnants are in workable sizes, with many that will easily fit most room dimensions; there are even some large enough to cover two or three rooms. Dick's has a separate corner devoted just to area rugs, from inexpensive and small up to the "real thing." You can get something super cheap if you're just nesting in a place until the next move. Delivery charges are reasonable, usually $15–$25 depending upon distance. Directions: From 880 take the 66th Avenue Exit west to Oakport, turn right, and follow one mile to Lesser.

Floorcraft

470 Bayshore Boulevard, San Francisco. (415) 824-4056.
M–F 8–6, Sat 8:30–5, Sun 10–5. MC, VISA, AE, DIS.
Parking: street.
You'll find about 1,000 remnants in easy-to-see racks. Your best prices are on the "weird" sizes, because it's harder to sell a 7-by-20-foot rug than a standard 10-by-12-foot. Ditto for

vinyl remnants. The selection covers about every type of carpet, including wool berbers, commercial carpets, graphics, loops, textures, and plush. Installation, cutting, binding, and delivery are provided. Kitchen remodelers will want to compare prices on Floorcraft's midpriced kitchen cabinets from Diamond, Omega, and Dynasty. You may be surprised to find that you'll save at least 10% off all those other "deeply" discounted prices advertised everywhere else, and maybe more on custom orders. Expect at least 15% lower prices than the warehouse super stores on custom orders for tubs, faucets, and toilets from Kohler, Moen, and Delta.

Remnant World Carpets

5158 Stevens Creek Boulevard (at Lawrence Expressway),
San Jose. (408) 984-1965. M–F 9–9, Sat 10–6, Sun 11–5.
MC, VISA, DIS, AE. Parking: lot.
(Other store: Kaleidoscope Quality Carpets, White Road Plaza,
1054 S. White Road, San Jose.)
You'll find over 2,000 remnants from leading mills at good prices. Want a take-it-with-you rug? Have it bound to your specifications. If you lack the fortitude to lay it yourself, you can have it installed. You can also special order carpets from samples at very nice discounts, or pick up a bound area rug or hall runner from this extensive selection. Finally, check the vinyl flooring in rolls and remnants.

Wood Bros.

221 N. 16th, Sacramento. (916) 443-2031. M–Sat 8:30–5:30.
MC, VISA. Parking: lot.
Wood Bros. has a huge showroom with rolls of carpets and vinyl flooring from major manufacturers (Trust Mark, Mohawk Excellence, Salem, Lees, Cabin Craft, Philadelphia, Evans & Black, Armstrong, Tarkett, Congoleum, Mannington, and more). The prices are already good, yet the staff is always willing to dicker a little. Its best bargains are in the annex, where remnants are neatly organized by size up to 12 by 30 feet. Each piece is priced. (It drives me nuts when stores don't tag carpets, requiring you to ask for a price over and over again.) You'll be referred to licensed contractors for installation.

Helpful Hints

Bert's Carpet Workroom

1751 Tennessee Street, San Francisco. (415) 641-8255.
M–Th 9–4:30, Fri 9–3. Cash/Check. Parking: street.
Stretch your decorating dollar by making the best use of
remnants or old carpeting. Maybe you're cutting down wall-
to-wall carpeting to use in a bedroom, or you have some
good remnants left over from a new carpet installation and
you want to make runners or small area rugs. Worse-case
scenario—your dog has chewed the edges of your expensive
Oriental carpet. Call Bert's, one of the few companies around
that specializes in binding. Binding is $3.25/yard; serging is
$3.75/yard; fringing is $5/yard. Ask about costs on carpet
repairs or a full line of Oriental fringe. Also, serging and binding of sisal carpets.

Also See

Under Furniture and Home Accessories—
Catalog Discounters, General Furnishings:
All listings

Under Furniture and Home Accessories—
Furniture Clearance Centers:
Macy's Furniture Clearance Center

Dinnerware and Kitchenware

General

Avery's

3666 Stevens Creek Boulevard, San Jose. (408) 984-1111,
(800) 828-3797. M–Sat 10–6, Sun Noon–5. MC, VISA. Parking: lot.
Bargains go hand-in-hand with extra-special benefits at
Avery's—courtesy strollers for the tots, fresh-brewed comple-
mentary gourmet coffee, and starched linen hand towels in
the lovely restroom. Avery's may have changed its pricing on
some categories to appeal to bargain hunters, but it retains
its lovely ambiance, fine selection of giftware, tasteful merchandising, and gracious service. The realities of the marketplace
prompted its new discount policy: 30% off retail on most patterns of fine china (Noritake, Villeroy & Boch, Wedgewood,
Spode, Lenox, Fitz & Floyd, et al.); 25–30% off retail on stainless and silverplate flatware; 30–50% off on sterling flatware;
and discounted stemware (excluding Waterford and Baccarat).
A 50% discount applies to any leftovers, closeouts, whatever,
found in its clearance room. Brides will want to register! Throw
in its courtesy gift wrap, shipping, 800 number, and in-stock
availability of most patterns and you end up with a full-price
service and real values—a winning combination. Avery's is
located behind Kiddie World at the back of the parking lot.

Chef's Cordon Bleu

1135 Industrial Road, San Carlos. (415) 637-8405.
M–Sat 9–5. MC, VISA. Parking: lot.
(Other store: 28 Westlake Mall, Daly City.)

This store serves as an outlet for plain and patterned Cordon Bleu porcelain dinnerware and bakeware. New inventory (overruns, discontinued patterns, slightly imperfect pieces) is added weekly, so you may want to visit more than once. Since the line is frequently featured in major store sales and promotions, the discounts vary accordingly, but you can count on 50% off "regular" retail—maybe more in the case of missing lids and other such incomplete items. This outlet also caters to restaurant chefs and gourmet cooks; professional equipment and kitchenware are discounted about 20% off retail (even Calphalon, Le Creuset, All Clad, and Cuisinart). Along with the more popular items, you'll discover hard-to-find baker's equipment like oversized pie plates (up to 12-inch), along with cake-decorating supplies, gadgets, utensils, pot racks, knives, springmold pans, butcher-block carts, and other kitchenware. You can really get serious about cooking and buy a Wolf or Viking range at discounted prices.

Chicago Cutlery Etc.

Outlets at Gilroy, Gilroy. (408) 842-3810. Daily. MC, VISA.
Parking: lot.

Whether you're cutting up tomatoes or a side of beef, you'll find a suitable knife at Chicago Cutlery at below department store sale prices. You'll also find Wagner cast-iron skillets, Magnalite professional cookware, Colonial candles, and lots of other goodies. Your best buys are the discontinued items and seconds (not functional flaws; usually discolored wood handles on the knives or minute scratches on the Magnalite pans).

Cookin'

339 Divisadero (bet. Oak and Page), San Francisco.
(415) 861-1854. T–Sat Noon–6:30, Sun 1–5. MC, VISA.
Parking: street.

This fascinating store is piled, stacked, jammed, and crowded with "recycled gourmet appurtenances," or, in plain English, used cookware. If what you want isn't made anymore or you can't locate it anywhere, it may be here. I'm not sure Cookin' qualifies as a bargain store, since the "old" things sometimes cost more now than they did originally, and many secondhand items are superior to the new stuff. The brands that made up Mom's or Grandma's kitchen are still available, but they're often made overseas and don't reflect the same quality. If you want anything copper, there's plenty. Cast iron, stock pots, bakeware, old measuring cups and utensils, exotic pastry items, molds, grinders, and more are sure to tempt. Count on dinnerware, soufflés, casseroles, custards, coffeemakers, waffle irons, glassware, and china. Not everything is old; occasionally there are closeouts at 25–45% discounts. Love the expensive professional-grade French pastry molds, bags, tips, and stuff for those Cordon Bleu recipes. If you're cleaning out your kitchen or disposing of an estate, call the owner, who's always on the lookout for good stuff.

Copper Kitchen

21 Princess Street, Sausalito. (415) 331-1919.
Daily 11–5 (closed Wed). MC, VISA, AE. Parking: street/pay lots.
Designers and restaurateurs are beating a path to the Copper Kitchen to buy the old Greek and Turkish molds, pails, bowls, buckets, and assorted pieces to use as fireplace pots, planters, or decorative accents. Old Turkish turban molds that sell here for $15 are often sold for $40–$50 in San Francisco's specialty boutiques. True to its name, you can find just about anything made from copper. From heavy, new French cooking pots (usually 25% off that famous cookware store's regular prices), new molds, graters, tea pots, crepe pans, fry pans, stock pots, strainers, cookie cutters, wine coolers, pot racks and hooks, plus lots of charming, slightly tarnished old copper cookware. (Old pieces that have worn out their tin lining are not suitable for cooking, but they add wonderful charm to any decor.) Everything is discounted a little to a lot (some new pieces just a modest 10%–20%); however, there's always a sale posted on a particular group of copper something. The best prices are always on the old pieces—the Greek owner utilizes his direct connections to the "old country" to acquire these goods. You can shine up those old pieces, but I like them the way they are. Charming little store with the best copper selection in the Bay Area, and a good reason to visit Sausalito.

Corning Revere Factory Store

Great Mall of the Bay Area, Milpitas. (408) 934-9070. Daily.
MC, VISA, DIS. Parking: lot.
(Other outlets: Folsom, Gilroy, Milpitas, Petaluma, Tracy,
Vacaville centers.)

Corning and Revere products are the emphasis at this store:
Visions cookware; Corelle dishes (open stock and boxed sets);
Pyrex everything; Corningware bakeware and separate replacement lids; Revere bakeware and copper and aluminum disk
bottom pots and pans. The big discounts apply to Corning's
and Revere's own lines, typically 20–60% off retail. The best
buys are on 24- or 32-piece sets, such as Corelle and Corningware, in plain boxes.

Cyclamen Studio Outlet

1825 Eastshore Highway, Berkeley. (510) 843-4691.
M–Sat 11:30–5:30. Cash/Check. Parking: lot.

Julie Sanders's whimsical ceramics appear in stores like Henri
Bendel, Marshall Field, and their Bay Area equivalents. Stop in
to buy seconds, prototypes, and sample pieces. These ceramics
are divided into dinnerware, platters, bowls, mugs, pitchers,
and vases. Each piece is handpainted and unique. Inspirations
for her designs come from the great artists of the nineteenth
and twentieth centuries, French Renaissance architecture,
Mission furniture, and African textiles; combining sculptural
shapes only adds to their originality. Five-piece place settings
of dinnerware range at retail from $90 (solid colors) to $200.
At the outlet, you're unlikely to find complete place settings
all in one color, but you can expect a fun forage for accessories.
Platters and other serving pieces in brightly colored glazes
with dramatic designs, some with touches of gold, make wonderful gifts. The platters may range from $36 to $90 and lend
themselves to serving many ethnic foods that are so popular
in today's menus. Prices wholesale or below. All sales final.
Shipping available, including boxes. Outlet faces the freeway.

Dansk Factory Outlet

801 Main (Dansk Marketplace), St. Helena. (707) 963-4273.
Daily 10–6. MC, VISA. Parking: lot.
(Other stores: Carmel (408) 625-1600; Tahoe Truckee Factory Stores,
Truckee (916) 582-0938.)

Dansk stores showcase all the products made by this fine
company. Its lines are particularly appealing for their clean

contemporary designs and functionality. Prices are typically discounted 30–60% on discontinued groups and factory over-runs. The stores are fun to visit, beautifully merchandised, and brimming with colorful, well-priced bargains. My favorite Dansk purchase: the 18-piece wine glass set packaged in a handy box with drawers that functions neatly as a storage unit.

David M. Brian
1126 Broadway Plaza (at S. Main), Walnut Creek.
(510) 947-1991, (800) 833-2182. M–F 10–9, Sat 10–6, Sun
11–5. MC, VISA, AE. Parking: lot.
I think of David M. Brian as the Gump's of Contra Costa County. It's a pleasure to peruse its elegant home accessories, decorative fine art, giftware, dinnerware, kitchenware, and linens. It's not a bargain store, but one bargain angle may be of interest to you—30% discount on all sterling silver and silverplate flatware by Towle, Reed and Barton, Wallace, International, Oneida, Gorham, Lunt, and Kirk Stieff, with interest-free, easy payment plans. Another plus is that almost every pattern is in stock. If you're buying a present, you'll love the free giftwrap and free shipping within the Bay Area—just another aspect of this first-class store! Phone orders accepted.

Elegant Glass Factory Outlet
109 Cooper Street, Santa Cruz. (408) 427-4260.
M–Sat 10–6, Sun 11–5. MC, VISA. Parking: street/lot.
You've seen Annieglass in the finest stores and craft galleries across the country. Famous for its Roman Antique textured glass dinnerware with 24K gold bands, the company offers fourteen distinct lines of dinnerware and home accessories. The glassware is completely handmade and signed. At Annie-glass's new outlet, you'll have a chance to buy seconds at about 40% off retail. This is a very nice source for wedding gifts (serving bowls and hors d'oeuvres platters). You can have a personal inscription written on the underside of the rim. A dinner plate that retails for $40–$50 will be priced about $25–$30. Serving pieces are $58–$125. You can also special order first-quality Annieglass.

Famous Brands Housewares

Factory Stores of America, Vacaville. (707) 451-8546. Daily.
MC, VISA, AE, DIS. Parking: lot.
(Other outlets: Gilroy, Lathrop, Tracy centers.)
Here you'll find everything Rubbermaid, closet accessories
and organizers, picture frames, bakeware, cookware, gadgets
galore, potpourri, kitchen linens, pots, pans, serving dishes
and platters, glassware, microwave cookware, laundry room
necessities, giftware, and more. The store offers promotional
items, discontinued styles, closeouts, and regular merchandise
at 20–70% discounts. It's a subsidiary of the Lechters stores.

Farberware Outlet

Factory Stores of America, Vacaville. (707) 452-0533. Daily.
MC, VISA. Parking: lot.
(Other outlet: Lathrop center.)
You'll be blinded by the gleam of Farberware's stainless
steel pots and cookware as you wander through this outlet.
Discounts are 25–40% off on most items, but can go as high
as 60% off retail. Farberware also makes small electric appliances like toasters, coffeemakers, hand mixers, and tea kettles,
as well as mixing bowls, measuring cups, etc., all offered at
minimal to large discounts.

Franmara

4155 Stevens Creek Boulevard (at Kiely next to LeeWards),
Santa Clara. (408) 244-4464. M-Th, Sat 10-6, F 10-8, Sun 11-5.
MC, VISA, DIS, AE. Parking: lot.
(Other stores: Great Mall of the Bay Area, Milpitas;
570 Work, Salinas.)
This is an outlet for Franmara, an importer of porcelain dinnerware, corkscrews, barware, and top-of-the-table items. Pillivuyt
("pilly-vwheat") French porcelain, its largest line of dinnerware, has over 3,000 distinct pieces and offers a European
look. Pillivuyt's traditional and contemporary designs and
multifunctional qualities have made it a favorite with great
cooks around the world. Each piece can go directly from
the freezer to the oven or microwave. You'll find first-quality
overruns and discontinued products here, sold as open stock,
in plain brown boxed sets or by the place setting. Since this is
the Mercedes-Benz of dinnerware, prices reduced at 40–60%
may still be higher than the cheaper lookalike versions at
popular import stores. However, there's a world of difference

in the quality. Patterns come in plain white, or very special and decorative. By far the most interesting items to me were the accessory pieces common to restaurants but not normally available in other dinnerware services. If you've always wanted a custom-designed set of dinnerware, inquire about Franmara's custom program; after all, that's what it does every day for its extensive trade clientele. Don't miss the "leftovers" from its barware and corkscrew line, the cookware, cutlery, and flatware purchased to round out the selection.

The Goodbuy Store, Taylor & Ng Outlet

2919 Seventh Street (one block north of Ashby), Berkeley.
(510) 849-1000. M–Sat 10–5, Sun 11–4 (seasonal hours vary).
MC, VISA. Parking: street.

Taylor & Ng has a neat little outlet near Whole Earth Access. If you're into Chinese cooking, you'll find everything from A to Z: woks, steamers, wok utensils, brushes, cleavers, and more. Coffee drinkers may want to try an espresso or cappuccino machine. Stock up on cookware and serveware; mugs; well-priced Le Carp blue and white serveware for Asian dishes; a multitude of linens (aprons, kitchen towels, mitts, pot holders); baskets; stovetop sandwich makers; wine racks; silk flowers; specialty foods; cutlery; and cookbooks. Exchanges with receipt for store credit only. Store may be relocating; phone first.

Gorham Outlet

801 Main Street, Dansk Marketplace, St. Helena.
(707) 963-7532. Daily 10–6. MC, VISA. Parking: lot.

The Gorham Outlet absolutely glistens with sterling silver, silverplate, crystal, and china. It sells overstock, discontinued patterns, and seconds at 20–60% off retail. Many china patterns are sold as 20-piece sets (best discounts) or may be purchased as open stock. You'll find sterling gift items and baby gifts. Silverplated Revere bowls, crystal bowls, boxes, candlesticks, and Gorham dolls both gift and collectible (numbered and signed), are also popular. There are in-store specials in each category at all times. It will accept UPS orders on inventory in stock, but can't accept special orders for first-quality patterns or items not in the store.

Heath Ceramics (Factory Outlet)

400 Gate 5 Road, Sausalito. (415) 332-3732. Daily 10–5.
MC, VISA. Parking: lot.

The Heath Factory Store could well be the focal point of a trip to Sausalito. Overruns and seconds of tile for flooring, counters, and walls are available in extraordinary colors and textures at very worthwhile savings. The dishes and heat-tempered cookware that do not pass its high standards are sold for 40% below retail prices. You'll find new glazes reflecting the latest looks in home-decorating trends plus whiteware (dinnerware) in all shapes and special one-of-a-kind decorated plates. These savings are apt to keep you coming back to round out your dinner settings, to buy gifts, to purchase tile for a remodeling project, or to introduce a friend to the experience.

Heritage House

2190 Palou Avenue, San Francisco. (415) 285-1331. M–F 10–6.
MC, VISA, DIS. Parking: street.

Heritage House offers some special benefits that make it a solid alternative to the popular mail-order discount companies. First, the selection, which is distinguished by the many premium lines of imported European (some handpainted) lines of china, stemware, and flatware and others that bear prestigious American designer names. It may only be able to offer minimal (10–20%) discounts on these lines, but that's better than none at all (and many are not available through mail order). On the more mainstream lines sold in department stores everywhere, prices are sometimes a tad higher than many mail-order companies, but still very competitive. If you're adding to your patterns, the staff is helpful about advising you when the manufacturers have scheduled sales and special promotions, so you can time your purchases for maximum savings. Brides get very special treatment, with a complete registry program plus a telephone registry program for out-of-area brides. Appointments are preferred for bridal consultations; with hundreds of patterns to choose from and combine, you'll appreciate the staff's expertise in helping you through the process of choosing the patterns you'll live with for many years. There are only two or three very upscale retail stores around the Bay Area that have a selection that rivals what you'll find here. Stop in too if you're shopping for tasteful gifts. The company has a most unlikely location in an industrial park in the Bayshore area. It's modest exterior is in complete contrast to the beautiful showroom you'll encounter once you go through the doors. From downtown, take the Army Street/Bayshore Exit to Bayshore. Turn left on Oakdale, right on Barnveld, and left on Palou.

Janus

261 Main Street, Los Altos. (800) 697-3500.
M–F 10–6, Sat 9:30–5:30, Sun Noon–5. MC, VISA.
Parking: street/rear lot.
Use the Janus 800 number to take the legwork out of gift buying. Or stop in and find a beautiful store featuring fine china, crystal, flatware (stainless, sterling, and silverplate), and giftware, with a discount policy that rivals many of the best mail-order companies. A few patterns in a few lines are not discounted, but 20% discounts are offered on Jean Couzon stainless (no one else does that). Minimum discounts start at 20% off retail, some are around 40%, and occasionally even more when manufacturers' promotions are added. Brands include Wedgewood, Christian Dior, Spode, Fitz & Floyd, Lenox, Noritake, Dansk, Villeroy & Bach, Royal Doulton, Reed & Barton, and other famous lines. Janus will ship anywhere!

The Kitchen Collection

Factory Stores of America, Vacaville. (707) 446-7823. Daily.
MC, VISA, DIS. Parking: lot.
(Other outlets: Gilroy, Lathrop centers.)
The Kitchen Collection is a factory store for Wear-Ever and Proctor-Silex. Everything in kitchen essentials is covered, including other brands like Meyer, Lincoln, Wilton, and Anchor Hocking, all at a good price. There's a complete array of Wear-Ever pots and pans, pressure cookers, roasters, cake pans, and indispensable small electric appliances like toaster ovens, coffeemakers, juicers, popcorn makers, portable mixers, griddles, electric frying pans, woks, and Crock-Pots, as well as less essential but still useful devices. Sign up for its mail-order discount catalog.

Le Creuset Factory Outlet

Factory Stores of America, Vacaville. (707) 453-0620. Daily.
MC, VISA, DIS, AE. Parking: lot.
Le Creuset cookware is exactly what you need for cooking comfort foods: stews and brews that need long, slow, simmering or baking. If price has kept you away, check out the bargains on

everything familiar (and unfamiliar) this company makes. First-quality pieces are discounted about 40%, seconds about 50%, and discontinued pieces and liquidations as much as 70% off retail. Don't pass up other the culinary accessories like the never-fail screwpull corkscrews, woks, and storage containers. Ships UPS anywhere!

Le Gourmet Chef

Petaluma Village Factory Outlets, Petaluma. (707) 766-8893.
Daily. MC, VISA. Parking: lot.
(Other outlets: Folsom, Napa, Pacific Grove centers.)
An irresistible store for browsing, buying, and, to a lesser extent, bargains. The latest in gourmet cookware, gadgets, and accessories are almost as tempting as the gourmet edibles in jars, packages, bottles, and boxes (sauces, mixes, jams, marinades, vinegars, etc.). Most of the nonfood merchandise comes from American Direct Outlets, a company that has provided many vendors with a way to unload overruns, discontinued products, and more. Some famous names: Cuisinart, Krups, Cushionaire, and Rowenta. Give your kitchen a culinary update by selecting some new fine cutlery, gourmet cookware, microwave bakeware, glassware, small electronics, kitchen gadgets, or accessories (picture frames, salt and pepper shakers, mugs, cleaning aids, et al.). Except for kitchen gadgets and edibles, everything is priced to compete with department store sale prices.

Lenox Factory Outlet

Outlets at Gilroy, Gilroy. (408) 847-1181. Daily.
MC, VISA, AE, DIS. Parking: lot.
Hurrah! Three cheers! Lenox has opened a large, elegant, and well-stocked store. China, stemware, giftware (vases, picture frames, candles, etc.), and a nice selection of table linens and place mats. Since Lenox now owns Gorham, you'll also find stemware, flatware (stainless, silverplate, and sterling), and Gorham giftware. "Exclusives" to the outlet include paper products (napkins, paper plates, etc.) that coordinate with Lenox china patterns. Prices are discounted 30–50% off retail. Everything is almost invisibly marked as a second, yet the merchandise may in fact be first-quality surplus or closeouts. Tables are filled with stacks and stacks of everyday dinnerware and fine china, including some of the most popular patterns made by Lenox. These are sold on an open stock basis. Phone

quotes and orders are accepted on the store's inventory; however, no special discounts are offered on merchandise that may not be carried in the outlet. Note: For invitations to extra savings make sure you're on the Lenox mailing list. UPS shipping anywhere!

Marjorie Lumm's Wine Glasses

112 Pine Street, San Anselmo. (415) 454-0660.
M–F 10–4; weekends by appt. MC, VISA. Parking: municipal lot.
The serious wine buff doesn't want cutwork or ornamentation on glasses obscuring the color and clarity of wine. If you're as serious about your wine glasses as you are about your wines, you'll want to pay a visit to Marjorie Lumm's warehouse/store. She has been at the helm of her own mail-order glass company for twenty-seven years. Most of her glasses retail between $5 and $15; the most expensive is the Riedel Sommelier Burgundy at $42. Bargain hunters will want to scrutinize the seconds, reduced 50% off retail. You may also find discontinued first-quality glasses sold at a considerable discount. Glasses can be engraved for a modest charge and chipped or broken glasses can be repaired. Call first about availability and store hours. Write for her catalog: P.O. Box 1544, San Anselmo, CA 94979.

Mikasa Factory Store

1239 Marina Boulevard, Marina Square, San Leandro.
(510) 352-1211. M–F 10–9, Sat 10–6, Sun 11–6. MC, VISA.
Parking: lot.
(Other outlets: Anderson/Redding, Gilroy, Napa, Petaluma, South Lake Tahoe, Tracy, Vacaville centers.)
You have a chance to buy everything Mikasa here. Since it makes over 300 patterns of dinnerware alone, you know there's a lot you haven't seen before. You'll also be energized by the prices, a tempting 20–50% off retail. At the outlet you'll find dinnerware, casual to fine china; casual and formal stainless flatware; cookware, bakeware, and casseroles; canisters; crystal stemware and giftware; linens; tea kettles; pots and pans; vases; houseware; and more. Using Mikasa's special order desk is the best way to order additional settings or pieces. UPS shipping available. Sorry, no giftwrap; all sales final.

Oneida Factory Store

Factory Stores of America, Vacaville. (707) 448-5804. Daily.
MC, VISA. Parking: lots. (Other outlets: Anderson/Redding,
Gilroy, South Lake Tahoe centers.)

You can't miss the Oneida Factory Stores, with their dazzling displays of silverplated goods. You'll find overruns, vendor returns, excess inventory, and some seconds in traditional silverplated hollowware, stainless and gold-electroplate flatware, gift items, leaded crystal stemware and accessories, as well as melamine children's giftware. Expect 50–70% discounts off original retail on everything. Tea sets, serving trays, casserole holders, picture frames, candle holders, most patterns of Oneida flatware, and food warmers are plentiful. Almost every item displayed is available in prepacked gift boxes.

Pfaltzgraff Factory Store

Factory Stores of America, Vacaville. (707) 446-4984. Daily.
MC, VISA. Parking: lot.
(Other outlets: Gilroy, South Lake Tahoe centers.)

If you want to pick up serving pieces, replace broken dishes, or add to your sets, stop by Pfaltzgraff Factory Store. Current patterns are discounted a modest 15%, but seconds packaged as "brown box specials" save you a lot more. You'll find glassware from Durand, Anchor Hocking, Arcoroc, and Libbey at modestly discounted prices. Also crystal stemware, flatware sets, knives, utensils, and lots more. Charming store, but I'd like to see bigger discounts.

Reed & Barton

Outlets at Gilroy, Gilroy. (408) 847-5454. Daily. MC, VISA.
Parking: lot.

Just what you'd expect from Reed & Barton: stainless and sterling silver flatware, silverplate, serving pieces, hollowware, storage chests, and more. The inventory is first quality, overruns, discontinued, and slightly irregular (usually on the silver chests). Discounts range from so-so to impressive. Also, Sheffield silverplate serving pieces and Belleck china giftware from Ireland. A lovely store with an accommodating staff. Phone orders accepted.

Robin's Nest

116 E. Napa (just off the Plaza), Sonoma. (707) 996-4169.
Daily 10–6. MC, VISA. Parking: street.
Going to the wine country? Then stop off here for kitchenware, giftware, dinnerware, Maxim electrics, gourmet cooking
accessories and foods, small appliances, and culinary linens
for 15–30% off retail (selected markdowns to 60% off retail).
The best buys are on seconds, closeouts, discontinued items,
and samples.

Royal Doulton

Factory Stores of America, Vacaville. (707) 448-2793. Daily.
MC, VISA, AE. Parking: lot.
(Other outlet: Pacific Grove center.)
This Royal Doulton store is a treasure of fine china, giftware,
and collectibles sold at discount prices. Slightly imperfect and
first-quality active patterns of Royal Doulton, Royal Albert,
and Minton china are sold at 40% discounts. Patterns not in
stock can be special ordered and shipped to your home.
Don't expect to find recently introduced patterns in stock.
You may find recently discontinued patterns. Beatrix Potter,
Brambley Hedge, Bunnykins, Toby Jugs, Character Jugs, and
Crinoline Ladies giftware are sold at 20% discounts. You'll also
find Royal Albert giftware and some crystal. Keep your eyes
peeled for "extra specials" and markdowns around the holidays.
You can special order anything in Royal Doulton, Royal Crown,
or Derby. Don't worry about getting your china and giftware
home: they ship via UPS anywhere, and most items are sold in
gift boxes.

Silver & More

Factory Stores of America, Vacaville. (707) 451-2114. Daily.
MC, VISA. Parking: lot.
(Other outlets: Gilroy, Milpitas centers.)
At Silver & More you'll find displays of current silver, silverplate, and stainless flatware patterns from Towle, Wallace, and
International Silver at 50% discounts, plus Gorham, Reed &
Barton, Lunt, and Kirk Stieff competitively priced with the
best mail-order companies. If all goes as planned, by the time
you're reading this you'll also find Waterford, Baccarat, Lladro,
and Hummell at 20% below department store prices. These
companies make several qualities of silverplated giftware and
hollowware: a lot of budget-priced trays, bowls, and candle-

sticks that offer the gleam but may not have the weight or quality engraving found on the better groups in stock. Check the table where you may find ice tea spoons, butter knives, serving pieces, and other items in popular patterns priced individually and very cheaply. Also check for special promotions of one kind or another offered every week.

Union Street Glass Outlet

2670 Union Street (off Grand Avenue near Cypress), Oakland. (510) 451-1077. M–F 10–4. (Sat and Sun before Christmas holidays). MC, VISA. Parking: street.

Union Street's Manhattan stemware design won the prestigious Niche design award in 1994. It's no wonder this line has become so popular with discriminating consumers. Its goblets, barware, bowls, and vases are elegant—and expensive: goblets retail for about $50 each. Each piece is hand-blown, signed, and dated. It's hard to figure what makes a second, since subtle variations on each piece enhance and emphasize the handmade look. Most collections here are embellished with 23K gold that will not scratch or wear off. You can choose goblets that have jewel tones drawn through the stem with gold-leaf permanently fused into the design. For maximum versatility, the clear glass and gold-leaf treatments are the ultimate in elegance. From my perspective, the seconds at $10–$20 per stem, $5–$10 for a piece of barware, paperweights for $10, and bowls and vases at $35–$150 are genuine bargains. Note: This line works beautifully with Annieglass dinnerware. If you stop by and the door is locked, push the buzzer.

Villeroy & Boch Outlet

Petaluma Village Factory Outlets, Petaluma. (707) 769-9029. Daily. MC, VISA. Parking: lot.
(Other outlet: Tahoe/Truckee center.)

If you're cruising up 101, take time out to visit the Villeroy & Boch Outlet, where shoppers delight in 20–70% discounts off retail (most dinnerware discounted at least 35% off retail). You'll find seconds and current pattern overruns, but it's unlikely you'll find its newest patterns. The company makes about sixty patterns; at the outlet you'll find about twenty-five, including many of its best-known patterns, like Basket, Petite Fleur, Amapola, Siena, Iris, Mariposa, Alba, Delia, Botanica, Molina, and its two popular Christmas patterns, Naive and Holly. You can buy a piece or a place setting from open stock.

You'll find more porcelain than bone china patterns, and you're limited to the patterns in stock; no special orders for other patterns. However, you can call and order anything in stock and have it shipped UPS to your home. Villeroy & Boch also makes 24% lead crystal stemware. Prices on seconds and over-runs range from $6 to $18. Exchanges with receipt are allowed within two weeks.

Mail Order

Many mail-order companies offer the best of both worlds: good service and good prices on fine and everyday china, flatware (silver and silverplate), hollowware, crystal stemware, fine giftware, better jewelry, and collectibles. Check the back pages of almost any home magazine for starters. If a local retailer is having a special 40%-off sale, then you may save just a few dollars. To avoid problems, keep careful records and copies of your order, ask for an estimated shipping date, and make sure you understand the company's return policy. There are trade-offs. For those starting or completing their own sets of china, crystal, or silver, there's no Club Plan to spread the payments without interest. On the plus side, you may avoid the California sales tax (pending legislation); you can use toll-free 800 numbers to place your order; most companies have a national bridal registry; and shipping and insurance charges are very reasonable. The following companies have good track records based on my experience. Each may have slightly different pricing, availability, and shipping charges, so it's a good idea to get on the mailing list of each.

Ross-Simons
(800) 556-7376; fax (401) 463-8181.
Always my first choice for mail order. Most major brands, in-stock inventory, and bridal registry. Also fine jewelry, watches, nice giftware.

Michael J. Fina
(800) BUY-FINA; fax (718) 937-7193.
Bridal registry, good prices, some hard-to-find (at discount) patterns in china and stemware, better housewares, and jewelry.

Midas China & Silver

(800) 368-3153.
Smaller catalog, but good values on china, flatware, and stemware. Status pens, estate silver specials, and bridal registry.

Thurber's

(800) 848-7237; fax (401) 732-4124.
Cover all your bases with this company's catalog. Bridal
registry and most mainstream china, flatware, and stemware
patterns offered at discount.

Also See

Under Giftware and Home Decor:
All listings

Under Linens:
Bed & Bath Superstore; Home Express

Under Jewelry and Watches:
Cresalia Jewelers Diamond Expertise

Under Appliances, Electronics, and Home Entertainment:
Whole Earth Access

Under General Merchandise:
All listings

Draperies and Window Coverings

American Draperies & Blinds Factory Sale

1168 San Luis Obispo Avenue, Hayward. (510) 487-3500.
Usually first Sat of May and Nov 8:30–4:30. MC, VISA.
Parking: lot.

American makes draperies and blinds; twice a year it opens its factory to the public to clear out miscellaneous stock, draperies in discontinued fabrics, production overruns, and odd sizes. Most draperies are priced between $20 and $60, a savings of 50–75%. Bring your rod sizes and lengths required. Expect traditional, three-pronged, French-pleated, lined/unlined draperies (double fullness), fan-folded and ready to hang with hooks inserted. You'll find a variety of colors, weaves, textures, and weights. Extrastrong miniblinds and verticals in alabaster and white are sold with a lifetime warranty in the twenty most requested sizes (custom sizes available, too). Its sales usually occur on the first weekends in May and November. All sales final. Call anytime during the year and ask to be put on the mailing list.

Crow's Nest Interiors

2100 San Ramon Valley Boulevard, San Ramon. (510) 837-9130.
T–F 10–4, Sat 10–2. Cash/Check. Parking: rear lot.

Since the fabric is the largest part of the total expense in drapery or other window treatments, Crow's Nest's 30% discount on fabrics helps considerably. Additionally, its workrooms provide excellent quality at fair prices. Three outside designers work on a consulting basis for $45/hour, which is refunded when the drapery order is placed. In addition to draperies, Crow's Nest discounts Ohline and Woodfold shutters 33%. You'll like the 25–30% discount on wallpaper and 20–25% on coordinating wallpaper fabrics. You'll find its prices on bedspreads, comforters, window seat covers, pillows, and upholstery equally pleasing. A two-thirds deposit is required with your order.

The Drapery Outlet

590 Taylor Way, Belmont. (800) 371-6100. M–F 8–5, Sat 9–1.
MC, VISA. Parking: street.

For years this company has filled drapery orders for major stores. This outlet has a drapery workroom, a fabric warehouse, and the experience to handle almost any type of drapery treatment. You save on several aspects of the job. First, on fabric, where markups are very modest. In addition to the in-house selection, you can plow through hundreds of sample books from major suppliers. You can go budget, better, or best; bring in your own fabric to have draperies made; or special order a fabric. You'll avoid the add-on markups taken by most major stores on every aspect of the job. If you need help, its consultants will come to your home with samples, make recommendations for design treatments, and take measurements. The company gets you started and inspired with its display of treatments. Choose custom trims from sample books and hang the draperies from discounted Kirsch rods. A 50% deposit is required before making the draperies; no charge for measurements if an order is placed.

Wells Interiors Clearance Center

41477 Albrae Street, Fremont. (510) 490-6924.
M–F 10–6, Sat 10–5, Sun 11–5. MC, VISA. Parking: lot.
(Other stores: fourteen stores in Northern California;
check Geographical Index.)

If you don't mind spending a little time scrounging to unearth your bargains, Wells Interiors offers hard-to-beat prices. This is where all the returns, double orders, customer mistakes, factory mistakes, etc. are sent from nineteen stores. Sizes and styles are limited, but even Wells's everyday discount prices are drastically reduced. For example, vertical blinds for patio doors that would normally sell for $80–$200 go for $50–$75. Wood blinds priced normally at $50–$200 per window are $25–$50 each. Keep your window measurements in your wallet so you can shop if you find yourself in the area. If you never get to the clearance center, stop by one of its fourteen Northern California stores. I have no trouble at all choosing Wells Interiors as a reliable source for value. I love the audacious signs posted in its stores comparing its prices to other local companies. Directions: From 880, take the Stephenson Exit west. Turn left at Albrae, and follow around curve. Outlet faces freeway.

The Yardstick

2110 S. Bascom Avenue, Campbell. (408) 377-1401.
M–F 9:30–8:30, Sat 9:30–6, Sun 10:30–5. MC, VISA, DIS.
Parking: lot.

If you need draperies right away or you want luxury window treatments at budget prices, check The Yardstick. It usually has about 3,000 ready-mades (guaranteed 2½ fullness) from its own workrooms available for you to take home and hang. There's also a complete custom window-covering department using popular fabrics from Waverly, Robert Allan, Richloom, Covington, et al. Home-decorating services include furniture upholstering, and there's a bridal department complete with fabrics, laces, and accessories. Free in-home decorating service anywhere from San Francisco to Monterey. Kirsch and Graber drapery rods are always 30% off the manufacturers' list prices. It also has a large dress yardage department.

Also See

Under Carpets and Flooring:
Lawrence Contract Furnishers

Under Furniture and Home Accessories—Catalog Discounters:
Most listings

Under Linens:
Factory Outlet

Under Fabrics—Home-Decorating Fabrics:
All listings

Trade Secrets

Trim the costs of drapery rods with a little subterfuge. (I got this idea from a treatment used in a model home.) Head out to the nearest home-improvement store and buy PVC pipe (the plastic pipe used in sprinkler systems) or galvanized pipe from the electrical department. Choose any width—1-inch, 2-inch, 3-inch, or whatever. The heavier galvanized pipe works better for longer rods and heavier fabrics. If the rods are not going to be entirely covered by the fabric, give them a decorative finish with spray paint. I've seen clever finishes achieved with a coating of Rustoleum spray paint followed by sponging with a faux paint kit. Some have covered exposed rods with a fabric casing, or glued marbleized or textured wallpaper around the pipes. Attaching the rods is not difficult. Mount the rod like any other rod, using drapery hardware. To have something stable to screw into, thread a length of board through the pipe. Pull the edge of the drapery around the mounting hardware and nail or staple into wall to cover end of rods, or create your own finial. Is it worth the bother? I priced galvanized pipe 2 inches wide and 10 feet long for $6.93, and PVC pipe 2 inches wide and 10 feet long for $4.15. That's a fraction of the cost of the "fashion" rods so popular in recent trends.

Flower and Garden

Calaveras Nurseries
1000 Calaveras Road, Sunol. (510) 862-2286. Daily 8–4:30.
MC, VISA. Parking: lot.
This firm grows many of the plants that it sells wholesale and directly to the public. Bring your list and landscaping plans and buy everything you need in one fell swoop at down-to-earth prices. Prices in 1995 were as follows: 1-gallon shrubs $2.95–$3.40; 1-gallon trees and vines $3.40–$4.40; 5-gallon shrubs $9.95–$12.90; 5-gallon trees and vines $14.95–$16.95; and flats of ground cover $9.95–$12.95. Call first to make sure that what you want is in stock. Delivery can also be arranged. For fall planting, time your buys for the Big Fall Clearance Sale!

Coast Wholesale Dry Flowers & Baskets
149 Morris Street, San Francisco. (415) 781-3034.
M–F 6–3, Sat 7–Noon. MC, VISA. Parking: private lot.
One glance at the warehouse and you'll get the feeling that they've scoured the forests and fields for unusual dry flowers such as hydrangeas, along with wreaths, oak leaves, pine cones, et al. Garlic braids, unique baskets, and potpourri create a fragrant shopping environment. Floral supplies and beautiful fancy ribbons are also available. Prices are in line with other flower market vendors.

Concord Silk Floral

2061 Commerce Avenue, Concord. (510) 682-8088.
M–Sat 10–5. MC, VISA. Parking: lot.

Allergies? Then your salvation is artificial flowers and greenery, but at bargain prices of course! If you have a resale number and are in the flower business, you'll get extra-special prices on all the flowers, floral supplies, plants, baskets, and faux trees here.

Cottage Garden Growers

4049 Petaluma Boulevard North (up Pine Tree Lane), Petaluma.
(707) 778-8025. Feb–Oct, daily 9–5; Nov–Jan, daily 10–4.
MC, VISA, AE. Parking: lot.

This nursery specializes in perennials, grasses, clematis, herbs, and many varieties of new and old antique roses. All plants are grown on the premises, ensuring consistent care and quality, as well as acclimation to the region. You'll find more than 400 varieties (most offered in 1-gallon cans). Prices are very reasonable—$4.95 each, or choose any six for $28. The more common varieties are also at the big discounters (K-Mart, Home Depot, et al.) at slightly lower prices, but Cottage Garden's plants are fuller and healthier, and get my money every time. If you have your heart set on a particular plant, call for availability and a list of all the plants carried.

Flower Terminal

Sixth and Brannan streets, San Francisco. Hours vary,
generally M–F 2–11 a.m., Sat hours for a few vendors 8–Noon.
Cash/Check. Parking: street/lot.

Several wholesale nurseries are located in this block, selling cut flowers, houseplants, greenery, and floral supplies to the trade and the public. Don't expect information or advice. Vendors have neither the time nor the personnel for retail services. You are required to pay sales tax unless you have a resale number. Highlights: Ira Doud and Floral Supply Syndicate are headquarters for ribbons, decorations, wrapping paper, wreaths, and other fixin's for holiday decorating, floral displays, or table decorations. Silver Terrace is the largest of several vendors selling cut flowers, foliage, and plants. While prices aren't "wholesale" to the public, many items are simply not sold elsewhere at retail. From October through Christmas, anxious shoppers crowd these dealers to get a head start on their holiday decorations. Note: Only people with resale numbers are allowed to park in the lot, and street parking can be a real problem!

Flowers Faire

360 Bayshore Boulevard, San Francisco. (415) 641-7054.
M–Sat 8:30–6:30, Sun 9–5. MC, VISA. Parking: street.
People who live and work in this area stop by here to pick up roses, tulips, or tasteful mixed bouquets. For decades, this quick-service, budget-priced operation has specialized in carry-away bouquets. You'll get more blooms for the buck here than at your local supermarket. Flowers Faire offers several reasonably priced packages for weddings based on the use of seasonal flowers—and additional savings if it doesn't have to deliver. You can have it your way, but some flowers will cost more. If you become a frequent customer, you'll want to pick up a discount card.

Lisa Arnold Nursery Sales

9950 Calaveras Road, Sunol. (510) 862-9009.
M–F 7–4, winter, Sat 8–4; spring/summer, Sat and Sun 8–4.
Cash/Check. Parking: lot.
For a big landscaping job, go where the pros—landscape contractors and nurserypeople—go. Bring your "want list" and fill your trunk with trees, shrubs, ground covers, color, and specialty items like Japanese maples, bonsais, and palms. Some prices: flats $8.50–$11.50; 1–gallon $2.50–$4.50; 5–gallon $7.50–$16.50; and 15–gallon $30–$50.

Nor Cal Pottery

2091 Williams Street, San Leandro. (510) 895-5966.
M–F 10–4. Cash/Check. Parking: lot.
Nor Cal is an importer and distributor of pots and planters. It also imports many unique pots and planters used by landscape architects and interior designers. Since most of its pots are terra-cotta imported from Italy, a fair amount of seconds are accumulated—damaged in shipping, with cracks or chips. These seconds are usually 50% off retail. Occasionally, special pots get damaged, and then prices may be dropped to 75% off retail. There are bargains aplenty. You'll want to poke around each stack and pallet of pots, but ignore the excess first-quality inventory also stacked outside at full retail. At times, I've spotted fairly large terra-cotta pots (seconds) priced at $5 (well below wholesale). If you approach Nor Cal with an "I'll take pot luck" mindset, you'll probably be more than satisfied. Directions: From 880, take the Marina Exit west. Turn right at Merced, left on Williams.

Ortiz Pottery Outlet

425 South Market Street, San Jose. (408) 286-3661.
T–Sat 9–6, Sun 10–3. MC, VISA. Parking: lot.
Behind San Jose's Convention Center, the refurbished Mercado San Jose Shopping Center is taking shape. This outlet offers pallets, tables, and stacks of pottery containers, such as Italian terra-cotta, Gainey ceramics in over fifty colors, and Mexican and Chinese pottery. These are closeouts and seconds at nicely discounted prices. Inventories from other manufacturers produce an ever-changing selection. Look for statuary items such as fountains and birdbaths. You'll appreciate the umbrellas over the pottery yard on rainy days.

Planter Technology

999 Independence Avenue, #E, Mountain View. (415) 962-8982,
(800) 542-2282. M–F 7–5. MC, VISA. Parking: street.
Planter Technology makes Natural Spring Controlled Watering Planters. These planters have a double wall that holds water inside. Water enters through the base of the planter but is controlled through a sensor that detects when the soil is dry. The plant itself controls when and how much water it receives depending upon its individual needs. The planters are more expensive than most self-watering pots. Buying direct on a cash-and-carry basis yields a 20% discount. To avoid sticker shock, here are a few prices. For the most popular colors in the Natural Spring series (ivory, satin black, Italian terra-cotta, deep blue, hunter green, burgundy): 8-inch planter at $14.20; 11-inch at $22.60; 17-inch at $60.76. They are a little pricey to be sure, even though prices have been reduced from prior years! If you frequently replace house or patio plants or otherwise have difficulty keeping plants watered correctly, the cost may be worthwhile. For information, or to order, call (800) 542-2282. No discounts on phone orders.

Pottery & Floral World

685 Brannan Street (at Sixth Street), San Francisco.
(415) 543-5455. M–Sat 8:30–5, Sun 10–4. MC, VISA, AE.
Parking: rear lot.
Customers become regulars as every visit produces new treasures. Company buyers are on the prowl for surplus and slightly imperfect inventory from manufacturers and importers to keep its three West Coast stores well stocked. They're successful, too! The pottery yard is stocked with standard

Mexican terra-cotta pots, as well as unusual large urns (many with distinctive finishes), statuary, fountains, outdoor benches and tables. Artificial flowers, mostly silk, are always in good supply at great prices. You'll also find giftware (love the surplus dinnerware from L.A. Pottery), baskets, Chinese pots, cookie jars, wax fruit, bath accessories, holiday ornaments and decorations. Shoppers hurry in each fall for decorations and fixin's, then line up early for post-Christmas sales, and return again in late spring for last-chance markdowns. Love those parking spaces at the back of the store!

Pottery Products Outlet

15715 Hesperian Boulevard, San Lorenzo. (510) 481-1902.
M-F 10-6, Sat 10-7, Sun 11-5. MC, VISA. Parking: street/lot.
When warm weather rolls around and you're in a potting mood, you'll find good buys on an ample selection of planters and pots. True to its name, you'll find pottery aplenty. Some of its merchandise is classified as seconds (usually the stoneware or ceramic pots); it also carries first-quality bargains in odd lots, closeouts, and direct purchases at discount prices—a consequence of its wholesale business. A 6-inch standard clay pot sells for about 74¢. You'll find hand-thrown stoneware pots, Southwest plaster vases, architectural ceramics, statuary, birdbaths, and wrought iron. Everything is discounted 20–50% off!

Remember with Flowers

24901 #B Santa Clara Street (off Jackson and Highway 92),
Hayward. (510) 784-8990. M-T 6-8, W-Sat 6-10, Sun 8-6.
MC, VISA. Parking: lot.
(Other store: 1553 A Street, Hayward.)
Remember with Flowers is a clearinghouse for fresh-cut flowers, selling surplus inventory from the Flower Market and local growers every day. Flowers are graded for shipping (1–5); Remember with Flowers buys flowers that have passed their tolerance for cross-country shipping (a 3 grade), but they're not bloomed-out or tired. All flowers are sold in bunches of ten or two dozen stems, the wholesale norm. Shop prepared to select the best of what's available. You may find freesias, chrysanthemums, hybrid lilies, alstromeria, roses, and baby's breath at about half the price of the supermarket. If you need just a one-day display of flowers, you may find everything you need in the markdown buckets near the front door; prices are reduced another 50% or so.

A Separate Arrangement
5758 Shellmound Street, Emeryville. (510) 653-7227. Daily 9–6. MC, VISA. Parking: lot.

East Bay shoppers don't have to cross the bridge to find super buys on fresh-cut flowers. Just take the Powell Street Exit east off I-80 to the first light, turn right, and head for the orange building behind Lyon's restaurant. This good-sized shed-type building is filled with buckets of flowers and some house plants. The company supplies many flower kiosks in supermarkets and other retail operations with ready-to-go bouquets and bunches of individual blooms. The leftovers are sold to the public at deeply discounted prices. In spring 1995, a half dozen tall red roses were $7.50; Casablanca lilies were $4.50/stem; tulips 5/$3.50; alstromeria 5/$2.75, and a bunch of baby's breath $1.50. Wow! Inquire about flowers for weddings or other special events (bouquets or centerpieces). Accommodating staff.

Smith & Hawken Outlet
1330 Tenth Street, Berkeley. (510) 525-2944. F, Sat, Sun 10–6. MC, VISA. Parking: lot.

Smith & Hawken's outlet is partitioned from its very attractive full-service retail store and nursery. It has a separate entrance and offers merchandise in garden furniture, distinctive gift and dinnerware items, garden tools, plant food and fertilizers, fireplace tools, garden books, some apparel, and much more in the way of esoteric gardening and decorative items. Some merchandise may be slightly damaged or irregular, but most is discontinued catalog inventory reduced 25–75% off retail. Note: I've found that hours change from time to time, so maybe call first.

Ssilkss
635 Brannan Street, San Francisco. (415) 777-1353. Daily 8–5. MC, VISA. Parking: lot.

Ssilkss, an importer, wholesaler, and manufacturer of artificial trees, stocks an impressive inventory of silk flowers, plants, and trees and offers the same discounts to everyone. Ssilkss makes a variety of artificial trees up to twenty-five feet tall: ficus, palms, flowering trees, and bonsais. Complete your presentation with baskets and dried material to coordinate with the silk flowers and greenery. Christmas starts in August here with an extensive display of Christmas trees 4 to 15 feet tall and grapevine reindeer up to 6 feet tall.

Sunflower Wholesale Floral Supply

1243 Boulevard Way, Walnut Creek. (510) 947-0543.
M–F 9:30–4:30, Sat 10–4:30. MC, VISA. Parking: lot.
East Bay floral designers and wannabees flock to this upscale
operation to get the very best in floral supplies. Word has spread
that this is the place to go for inspiration, unique and high-
end flowers and fixings. Amidst the abundant floral displays are
sample arrangements created by Sunflower's talented in-house
designers that reflect the latest trends and sophistication in
flowers, colors, and foliage. If you're clever at duplicating, but
shortchanged in creativity, you'll welcome the ideas that are
provided. If you're lazy or in a rush, you can buy the ready-to-
go arrangements that are very reasonably priced considering
the level of originality. I found prices competitive and sometimes a bit higher than some vendors at the San Francisco
Flower Mart, but you get so many extras at Sunflower: excellent customer service and free advice, unique blooms (dried,
paper, and silk), beautiful ribbons (silks, French wired, and
other high-end exotics that can be quite pricey), distinctive
containers and objects for showcasing your arrangements
(baskets, bowls, bird cages, papier-mâché boxes, twig chairs),
wreaths made from out-of-the-ordinary materials, and some
elegant home accessories (window boxes, stands, statuary,
topiaries, pots, vases, etc.). I saw many things that I haven't
seen at other floral supply outlets, which is what makes this
company so special. There is a two-tiered pricing structure.
Wholesale buyers must have a valid California resale license,
and the general public pays the listed retail price (with additional discounts for quantity purchases). Hands-on classes
with an emphasis on basic floral design techniques are offered
one Saturday each month for a modest $10 fee. Martha
Stewart would love this place!

Also See

Under Art, Craft, and Hobby Supplies:
Fantastico

Under Home Improvement:
Home Depot

Under General Merchandise—Membership Warehouse Clubs:
Price/Costco

Furniture and Home Accessories

In this chapter, I've separated the listings into logical groups. All the stores mentioned offer substantial savings. Some have large showrooms with backup warehouse stock, allowing you to buy furniture directly off the floor, while others may have minimal or no stock on display and do most business through catalog orders. A few are clearance centers for full-service retail stores. When stores have focused on a particular category of home furnishings, e.g., office or baby furniture, I've created a separate section for them.

It's important to understand the system when buying furniture. When you place a custom order (as opposed to buying in-stock inventory) you usually have to wait anywhere from a few weeks to several months for delivery. The store you're buying from often has no control over turnaround time. For instance, the fabric you've chosen for a new sofa may be out of stock at the factory, or delivery may be delayed until the manufacturer schedules another production run. Often the store won't be aware of these problems until the piece is ordered from the manufacturer. Once the furniture arrives, there may even be additional delays if freight damage has occurred and the piece must be "finished" or "deluxed." It's hard to fathom how a china cabinet can be sent without shelves or hardware, but it does happen. When something goes wrong, it may seem to take forever to sort everything out. In most cases, the only way the store can alleviate the aggravation is to keep you informed. Patience is required when placing a custom order, whether you're trying to save a few hundred dollars or several thousand dollars on your furnishings.

Catalog Discounters

The businesses in this section sell furnishings primarily from manufacturers' catalogs rather than from in-house stock. They offer some of the best alternatives to high retail prices. The operations I have listed are all similar in that they take a small markup. Many eliminate costly services and forego advertising. Some of these places have no furnishings at all to show; others have quite a few. Buying furniture this way will usually enable you to save 20–40%. The discounts offered by these stores differ by degrees. Some offer little more than a very low price, while others combine a high level of service and design support with slightly higher prices. I'm confident that you'll be able to find the store that most fits your needs among the ones I've listed. Most have no credit plans other than MC or VISA. These stores may also focus heavily on two or three categories of furnishings. Therefore I've cross-referenced them under the carpets, appliances and draperies sections, or in instances where I felt it was more appropriate, I've placed the stores' listings in those categories. Note the cross-references to consider all your options.

Alioto & Associates

644 Third Street West, Sonoma. (707) 996-4546.
M–Th 9–5; F, Sat, eves by appointment. Cash/Check. Parking: lot.
Alioto & Associates maintains a low profile compatible with Sonoma's pastoral image. Although the exterior resembles a new apartment house, the showroom is quite lovely. You'll find several room groupings complete with tasteful accessories providing a tempting assortment of furnishings from the manufacturers it represents. Showroom prices reflect the manufacturers' suggested retail listing; you'll have to ask for the discount price. Of course, you can buy off the floor, but chances are you'll end up purchasing from its catalog resources. Alioto has an extensive selection of wallpaper books (average 25% discount); carpet and flooring (vinyl) samples from leading manufacturers; window treatments (blinds, pleated shades, woven woods); and fabric samples for draperies and upholstery. Alioto works with new homeowners and remodelers at the blueprint stage to help them avoid expensive mistakes. It controls costs by operating with a minimal markup, doing business on a cash basis, and being family owned. Using its interior design service, you can completely decorate your office

or home. In addition to most major brands of high-end furniture, it can also order some "restricted" brands, although the discounts may be less. Phone quotes are given if you can provide all the specifics.

Angelus Furniture Warehouse

55 Fourth Street (off Oak), Oakland. (510) 268-0265.
W–Sun 10–5:30. MC, VISA, Credit plan. Parking: lot.
Angelus has an out-of-the-way location near Jack London Square, close to 880. It buys closeouts and current lines of furniture from major manufacturers and passes on deep discounts from its no-frills store. The selection and quality runs from budget to better with brands like Bernhardt, Bassett, Douglas, Stanley, Lexington, Highland House, Stearns & Foster, Pulaski, and Universal. Shop for living room, dining (and dinettes), bedroom (including teens' sets), occasional furniture, leather, and wicker. The case goods category (bedroom, casual, and formal dining room furniture) is excellent. Upholstered furniture and children's furniture lines are well priced, and many other fabrics or lines can be ordered from catalogs for discounts of 25–35%. The styles include a little of everything found in today's market. Delivery is additional. Directions: From Hayward or San Mateo, take 880 north to Oak Street Exit, left on Oak Street, left again on Fourth.

Chett Gaida Interiors

80–B Carolina, San Francisco. (415) 558-9823.
M–F 9–4. Appt. preferred. Cash/Check. Parking: street.
Chett Gaida is a pro who combines personal design service with good values. He generally serves an upscale clientele prepared to pay for quality, evident in middle- to high-end furnishings like McGuire, Henredon, Umphred, Leathercraft, Aireloom, La Barge, Lane, Hekman, and others. If you're timid about making buying decisions involving thousands of dollars on furnishings you'll have to live with for years to come, you'll appreciate the time he's willing to spend with you. This includes visits to trade showrooms, design expertise, and even home consultations. If you're interested in investing in a fine handmade Oriental rug, he can arrange visits to reputable wholesale rug showrooms. Gaida offers a peace-of-mind alternative for those who simply can't do it on their own. Deposits of 50% are required with an order. Appointments preferred.

David Morris Co.

1378 Sutter Street (bet. Franklin and Van Ness), San Francisco.
(415) 346-8333. M–F 9–5:30, Sat 10–2. MC, VISA, 30- to 90-
day interest-free payment plans. Parking: street.

You'll see just a few sample pieces of furniture on the floor,
but David Morris offers good savings on custom orders from
major catalogs. It does a tremendous carpeting business and
works closely with insurance companies on replacement
claims. If carpeting is your top priority, you'll want to settle
down with sample books from just about every carpet company.
Inquire about Karastan and its Persian and Chinese carpets.
Selecting new draperies or window treatments is a piece of
cake. If you must see before you buy, you can arrange a pre-
view trip to the Furniture Mart. It also sells well-known brands
of kitchen and laundry appliances, TVs, VCRs, and stereos.
You'll save 30% on almost all purchases, including freight and
delivery.

Deovlet & Sons

1660 Pine Street (bet. Van Ness and Franklin), San Francisco.
(415) 775-8014. M–Sat 8–5:30. MC, VISA. Parking: street/pay lots.

This store has been around for over fifty-five years and for
good reason. The grown-up children of its original customers
now get the same good values, prices, and service that their
parents received years ago. You may have to ask someone to
turn on the lights on the second and third floors for a good
look at the bed, dining, breakfast, and living room furnishings.
You'll find displays of very moderately priced goods in upholstered lines and case goods for bedroom and dining room,
major lines of kitchen and laundry appliances (including Wolf,
Viking, Gaggenau, Dacor, and Sub-Zero), and vacuum cleaners.
It leans toward traditional and includes Victorian-inspired
reproductions in upholstered furniture and case goods, and
many oak pieces. It can usually offer immediate delivery on
appliances and bedding. You'll find excellent prices on its large
selection of carpets from several major mills, and count on a
25–30% discount off retail.

Dicker Furniture

37235 Fremont Boulevard, Fremont. (510) 797-8884.
T-Sat 9-6, Sun Noon-5 (eves by appt.). MC, VISA. Parking: lot.
Dicker Furniture has been around for years and years. Every
square inch is jammed with transitional and traditional furnishings and accessories (some Victorian reproductions, too).
Nicely framed prints, mirrors, and clocks, some very elegant and
ornate, cover the walls. You'll find lots of lamps, occasional
tables, accent chairs, sofas, formal dining sets, some recliners,
bedroom furniture, grandfather clocks, and more. Dicker keeps
good company, selecting manufacturers like Cavalier, Kimball,
Lincoln, Stiffel, Dunhill, Century, Pulaski, Perfection, Hammary,
Weiman, Highland House, Sumter Cabinet, Hooker, Lexington,
Jasper Cabinet, Lane, Bernhardt, Heritage House, American
Drew, and Waterford, and even more in its catalog library.
Prices are very competitive with all the others listed in this
chapter. You'll always get a "sale" price that is 25-40% off
retail on most lines, including all freight and delivery charges.

Don Ermann Associates

699 Eighth Street, Suite 100A, San Francisco. (415) 621-7117.
M-F 9-5. MC, VISA. Parking: lot.
Don Ermann's new setting in the San Francisco Fashion Center
represents an attempt to simply his life and business. Old
timers may miss his elegant showroom, but they'll still find
the enticing pricing that kept them coming back time and
time again over the years. Like most other outfitters that offer
quality furnishings at discount prices, Don and Joan Ermann
can help you make your way through an extensive collection
of furniture catalogs. You can purchase better lines of home
furnishings, plus carpets, floor coverings, draperies, fabrics,
executive office furniture, and wallpapers. The lines it carries
are impressive. Some high-end examples are Brown Jordan,
Century, Hammary, Hekman, Glass Arts, Hickory Chair, La
Barge Mirror, McGuire Rattan, Taylor Woodcraft, and Dunhill.
Serious customers are taken to the Galleria or Showplace
Square to evaluate potential choices. I found Don Ermann's
staff to be most accommodating: never pushy and very
knowledgeable. Pricing is straightforward. The store subtracts
40% from the retail price (from factory-published lists, not
inflated retail lists). Delivery charges additional. If your time is
precious, make an appointment so someone will be available
to give you their undivided attention.

Eastern Furniture

1231 Comstock, Santa Clara. (408) 727-3772.
M, T, Th 9:30–8; W, F, Sat 9:30–5:30; most Suns Noon–5.
MC, VISA. Parking: lot.
Eastern has 50,000 square feet featuring galleries by Century, Hickory-White, Bernhardt, Leathercraft, and Harden. You'll find leather furniture; youth furniture from companies like Lexington and Stanley; mattresses from Serta; recliners from Braddington-Young; plus many informal dining sets and occasional tables. Filling in the spaces are upholstered sofas, chairs, sectionals, entertainment centers (RCA entertainment centers and components a specialty), and accessories. Its nearby warehouse's backup inventory may save you a possible three-month minimum wait. You can special order merchandise from the approximately 200 manufacturers it represents. The discount is 35% off the manufacturer's list price on most furniture lines carried. Beautiful showroom with elegant displays. Interior designers available.

Gallery West

1355 Market Street (at Tenth Street), San Francisco Furniture Mart II, San Francisco. (415) 861-6812. T–F 9:30–4:30, Sat 10–4. MC, VISA, Financing. Parking: validated basement garage weekdays, street on Sat.
At Gallery West you'll have access to the wholesale showrooms of the Western Merchandise Mart. Browse through manufacturers' catalogs of sofas, chairs, bedroom and dining room pieces, occasional tables, lamps, accessories, draperies, window coverings, carpeting, and vinyl or hardwood flooring. Serious customers get to view possible selections in Mart showrooms in the building or at Showplace Square. The staff can provide complete design services at no extra cost when combined with major purchases. The usual discount reflects 30–40% off the prices in conventional retail stores. As a factory representative for Highland House and Designer Gallery Ltd. (upholstery), Hekman Furniture, Sumpter Cabinet and Howard Miller (clocks, curios), and James Moder crystal chandeliers, Gallery West offers special discounts on these lines. Delivery is extra. You'll have to stop at the desk in the main lobby to get the okay to visit the Gallery West showroom. This building is not open to the general public.

Giorgi Bros.

212 Baden Avenue, South San Francisco. (415) 588-4621.
M–Sat 9–6, F until 9. MC, VISA, Financing. Parking: street/lot.
Giorgi Bros. is not an elegant store. To earn that description, it would have to carpet, paint, and triple its space to provide room for lovely vignettes that would do justice to the furnishings it sells. As it is, the store is usually crammed with about one hundred sofas, approximately fifty bedroom and fifty dining room sets, entertainment cabinets, grandfather clocks, mattresses, appliances, floor coverings, chairs, occasional tables, and more. Its buyer does an impressive job selecting fabrics for the upholstered pieces on the showroom floor. Additional inventory is kept in a nearby warehouse, helpful if you're in a rush. If you want to select your own upholstery pattern or finish, you can custom order through the catalogs. Across the street in the annex are informal kitchen and dining sets, children's furniture, and other articles. You'll see moderate-to high-end lines like Century, Hickory-White, Vanguard, Flex Steel, Bernhardt, Wexford Collection, Pennsylvania House, Lexington, Hammary, American of Martinsville, Weiman, Pulaski, Classic Leather, Stanley, Lane, Hekman, Harden, La Barge, Burton James, and dozens more. Tags list Giorgi's discount price (at least 33% off prevailing retail), plus manufacturer's name and model number. With all this emphasis on its classy furniture selection, it's easy to overlook the appliances, home electronics, and floor coverings (carpet, vinyl, hardwood) at very competitive prices. Looking forward to completion of its fifty-space parking lot across the street from the main store.

House of Values

2565 S. El Camino Real, San Mateo. (415) 349-3414.
T–Sat 9:30–5:30, F eve 7–9. MC, VISA. Parking: street.
Just when I think I've seen everything at House of Values, I'm directed out the door and down the street to the next showroom. There's an outstanding selection of furnishings that reflect all the latest design trends (including new shabby chic slipcovered upholstery and Shaker-style pine, maple, and cherry tables and cabinets). My comparison surveys earned it high marks on pricing and values. Although it sells no carpeting or draperies, its in-store selection of fine-quality bedroom and dining room furniture, entertainment cabinets, occasional tables, lamps, upholstered goods, brass and iron beds, and

mattress sets is quite extensive. Some famous names: Century, Hickory, White, Harden, Bernhardt, Burton James, Hekman, Garcia Imports, La Barge, Highland House, Lexington, Stanley, Lane, and more. You can save a minimum of 35% (including freight and delivery). If you find the perfect piece on the floor, it's yours as soon as delivery can be arranged. You can custom order "designer lines" of furniture from its catalogs or show-rooms at Showplace Square and designer fabrics by the yard for your own home-decorating projects. Need help? Then you'll appreciate the interior design service available at no extra charge. Worth a visit from anywhere in the Bay Area.

The Interior Warehouse

7077 Village Parkway, Dublin. (510) 829-7280, (800) 547-8614. T–F 10–5, Th eve by appt., Sat 11–4. MC, VISA. Parking: lot.

This charming catalog furniture buying service has several choice pieces of upholstered furniture on its floor; hundreds of furniture catalogs; fabric, flooring and carpet samples; window treatment displays; and wallpaper books. Even better, it's comfortable. The sales staff is friendly, knowledgeable, helpful, and very low-key. Members of its entourage include Henry Link, Bernhardt, Pulaski, Lane, Hickory Tavern, Hekman, Umphred, Fremarc, Dino-Mark Anthony, Brown Jordan, Cal Mode, Chapman, Weiman, La Barge, Habersham Plantation, McGuire, Stanley, and many more. The discounts on these lines are 25–40% off manufacturers' suggested retail. On wallpaper and fabrics in sample books, discounts are 15–30%, or occa-sionally more when the manufacturer is having a special pro-motion. Its drapery and upholstery swatch selection is one of the finest in the East Bay. Carpeting is sold for 10% over cost. Ohline and Woodfold custom shutters are 30% off! Resident designers can provide in-home consultations at approximately $60/hour. Directions: From 680 (north of 580 interchange) take the Alcosta Exit east of Village Parkway, and turn right.

John R. Wirth Co.

1049 Terra Bella, Mountain View. (415) 967-1212, (408) 736-5828. T–F 11–6, Th until 9, Sat 11–5. MC, VISA. Parking: lot.

If you're asked for a referral at the desk, just mention *Bargain Hunting in the Bay Area*. Then you can join South Bay and Peninsula residents who want to stretch their home-furnishing dollars on living room, dining room, bedroom, and outdoor patio furniture, mattresses, and accessories. You can spend hours eyeballing the wallpaper books, fabric swatches for draperies or upholstery, and an almost overwhelming selection of carpet (including area and Oriental), vinyl or hardwood flooring samples, even custom kitchen cabinets. Wirth can handle any window covering or treatment, including shutters. For additional choices on home furnishings not in the showroom, you can go to catalogs. The salespeople are experienced, helpful, and not pushy. The prices on furnishings (including freight and delivery) are discounted on the average about 35%, and up to 50% on some showroom clearance merchandise. Note: No phone quotes, sales usually final, full payment expected before delivery, and the hours are atypical. Directions: Heading south on 101, take the Shoreline Exit west. Terra Bella is the first street on the left; go one and a half blocks.

Leon Bloomberg Co. & House of Karlson
80 Carolina Street, San Francisco. (415) 863-3640.
By appt. only, M–F 9–5. Cash/Check/VISA. Parking: street.
Leon Bloomberg won't stay retired. He closed his furniture store a few years ago. Now he's back, leasing space from the San Francisco Furniture Gallery. His catalogs cover everything from patio furniture to bedroom sets (some hard to find at discount). There are also books of carpets and flooring samples. Leon and his staff work by appointment. A qualified interior designer is available to help with selections of furnishings and treatments: custom rugs, reupholstering, finishing, window treatments, and bedcovers. Call first to discuss your needs and budget so that when you visit they can be prepared with suggestions or tell you whether they have access to the lines you have already selected. Phone quotes provided if you've got all the specifications. Naturally, savings are your incentive for checking in, and you can probably expect a solid 35% off retail. A 40% deposit is required to place an order; balance due on delivery.

Millbrae Furniture Company
1781 El Camino Real, Millbrae. (415) 761-2444.
T, Th 10–6, W, F 10–9, Sat 9–5. MC, VISA.
Parking: street/city lot (side of building).
To be in a position to provide good value, it helps when you own your own building and warehouse. That way, you have the space to take advantage of special discounts on volume

purchases when manufacturers make their offers. Millbrae Furniture fits the bill on both counts. Millbrae manages to cram in a good selection of furniture, appliances, bedding, carpets, draperies, and Sony and Hitachi TVs, making this a one-stop resource for consumers. On the first floor you'll find upholstered goods. Go up to the second floor to bounce on the bedding and check the dining and bedroom groupings. Finally, explore the basement for recliners and appliances. You can buy moderately priced furniture right off the floor, or mosey over to its back room, where there are cabinets full of manufacturers' catalogs that provide additional resources. On most items the savings run about 30% off prevailing retail prices; however, appliances are 10% over cost. The appliance department has undergone a facelift to showcase its upscale Sub-Zero, Dacor, and Wolf lines, plus other consumer favorites. Like most discounters, this store rarely advertises but does a steady business based on referrals.

Noriega Furniture

1455 Taraval Street (at 25th Avenue), San Francisco.
(415) 564-4110. T, W, F 10–5:30, Th 1–9, Sat 10–5.
MC, VISA, DIS. Parking: street.

Noriega Furniture is appealing for its beautiful showroom, personal service, and decorator consultants. The specialty here is expensive, high-quality furniture. Its manufacturers' catalogs offer furniture, carpets, draperies, wallpaper, beautiful artwork, and accessories at savings of at least 20% and as much as 33%. It is one of the few resources in the Bay Area discounting Lladro and Hummel, as well as Waterford and Lenox lamps. Noriega also features Stickley Mission Oak furniture, Arts and Crafts lamps, and pottery. You can purchase European, American, and Oriental reproductions and accent pieces; distinctive accessories like etchings from Eidenberger and Kasmeir; museum replicas; and original antique prints and drawings. Overall, you'll be dazzled by traditional furnishings from companies like Henredon, Karastan, Karges, Kindel, Marge Carson, La Barge, Widdicomb, and others. If you need help, its decorators will go to most Bay Area communities with samples. Located in the Sunset/Parkside district, one mile north of Stonestown Shopping Center.

Peck & Hills

701 66th Avenue, Oakland. (510) 632-6027.
Cash/Check/Credit plan. M–Sat 9–4:30. Parking: lot.

Almost an endangered species, Peck & Hills has survived when many other upscale furniture retailers have vanished from the scene. Owned by the same family since 1896, its tradition of showcasing some of the best lines of traditional (eighteenth-century, French, neoclassic, etc.), country and transitional furnishings for the more formal rooms in our homes has resulted in a loyal following of sophisticated consumers. This is where to go when you've decided to buy "forever" furniture—with quality that will last and be passed down to the next generation. (Even with its fair pricing, most of the lines sold here may be out of reach for younger first-time homeowners.) While the building (next to the Oakland Coliseum) is nondescript, its 27,000-square-foot showroom filled with tasteful vignettes is as lovely as any found at Showplace Square. It's a wonderful source for finding distinctive accent pieces—a handpainted armoire, neoclassic demi-lune, dramatic coffee table, or occasional table—pieces that add spark and character to a room, resulting in that perfect eclectic note. Some new lines reflecting the Arts and Crafts resurgence and the country-inspired lines (better quality and more sophisticated than much of what you see on the market) reveals how discriminating the company is in its choice of manufacturers. Expect an impressive selection of sofas, chairs, sectionals, and recliners along with cabinets, dining room furnishings, tables, and accessories. All the beautiful furniture displayed is for sale (some dining groups must be purchased as a set). The floor samples also provide an indication of the quality, feel, and finish from more than fifty manufacturers—important when you're contemplating a custom order. You can rely on its staff of professionals to give you the time, expertise, and design consultation that takes some of the anxiety out of making live-with-forever decisions. Home consultations are available at an additional charge (usually applied to purchase when an order is placed). At Peck & Hills you've got it all: good prices, extensive and gracious service, convenience and excellent selection. No phone quotes. Directions: From 880, take the 66th Avenue Exit east.

R & R French Bros.

333 Alabama (at 16th Street), San Francisco. (415) 621-6627.
M–F 9:30–6, Most Sats 10–3. Cash/Check/MC. Parking: street/lot.
French Bros. is an excellent resource for home furnishings, floor coverings, draperies, and window coverings at very special discounts. To begin with, study its showroom samples, which give a tiny taste of the companies it represents. Then browse through its library of catalogs and, if necessary, make an appointment to visit wholesale showrooms, where you can get the complete picture on the lines you have under consideration. Here's a partial list of the manufacturers represented: Stanley, Bernhardt, Pulaski, Lane, American Drew, Dino-Mark Anthony, Barcalounger, Henredon, Coleman of CA, Baker, Bassett, and Lexington. Its extensive carpet and vinyl flooring selection includes a wide range of residential and contract carpeting. As it is displayed gallery fashion, you won't have to exhaust yourself hauling heavy sample books around. Expect good service on window treatments, whether you're in the market for miniblinds or fashion drapery treatments. Finally, the prices on major lines of bedding are right on target for bargain hunters.

Richardson's

2368 Concord Boulevard (at East Street), Concord.
(510) 685-8613. MC, VISA, Financing.
M–F 9–6, Th until 7:30, Sat 9–5:30, Sun Noon–5. Parking: lot.
It's true that your home reflects your personality, your tastes and your aspirations. That doesn't mean you have the talent to make that happen. Richardson's staff of design professionals is on hand to help you through the process of choosing furnishings, whether it's just one special piece, an entire room, or a houseful. Free in-store design consultations combined with pricing that usually saves you 25–35% off manufacturer's list prices (including freight), and a beautiful showroom filled with tasteful furnishings ensures that consumers are on the right track in obtaining solid values and service. You'll want to start by considering all the furnishings in its carefully selected display of classic, country, traditional, transitional, and eighteenth-century furniture, tastefully grouped in this-is-how-it-will-look room vignettes. The furniture is enhanced by beautiful accessories (mirrors, pictures, lamps, accent pieces, and other decorative items). If it's on the floor, you can take it home or have it delivered immediately. Otherwise, you can sit down

with a designer at one of the conference tables and consider other options from its catalog library. Century, Harden, Lexington, Lane, National Mt. Airy, Barcalounger, Burton James, Stanley, American Drew, Virginia House, and others add up to an impressive collection of manufacturers including some that are not seen everywhere you go, a plus in my book. Finish the project by choosing window treatments and wall coverings. Special orders require a 25% deposit, balance due on delivery. Inquire about additional design services. No phone quotes.

Western Contract Interiors
1702 Park Avenue, San Jose. (408) 275-9600.
M–F 8:30–5:30, Sat 11–5:30. Cash/Check. Parking: lot.
If you're past the start-up phase of furnishing your home and are in search of quality furnishings at significant savings, you'll be in good hands here. When you want to sit down and get serious with your queries, I suggest making an appointment with a staff designer. You're welcome to stop in anytime to work through the array of books and samples. Western's lovely showroom has sample pieces of furniture for starters and tasteful accessories, but it's hardly representative of the total resources available. You can order window coverings, mattress sets, bedspreads, carpeting, and furniture for any room in the house, or patio furniture for outside. Western has a contract division that you can also use as a resource for business and home office furnishings. Many Silicon Valley executives have ordered ergonomic seating, including chairs from Herman Miller and other leading manufacturers. About prices: Expect to save 25–40% off manufacturers' retail list prices on most lines.

Also See

Under Carpets and Flooring:
Lawrence Contract Furnishers

General Furnishings

If you're into dollar-wise decorating, there are familiar stores all around the Bay Area that offer stylish furnishings and accessories at "getting-started" prices. Stores like Cost Plus and Pier 1 offer low-cost furnishings—kitchen sets, informal chairs, tables, and sofas, plus the accessories and accent pieces to fill the empty spaces in your rooms. The Bombay Company is an excellent resource for accent pieces and accessories for those in the traditional mode.

Bellach's Leather Furniture
1600 Van Ness (at California), San Francisco. (415) 474-7444. M–Sat 10–5:30, Sun Noon–5. MC, VISA, Credit plans. Parking: lot. (Other stores: Concord; Novato; Sacramento; Sunnyvale.)
Bellach's offers discounts of 30–40% off manufacturers' list prices and backs them up with a price guarantee. It carries leather sofas, chairs, recliners, sofa beds, and sectionals from industry leaders, including Emerson, Natuzzi, Eknorness, Executive, Klaussner, Leatherman's Guild, Cameo, Himolla, Elite, Stylecraft, and others. Its stores cater to both the contemporary and traditional customer. The manufacturers' labels are right there so that you can comparison shop its prices.

Bob's Discount Wood Furniture
2078 San Pablo Avenue (bet. University and Addison), Berkeley. (510) 848-6662. M–Sat 10–6, Sun 11–5. MC, VISA, DIS. Parking: street.
Need cabinets to store your collection of compact discs, books, or videotapes? This store has carved out a niche in the unfinished furniture business as a specialist in bookcases. You can get custom sizing on most cases and cabinets here. Your choice of wood is determined by your budget: basic pine for budget buyers; veneers of alder or oak for better quality, and solid oak or alder for best. You can buy off the floor from an extensive inventory of cases in many standard sizes: widths from 18 inches, heights to 96 inches, and standard depths at 9 and 12 inches. You may want a custom depth for compact discs. Buy unfinished cases or spend about 10% more for several options in stains or clear sealers. Glass or wood doors on some styles, also fixed or adjustable shelving. Prices are very good across the board. I particularly liked the extra quality features like mounting rails to anchor tall cases to walls. Finally, there are many

options utilizing cabinet bases with bookcase tops—lots of versatility! Call for phone quotes, but take measurements first.

Busvan for Bargains

900 Battery Street, San Francisco. (415) 981-1405.
M-Sat 9:30-6, Sun Noon-6. MC, VISA, Revolving charge.
Parking: validated and pay lots.
(Other store: 244 Clement Street, San Francisco.)
Although not your typical furniture store, Busvan carries almost anything from its somewhat tired, but too busy to remodel store: furniture, appliances, rugs, pianos, antiques, paintings, books, bric-a-brac, and office furniture. The main floor is filled with new, discount-priced upholstery and mattress sets at excellent prices. The top floor is crowded with bedroom, dining room, and accent furniture in the budget to moderate price ranges, and occasionally some exceptional one-of-a-kind accent pieces (trade samples). Nestle your preteen or adolescent in style from its expanded selection of bedroom groups. Busvan offers a sea of RTA (ready-to-assemble) or lifestyle furniture, especially desks, bedroom pieces, computer furniture, bookcases, and entertainment centers. Its solid-pine unfinished furniture is priced to make other stores blush. Opportunistic buys lead to an eclectic selection of floor samples and factory closeouts. The basement features used furniture at rock-bottom prices. Although the staff is friendly and helpful, the size of the store makes it primarily self-service. All sales final. Reasonable delivery charges or bring your own van; Busvan will pad your furniture and stash it in or on your vehicle for free.

Commins Design Group

990 Grant Street, Benicia. (707) 745-3636.
Th-F 10-5, Sat-Sun 11-6. MC, VISA, AE. Parking: lot.
Commins's warehouse showroom in Benicia is an extension of its furniture manufacturing and design company. The company sells direct to consumers out of its impressive selling space at its factory. For contemporary furnishings that embrace classical design elements, a trip is mandated. Everything speaks of nature and the organic, with elegant faux finishes on all the pieces. I loved the dramatic chests, étagères, entertainment cabinets, wall units, consoles, bedroom systems, and glass-top tables with architectural pedestal bases. The many accessories on hand are from local artisans and importers, selling for

appreciably lower prices than elsewhere. Altogether, this upscale collection of distinctive furniture and accessories is in no way ordinary or predictable. You can acquire prototype samples, buy pieces off the floor, or opt for a custom design that allows you to choose the color of the finish and possibly some design modifications at no extra charge (or a very modest one). In this way you'll save about half of what you would have paid a designer or showroom. Also, glass tops for anything at really good prices.

Cottage Tables Co.

550 18th Street (off Third), San Francisco. (415) 957-1760.
M–Sat 1–5. MC, VISA. Parking: lot.
Tony Cowan builds superior-quality tables in the old tradition— from solid wood using dowel-and-glue construction. Each table is custom-made. A table that you buy from him will become a family heirloom. There's no inventory on hand other than several sample tables to show the quality of his work, some style variations, and the woods and finishes used. A reasonably formal, solid cherry plank table 36 by 72 inches was priced at $1,200; a country pine table 33 by 60 inches was $875. You can have tables made in maple, walnut, pine, cherry, or oak; in styles conveying a contemporary, country, traditional, or transitional feeling; in a variety of leg styles; and you can add a silverware drawer for about $150. Tony does not make chairs, but keeps several on hand that he can order for you from manufacturers' catalogs. He sells the chairs at cost, which amounts to almost a 50% discount to you—a nice accommodation for his customers. A 50% deposit is required with your order.

Discount Oak Furniture

375-A Third Street, San Rafael. (415) 453-6078.
M–F 10:30–6, Sat 10–5. MC, VISA, DIS. Parking: lot.
You'll find oak furniture with an emphasis on furnishings for the home office, plus entertainment systems, wall systems, stereo cabinets, TV stands, and bookcases priced at about 25% below competitors. You can buy everything from budget-priced oak veneer over pressed wood to solid oak in a variety of finishes. Farmhouse tables and chairs, ball-and-claw tables, trestle tables, and other styles more contemporary and transitional are perfect for the informal rooms in your home and ready to go. You'll find entertainment cabinets in all configurations. All furniture is assembled and can be purchased right

off the floor for immediate delivery. You can special order other options from manufacturers' catalogs. This is a good place for younger couples getting started and anybody who wants good value.

Discover Design Resource Center
2 Henry Adams Street, San Francisco. (800) 877-8522.
M–F 10–5. Parking: street/pay lot.
Many Galleria and Showplace Design Center showrooms, formerly open to the trade only, now welcome the public to view the finest in home furnishings. Each showroom posts signs defining its admittance and purchasing policies. All public visitors must first visit the Discover Design Resource Center on the Showplace Design Center Fourth Floor, where they may purchase a Discover Design picture badge for $20 annually or receive a day pass. A Design Resource Guide takes visitors through the categories of merchandise, explaining showroom regulations and offering tips on custom ordering and working with design professionals. Remember, these are not retail stores; the multitude of choices can send you into sensory overload. The responsibility for choosing fabrics, frames, and finishes may require more expertise than you have, and if you're not satisfied with your efforts, you're out of luck, since all sales are final! You may discover that although access is illuminating, your best aesthetic and financial result comes from consulting a design professional.

English Garden Furniture & Old Country Lighting
128 Mitchell Boulevard, San Rafael. (415) 492-1051.
M–Sat 11–4, Sun 11–4 (call to verify). Cash/Check. Parking: lot.
English Garden Furniture captures the look of Victorian garden furniture and will last for years. It duplicates elegant designs from the 1700s to today in cast aluminum. The tables, chairs, and benches in these historical patterns reflect charm and grace, and beautifully enhance traditional decors and gardens. The company has built furniture for the Embassy Suites Hotels and many historical mansions, gardens, and other public places. It also serves discriminating consumers who want good value and good design that's out of the ordinary. Once you understand the quality of this furniture, the prices appear reasonable. When it comes to top-of-the-line garden furniture, you can find similar styles in each of the three major manufacturers' lines. A chair from English Garden Furniture at

$195 is comparable to one that may be priced closer to $700. Charming dining sets (table and four chairs) in various patterns are available for $795 to $1,300. Tables are sold in small dimensions or large and some are available with glass tops. The company also excels in its selection of garden benches, light fixtures, chandeliers, lampposts, urns, pot racks, authentic European French doors, and anything custom you might desire. Remember, the furniture and accessories are every bit as lovely indoors as out. If you've passed the plastic-and-webbing stage, and you're willing to invest in a lifetime set of garden or patio furniture, then you may want to consider this source before making any final selections.

Furniture Express Outlet

667 Folsom Street (bet. Third and Fourth streets), San Francisco.
(415) 495-2848. M–F 11–7, Sat 10–6, Sun Noon–5.
MC, VISA, AE. Parking: street.
Folks on the prowl for inexpensive furnishings will find most of what they need right here. There are easily assembled computer workstations, desks, TV carts, dressers, bookcases and shelving units, microwave/utility carts on casters, solid maple tables, affordable dressers and pine bedroom furniture (finished and unfinished) for teen or children's rooms, and home entertainment centers (as low as $39). This is not forever furniture, but the overall quality/price/value equation is solid and the prices are very appealing for budget decorating. Prices on many pieces were about 30% below those in a local department store "sale" ad posted on the wall. Everything is sold in boxes. Delivery can be arranged.

Futon Shop Factory Outlet

1011 25th Street, San Francisco. (415) 863-9696.
M–Sat 9:30–5:30, Sun 11–5. MC, VISA, AE, DIS. Parking: street.
The Futon Shop has twenty-two stores and this one clearance center. You won't find any special pricing on the futons, but you can find a discontinued frame, a slightly damaged floor sample (usually finish flaws or scratches), and out-of-box frames. Savings are 30–50% off original retail. Selected close-outs on futon covers are also discounted. Delivery is available for an extra charge.

Lafayette Furniture

3311 Mt. Diablo Boulevard, Lafayette. (510) 283-8460.
M–Sat 10–5:30, Wed until 7, Sun Noon–5. MC, VISA.
Parking: lot.

The building is just a cut above a warehouse, crowded with furniture that leaves no room for spacious and tasteful vignettes. I recognized many well-known lines that capture the look and style of more expensive high-end brands. Strata-lounger, Cavalier, Dino-Mark Anthony, Flex Steel, Lane, Dixie, Pulaski, and Taylor Woodcraft are a few examples. You can buy off the floor or custom order from catalogs. A lot of space is devoted to family room furnishings, but more formal living room chairs and sofas, formal and informal dining room sets, bedroom sets, and accessories are adequately represented. The styles: traditional, country, transitional, and contemporary. Count on savings that add up to about 30% depending on whose prices you use for comparison.

Lamps Plus

4700 Geary Boulevard, San Francisco. (415) 386-0933.
M–F 10–9, Sat 10–6, Sun 11–6. MC, VISA, AE. Parking: street.
(Other stores: Pleasant Hill; Sacramento; San Jose;
San Lorenzo; San Mateo; San Rafael.)

Lamps Plus benefits from volume purchasing power (it's the biggest distributor of Stiffel lamps in the country). It offers a lot and while it can't be all things to all people, it comes close. I spotted the ordinary, ho-hum, and familiar styles seen in most home-furnishings stores, and some extra-special lamps and fixtures. If you want a classic-styled brass lamp, you can find it in budget-, mid-, and higher-priced versions, all representing solid values. Can't complain about these manufacturers: Koch & Lowy, Halogen, Westwood, Fine Arts, Geo. Kovacs, Stiffel, and ceiling fans from Casablanca and Hunter. Pacific Coast Lighting is the Lamps Plus line of fixtures and lamps. The values are excellent on this line when comparing prices to similar styles of lamps and fixtures from other vendors. If you need track lighting, office desk lamps, or lighting fixtures, you'll find them at solid discount prices. Casablanca fans are usually about 25% off prevailing retail, even more during special sales. Lamps Plus can also special order fixtures from catalogs. Finally, it has about the biggest array of replacement lamp shades I've spotted in the Bay Area.

Mancini's Sleep World

968 El Camino Real, Sunnyvale. (408) 245-6251.
M–F 10–9, Sat and Sun 10–6. MC, VISA, DIS. Parking: lot.
(Other stores: Los Altos; San Jose.)
South Bay mattress shoppers can get a fair price from Mancini's. They'll also find one of the best selections from Serta, Sealy, Simmons, and Spring Air. The staff can give you the low down on the differences between brands and qualities so that you can make an informed decision, whether you're buying budget or top-of-the-line. Check the bulletin board, where ads are posted from its competitors (one way to show that its pricing is solid). Prices include delivery, removal, and disposal of old mattress sets. Mancini's also sells adjustable beds, futons, bed frames, headboard sets, and a nice selection of children's furniture (lots of bunk beds).

National Mattress Clearance Center

15430 Hesperian Boulevard, San Leandro. (510) 481-1623.
M–F 9–7, Sat 9–6, Sun Noon–5. MC, VISA, DIS, AE. Parking: lot.
National, in business for sixty-five years, has such a large collection of mattresses and box springs that it could host a slumber party for hundreds. Its huge mattress department has two sections. First, you'll find new Simmons, Sealy, Serta, and Spring Air mattress sets at about 20% below the advertised department store "50% off" sales. Every manufacturer offers price groups ranging from budget to ultrapremium. So wherever you fit, you'll be sure to find a terrific value. You can do even better if you're willing to consider mattresses from the "as-is" area. This is where you'll find legitimate factory seconds and mismatched sets. Defects or flaws are carefully pointed out and explained when you're making a choice. Some flaws are obvious, but many are not. Factory seconds also carry a warranty, but for a shorter time. I spotted a top-of-the-line, king-sized set priced at half National's discount, first-quality price.

Rivertown Furniture

307 G Street, Antioch. (510) 754-9900. M–Sat 10–5:30.
MC, VISA, DIS, Financing. Parking: street.
Rivertown Furniture offers savings of 25–40% on its moderately priced home furnishings. If your taste runs to traditional, you'll probably feel at home with the selection of oak or cherry bedroom and dining room furniture groups surrounded by hutches, entertainment cabinets, occasional tables, brass beds,

upholstered furniture, collectibles, and porcelain dolls. If you know manufacturers by name, consider these sources: Wesley Ann Brass Beds, Lane (recliners), Richardson Bros. (oak), Lexington, Kenwood, Pulaski, Hooker, Dino-Mark Anthony, Vargas, Trend Manor, Dixie, Mastercraft, Flex Steel, and Fairchild. The new in-store gallery of Thomas Kinkade and Marty Bell signed lithographs is appealing to many customers. Buy right off the floor or custom order from the catalogs. For special orders a $100 deposit is required; delivery is extra.

Roney's Furniture
14000 Washington Avenue, San Leandro. (510) 352-4074. M–Sat 9:30–6, Sun 11:30–6. MC, VISA. Parking: lot.
Roney's warehouse (a former National Guard armory) is stuffed. The emphasis is on traditional or transitional furniture from major manufacturers. Prices are nicely discounted, whether you buy a piece off the floor or opt for a custom catalog order. If you need it yesterday, you can buy sofas, chairs, tables; living room, bedroom, and dining room furniture; entertainment cabinets, recliners, lamps, and accessories. Whether you're buying your first piece of furniture with a minimal budget or upgrading, Roney's offers many options for most budgets. Expect a small delivery charge. If you're in the mood for a good browse with the hope of finding a great bargain, give Roney's a whirl; you're sure to become a regular.

Sleep Shop Ltd./Kids & Teenz Ltd.
1530 Contra Costa Boulevard, Pleasant Hill. (510) 671-9400. M–F 10–9, Sat 10–6, Sun 11–5. MC, VISA, DIS. Parking: lot. (Other stores: Antioch; Dublin; Lakeport.)
This very complete store makes a profit through volume sales rather than high markups. A diverse selection of brass and iron beds (at least thirty-six models) and daybeds (about twenty-four models) are available from Elliotts, Wesley Allen, Fashion Bed Group, and Elm Creek. Sleep tight on mattress sets from Simmons, Serta, Sealy, and King Koil that are always available at less than department store sale prices. It aggressively discounts special buys and mattress sets with discontinued covers. Delivery charges are minimal. If your tots are ready to leave their cribs, check out the extensive selection of youth, teen, and juvenile furniture in the Kids & Teenz Ltd. department. With eighteen vignettes and more than sixteen bunk beds on display, you can find just the right look to suit your child's

personality. Parents appreciate that many companies are offering suites of furniture with classic and clean lines that can leave home with the kids when they set up their own households. Stanley, Camelot, Nordwins, Boyd, Silver Eagle, Vaughn, and Tempo are companies making the grade at Kids & Teenz Ltd. Special orders may take a few extra weeks or months, but the prices discounted at least 30% make the wait worthwhile.

Stanford Fine Furniture & Designs

6925 Central Avenue, Newark. (510) 745-9962. M–F 8:30–5. Cash/Check. Parking: lot.

If you want to achieve a designer look in upholstered furniture without designer prices, go where designers go: Stanford Designs. This company makes its own lines of sofas and does a lot of custom work. (Loved the new shabby chic style, a slightly loose slipcover over a muslin covered sofa.) There are several ways to get a deal at Stanford. First, sample pieces can be purchased off the factory salesroom floor. Next, you can go back to the warehouse and check the inventory of discontinued fabrics. Pick your sofa, sectional, sleeper, or chair style, your fabric, and your quality—you'll get such a deal! Pay extra and you can have coil spring construction, down pillows, and so on. Otherwise, Stanford uses kiln-dried hardwood frames, double bracing, HR 30 foam cushions with a ten-year guarantee (even the best companies often use only 1.85 density foam), and lined skirts. Shopping this way takes a little initiative. If you're trying to achieve a certain look, bring in a picture, find the fabric, and prepare yourself for extra customization charges. You'll still come out way ahead. A 50% deposit is required with the order, balance before delivery.

Tradeway Stores

10860 San Pablo Avenue, El Cerrito. (510) 529-2360. M–F 9–6, Sat 9–5:30. MC, VISA. Parking: street.

At Tradeway you'll find discounts on high-end pieces and some fairly ho-hum furnishings. It has contracts with several manufacturers like Thomasville, Dixie, Hammary, Broyhill, Universal, American Drew, Lexington, Bassett, American of Martinsville, and others. When furniture isn't delivered to a retailer for whatever reason, the manufacturer avoids shipping it back across the country by redirecting it to Tradeway. Everything is "detailed" (repaired) if necessary and then priced at about 40–50% off original retail. Anything marked "as-is" has been part of a redirected inventory. Other furniture lines are also stocked to balance out this unpredictable incoming inventory. For the most part they're budget- to moderate-priced lines of upholstered furniture; dining and bedroom furnishings are also discounted. The furnishings are jammed haphazardly into several rooms on two levels. If you're looking for farmhouse-style kitchen tables, inexpensive dinettes, bunk beds, student desks, or family room sofas, Tradeway has lots of potential. Also a good selection of bedroom and dining room furniture. Delivery on purchases over $750 is free from San Leandro to Vallejo; otherwise delivery is priced according to distance.

Way to Go

2107 Broadway, Redwood City. (415) 306-1144.
M–Th 10–8, F 10–5:30, Sun 10–6 (closed Sat). MC, VISA, DIS.
Parking: rear lot.

Putting theory into practice has been successful for the enterprising young owner of this store. (His concept was developed and presented for his Master's thesis.) Way to Go is a boon to the just-getting-started crowd and for those who want attractive, functional furnishings at no-nonsense prices. Everything in this store is sold in a box, whether it's a large 8-foot home entertainment three-piece cabinet system or a small kitchen utility cart. More than 300 assembled pieces are displayed for a buyer's consideration. Six of the best American manufacturers of ready-to-assemble furniture supply the goods, including Sauder Woodworking, O'Sullivan, and Bush Industries. You'll be surprised at how sophisticated and attractive RTA furniture has become. Many pieces are assembled with clips and fastenings, while some need a little glue to finish the process. (The owner suggests that all you need is a lot of patience and a margarita to see you through the job.) Many popular wood finishes and furniture styles are represented so that it's a simple proposition to find something that fits right into your decor. Oak, cherry, honey maple (Shaker-style pieces), black or white matte, white-washed finishes, etc. are available on most types of furniture. You carry out boxes and assemble computer workstations, bookcases, microwave, VCR or TV carts, entertainment centers, beds, dressers, cabinets, hutches (dining room or kitchen), and assorted, versatile storage pieces. You can pay as little as $75 for an oak entertainment center, or $359 for a Shaker-style honey pine–finished unit. Prices are backed up with a price guarantee, and (if you're all thumbs) assembly can be arranged for an extra fee. Unopened boxes can be returned within ten days for a store credit. Delivery service available for a fee.

Wood Creations

132 Cochrane Plaza, Morgan Hill. (408) 776-7574.
M–Sat 10–6, Sun Noon–5 (closed Wed). MC, VISA. Parking: lot.
Wood Creations may not offer the "bargains" that so many other furniture listings do, but it solves so many customers' dilemmas that I believe a referral is justified. This company loves the customer whom everyone else sends away empty-handed. If you've searched in vain for an entertainment cabinet for your stereo system, wall unit, computer work-station, or desk, Wood Creations is your final option. You can start from its line (Furniture by Doan) in contemporary, tradi-tional, and Shaker styles of bedroom furniture, desks, computer desks, entertainment centers, bookcases, chest and platform beds, or bring in your own design. Wood Creations will build in pine, oak, and birch. Specialty woods may be used at a premium price, dependent on the size of the order. Custom pieces are stained in its finishing shop. A simple cabinet for TV and VCR starts at about $500; bookcases start at $75; a complex, highly crafted unit to cover an entire wall may go up to $3,000 plus. Since this company is located about twenty miles south of San Jose on 101, I recommend that you call first to discuss your custom project and make sure that they can do what you want. Delivery charged according to distance.

Mattress Buyers Beware

Beware the mattress "discounters" that have proliferated around the Bay Area. Ads promising hard-to-believe prices are most often a lure to an aggressive bait-and-switch sales pitch. It seems that some sales personnel have the attitude that "if you can't sell them, insult them." Mattress sets from major manufacturers sold at these outfits are often made expressly for the discounters. From my comparisons, you can buy better quality and receive greater value when purchasing a mattress set from the sources listed here.

Hints for savvy shopping

When you canvass the market for mattress sets, you're likely to end up very confused by the many names from the same manufacturer you find at different retail stores. Large stores and chains with volume accounts usually pick their own names for the manufacturers' groups they buy; they may also decide upon special fabric patterns and colors for the ticking. Most independents will sell mattress sets with the manufacturers' original names. By carefully studying the components displayed in a manufacturers' cut-out samples, i.e., the number of coils, turns and gauge of the coil; weight, thickness, composition, and layers of the cushion elements; type of suspension system; and relative price range, you'll soon figure out that a specific manufacturer's Pontiac Supreme at Store A is equivalent to Buick Ultra at Store B and on a par with Oldsmobile Maximum at Store C. Many manufacturers have enlarged the selection at the high end of the market, offering mattresses with more design and comfort features, and accordingly higher prices.

Also See

Under Appliances, Electronics, and Home Entertainment:
Whole Earth Access

Under General Carpets and Flooring:
Pioneer Home Supply

Under Linens:
Dreams

Baby and Juvenile Furniture/Equipment— New and Used

You might as well decide where to shop for baby furniture and equipment on the basis of convenience and selection, unless you want to go endlessly in circles, comparing prices to save a few bucks. It's a very competitive market—kept that way by manufacturers who closely control distribution of various style groups to selected retailers. The following stores are all very competitive and noteworthy for keeping prices as low as possible. I've included stores that also sell quality used furnishings along with the new. Other Bay Area resources for budget to moderately priced baby furniture and equipment: Toys 'R' Us, Best Products, Wal-Mart, K-Mart, Price/Costco, and Burlington Coat Factory (some stores).

Babies Unlimited

5627 Paradise Drive, Paradise Center, Corte Madera.
(415) 924-3764. M–Sat 10–5, Sun Noon–4. MC, VISA, AE, DIS;
Trade. Parking: lot.
It's hard to navigate around this floor crowded with new and quality used baby furniture and equipment. Along with basic needs such as cribs, playpens, high chairs, and strollers, you'll find items like wicker bassinets, baby carriers, and snuggle pouches. New merchandise from Graco, Aprica, Crib 4 Life, Gerry, Nuline, and Century is nicely discounted. You can also special order from catalogs. Grandparents will scan the used selection to set up their when-baby-visits nest. Trim your costs with unfinished baby dressers, priced at $129–$159. The rental policy on all furniture and equipment is of special interest to relatives of babies.

Baby Super—Rockerworld & Furniture for Kids

1523 Parkmoor Avenue, San Jose. (408) 293-0358.
M–W, Sat 10–6, Th–F 10–8:30, Sun Noon–5. MC, VISA;
Layaway. Parking: lot.
(Other store: Baby and Kids Bargain Warehouse,
1881 W. San Carlos, San Jose.)
Almost supermarket-sized, this store is great for one-stop shopping. It offers an extensive selection, both in quality and quantity, of baby and toddler equipment and furniture for tots and the juvenile market. Buy everything you need for the first eighteen months: infant clothing, diapers, blankets, cribs, high chairs, porta-cribs, adult rockers, playpens, car seats, and more. There's a complete furniture selection for infants through teens. Crib suites (cribs, dressers, changing tables, etc.) and youth furniture add up to one of the best selections of furnishings found anywhere in the Bay Area. John Boyd, Kemp, Stanley, Dixie, Henry Link and Childcraft, Play Space, Morigeau, Berg, and Vermont Tubbs are some of the lines. Furniture prices are nicely discounted. The selection of rockers and gliders is appealing. They're great all the time, for anyone. Be sure to check the Baby & Kids Bargain Warehouse, where discontinued merchandise, floor samples, and more budget-priced lines of goods are sold.

Baby World

5854 College Avenue, Oakland. (510) 655-2950.
M–F 10–6, Sat 10–5, Sun Noon–5. MC, VISA. Parking: lot.
Baby World provides new and used children's equipment, furniture, and toys. There's a wide array of riding toys (try to leave without one if you're shopping with your toddler). The playthings range from popular classics up to the latest in high-demand amusements. This is an excellent source for grand-parents who need to set up a baby room. The selection of cribs, playpens, bassinets, high chairs, and car seats is quite extensive. The prices are great!

Children's Furniture Warehouse

525 66th Avenue, Oakland. (510) 562-9876.
M–Sat 10–5, Sun Noon–5. MC, VISA; Layaway. Parking: lot.
The selection itself makes Children's worth a visit. For best buys check the Clearance Corner for extra markdowns. Thanks to its large warehouse for backup, most items are in stock for immediate use. Prices on cribs were competitive, but often a little higher than some of the other stores in this section. You'll find displays of toddler-sized play tables, chairs, and other furniture to coordinate with the various styles of cribs, adult rockers, and all the baby equipment on your list.

Kids Again

11837 Dublin Boulevard (Dublin Square Shopping Center), Dublin. (510) 828-7334. M–Sat 10–5, Th until 7, Sun Noon–4. MC, VISA. Parking: street.
Kids Again sells new brand-name lines of baby and youth furniture at discounts up to 40% off retail. After browsing through its showroom filled with infant, child, and teen furni-ture, extend your options even more by turning the pages in manufacturers' catalogs. Special orders involve a few months for delivery, but you'll end up delighted with your savings. Sev-eral popular lines of crib and juvenile bedding (sheets, bumper pads, dust ruffles, quilts, shams, et al.) can be ordered from catalogs at 10–25% off suggested retail. Kids Again is also a consignment store—a big one, too. Buy or sell your children's clothing (sizes 0–10), toys, furniture, and equipment or your still wearable maternity clothing. Fashion Court is set aside for consignment clothing for women with an emphasis on better quality, classic, casual, career, and special-occasion clothing.

Leonard's Tot Shop

736 First Street, Benicia. (510) 682-5888, (707) 745-0438.
M–F 10–6, Sat 10–5, Sun Noon–4. MC, VISA. Parking: street.
This store is jammed with clothing, infant furniture, equipment, and accessories. Bargains on clothing happen only during its special sales (two or three times a year). You'll find a good selection of cribs starting at about $150. Save approximately 25% off on the linen sets. You'll find wallpaper books that coordinate with several of the linen sets it carries. The Tot Shop offers better discounts with its special promotions on certain cribs and equipment.

Little Tots New & Used

1882 N. Milpitas Boulevard, Milpitas. (408) 946-0499.
M–Sat 10–5. MC, VISA, DIS, AE. Parking: lot.
This is a tiny store, jammed with good buys on baby equipment and furniture, priced to be very competitive, often because they are purchased from trade show displays. I was most interested in the selection of used items that are usually in very good condition and at half the price of new items.

Lullaby Lane & Kids Furniture Clearance Center

570 San Mateo Avenue, San Bruno. (415) 588-7644.
M–F, W until 9, Sat 10–5:30, Sun 11–5. MC, VISA, AE.
Parking: street/rear lot.
(Other store: Kids Furniture [juvenile only],
532 San Mateo Avenue, San Bruno.)
Opened in 1947, Lullaby Lane is now three separate operations. First stop for bargain hunters is its clearance center, where closeouts, floor samples, discontinued, and slightly damaged items are sent over from its two other stores and sold for up to 50% discounts off regular store prices. Next, the main store, a few doors away at 556 San Mateo Avenue, has an extensive selection of baby "everything." Think you can save more elsewhere? Take Lullaby Lane up on its offer to meet any price. Kids Furniture, just a few doors from its main location, is filled with nicely discounted juvenile furniture.

Also See

Under Furniture and Home Accessories—Catalog Discounters:
All listings

Under Recycled Apparel:
General information

Furniture Clearance Centers

Brooks Rents Clearance Center
30985 Santana Street, Hayward. (510) 487-8333. F–Sun 10–6 (hours subject to change). MC, VISA, AE. Parking: lot.
This operation is geared toward liquidating Brooks's rental returns at prices that must surely appeal to those reluctant to furnish rental property with new and expensive furniture. College students make do very nicely—one I know of bought a sofa, chair, TV cart, kitchen table, and two chairs for less than $150. Not everything is used, old, or tired; occasionally new, discontinued rental lines are available at substantial discounts. You can also find used refrigerators, washers and dryers, TVs and stereo systems. These appliances have a thirty-day exchange warranty. Brooks can also help you outfit your office. Delivery is extra. Directions: From 880, take Whipple Exit east. Left on Wiegman, right on Zephyr, left on Santana. Brooks occasionally takes its inventory to other cities in the Bay Area or outlying areas (Sacramento and Stockton), for huge tent or parking lot sales. Watch local papers or have your name put on its mailing list.

Cavanaugh Gallery Outlet
415 Main Street, Half Moon Bay. (415) 726-7771. Daily 10–6. MC, VISA. Parking: lot.
I've been charmed and impressed with the lovely presentations of traditional furnishings and accessories at the Cavanaugh Gallery stores. Success leads to excess, which leads to an outlet. Good! If you're smitten with the orientation of these stores— solid wood Amish-inspired furniture, the tasteful and cozy upholstered collections, the quaint accessories—then visit the warehouse. You'll find tables, armoires, beds, chairs, sofas, and more. Discounts are 25–40% off store retails. The larger discounts are applied to one-of-a-kind, discontinued, seasonal,

or slightly damaged furniture, accessories, gift items, and artwork. Delivery charges are reasonable and vary with distance.

Cort Furniture Rental Clearance Center

2925 Mead Avenue (off Bowers), Santa Clara. (408) 727-1022.
M–F 10–7, Sat–Sun 10–5. MC, VISA, AE. Parking: lot.
(Other store: 600 Dubuque, South San Francisco.)
Sometimes you need budget-priced furniture ASAP! Cort's
"retired furniture" goes on sale when a line has been discontinued from its rental inventory or the pieces are too tired
to pass muster with rental customers. In any case, you'll save
30–70%. The rental business has gone upscale, so the better
the quality and condition of the item, the higher the price.
Sofas, lamps, mattresses, pictures, and just about anything
Cort rents might be found, but no appliances. Most furnishings come from midprice manufacturers. You'll also find office
furnishings. Delivery is extra.

Limn's Furniture Clearance Center

290 Townsend Street, San Francisco. (415) 543-5466.
M–F 9:30–5:30, Sat–Sun 11–5:30. MC, VISA. Parking: lot.
Limn is a specialty furniture retailer whose furnishings reflect
best-quality European manufacturers, including more than
300 Italian firms often found in Metropolitan Home. Its style
is classic contemporary, is design oriented, and appeals
particularly to architects and a younger, affluent clientele.
The Townsend Street retail showroom is filled with distinctive
and unusual furnishings. Many of the contemporary pieces
provide the eclectic note needed to spark a ho-hum room. All
this superior design comes at a big price, which is why it's worth
checking the warehouse on weekends for chairs, sofas, lighting, stools, and tables that may be discontinued, at drastically
reduced prices (more than 50% on many pieces). Delivery
service available.

Macy's Furniture Clearance Center

1556 El Camino Real, South San Francisco. (415) 878-0802.
W–Sun 11–6. MC, VISA, Macy's Card. Parking: lot.
You will find good buys on Macy's furniture, rugs, luggage,
and vacuums. I spotted reductions of at least 30% off original
retail and many pieces at 50%. Numerous occasional tables,
entertainment cabinets, reproduction antique pieces, and
mattress sets add to the selection's appeal. If you spot a really

good buy, snatch it up or someone else will. Of course, you'll also find damaged, soiled, or discontinued furnishings. There is usually a very good selection of area rugs that represent styles or patterns pictured in Macy's ads in previous months. Since this is a warehouse, wrap up in a warm sweater before setting out. All sales final.

Sears Furniture & Appliance Outlets

1982 West Avenue (at 140th), San Leandro. (510) 895-0546.
M–F 10–7, Sat 9–6, Sun 11–5. DIS, Sears Card. Parking: lot.
(Other store: Hillsdale Mall, San Mateo.)
Sears' warehouse showroom in San Leandro features returned and (slightly) freight-damaged furniture at reduced prices. The customer returns have been reconditioned, and all bedding sterilized. There are usually more than 300 large appliances with minor dents and scratches, TVs (your best buys here), and furniture, vacuums, upholstered pieces, and mattresses. Sears sells its own and other brands of appliances. One-year warranty and maintenance agreements on appliances are available. The San Mateo outlet is much larger and neater with more upholstered furnishings and case goods (audiovisual cabinets, dining, etc.). 20–50% discounts prevail on discontinued floor samples. Check each tag for a definition of the status of the merchandise: new, used, damaged, discontinued, or sanitized. Referrals for delivery and installation available.

Sunrise Interiors Clearance Center

831 B Street (at Third), San Rafael. (415) 456-3939.
T–Sat 10–6, Sun Noon–5. MC, VISA. Parking: street.
Sunrise Interiors is one of my favorite home furnishings stores. It's beautifully merchandised and tasteful, reflecting the latest design trends. Even though I don't consider it a bargain source, I've found in past comparison surveys that its markups are very fair. When you combine its services with its prices, it's a reasonable option if you need the design help you won't get from discounters. There's a "lowest price" guarantee, but since everything is coded to a paranoid degree, it's hard to comparison shop. Be sure to evaluate the special purchase items selected for exceptional value and style and marked with Sunrise's gold tag. You can find some solid bargains among the odds 'n' ends in its clearance room. Pieces have been marked down at least 30% off full retail or more often 50%, even a few up to 70% off. I spotted really sensational buys on wing-

back chairs, pine blanket chests, slipcovered sofas, lamps, decorative pillows, occasional tables, accessories, etc.

Thomasville Outlet
Address of new location pending.
The dilemma: At press deadline, the new location of the Thomasville outlet was not confirmed. The company is hoping to complete negotiations for an outlet at Heritage Square in Concord by August 1995. (Call your local Thomasville Gallery store for confirmation.) Some changes are expected at the new outlet operation due to the company's new pricing policy for its full-price Gallery stores, aimed at making furniture prices more consumer-friendly. This is likely to reduce the range of discounts offered by the previous outlet. However, the outlet will continue to receive truckloads of furniture from its factory back East: canceled orders, discontinued, samples, surplus inventory, and, occasionally, slightly damages pieces, plus left-overs from local Thomasville Galleries. The outlet will offer a "what you see is what you get" selection—some bedroom or dining suites may not be complete. Expect many very nice sofas, chairs, and occasional tables. Prices will not include delivery. Everything will be sold as-is. For a reasonable fee, damaged pieces can be repaired. All sales final.

Office Furniture

Berkeley Outlet
711 Heinz Street, Berkeley. (510) 549-2896. T–Sat Noon–6. Cash/Check. Parking: street, limited on-site.
This outfit gives new meaning to being "tucked away." It's piled and jammed with office furnishings that range from old and ugly to nearly new and up-to-date. Bay Area corporations rid themselves of used office furniture by selling to companies like this one. Because it buys in huge lots and provides no services, prices are very low for better-quality pieces like heavy-duty file cabinets from insurance companies (they take a lot of use). You'll spot brands like Steelcase, General Fire-proofing, Knoll, Allsteel, Art Metal, Herman Miller, Hayworth, and Hamilton. Most of the items are geared for offices or businesses where real work is done, rather than providing front-office glamour or image. Customers are referred for delivery services.

Big Mouth

1129 Airport Boulevard, South San Francisco. (415) 588-2444.
M–F 9–5:30, Sat 10–4. MC, VISA. Parking: lot.

With a name like Big Mouth you might expect lots of fast talk and hustle; instead you'll find seasoned experts who buy used office furniture at a bottom price, and pass on the savings to you. If you need top-notch, firesafe, lockable files with full suspension, there's always a good selection on hand. You might be surprised that used file cabinets are sometimes as expensive as new until you realize that there's a wide range in quality and durability. It's easy to find a new four-drawer cabinet for around $100, but chances are it does not compare to a used commercial-quality one. Check in for desks, chairs, tables, and lots of odds and ends. Good deals are frequently offered on slightly damaged new desks. If you must have new furnishings, a visit can be arranged to a wholesale distributor to make your selection; Big Mouth will place the order and give you a very substantial discount. Extra discounts for large lot orders.

The Desk Depot

89 Pioneer Way, Mountain View. (415) 969-3100.
M–F 9–6, Sat 10–5. MC, VISA, AE. Parking: lot.

This place specializes in used office furniture. You can also buy computer furniture, partitions, chairs, coat trees, tab card files, chalkboards, school desks, and wastebaskets. Some new pieces are stocked at 20–40% off list price.

Rucker Fuller South

601 Brannan Street, San Francisco. (415) 495-6895. M–F 8–5.
MC, VISA. Parking: lot.

If you're starting business in a day or two, don't worry; whiz by, do your shopping and arrange for immediate delivery. There's also a large selection of used stock. The savings on the samples and closeouts range from 40% off retail to below cost. The used furniture is priced according to condition and original price; save 40–60% off original cost. If you're lucky you can pick up a Steelcase file cabinet at about 50% off. There's not much in computer furniture, but lots of desks, credenzas, files, tables, and chairs for any use. Delivery will cost.

Sam Clar Office Furniture

341 13th Street (bet. Webster and Harrison), Oakland.
(800) Sam Clar. M–F 8:30–5:30, Sat 10–4 (Dublin and Concord).
MC, VISA. Parking: validated at Merchants Garage on Webster.
(Other stores: 1221 Diamond Way, Concord; 6801 Dublin
Boulevard, Dublin.)

Some of the office furnishings in Sam Clar's bargain basement
have the "uglies," but they're functional and cheap. Others are
nearly new, with today's business look, but of course they're
more expensive. Everything is priced and, for the most part,
firm. Many customers head right for the new "factory seconds"
(desks, files, and more) unloaded by a major manufacturer and
priced about 40% lower than if in perfect condition. You
can often save by combining new merchandise from the main
floor with used articles from the basement.

Also See

Under Furniture and Home Accessories—
Catalog Discounters, Clearance Centers:
All listings

Under Office Supplies:
Arvey Paper Co.; Office Depot; OfficeMax

Under General Merchandise—Discount Stores:
Price/Costco

Used Furniture

Cottrell's

150 Valencia Street, San Francisco. (415) 431-1000.
M–F 9–5:30, Sat 9–4:30. MC, VISA. Parking: street.

The interior is gloomy and the dust level is high, but there's a
vast inventory ranging from new to almost ancient furniture—
some good, some downright ugly, and most well priced. With
a little inventiveness, those willing to take paint brush to
wood may end up with a real conversation piece. Delivery in
the City is free on purchases over $100.

Harrington Bros. Inc. Moving & Storage

599 Valencia Street (corner 17th Street), San Francisco.
(415) 861-7300. M–Sat 8–6. MC, VISA, AE. Parking: street.
Twentysomething apartment dwellers do well at Harrington
Bros. when they're furnishing their apartments—lots of possibilities if the goal is to create an eclectic, Art Deco, or contemporary environment. Harrington Bros. is bright, cheery, and
chock-full of furniture and accessories from the '20s through
the '50s. I saw furniture that's gone from very much the rage,
to really tacky, and back again. Harrington's furniture is well
priced and most of it comes from estate sales. While the older
pieces have the most personality, there's also a selection of
more recent used furniture.

Home Consignment Center

1901-F Camino Ramon, Danville. (510) 866-6164.
M–Sat 10–6, Sun Noon–5. MC, VISA, ATM. Parking: lot.
The Home Consignment Center has an advantage over other
consignment furniture stores—its size and space. Trucks deliver
new "old" furniture twice a day. The furniture comes from
model homes and from local homeowners (many have been
referred by interior designers who are helping clients make
way for the new), and include new furnishings from design
showrooms and manufacturers' reps. The furniture is displayed
for forty-five days, then offered for sale at auctions held at
the store. The consignee receives 60% of the selling price off
the floor, or 75% if the item is brought directly to auction.
The staff works closely with owners to determine appropriate
pricing and presents any offers that may be made by customers. Stop by and you'll find furniture that is elegant and
updated (*Architectural Digest* quality), and some easily identi-
fied as being "trendy" from the '70s and '80s (Mediterranean
bedroom sets, whitewashed oak dining sets, pecan occasional
tables, glass and enamel, etc.). Also, many nice sofas, occasional chairs, accent pieces, children's bedroom furniture, and
dining room sets. I was intrigued by the display of chandeliers
that offered some great buys. It's nice to find a place where
one can take that perfectly good lighting fixture that just
doesn't fit your decor. Check the walls around the store for
original paintings, lithographs, wall decor, etc. Occasional old
furniture pieces with personality, even a few antiques, and
area rugs make an appearance now and then. Delivery is extra,
also charges for consignment pickups. Directions: From 680,

take Crow Canyon Exit east to first light. Turn left on Crow Canyon Place, go one or two blocks, curve left on Camino Ramon. (Center behind large Marshall's store).

Judith Frost and Company

81 Encina Avenue, Palo Alto. (415) 324-8791. T, W, Sat 10–4, and by appt. VISA (checks preferred). Parking: street.
Judith Frost has gathered an appealing collection of quality consignment furniture and decorative items for the home, garden, or office. Anything goes, as long as it's quality. Upon completion of a sale, the original owner receives 60% of the price. When pieces are too large to move into the store, pictures are posted on a bulletin board for prospective buyers to consider. Count on a nice selection of old pieces, antiques, occasional chairs, new and used sofas, and Oriental accessories. This is a somewhat elitist collection with prices that range from $5 (on accessories) to thousands. Note: The store may be relocating, so call before visiting.

Maggie's Drawers

121 S. Murphy Avenue, Sunnyvale. (408) 730-9300.
T–Sun 10–7. MC, VISA. Parking: street.
South Bay furniture buyers might want to cruise through Maggie's Drawers. Maggie, a designer, maintains a studio-style consignment furniture store and design office where other designers send their goofs or sample pieces (including gifts and accessories) from mansions after "Showcase" tours/exhibitions. Some upscale furnishings come from individuals. Prices are set at about 60–70% off original prices.

Popik Furniture Co.

935 Main Street, Redwood City. (415) 368-2877.
M–F 9–5:30, Sat 9–5. MC, VISA, AE, DIS. Parking: street.
The children and grandchildren of Popik's original customers have sustained this business for fifty-four years. The original family is still at the helm, supplying Peninsula shoppers with new and used furniture. Furniture is bought outright and then most pieces are "spruced up" in the refinishing shop in the back of the store. At first glance it may not be obvious that much of the furniture is used. It's unlikely you'll find antiques, but many pieces are definitely "vintage." If you're set on finding a piece to slipcover, stencil, or personalize with a faux finish, this is a good place to start. After fifty-four years, the

interior of the store is a little tired, and furniture is crammed throughout. Bargain basement–quality furnishings reside side by side with some real jewels. New furnishings and bedding are geared for the budget crowd rather than an upscale market, but the prices are all nicely discounted. Free delivery. If you have furniture to sell, call to schedule a home evaluation (no tired sofas wanted).

Take It or Leave It

210 N. Santa Cruz Avenue (downtown area), Los Gatos. (408) 354-4567. T–Sat 10–5:30, Sun 11–4. MC, VISA, AE. Parking: street, rear lot.

At Take It or Leave It, you'll find a pleasing mixture of "old pieces," antiques, and still attractive used furniture. I thought prices a little high on some pieces, but you can always make an offer. Most used pieces are priced 50–70% off original retail; antiques priced a little less than prevailing market prices. Some pieces are new, others bring to mind trends from years past. More options can be seen in the photo album showing furniture pieces that local residents want to sell.

Also See

Under Furniture and Home Accessories—
Furniture Clearance Centers:
All listings

Giftware and Home Decor

Clay Art Ceramics Outlet

239 Utah Avenue, South San Francisco. (415) 244-4970.
M–F 9–3. Cash/Check. Parking: street.
Clay Art/About Face makes ceramic masks, banks, bathware,
and houseware (teapots, cookie jars, salt and pepper sets,
mugs, tissue dispensers, candlesticks and toothpick holders)
sold through gift shops around the country. The decorative
ceramic masks are made in about seventy different images,
including the company's original limited editions. These can get
very expensive with the addition of feathers, jewels, or other
design elements. The tabletop and home accessories collections
combine functional creativity with sophisticated whimsy. Lots
of animal motifs. Everything in the seconds room is discounted
about 50% off wholesale and the flaws are no big deal (usually
painting defects).

Cody Collection Outlet

1607 Jackson Street (between Polk and Van Ness), San Francisco.
(415) 921-8521. Th–Sat Noon–5. Cash/Check. Parking: street.
Part of the charm of this outlet is found in its petite size—
a small space set aside to showcase the treasures that make up
the Cody Collection. The discriminating stop by, open the iron
gate, and search the displays for new pieces that will enhance
their homes. Everything is imported and sold through upscale
stores noted for providing the "details" of today's lifestyles
and environments. Look closely and you may see some of these
beauties pictured in *Elle Decor, Victoria, Vogue France,* and
WWD. Although the designs may change with each season's

collection, there's usually a smattering of candlesticks, picture frames, decorative boxes, whimsical straw sun hats, napkin rings, balls, bowls, decorative plates, chandeliers, light fixtures, gold and silver shelves and mirrors, topiaries, ornaments, and lots of other goodies. Everything is categorized as samples, seconds, prototypes, overstocks, one-of-a-kind, or discontinued and priced at wholesale! Wonderful source for unusual and tasteful gifts.

Cohn-Stone Studios

5755 Landregan Street, Emeryville. (510) 654-9690.
M–F 10–5:30 (closed 1–2:30). MC, VISA. Parking: street.
The artists at Cohn-Stone studios have earned a reputation for quality and design. Their contemporary handblown glassware, distinctive bowls, vases, perfume vials, paperweights, and plates have been exhibited in some of the nation's top galleries and fine arts specialty stores. Save 50% on seconds that may have a bubble or a scratch; they may be too big or too small, experimental, or discontinued. There's a good range of gift-priced beauties from $10 to $200, although some very special pieces may be priced from $300 to $750 (lamps). Anything made by Cohn-Stone is destined to be a tasteful, timeless gift or a wonderful accent for your home. All sales final.

Collectibles Outlet

1899 W. San Carlos Street, San Jose. (408) 288-6027.
M–F 10–6, Th until 9, Sat 10–5, Sun Noon–5. MC, VISA.
Parking: street.
For classy collectibles you can't do better than the Collectibles Outlet. Here are just a few of the names: Hummel, Lladro, David Winter and Lilliput cottages, Precious Moments, Dept. 56, Royal Doulton, Waterford, Nao, Swarovski, Boyd Bears, plus many other brands of status bears and dolls (Madam Alexander, too), and more! Naturally, your first question should be, "Are these authentic?" The answer: Yes! The proof: the registered trademark on each piece. Even though most of the inventory is discounted starting at 15% off retail, prices may be as much as 40–70% off original retail on special purchases and close-outs set out in the clearance room. The Collectibles Outlet is simply marvelous!

Crate & Barrel Outlet

1785 Fourth Street, Berkeley. (510) 528-5500.
M–Sat 10–6, Sun 11–6. MC, VISA, AE, DIS. Parking: lot.
Picture what you find in Crate & Barrel's "lifestyle" stores: bright, contemporary, and functional home accessories. Out-of-season, discontinued, and occasionally damaged goods are sent to the outlet from its full-service retail stores. Discounts are 20–70% off original retail, although many discounts are in the more modest 25–30% range. Check every nook and cranny of this colorful and creatively merchandised outlet. Crate & Barrel's popular basic stemware and barware are carried at retail store prices. Returns and exchanges.

Evans Ceramics Gallery

55 W. Grant Street, Healdsburg. (707) 433-2502.
Wed–Sun 10–5. MC. Parking: street.
Evans Ceramics produces designer vases and art pieces in raku, a firing process in which exotic finishes are achieved by pulling pieces directly out of a yellow-hot kiln. Evans's gallery is filled with one-of-a-kind prototypes, seconds, and overruns at clearance prices. The 20–70% markdowns vary with the status of the pieces. Most pieces are marked down 50% or more. Evans's art evolves with design trends. Newer pieces and color palettes are continually being developed. The latest? The beautiful Glass Art line.

Home Again

1268 Marina Boulevard, Marina Square, San Leandro.
(510) 352-4758. M–F 10–9, Sat 10–7, Sun 11–6. MC, VISA.
Parking: lot.
(Other outlets: Anderson/Shasta, Folsom, Gilroy, Lathrop,
Milpitas, Napa, Pacific Grove, Petaluma, South Lake Tahoe,
St. Helena, Truckee, Vacaville centers.)
With average 20% discounts, this barely qualifies as a "bargain" resource, but the merchandise is quite appealing. Pick up an "adornment" for your home from the collections, which include silver, crystal, table linens, afghans, picture frames, framed art, brass, potpourri and fine soaps, candles, whimsical gifts, stationery, and more. The merchandise enhances decors in traditional, country, romantic, or Southwest modes. Save your gift boxes, since Home Again has none to offer.

Lundberg Studios

131 Old Coast Road, Davenport. (408) 423-2532. Daily 10–4.
MC, VISA, AE. Parking: street.
Lundberg Studios is the recognized leader in Tiffany art glass reproductions. Pieces sell in fine galleries and world-renowned stores. A Lundberg paperweight retails $200–$400, a Tiffany-style lamp also in the hundreds! At any time in the studio there are usually seventy-five to one hundred seconds that are discounted about 50%. Lamps, paperweights, vases, crystal, and glass perfume vials may have minor flaws or they may be discontinued. In exchange for the seconds' low prices you may have to forego Lundberg's prestigious signature. If you are an art glass collector, the trip to Davenport will be worthwhile.

Maslach Art Glass Studio & Seconds Store

44 Industrial Way, Greenbrae. (415) 924-2310.
T–Sat Noon–4. MC, VISA. Parking: street.
The elegant displays in this outlet showcase the many original pieces and goblets produced by Maslach. What's not readily apparent is that most of these beauties are seconds reduced about 50% (goblets starting at $34). Seconds in Maslach's distinctive marbles are $5–$40. You may find dichroic scent bottles, paperweights, bowls, and sculptures that will make beautiful gifts. Great wedding presents!

Nourot Glass Studio

675 E. H Street, Benicia. (707) 745-1463.
M–Sat 10–4, Sun Noon–5. MC, VISA. Parking: street.
Works by Nourot are in the collection of the Corning Museum of Glass. If you would like to own a museum-quality piece of art glass that is individually crafted in the ancient tradition, be sure to get on the Nourot mailing list for special promotions where selection is best and bargains abound. Special sales events are scheduled on the weekend before Mother's Day, the second weekend in August and the first weekend in December. Retail prices are steep, but the quality is impeccable. Sale prices reduced 50% make them more affordable.

R. Strong Glass Studio & Gallery

1235 Fourth Street (at Gilman), Berkeley. (510) 525-3150.
M–Sat 10–4:30. MC, VISA. Parking: street.
Randy Strong designs and creates distinctive handblown goblets, vases, sculpture, and paperweights, many of which

have 22K gold leaf fused to the glass. His unique works are seen at fine exhibits and in arts and crafts magazines. Prices at the studio's gallery are 10–75% off regular retail prices. The outlet's prices range from $15 to $58 for goblets and paperweights (seconds); special sculptures and platters can cost more (first-quality pieces are also available at slightly higher prices). The studio also features some special works by other artists at reduced prices. The main entrance to the studio is on the side of the building.

San Francisco Music Box

Great Mall of the Bay Area, Milpitas. (408) 956-9427. Daily.
MC, VISA, DIS, AE. Parking: lot.
You'll love the melodic greeting from dozens of music boxes when you enter this outlet, which serves as a combination clearance center and retail store. Not everything is discounted—look for tags or display signs with red dots to zero in on the special discounts. Music boxes come in any number of surprising configurations: mugs, figurines, key chains, water globes, stuffed animals, masks, trinket boxes, picture frames, and more. Don't worry, closeout or discontinued merchandise will be in working condition.

Smyers Glass Studio

675 E. H Street, Benicia. (707) 745-2614.
M–Sat 10–4 (daily Nov and Dec). MC, VISA. Parking: street.
Smyers Glass is known throughout the country for its fine handblown stemware. A favorite of young brides and those who love to entertain, Smyers glass is sold in fine stores such as Neiman Marcus, Gumps, and Nordstrom. In addition to his handblown stemware, Stephen Smyers creates beautiful paper-weights, bowls, vases, and perfume bottles. Seconds in the studio sell for 50% off retail. Special sales the first weekends in May and December offer exceptional buying opportunities.

Tuesday Morning

239 Third Street, Montecito Plaza, San Rafael. (415) 453-9816.
All stores: M–Sat 9:30–6, Th until 9, Sun Noon–6.
MC, VISA, DIS. Parking: lot.
(Other stores: Danville; Sacramento; San Jose; San Mateo; Saratoga; Sacramento; Walnut Creek.)
Texas-based Tuesday Morning has built its success and reputation on the uniqueness and quality of its inventory. After

years of stories from out-of-state friends, my expectations for this company were unreasonably high. Prices are promised to be 50–80% off original retail on excess inventories from manufacturers around the world. If you currently shop at other discounters like T.J. Maxx or Marshalls, the prices on some merchandise may be merely competitive or much better. Everything is relative! The company's opening "events," held four times a year, draw shoppers attracted by the prospect of buying both the expected and unexpected: Oriental rugs; crystal and silverplated giftware; housewares; porcelain lamps; bed, bath, and table linens; paper products; Christmas and holiday paraphernalia; baskets; children's toys and apparel; men's furnishings; even some furniture. You'll see some very famous names attached to the inventory. Everything is first quality. Wow! Cash refunds and returns allowed. Selections vary from store to store. Special shopping opportunities are offered to selected mailing list customers (big spenders). Opening events scheduled generally for mid-Feb/March, May/June, mid-Aug/Sep, and mid-Oct/Dec.

Zellique Art Glass

701 E. H Street, Benicia. (707) 745-5710. M–Sat 10–4.
MC, VISA. Parking: street.
Zellique offers handblown art glass designed by Joseph Morel and other craftspeople. If you don't mind a slight imperfection that you probably can't even see, then you'll save about 50% off retail. The collection includes paperweights, perfume bottles, bookends, vases, individual sculptures, bowls, and lamps. For the best selection, schedule a visit when Zellique, Smyers, and Nourot join forces for special open house events on the weekend before Mother's Day and the first weekend in December. Get on their mailing list for these special events.

Also See

Under General Clothing:
Burlington Coat Factory; Marshall's; T.J. Maxx

Under Jewelry and Watches:
Cresalia Jewelers Diamond Expertise

Under Dinnerware and Kitchenware:
Dansk Factory Outlet; Mikasa Factory Store

Under Linens:
Home Express; Linens 'n' Things

Under General Merchandise:
All sections

Under Special Sales and Events:
Most listings

Home Improvement

When it comes to home-improvement projects, it's hard not to mention HomeBase and Home Depot. These two warehouse stores dominate the market with vast selection and deep discount pricing. Similar in operation, they offer an in-depth selection of everything you need to build and fixture a home from the blueprint stage to the final step of landscaping and fencing. Most consumers are satisfied with the overall quality offered in the selection of products. However, if you're looking for more luxurious and expensive products, you may have to use specialty sources and forgo any hope of a bargain. Considering the sheer number of people who besiege these stores every day, both companies do a fair job with service, but they'd have to triple the staffing to provide the one-on-one attention that most of us would like. To that end, each company offers many special events for do-it-yourselfers. Think of these stores when buying plumbing, fencing, paint, tools, lighting fixtures, lumber, paneling, windows, sprinkler systems, hardware, garden equipment and supplies, window blinds, flooring, kitchen and bath cabinets and fixtures, electrical, patio furniture, barbecues, and more, more, and more.

Black & Decker

Factory Stores of America, Vacaville. (707) 453-1256. Daily. MC, VISA. Parking: lot.
You'll discover that Black & Decker makes lots of helpful and innovative gadgets and Handy Andy aids in addition to its well-known line of tools and garden equipment. Everything in the outlet is priced at least 25% off retail. (The company sets

prices to undersell its competitors.) You'll see "service products" (reconditioned items that carry a full two-year warranty and often sold at 50% off retail); blemished cartons; and discontinued models. It may be worth a visit to buy a new cordless drill, palm grip sander, router, Workmate, variable speed drill, power miter saw, circular saw, Groom 'N' Edge garden trimmer, buffers, hedge trimmer, or One Touch Lawn Mower. Black & Decker gets into the kitchen in a big way; you'll also find a variety of small electrical appliances at the same discounts.

Caldwell Building Wreckers

195 Bayshore Boulevard, San Francisco. (415) 550-6777.
M–F 8:30–5, Sat 9–4:30 (Nov–Feb M–F 8–4:30). MC, VISA.
Parking: street.
Caldwell Building Wreckers recycles building materials and offers new distributor's closeouts plus seconds and liquidated stock. It's a labyrinth of rooms stocked with both new and used building materials. I was impressed with the variety in the hundreds of new windows and doors (exterior and interior). You'll discover well-known brands in wood frame windows and patio doors, most dual glazed (French door units, too). Also check out the decorative molding. You can go basic and budget-quality, or trade up to something really special and upscale. Either way, you'll be saving considerately. You can trim your building costs by buying recycled lumber, plywood, beams, mirrors, used bricks, cobblestones, occasionally slabs of granite and marble. The lumber is fully dried, avoiding the twisting that occurs later if it's too green. Also, Caldwell can custom cut special beams or sizes for you. I can't get too excited about used toilets, sinks, or bathtubs (unless they're Victorian style), but they're in stock, too. Delivery can be arranged.

Ceramic Circus

438 Francisco Boulevard W., San Rafael. (415) 456-0282.
M–Sat 9–4:30. MC, VISA. Parking: lot.
You'll find Ceramic Circus in back of Tilecraft, an upscale tile company. It's a familiar story—special purchases, seconds, returned, and discontinued items. Discounts are 50–70% off original retail. You'll find more floor tiles than anything else, but there are some countertop and wall tiles. I noted one flooring tile marked down from $4.50 to $1.90. The selection is limited, so while it's probably not worth driving a long way, stop by if you're in the area. Note: The entrance is on Rice Street.

Designer's Brass

280 El Camino Real, San Bruno. (415) 588-8480.
M–F 8:30–5:30, Sat 9–5. MC, VISA, ATM. Parking: lot.
Check out Designer's Brass if you're replacing nondescript bath
and kitchen fixtures. With luck you'll find something you like
among the many discontinued bathroom or kitchen faucets,
fancy front door locks, and indoor knobs, all deeply discounted.
If you buy regular inventory, discounts vary with the amount
of sale ($100 and over). This outfit carries status brands that
ordinarily cost far more than the budget to moderate models
at HomeBase, et al. Very nice selection of the latest in kitchen
and bathroom fixtures and accessories (pulls and knobs for
cabinet doors).

Hess Trim Center

930 California Avenue (off Commercial), Sunnyvale.
(800) 559-1454; fax (408) 481-9056. M–F 7–5, Sat 9–4.
MC, VISA. Parking: lot.
Hess Trim Center is a specialty operation, offering quality,
price, and selection: everything in the way of trims, mouldings, fireplace mantels, etc. in a variety of woods—primed,
paint grade, and stain grade (more expensive). Also in stock
are forty patterns in new woods: maple, cherry, walnut,
mahogany, and white oak. My comparisons revealed that its
prices were often lower than at warehouse stores, or at least
competitive. If you're intent on adding charm to your home
with some architectural moulding, visit or request a catalog.
Catalogs do not list prices, which vary depending on fluctua-
tions in the marketplace and quantity ordered.

Ken's Glass

2905 Senter Road (at Lewis), San Jose. (408) 578-5211.
M–Sat 9–5; always closed W and Sun. Cash/Check. Parking: lot.
Ken offers great prices because he cuts corners: no secretary,
virtually no overhead, no delivery, no installation, no cutouts
on glass or mirrors (although he will trim edges to size), and
cash-and-carry. Ken stocks first-quality glass and mirrors, as
well as seconds with a substantial price differential, in all sizes
and shapes. He has a good selection of precut sizes of glass
and mirrors for shelving, picture frames, rounds for table tops,
and mirrored closet doors. Look for bronze and clear beveled
mirrors. Check all his bargains before deciding; you'll find many
price options (40–80% discounts), whether you're covering an
entire wall with mirror or simply replacing a broken window.

The Kitchen Table

151 Third Street, San Rafael. (415) 453-2662.
M–F 9–4, Sat 9–2. Cash/Check. Parking: street.

This small shop is hardly more than a shed. The floor is covered with sawdust (you may be too by the time you leave), and the smell of glue pervades the air. You'll see work in progress: butcher-block tables and countertops being built. Each butcher-block item is made to the customer's specifications. Drawers, knife racks, wine or glass racks, shelves, microwave platforms, and more can be made to accessorize the tables. Since they're handmade, you won't find the smooth edges and perfectly finished surfaces typical of mass-produced butcher-block products; these are more like antiques. They're finished in urethane seasoned with nontoxic peanut oil or paraffin. Custom services are usually costly, but not here. You may save 40–60%, depending on where you do your comparison pricing. A table 48 inches long, 24 inches wide, 4 inches thick, any height, runs $190; one 27 inches long, 18 inches wide, 4 inches thick is $90. Orders can usually be filled in a couple of weeks. Call for a phone quote.

Major Lines "As-Is" Warehouse

235 Bayshore Boulevard, San Francisco. (415) 647-9066.
M–F 8–5, Sat 9–4. MC, VISA. Parking: lot.

If you're clever you can do a lot with the options available at Major Lines, distributor for Merillat custom kitchen and bathroom cabinets. This midpriced line offers standard features like roll-out trays, a furniture-quality finish, and wipe-clean interiors. There are several styles, finishes, and cabinet fronts available. You can buy veneers or solid wood face frames or practical, easy-to-clean melamine laminates. The bargain angle starts when you enter the warehouse, where discontinued (some just with style modifications), slightly damaged, or otherwise marked-down cabinets are shown. At times, you may find enough cabinets in one style to completely outfit a kitchen or bath. More often, you'll find just a cabinet or two for the utility room, small bath, etc. Prices are about half off contractor pricing. (Saw many pieces at $49.) All sales final.

McIntyre Tile Co.

55 W. Grant Street, Healdsburg. (707) 433-8866.
M–F 9–4, Sat 10–4. Cash/Check. Parking: street.

McIntyre Tile is sold directly through architects and interior designers. Its handcrafted, high-fired stoneware and porcelain tile is available in many beautiful colors, at about $10/square foot. Call and request a selection of samples in your color range. If you see one you like, inquire about its seconds, which are half-price (about $3/square foot) and may be off-color or slightly warped, but otherwise structurally sound. Allow plenty of time to pick and poke through the seconds. Note: The store closes for lunch 12:30–1:30. Get on its mailing list.

The Moulding Company

2308-C Bates Avenue, Concord. (510) 798-7525.
M–F 8–5, Sat 10–4. MC, VISA. Parking: lot.

East Bay consumers should stop by this warehouse (wear sweaters on warm days) to select mouldings or decorative trims. Most mouldings (crown, base, casings, cove, etc.) are available in finger-jointed pine (paint grade), stain grade, and primed. A few mouldings are stocked in oak, while other woods are available by special order (including mantels, columns, and pillars). Sorting out the choices is made easier by reviewing the company's six-page catalog, which illustrates the type, dimension, and style of its moulding. (This will be mailed on request.) The company supplies many smaller establishments with moulding for resale, sells to many contractors, and offers consumers pricing that's substantially lower than the local home-improvement superstores. My comparison surveys revealed savings of about 35–40% on average. You can send your contractor in to make purchases, or, if you're a deter-mined sort, do it yourself. It's not that hard to do if one plans each cut carefully and practices first on an extra length of moulding. If you're doing several rooms, an investment in a chop saw makes the whole enterprise easier. Delivery is free in Contra Costa County and to other areas on larger orders. Location: Bates is off Port Chicago Highway (about one-half mile west of Price/Costco on Bates).

Nissan Tile Clearance Center

364 Bayshore Boulevard, San Francisco. (415) 641-4500.
M–F 8–5, Sat 8–2. MC, VISA. Parking: street.

Nissan is a major importer of ceramic tile, porcelain, granite, and slate and distributes to tile contractors and retail stores. Not everything in its small clearance center is discounted, but you can save 30–50% on odd lots, closeouts, and discontinued stock. Usually these leftovers have no trim pieces to match, limiting their application. Pick up supplies and all the free advice you need. Look for weekly sale specials.

Norstad Pottery

253 S. 25th Street, Richmond. (510) 620-0200.
M–F 9–5, Sat 10–3. MC, VISA. Parking: lot.

Norstad Pottery produces distinctive, beautiful, and functional high-fired stoneware tables, planters, and vases, plus bath, kitchen, vegetable, and bar sinks that are handcrafted from stoneware clay fired to approximately 2,400°. Each piece is hand-thrown and decorated; therefore, each is different. Norstad's dinnerware, platters, and baking and serving dishes appeal to those shopping for contemporary, aesthetic designs. Its sinks and stoneware are typically sold through architects and specialty tile and bath showrooms. Bargain hunters check the Richmond showroom for seconds that may have slight color imperfections or something as minor as a pinhole in the glaze. These are visual flaws that don't impair product integrity. Discounts on seconds are 25–40% off retail. Catch sales in April and early December when everything is reduced 25% and seconds are reduced an additional 40%.

Post Tool & Supply

800 E. Eighth Street, Oakland. (510) 272-0331.
M–Sat 8–5, Sun 10–3. MC, VISA, DIS. Parking: street.
(Other stores: Fremont; Modesto; Sacramento; San Francisco; San Jose; San Rafael; Santa Rosa; Stockton.)

Post is all set up for serious tool users, offering high-quality brands: Milwaukee, Skil, Hitachi, DeWalt, Ryobi, Porter-Cable, Makita, and others. You'll usually find drill presses, bench grinders, table saws, hand tools, jacks, vises, wrenches, socket sets, electric tools, air tools, electric saws, lathes, and tool boxes. Everything is fully guaranteed and comes in the original factory packaging. Prices are sometimes a tad higher than at Home-Base or Price/Costco, but the trade-off is expanded selection, customer service, and support.

R.V. Cloud

1217 Dell Avenue (Irrigation) and 3000 S. Winchester
(Plumbing), Campbell. Irrigation, (408) 374-8370; Plumbing,
(408) 378-7943. M–F 8–5. MC, VISA. Parking: lot.

When landscaping your yard and installing a sprinkler system,
stop by R.V. Cloud, a major wholesaler of irrigation supplies
for contractors and perfect for do-it-yourselfers. Do everyone
a favor and do some homework first: the staff is busy! You can
buy pipe, fittings, sprinkler heads, timers, regulators—in short,
everything you need. You'll pay about 10% more than contractors, which will save you about 20–30% off the prices at
building supply stores. The plumbing department is through a
separate entrance at the other end of the building. You can
order plumbing supplies, water heaters, pumps, and bathroom,
kitchen, and laundry fixtures (toilets, sinks, tubs, and faucets)
from catalogs. Kohler, Price Pfister, Moen, Delta, Grohe, and
others are stocked. R.V. is a good source for high-end fixtures.
Keep an open mind and you may find really special prices on
discontinued fixtures that offer quality you probably can't
afford if you buy current stock. Special plumbing fixtures for
the handicapped can be ordered. The quality ranges from
standard to superlative. The merchandise comes in sealed
boxes, so be sure to research style and color selections before
coming in. Local delivery can be arranged for a nominal fee.
Note: It's not open on Saturdays.

Raffles Fans

1244 Fourth Street (corner of Fourth and C), San Rafael.
(415) 456-6660. M–Sat 10–5:30. MC, VISA. Parking: street, lots.

Raffles specializes in ceiling fans and offers everything savvy
value-conscious shoppers need: expertise, good service, and
competitive prices. Raffles sticks with the proven leaders in
the field: Casablanca and Emerson. Prices range from $99 to
$2,500. Most sales fall in the $199–$500 range. It's important
to evaluate first what charges are involved in installation, particularly if a new ceiling outlet must be put in. When shopping
around, be sure to compare apples to apples. Some stores may
quote prices that do not include fan blades, a light fixture, or
fitting. Raffles offers good discount prices up front and stands
behind its prices with a price guarantee "to meet or beat any
advertised or written quote."

Stonelight Tile Factory

1651 Pomona Avenue, San Jose. (408) 292-7424. Sat 9–5. Cash/Check. Parking: lot.

Stonelight Tile is a glazed tile with an unusually dense body, made chiefly of natural clays instead of talc (used in most commercial tile) for a natural look that contributes to its great popularity among architects and designers. Stonelight's "boneyard" has stacks of leftovers and seconds (surface irregularities, color imperfections, or chips). The savings are considerable: Normal retail for these tiles is in the neighborhood of $7.50–$25/square foot. Seconds sell for 50¢ to $2.50/square foot and overruns are $3–$5/square foot. You may have to pay full price for trim pieces if they are not in the seconds or overrun selection. Boxes cost, so bring your own. Finally, do yourself and the busy staff a favor—take measurements and have quantity estimates ready before visiting.

Western Hardware & Tool Company

1947 Carroll Avenue, San Francisco. (415) 468-4530. M–F 8–5, Sat 9–4. MC, VISA. Parking: lot.

Western is a major supplier of tools for lineworkers, electricians, auto mechanics, carpenters, iron and steel workers, as well as manufacturing and industrial plants in Northern California. These are industrial-rated and may cost more than home-rated tools, even at discount. However, prices here are substantially discounted from manufacturers' lists. On products that serve both the industrial and home markets—Stanley tapes, vise grip sets, block sanders, saws, hammers, and other hand tools—prices are competitive with the warehouse stores. Western has no sales gimmicks or loss leaders, just low dealer prices every day.

Getting the Job Done—Helpful Hint

The Trades Guild
*Alameda County (510) 547-3337; Contra Costa County
(510) 820-2766; Marin County (415) 454-5272;
and San Francisco County (415) 777-3337.*
The Trades Guild is a free consumer referral service that leads
you to contractors for just about any home improvement or
repair service that's under consideration. They will give you
the names and phone numbers of members who work in your
area. Contractors referred by the Trades Guild must meet strict
membership criteria before they can be referred to the public.
Contractors must be licensed by the state and bonded. The
Guild verifies all insurance information, checks for complaints
on file with various consumer agencies, requires a personal
interview at the contractor's place of business, and requires
five written references from previous customers. There is no
charge to consumers—the service is supported by membership
dues. The next time you need a carpenter, tree trimmer, painter,
carpet installer, landscaper, plumber, electrician, someone
for earthquake retrofitting, etc., give them a call. This service
provides a peace-of-mind alternative to plucking names
willy-nilly out of the Yellow Pages.

Also See

Under Carpets and Flooring:
Floorcraft

Linens

General Linens

Bed & Bath Superstore

555 Ninth Street, San Francisco. (415) 252-0490.
M–F 9:30–9, Sat 9:30–7, Sun 10:30–7. MC, VISA. Parking: lot.
(Other stores: 590 Second Street, Oakland;
2675 Santa Rosa Avenue, Santa Rosa.)
Of course, it has linens from brand-name manufacturers, even some designer lines. Prices are discounted 20–40% on current, first-quality merchandise every day. You can give the bathroom the once-over, too. You'll find a wonderful collection of closet organizers and gadgets. Don't miss the houseware and kitchen department. Farberware, Fitz & Floyd, Mikasa, Rubbermaid, and Copco are a few of the lines in dinnerware, cookware, accessories, and giftware. All the stores are beautifully merchandised and well stocked, although sometimes it takes a ladder to reach the nearly ceiling-high shelves.

Bedspread Image

39201 Farwell Drive, East Mowry Shopping Center, Fremont.
(510) 795-0539. M–F 11–7, Sat 11–6, Sun 12:30–5.
MC, VISA. Parking: lot.
Bedspread Image should definitely be on your list of places to shop for bedspreads, daybed cover sets, sheet sets, and decorative pillows. Bedspreads and comforters from major mills are discounted 15–35% off retail. Prices on bedspreads range from $49 to $329 (for a top-of-the-line custom spread). The selection caters to most decors, from country cute to nouveau contemporary.

California Kid's Factory Outlet

621 Old County Road (two blocks south of Holly), San Carlos.
(415) 637-9054. T–Sat 9–4. MC, VISA, DIS. Parking: lot.
This company makes crib and twin bedding and accessories.
You can save 50% on discontinued coordinated sheets, dust
ruffles, comforters, bumper pads, and crib pillows; occasionally
you'll find window curtains, wall hangings, and liners for
bassinets. The patterns are delightful, ranging from demure
and feminine to bright, bold, and cheerful. Some merchandise
is sold in sets. The day bed linen sets insure that California
Kid's will not be left behind as its clientele grows older. Cribs
and twin beds are available, too.

Decorator's Bedspread Outlet

5757 Pacheco Boulevard, Pacheco. (510) 689-3435.
M 10–7:30, T–Sat 10–6, Sun Noon–5. MC, VISA, DIS. Parking: lot.
(Other Stores: Fair Oaks; Pleasanton.)
Here's a selection of bedspreads, goose down comforters,
daybed ensembles, dacron-filled comforters, decorator pillows,
and dust ruffles, offering depth and variety to suit almost
everyone's taste and needs (there are many high-quality bedspreads for upscale shoppers). If you're also covering windows,
consider ready-made draperies at prices lower than major
store sales. On regular, first-quality merchandise, you'll save
approximately 25% off prevailing retail. On custom orders you
can save 30–40%.

Discount Depot

2020 San Pablo Avenue, Berkeley. (510) 549-1478.
M–F 10–7, Sat–Sun 10–6. MC, VISA, DIS, AE. Parking: street.
(Other Stores: 520 Haight, San Francisco;
5350 Clayton Road, Concord.)
Discount Depot comes in handy for new Cal students building
their nests. They can pick up affordable linens and simple furnishings, a discount-priced futon and frame (budget to better
versions), or a carton containing some of the contemporary
RTA furnishings that make up much of the inventory. Usually
a screwdriver is the only tool needed to put together a computer desk, end or coffee table, cart, bookcase, small eating
table, etc. Find starving student discounts on pillows, tablecloths, sheet sets, towels, and throw rugs. Delivery can be
arranged for about $25 to areas within reasonable distance
from each store.

Dreams

921 Howard Street (at Fifth Street), San Francisco.
(415) 543-1800, (800) 419-1200.
M–F 10–8, Sat 10–6, Sun Noon–5. MC, VISA, AE, ATM.
Parking: free adjoining lot or street.

For starters, Dreams is a great place to shop for down comforters and other down products (feather beds, pillows, etc.). Since all comforters are made on-site, you can specify the weight of the fill, the design stitch, the covering fabric—allowing you to buy budget to top quality. The price you pay for whatever you choose results in excellent value and solid bargains. There's also a ready-to-go selection. You can decide on the type of down fill by examining the various down products on display. More information is provided by the staff on fill power and loft, and the thread count and fiber detail for the covering. You can also bring in your down comforter to be cleaned by Dreams's German down-cleaning plant, which gently refluffs old down as it cleans. The service department can replace or repair your comforter cover (pillows too) and add or delete fill for reasonable charges. There's a very nice discount fabric selection for making duvet or futon covers, or you can bring in your own fabric or sheets to have one made. It costs about $25 to sew up most duvet covers and often takes no more than fifteen minutes (seamstresses on-site work with amazing speed). If you need odd-size linens or bed coverings, bedskirts, shams (any kind of bedding accessory), or window treatment, your problems are over. Dreams also sells brand-name sheets, comforter sets, dust ruffles, duvets, pillows, futon covers, etc. I spotted many popular patterns and some very special and luxurious fabrications. Prices held up when compared to other local linen discounters and mail-order companies. Competitively priced mattress sets; brass and metal beds (including daybeds); and a tasteful selection of throws, afghans, and decorative pillows round out the selection—all nicely discounted.

Factory Outlet

29 Colma Boulevard, 280 Metro Center, Colma. (415) 992-0311.
M–F 10–9, Sat 10–7, Sun 11–6. MC, VISA, DIS. Parking: lot.
The Factory Outlet is worth a visit when shopping at the 280
Metro Center. It's the place to go when you're doing windows
on a budget. Ready-made draperies, curtains, panels, pleated
shades, and window coverings are promotionally priced every
day. Others will want to consider the brand-name towels, rugs,
bath accessories, shower curtains, sheets, pillows, comforters,
bedspreads, shams and dust ruffles, blankets, mattress pads,
table linens, and decorator pillows.

Fieldcrest Cannon

Folsom Factory Outlets, Folsom. (916) 351-0849. Daily.
MC, VISA. Parking: lot.
I found excellent buys here in every category, including scatter
rugs, blankets, sheets, comforters, and towels. The selection
of table linens was not very extensive, nor were the discounts
great. Price tags specifying "compared to" are first quality;
those saying "if perfect" are irregulars. The best buys are on
irregulars, with 40–60% discounts off retail. The flaws were
not obvious; in fact, I couldn't identify any. Loved the discounts on the upscale line of Charisma sheets. Returns for full
refund or charge card credit with receipt. Beautiful store!

Home Express

39125 Fremont Hub, Fremont. (510) 795-7111.
M–F 10–9, Sat 9:30–9, Sun 11–7. MC, VISA, DIS, AE. Parking: lot.
(Other stores: Citrus Heights; Concord; Dublin; Fresno;
Rohnert Park; Sacramento and South Sacramento; San Jose;
San Leandro; Santa Clara.)
Home Express can fill your linen needs for dining, kitchen, bath,
and bedroom with better-quality, brand-name merchandise
at discounted prices. You'll find linens, kitchenware, housewares, gadgets, gourmet foods, RTA furniture, small electronics,
organizers for every room, patio furniture, barbecue gear,
vacuums, and more. Shoppers appreciate the stores' pleasant
ambience, tasteful seasonal displays, and sizzling new trends
in home decor. Everyday prices are equivalent to department
store sale prices, with familiar brands at discounts of 10–60%
off regular retail.

Linen Factory Outlet

475 Ninth Street, San Francisco. (415) 431-4543.
W–F Noon–4, Sat 10–4. MC, VISA, DIS. Parking: street.
Linen Factory Outlet is connected to Western Linen, which
sells textiles for kitchen, bed, and bath to department stores,
hotels, restaurants, caterers, and small specialty stores. Being
small, it can fill orders for special sizes that are often hard to
buy from manufacturers. You'll find irregulars, overruns, and
discontinued items from its stock. Among these are the classic
bistro check tablecloth in many colors and European damask
tablecloths/napkins in 100% cotton. Look for imported items
such as famous British woolen blankets, throws, and flannel
bed linens. Quilters can get fabric scraps for 10¢/pound! Each
Saturday there are several items on special.

Linens 'n' Things

Great Mall of the Bay Area, Milpitas. (408) 934-9288. Daily.
MC, VISA. Parking: lot.
(Other stores: Citrus Heights; Roseville; Sacramento, San Jose.)
Bigger is better—especially as represented by Linens 'n' Things'
new superstore concept in Milpitas and San Jose. This power-
house national chain (more than 140 stores) offers 20–50%
discounts off department store prices every day and backs it
up with a price guarantee. Its stores stock a wide selection of
linens in every category for the home. That's just the beginning,
since its stores go on to provide "things" like picture frames,
framed art, everything for entertaining, kitchenware (pots, pans,
dishes, cutlery, etc.), small electronics, organizers, and tasteful
home accessories and accents. It relies on some of America's
leading companies to keep customers happy: Braun, Cuisinart,
Calphalon, Krups, Farberware, and linens from Laura Ashley,
Croscill, Waverly, Martex, Bill Blass, Adrienne Vittadini, and
others. It's not hard to duplicate a picture-perfect bedroom
with the coordinated groups of upscale linens in very current
patterns.

paper white ltd. Warehouse Sales

769 Center Boulevard, Fairfax. (415) 457-7673.
Quarterly sales. MC, VISA. Parking: lot.
paper white ltd.'s linens convey a romantic and nostalgic theme.
It designs and imports an expensive line in pristine white
linen, linen/cotton blends, and luxurious Italian cottons. Many
groups are lovingly trimmed with handmade lace, embroidery

appliqués, or cutwork. It's not hard to find linens that are similar to this line at much lower prices, but close inspection will reveal the difference—finer fabrics, superior embroidery, and designs that reflect owner Jan Dutton's discriminating design talent. If you're on paper white's mailing list, you'll get sale invitations that will lead to 40-60% markdowns on the "leftovers": discontinued items, slightly soiled or (insignificantly) flawed but always lovely linens. For the bedroom, you'll find duvet covers, window panels, dust ruffles, pillows, bedcovers, and shams; for the dining room, placemats, tablecloths, and napkins; plus home accessories, aprons, pillows, etc. Other treasures can be found in children's clothing: vintage-style dresses for girls in sizes 6mos to 12, cute outfits for boys from 6mos to Toddler 4, and, occasionally, christening outfits to last through several generations. Call or write for a sale notice. Scheduled 1995 sale dates: September 21, 22, 23; November 30; December 1, 2.

Ritch Street Outlet
688 Third Street, San Francisco. (415) 546-1908.
M–Sat 10–5. MC, VISA. Parking: street.
This colorful little outlet's good connections to a major Bay Area linen company means a ready supply of discontinued quilted placemats, napkins, aprons, oven mitts, potholders, towels, tote bags, and much more. Placemats at $2–$3 and napkins at $1.50–$2, available in solids and patterns, consti-tute the biggest part of the selection. Count on a few surprises and unexpected bargains, like porcelain and stainless steel cookware, mugs, music boxes, baskets, wood bowls, and other gift items. Prices are wholesale or less.

Springmaid Wamsutta Factory Stores
Outlets at Gilroy, Gilroy. (408) 847-3731. Daily.
MC, VISA, AE, DIS. Parking: lot.
(Other outlet: Vacaville center.)
Rather than going upscale like so many linen discount stores (accompanied by higher prices), this clearance outlet main-tains a bargain-basement image and about the lowest bed linen prices I've seen. The inventory is limited to closeouts and selected irregulars (not much in table linens); if you're not too particular about pattern or color, you'll find rock-bottom prices on sheets, mattress pads, blankets, pillows, comforters and bedspreads, and Pacific silvercloth. Exchanges and refunds with receipt.

Strouds

700 El Camino Real, 120 Menlo Station, Menlo Park.
(415) 327-7680. M–F 10–9, Sat 10–7, Sun 10–6.
VISA, MC, DIS, AE. Parking: lot.
(Other Stores: Corte Madera; Dublin; Newark; Pleasant Hill;
San Francisco; San Jose; San Mateo; Sunnyvale; Walnut Creek.
Outlets: Strouds Super Outlets; Tracy, Vacaville centers.)
Strouds is a specialty off-price linen operation that offers top-quality products at decent discounts on virtually everything for bed (including down comforters), bath, kitchen, and dining room. The selection includes current colors and styles (many top-of-the-line). Using its special order program, you can coordinate wallpaper, window coverings, and accessories with your linen selections. In-home service for custom window coverings. The Super Outlets in Vacaville and Tracy offer moderately priced linen lines, more special promotions, closeouts, and irregulars unique to these outlets. Also, clearance inventory from its full-line stores at great prices. Return policies are very liberal.

Warm Things Factory Store

180 Paul Drive (Terra Linda Industrial Parkway), San Rafael.
(415) 472-2154. M–Sat 10–5. MC, VISA. Parking: lot.
(Other Stores: 3523 Haven, Unit F, Menlo Park—open only
Nov–Apr; 6011 College Avenue, Oakland; 3063 Fillmore,
San Francisco.)
Everything from budget to best means everyone has warm and cozy nights! Warm Things provides all you need to know about loft, fill power, fabric, and design variables, plus good value. Its selection includes its top-of-the-line, European-style baffle construction in channel or box designs; 100% cotton cambric (270- to 335-thread count) covers; for lean budgets there are light- and medium-weight goose down comforters. Everything at its factory stores sells for 40–50% off its catalog prices. Warm Things also sells down pillows, featherbeds, boots, goose down bathrobes, wool mattress pads, slippers, many styles of down jackets, and Kennebunk throws. Duvet covers are available in many fabrications, including a lovely damask. Note: The Menlo Park store is open from November to April.

Mail Order

Local stores are limited in providing all your options for accessorizing, due to shelf and display space limitations. The companies below offer discounted prices, ranging from modest to very impressive, on a wide selection of linens in all quality ranges for children's and adult rooms. You're much more likely to see everything available in a particular pattern. You'll also find many esoteric bedding accessories and hard-to-find products. Call and request a catalog.

Touch of Class   (800) 457-7456

The Linen Source   (800) 431-2620

Domestications   (800) 746-2555

Home Etc.   (800) 362-8415

The Company Store   (800) 356-9367
(down specialty)

Also See

Under San Francisco's Factory Outlets and Off-Price Stores:
Esprit Factory Outlet

Under General Clothing:
Burlington Coat Factory; Marshall's; T.J. Maxx

Under Clearance Centers:
Most listings

Under Furniture and Home Accessories—Catalog Discounters, General Furnishings, Clearance Centers:
Most listings

Wallpaper

I'm all for saving money, but if you're going to use a local store's wallpaper books, do the right thing and give it your business. It's very expensive for independent dealers to maintain an inventory of hundreds of wallpaper books for customers. Your local store may indicate when sales are likely to occur, so saving money becomes a matter of timing if you can't use the resources listed below. Also check the listings under Furniture and Home Accessories—Catalog Discounters; General Furnishings; Fabrics; and other cross-references listed below for stores that maintain an extensive selection of wallpaper books, and then sweeten the process with nice discounts.

Elegant Clutter

702 Sycamore Valley Road West, Danville. (510) 837-1001. M–Sat 10–6, Sun Noon–5. MC, VISA, AE. Parking: lot.
Elegant Clutter is very popular in Contra Costa County for its discriminating and tasteful selection of home accessories, giftware, and furnishings sold in an elegant and gracious ambience. I'm only including it here because it offers 25% discounts on Kinney and Waverly wallpapers and fabrics. In terms of wallpaper, you can have both good prices and excellent service. Get on its mailing list for news about its mammoth spring warehouse sale when slightly damaged, discontinued, and excess inventory is sold for 40–75% discounts. Regulars line up early and have been known to prepare with champagne tailgate parties.

The Wallpaper Connection

Crow Canyon Commons, San Ramon. (510) 275-8055.
M-W, Sat 10-6, Th-F 10-7, Sun Noon-5. MC, VISA. Parking: lot.
This charming, cozy, boutiquelike wallpaper and home-decorating store has bins full of wallpaper (many with matching borders) discounted from 25–75% off retail ($10.99–$15.99). After you see these, spend some time leafing through the library of books from companies that read like a Who's Who of wallpaper. You'll save 20–35% on these offerings. Companion fabrics are discounted 15–20% off list. If Waverly is your line, you can also order comforter ensembles, draperies, and window treatments at 20% savings. If you need window coverings, bedding treatments, or a chair reupholstered, take a gander at the fabric swatch books. You'll save a little to a respectable amount depending on what you're ordering. Miniblinds and shades sold as well.

Wallstreet Factory Outlet

2690 Harrison Street (near 23rd Street), San Francisco.
(415) 285-0870. M-F 10-6, Sat 9-5. MC, VISA, AE.
Parking: street.
This is the City's best resource for wallpaper at bargain prices. In the front are about 1,000 current wallpaper patterns at 40–50% off retail book price. About 100 of these papers have matching borders and companion fabrics (typically priced at about $12.95/yard). Check the back room for occasional seconds, overruns, mill ends, and discontinued patterns at even greater discounts. Wallstreet stocks 500 wallpaper books for special orders at 25% discount. Its lovely displays and mockups help customers picture the finished room; its emphasis is on coordinating papers, fabrics, and borders. For best results, come with an open mind and prepare to be versatile. You can borrow samples for evaluation. If you start your decorating project with the wallpaper choice first, it's a cinch to coordinate the other elements.

Also See

House & Home

8

Eyewear

Focal Point
*2638 Ashby Avenue (at College), Berkeley. (510) 843-5367.
M–Sat 10–6, Sun Noon–5. MC, VISA. Parking: street.*
Focal Point provides a discriminating selection of unique eyeglass frames to a professional clientele. Many frames are fashion-forward, some are handmade, limited-production styles, while the details on the frames reflect the careful construction by their designers and suppliers. The small back annex offers bargain inventory; prices are reduced 50–90% off original retail. These markdowns are on discontinued styles or special purchases. Prices are $39–$99, most in the $59–$79 range. Good selection for men and women, for regular glasses or sunglasses, but smaller selection for children. Charges for single vision plastic or glass lenses are $69. German Zeiss lenses are standard. It takes three to five days to complete an order. The owner of Focal Point makes a convincing case for his use of superior (and somewhat costlier) lens products and he extols the quality of his service (optical grinding). He maintains that one-hour service is incompatible with a high standard of quality in filling prescriptions. I leave it to you to make your own determination.

The Optical Outlet

951 Market Street (bet. Fifth and Sixth Streets), San Francisco.
(415) 982-5106. M–Sat 9–5:30. MC, VISA, AE.
Parking: pay garages.

Designers supply The Optical Outlet with overstocks, discontinued styles, and samples at a deep discount, which the store passes on to its customers. Frames are priced about 40–60% off original retail. I spotted frames from Giorgio Armani, Beau Monde, Guess?, Polo-Ralph Lauren, Brendel, Kata, Alain Mikli, Cristian LaCroix, LA Eyeworks, Paul Stig, and others. Women and men get an equal share of bargains, with a smaller array for children with frames from Disney, Peanuts, and others. And you don't have to lose in the cost of lenses what you save in frames. As far as I've been able to determine, lens prices here are competitive with well-known Bay Area value-priced eyecare companies. All products are warranted against defects in manufacture, and the accuracy of prescriptions is guaranteed. Payment in full is required with each order (which takes about a week), or add $15 for same-day service.

Flea Markets

Attending flea markets has become a national weekend pastime. On any leisurely Saturday or Sunday, many families leave their all-too-peaceful homes to enjoy the harried, tumultuous bargaining and selling at a nearby swap meet or flea market. Here are some of the better-known markets in the area, held regularly throughout the year. Other markets occur on some other basis, maybe monthly or annually, and can be fantastic sources of bargains because they aren't as well attended as the listed ones. Check your local paper for notices of these events. Best bets: At either end of the Bay, the San Jose and Marin City Flea Markets maintain a reputation for the most reliable selection of everything from A to Z. Marin and the Foothill flea markets are distinguished by the number of artists and artisans who regularly offer some very original wares.

Berkeley Flea Market
Ashby BART Station Parking Lot (Adeline and Ashby), Berkeley.
(510) 644-0744. Sat–Sun 8–7. Parking: free. Admission: free.

Capitol Flea Market
3630 Hillcap Avenue (Capitol Drive-In), San Jose.
(408) 225-5800. Th 7–5:30, Sat–Sun 8–7.
Admission: $1 as walk-in, $2 per car.

De Anza College Flea Market
21250 Stevens Creek Boulevard, Cupertino. (408) 864-8946.
First Sat every month 8–4. Admission: free. Located in campus parking lots B and C; over 850 vendors. Parking: $2.

Foothill College Flea Market
12345 El Monte Road (corner Freeway 280), Los Altos Hills.
(415) 948-6417. Third Sat every month 8–3. Parking: $1.
Admission: free.
Good for antiques and collectibles, art, fine arts, floral
arrangements, books, jewelry, household stuff, etc.

Geneva Swap Market
Geneva Drive-In, 607 Carter (behind Cow Palace), Daly City.
(415) 587-0515. Sat–Sun 7–4. Parking: free. Admission: Sat 25¢,
Sun 75¢ per person.

Marin City Flea Market
Donahue & Drake (off 101, Marin City/Sausalito Exit), Marin
City. (415) 332-1441. Sat 6–4, Sun 5–4. Cash/Check. Parking:
lot, $2 charge. Admission: free.
Regular vendors sell prints, posters, T-shirts, antiques, handi-
crafts, ethnic arts, and sundry items. Note: A relocation of the
flea market in 1995 may occur due to redevelopment.

Midgley's Country Flea Market
2200 Gravenstein Highway South (off 101, west to Sebastopol
5 miles), Sebastopol. (707) 823-7874, (800) 800-FLEA.
Sat–Sun 6:30–4:30. Cash only. Parking: free.

Napa–Vallejo Flea Market and Auction
303 Kelly Road (off Highway 29, halfway between Napa and
Vallejo), Napa. (707) 226-8862. Sun 6–5. Parking: $2.
Admission: free.

San Jose Flea Market
1590 Berryessa Road, San Jose. (408) 453-1110.
W–Sun dawn to dusk. Cash Only. Parking: pay lot.
Admission: free.
The largest flea market in the United States, with the largest
number of regular vendors, offering a smattering of every
thing from clothes to furniture. Plants, pottery, toys, flowers,
T-shirts, and children's apparel are very popular.

Solano Drive-in Flea Market
Solano Way and Highway 4, Concord. (510) 687-6445.
Sat–Sun 7–4. Admission: Sat 25¢, Sun $1. Parking: free.

General Merchandise

Discount Stores

You don't always have to drive miles out of your way to go bargain hunting. Throughout the Bay Area, discount stores like Target, Wal-Mart, PayLess, K-Mart, and Pay 'N Save do a respectable job at pricing merchandise lower than full-service retail stores. Companies like Best Products and Service Merchandise advertise frequently, have many locations in the area, and consistently offer excellent values. They're good for all types of merchandise, particularly housewares, giftware, consumer electronics, jewelry, toys, and sporting goods. They cover almost every area except major home furnishings, apparel, and larger appliances. They are very competitive with each other, so comparative shopping pays off if you take the time to check catalogs before you buy.

Liquidators

Small liquidators abound all around the Bay Area, selling novelties, food items, health products, paper and party supplies, household goods, baskets, toys, whatever. In any case, it's hardly worth the time and expense of driving out of your way to shop at any one. Often they're named things like $1.99, Everything's a Buck, or my favorite, the 98 Cents Clearance Center Stores. Some stay strictly within the bounds set by their names; others have prices much higher than the names would suggest. By all means, cruise through the aisles of these stores if it's convenient. You may find some real deals, but sometimes you'll leave thinking it's all a bunch of junk.

MacFrugal's

200 Serra Way, Milpitas. (408) 946-9605.
M–Sat 9–9, Sun 10–7. MC, VISA. Parking: lot.
(Other stores: fourteen Bay Area locations,
check Geographical Index.)
MacFrugal's is strictly bargain basement. It buys carloads of closeout merchandise and sells at deeply discounted prices (40–70%). Goods include such diverse items as candles, linens, toys, books, houseware, giftware, and clothing. A great selection of Christmas ornaments and goodies is stocked every year.

Robert's Warehouse

430 Glacier Drive, Martinez. (510) 229-5540.
Members only: M–F 9–6, Sat 9–5, Sun 10–5.
Public one weekend each month Sat–Sun 9–5.
MC, VISA, DIS. Parking: lot.
Robert's Warehouse wholesales showroom and sales samples, manufacturers' overstocks, liquidations, and bankrupt inventories of new merchandise. The public is invited to shop one weekend a month; at that time you can buy for the same wholesale prices that dealers pay. Although you can never predict exactly what you'll find, you can expect candy, kitchen gadgets, silk flowers, used videos ($1–$20), stuffed animals, toys, books, wicker furniture, jewelry, stationery, houseware, bathware, figurines, music boxes, prints, crystal, and gifts for everyone. You'll save 50–75% off retail. To become a member, which allows you to shop weekdays, show your Price/Costco card.

Membership Warehouse Clubs

Almost everyone has a cluster of cards in their wallets, but probably none is more valued than a membership card to Price/Costco or Sam's Club. People in all economic and social levels consider themselves privileged to qualify for membership. By now thousands of Bay Area consumers have discovered the delights—and the hazards—of shopping at a warehouse club. Nearly everyone has a tale to tell along the lines of "I just went in to buy toilet paper and bought toilet paper and a new TV" or "Every time I shop, I end up spending an extra $100 to $200 on completely unplanned purchases." It's hard to resist the prices and the tempting selection of new items. "Grazing" down the aisles tasting vendors' new products guarantees that you'll leave with a full stomach and basket. Each club provides an extensive variety of consumer goods (electronics, computers, apparel, books, food, beauty, tires, housewares, giftware, fine jewelry, watches, tools, etc.) and office and institutional products, but don't expect an in-depth selection of anything. Each company makes buys at prices that allow it to undersell the competition. Trade-off: Many items are sold in extralarge quantities or packaged as multiples—a disadvantage for some individuals or small families. Surprisingly, the clubs manage to capture a fair amount of "high-demand" merchandise. At times, I've spotted Reebok, Adidas, and Nike athletic shoes, Liz Claiborne handbags, Guess? jeans, Rolex watches, Cross or Mont Blanc pens, Waterford crystal, and other items from consumers' "most wanted" lists. Each club continues to innovate and expand its offerings. Call for membership requirements. See Geographical Index for the Price/Costco or Sam's Club locations near you.

Special Sales and Events

A.S.I.D. Designers Sale

The Galleria, 101 Henry Adams, and The Showplace, 2 Henry Adams, San Francisco. (415) 626-2743. Sale dates in Jun and Nov advertised in major Bay Area newspapers. Sale hours: 10-4. MC, VISA. Parking: pay lots. Admission: $5.

Every year, A.S.I.D. (American Society of Interior Designers), sponsors two sales (in June and November) to benefit its educational fund. These sales are an opportunity to buy fine-quality, high-end furnishings at 40–70% off showroom list prices. Some designs appear to come right off the pages of *Architectural Digest* and others are comfortably familiar. If you're shopping for elegant pine armoires, chinoiserie, tansu, antique reproductions, lamps, framed prints or original art-works, wicker furniture, Oriental rugs, chairs, sofas, dining furniture, tables and occasional pieces, leftover fabrics, or just about any other home furnishing, you can anticipate tempt-ing items at these sales. Some are slightly damaged, but they're the exception. Many lines are not displayed through retail furniture stores, which makes the opportunity to see and buy the samples and rejects particularly appealing. A.S.I.D. members staff the sale and charge $5 admission to cover their costs. It's advisable to bring carpet, paint, and fabric samples for match-ing. Delivery arrangements can be made. Watch for announce-ments in local newspapers for these sales. The lines that start by 9 a.m. on Saturday are followed by a real crush during the first hours of the sale. Come Sunday for more elbow room and last-chance markdowns.

American Industrial Center Sale

2325 Third Street (bet. 20th and 22nd streets), San Francisco.
Sale info: (415) 621-1920. One-day Sat sale in Dec, 9–4.
Cash/Check. Parking: street.

Every year this cavernous industrial building, the American
Industrial Center, opens its doors to the public for a most
unusual sale opportunity. It's the place to go if you want to
scope out some unique bargains. Plan to spend a few hours
walking the halls, keeping your eyes posted for balloons, sandwich boards, and signs to lead you to the sale participants.
Each year the traffic increases as word spreads that this is the
only opportunity one has to buy certain very upscale merchandise. Because of market sensitivity, I can't mention companies
by name, but I can give a few clues to the types of merchandise
that you can find. For starters: an expensive line of handknit
sweaters for women and men; several fashion jewelry manufacturers (lines that sell under the glass at posh stores); home
accessories, including many sold through national catalogs
and at chic and trendy special boutiques locally; bath and body
products (many in elegant packaging); fashion hats; and
several charming lines of children's apparel. It's a different
environment, yet rest assured that security guards are on hand
to insure your comfort and safety. The sale is usually held on
the first or second Saturday in December. Sign up on someone's
mailing list so that you'll get sale announcements for future
sales. I'd start at the 2325 entry on Third Street (corner of 20th).
Look for sale flyers that identify the participants and spaces
where the doors will be open for your shopping adventures.

Concourse Sample Sales

The Concourse, between Seventh and Eighth streets, Brannan
and Townsend, San Francisco. Info: (415) 864-1500. Sat–Sun
Thanksgiving weekend; one Sat in May. Cash preferred/Checks
okay with many participants. Parking: pay lots. Admission $3.

Tenants of the Gift Center and Fashion Center, and many
importers, distributors, manufacturers, and designers rent booth
space at the Concourse for these mammoth events. Some
participants never show up anyplace else to sell their samples,
overruns, or leftovers. Each sale is frenzied from the moment
the doors open. The inducement for consumers? Wonderful
prices, usually 50% off original retail. Categories of merchandise: apparel for the whole family; body, bath, and beauty
products; baskets; giftware; silk plants; fashion jewelry; leather

goods; household goods; stationery; holiday decorations; home accessories; and more. Watch the *Chronicle* and *Examiner* for sale announcements and clip the $1-off coupon for admission.

Emeryville Stroll

Free stroll maps available at Doyle Street Cafe,
5515 Doyle Street (off Powell), Emeryville.
Stroll starts Thanksgiving weekend and continues
through first two weekends of Dec. Sat–Sun 10–5.

The Emeryville Stroll showcases the many designers, wholesalers, manufacturers, artisans, etc. who have facilities or studios in the area. The mix is unusual and eclectic. After picking up a map, you'll need your car to navigate the area. You may find sophisticated and contemporary men's ties; fine art glass (very fine vases, paperweights, bowls, etc.); wonderful hand puppets and stuffed animals; fun-themed string lights and night lights; contemporary glass oil-burning lamps; table linens; women's artwear and accessories; silk sachets, pillows, ribbons, and handcrafted personal accessories; fine-quality fashion jewelry, notecards, and handcrafted gifts; and assorted other gift-appropriate merchandise. Altogether, twenty-five to thirty-six individual companies open their doors for this popular event. Directions: Take the Powell Exit east from 80 to start the stroll. Parking is readily available throughout the area.

Fashion Center Sample Sales

699 Eighth Street (bet. Townsend and Brannan), San Francisco.
(800) STYLESF. Quarterly Fri and Sat sales. Cash preferred.
Parking: pay lots. Admission: $3.

Four or five times a year, usually in March, July, September, and November, the Fashion Center building "goes public." Over 300 sales reps have showrooms there and present more than 6,000 lines of apparel and accessories. On sale days (occasionally some Fridays, too), the reps set up booths in Exhibition Hall (lower level) to sell samples at wholesale prices to the public. Often reps have complete size ranges, since the companies they represent give them access to the entire line and size spectrum. By far the biggest selection is in women's apparel in all categories. Women who find limited choices in sample sizes can zero in on handbags, scarves, belts, and jewelry. Men's clothing includes a little of everything, from suspenders to bathrobes, and children's has overalls to precious party dresses. Dressing rooms are available on each aisle; selected booths have private dressing rooms. Plan ahead; most reps prefer cash, but many will accept checks with proper I.D. Because of safety and security considerations, strollers are not allowed. For free entry to five sales, early entry to Friday sales, buy a $12 Sample Sale Express Card. Don't worry about missing sale announcements usually placed in the fashion section of the Tuesday *Chronicle*; send your mailing list request to "Sample Sales," Fashion Center of San Francisco, 699 Eighth Street, Suite 2206, San Francisco 94103.

Firelight Glass Seconds Sale

1000 42nd Street, Emeryville. (510) 652-6731.
Daily 11–5 (Fri after Thanksgiving until Dec 23). MC, VISA.
Parking: lot on side of building.

Firelight Glass puts on a glow every year. The warehouse is always well stocked with tables of contemporary, clear-glass, oil-burning candles. It's a breathtaking display! I'd have to describe the quality-control inspectors at Firelight Glass as "picky, picky, picky" since I can't spot the flaws that make up the seconds sold at this annual factory sale. As seconds the candles are priced at 30–40% off (most at 40%), from $8 to $40. Many styles are offered in graduated sizes. Pick up just one, or a trio for a more dramatic display. I find these to be wonderful all-purpose gifts, and, generally speaking, they're appealing to almost everyone. Buy some just to tuck away for a "little gift" for some person or occasion later in the year. Go all the way and buy a small or large bottle of clean-burning Firelight lamp oil. The candles in cylinders, rounds, triangles, prisms, squares, cubes, obelisks, and other artful shapes come with a lifetime Fiberglas wick. Some candles are sold as sets with incentive pricing (usually three candles in graduated sizes), although these candles can be purchased individually. Whatever you buy, you'll appreciate the careful packing and boxing done at the counter. Add wrap and ribbon, and your gift is ready to go. Note: These boxes will not withstand the stress of shipping or mailing. Directions: Traveling north or south on San Pablo Avenue, turn east on 43rd Street. Go to Adeline, turn right, then turn left on 42nd Street. This company is located south of Powell Street off 80.

Furniture Mart Sample Sales

1355 Market Street (at Tenth Street), San Francisco.
Info: (415) 552-2311. One-day Sat sale dates
announced in May and Nov, 9–5. MC, VISA, AE.
Parking: pay garage off Market. Admission: $5.

It's hard to get past the desk and into the showrooms at San Francisco's Furniture Mart, but the doors open wide to the public during Sample Sales twice a year. The Mart has over 300 showrooms in two buildings (one ten-story, one eleven-story). The Mart reflects the entire spectrum of home furnishings and accessories—from tacky to terrific, from budget to best. Approximately sixty-five showrooms participate in each sale. Prices are close to wholesale, possibly less on some items. Expect to find a little of every category: area rugs, upholstered furniture, case goods (dining, bedroom, occasional tables), lamps, lighting, pictures, mirrors and great home accessories! Delivery service is available at extra cost. Watch the *Chronicle* and *Examiner* for sale announcements, or call to have your name put on the mailing list for sale notification.

Giftcenter Sample Sales

888 Brannan Street, San Francisco. (415) 864-SALE.
Dates: Sat sales in early Nov; usually in May
before Mother's Day. Admission: $3.

Tenants of the Giftcenter combine with other manufacturers' reps, importers, and distributors to present a tantalizing shopping excursion. Booths and tables are set up on four levels of the Giftcenter; you won't want to leave until you've canvassed each floor. Fashion jewelry, giftware, housewares, linens, bath and body products, kitchen items, novelties, picture frames, and gifts for any occasion are on display. Check the Pink Section of the Sunday *Chronicle/Examiner* for sale announcements and $1-off coupon for admission.

Kids' Benefit Sale

Sale site in San Francisco. Weekend in Nov.

The members of S.F. Childrenswear (a manufacturers' group) combine forces each November in a huge sale to benefit children's charities. The site of each sale changes, since the members rely on donated space for the event. If you're on the mailing lists of many children's outlets, you may get a sale announcement. Typically fifteen to twenty vendors participate; this is a wonderful opportunity to shop many manufacturers at once. Each company trims prices to the bone in keeping with the goals and spirit of the sale. Moms return each year to buy apparel for their children in sizes ranging from newborn to Girls 14. Check November issues of *Parents' Press* or *Peninsula Parent* for sale information, or write to In Cahoots, 5214-B Diamond Heights Boulevard, San Francisco, CA 94131, ATTN: Kids' Benefit Sale.

Nomadic Traders Warehouse Sale

1385 Ninth Street, Berkeley. (510) 525-5854. Daily 10–6,
Fri after Thanksgiving until Dec 31 (closed Christmas).
MC, VISA. Parking: street.

The focus at this sale event every year is on sweaters for the sporting crowd and their cold-weather activities. Sweaters are made and imported from Uruguay, Peru, China, Nepal, and other foreign locals. Original knits in natural fibers translate ethnic traditions into contemporary designs. Look for great colors (and neutrals); interesting designs and patterns; and light, medium, and heavyweight versions in many handknit and handloomed primarily unisex styles. Pick a cardigan, pullover, or vest. Sold through stores that cater to the outdoor industry, discounts at the sale are 25–60% off retail on current and past-season styles. Its new "fashion" sweaters in chenille, patchwork, and embroidered designs for women are very nice. Pick up a pair of warm socks, knit cap or hat, mittens, scarf, or blanket—other items imported by the company. In the past few years, the company has developed a tempting line of sports-wear, related separates and dresses for women (shirts for men). Made in Bali, the look is familiar—loose, unstructured, over-sized, and contemporary. Wonderful rayon fabrics, colors, and prints are discounted 30–60% off.

San Francisco Bay Area Book Festival

Concourse Exhibition Center, Eighth and Brannan streets,
San Francisco. (415) 861-2665. First Sat–Sun in Nov, 10–6.
Admission: adults $2/day, children 12 and under free.
Parking: street or pay lots.

The small press revolution started in the Bay Area. That's evident when you peruse the booths at the Book Festival, where these small presses showcase the fruits of their labors. Book lovers appreciate the opportunity to see many books that they may overlook when browsing through local bookstores. Mainstream publishers participate as well. Bargain hunters can fill their book bags with good deals, as most participants offer modest to maximum discounts on many of the titles in their inventory. Books range the spectrum of topics from A to Z (children's books included). Authors' readings and appearances combined with book-related events contribute to the appeal of this event.

Sporting Goods

Bent Spoke

6124 Telegraph Avenue, Oakland. (510) 652-3089.
T–F 11–6, Sat 11–5. MC, VISA, DIS. Parking: street.
The owners travel the state buying used bikes from various law enforcement auctions. That must account for the wide variety of "wheels"—with little pink girls' bikes, tricycles, 3-wheel bikes, mountain, hybrid, and road bikes filling up all the space in this store. Some bikes look like they've spent time languishing outdoors at the mercy of the elements, while others are like-new and spiffy. Prices start at $19 for kid's bikes, about $30 for adults. Bikes are reconditioned, and better bikes have a limited warranty. Budget-priced mass-market bikes (those sold at K-Mart, Toys 'R' Us, and other big chain stores or warehouse clubs) are not warrantied. Look around for special deals on new closeout models from manufacturers like Cignal, Jamis, Bianchi, Norco, and Nishiki. Bikes can be placed on consignment, but no bikes are bought directly from consumers. Good resource for families!

Demo Ski

509-B E. Francisco Boulevard, San Rafael. (415) 454-3500.
M–Sat 10–6, Th–F until 8, Sun 10–5. MC, VISA. Parking: lot.
Demo Ski rents and sells top-of-the-line skis, ski equipment, and snowboards for discount prices. Customers have the opportunity to try before they buy. During the summer it switches gears to sell in-line skates, water skis, and tennis rackets. Major brands include Burton, Rollerblade, Salomon, Nordica, H.O., and Wilson. When you're ready to buy, you'll save about

20–30% off on water skis and boards, vests, and accessories; 20–30% off tennis rackets (plan on $20 extra for professional stringing); 20–50% off snow skis and boots. Snowboards, in-line skates, and accessories are always 10–15% off. Demo Ski also offers 15–20% discounts on quality sunglasses from Vuarnet, Ray-Ban, Revo, Serengeti, Oakley, and Suncloud.

Fry's Warehouse Sports

164 Marco Way, South San Francisco. (415) 583-5034.
M-F 9:30-6, Sat-Sun 10-5. MC, VISA. Parking: street.
(Other stores: 4040 Pimlico Drive, Pleasanton;
1495 E. Francisco Boulevard, San Rafael.)
For golf or tennis, Fry's offers value, selection, and discounts on better pro shop lines of shoes, clothing, and equipment. Slip into shoes from Nike, Adidas, Wilson, K-Swiss, Foot-Joy, Reebok, or Dexter. Also, equipment from Wilson, Lynx, Power Bilt, Ping, Dunlop, Spalding, Hogan, MacGregor, Mizuno, Titleist, Cobra, Ram, Callaway, Daiwa, Cleveland, Yonex, and Taylor Made. These are not seconds or closeouts. While a discount operation, it provides tennis racket stringing and free club fitting with its golf swing computer.

Gus' Discount Fishing Equipment

3710 Balboa Street (bet. 38th and 39th), San Francisco.
(415) 752-6197. M-Sat 8-5. MC, VISA. Parking: street.
If words like "crocodile," "pencil popper," or "super duper" mean anything to you, read on. Gus' Discount Fishing Equipment is an experience! The prices entice regulars to stop in almost daily on their way to the water to see what's new. Serving as a West Coast wholesale distributor for Master, Ryobi, and Abu Garcia, Gus' also buys factory overruns, salvage losses, and inventory from liquidations. Everything is discounted 25–60% off original retail. You'll find equipment for salmon, trout, freshwater, saltwater, and surf fishing. The terminal tackle selection deserves careful scrutiny. Check the lures from Luhr Jensen, Bass Buster, Hopkins, Diamond Gigs, and Panther Martin. All rods and reels are guaranteed.

Karim Cycle

2801 Telegraph Avenue, Berkeley. (510) 841-2181.
M–Sat 11–6. (Selected Suns Noon–5). MC, VISA, ATM.
Parking: street.

This company's location close to the Cal campus is a definite
advantage. Students come in when the semester begins to buy
a bike and often return at the end of the year to sell it back
to Karim. The company is careful to protect the integrity of its
business. The seller's personal identification is required for
all transactions, and Karim clears all bike registrations with local
police departments. The selection covers bikes of all descriptions: mountain, road, and hybrids, 3-speeds, plus a few
children's and tandem bikes are usually in stock. Prices are set
according to condition and usually offer 40–60% savings
off original retail. Karim usually has a recent inventory print-
out with descriptions and prices of better bikes. In the $500-
plus range you might find Medici, Davidson Impulse, Puch
Mistral, Guerciotti, Bottecchia, and Tommansini. At $200–$300
you might buy a Raleigh Super Course or Competition, Nishiki
Prestige, Fuji Palisade, Univega Gran Sprint, or Centurion.
Mountain bikes start at $99. Before putting the used bikes
out for sale, each is reconditioned and further supported
by a thirty-day free service policy for any adjustments. Karim
also sells new bikes and always has several deeply discounted
closeout models in stock from well-known manufacturers.
Finally, you can often trade in your old bike on a new and
better model. Located three blocks north of Ashby at Stuart.

Las Vegas Discount Golf & Tennis

38 E. Fourth Avenue, San Mateo. (415) 347-6200.
M–Sat 10–5. MC, VISA, AE. Parking: pay lots.
(Other stores: Fairfield; San Ramon.)

Consumers can do armchair comparison shopping by checking
Fry's, Nevada Bob's, and Las Vegas ads to see which place is
offering the best deals. Las Vegas sells major brand-name gear
for golf and tennis. Golfers will find Ping, Powerbilt, Lynx,
Titleist, Hogan, MacGregor, Daiwa, Spalding, Mizuno, Yamaha,
Palmer, and Taylor Made among others. For tennis there's
Prince, Wilson, Yonex, Pro Kennex, Kneissl, Rossignol, and
Dunlop. Everything is discounted at least 20% and can be far
greater, depending on special buys. No extra charge for cus-
tom golf and tennis repair to handle any alterations.

Missing Link Annex

1988 Shattuck Avenue, Berkeley. (510) 843-4763. M–F
10:30–6:30, Sat 10–6, Sun Noon–5. MC, VISA. Parking: street.
The annex to Missing Link's popular retail store is where the
company keeps its rental bikes, trade-ins, and used bikes. If
the descriptive tags on each used bike are any indication, the
staff definitely has a sense of humor. Depending on the time
of the year, you'll find ten to thirty used bikes ranging in price
from $60 to $1,300 (about a 50% discount from original
retail). Occasional bike riders and very serious cyclists can find
road, mountain, or hybrids. Each bike is completely reconditioned and many come with a ninety-day warranty (a few are
sold as-is).

Nevada Bob's Discount Golf

1500 Monument Boulevard, Concord. (510) 680-0111.
M–F 10–7, Sat 9:30–6, Sun 10–5. MC, VISA, AE, DIS. Parking: lot.
(Other stores: Belmont; Fremont; Modesto; Rohnert Park;
Sacramento; San Jose; San Leandro; Stockton.)
With more than 300 franchise stores, Nevada Bob's has considerable volume purchasing power. It will also beat any
"verifiable" price on current pro line equipment. Each store's
experienced, professional staff ensures that customers are fitted
for their build and ability. Along with balls, bags, carts, accessories, and "extras," shoes at 30–50% discounts deserve your
attention. Give the apparel racks the once-over and you're sure
to end up looking like a golf pro at nicely discounted prices.

North Face Factory Outlet

1238 Fifth Street, Berkeley. (510) 526-3530.
M–Sat 10–6, Sun 11–5 (extended holiday hours).
MC, VISA. Parking: street.
(Other store: 1325 Howard, San Francisco.)
The North Face manufactures high-quality outdoor equipment
and colorful, long-lasting sportswear. Prices start at 20% off
retail and dive from there. These price reductions are applied
to seconds, overruns, discontinued items, and special make-
ups for its factory stores. Casual tops, pants, shirts, sweaters,
et al. for men and women (some unisex) can be classic or
colorful. You'll find Goretex and other high-tech fabrics in its
outdoor clothing, rainwear, and skiwear. North Face backpacks,
sleeping bags, fanny packs, tents, and duffels are always in
good supply and reduced 20–40% off. You'll even find hiking

boots, cross-country skis, and boots discounted. Soft luggage, carry-ons, and business cases made from sturdy cordura nylon are appropriate for both a Manhattan boardroom and a Jumla yak caravan. Get on the mailing list for its biggest sales, usually in May and November.

Play It Again Sports

1200 Contra Costa Boulevard, Concord. (510) 825-3396.
M–F 10–7, Sat 10–6, Sun 11–5. MC, VISA. Parking: lot.
(Other Stores: fourteen in Bay Area, see Geographical Index.)
At Play It Again Sports, most of what is sold is used; each Bay Area store may have a different mix of merchandise. Prices on used goods are discounted about 50% off original retail. You can buy, sell, trade, or consign equipment for football and soccer (including shoes), roller skates/blades, golf, exercise equipment and weights, water skis, street hockey, downhill/cross country and water skis, baseball/softball and racquet sports. No weapons or bowling balls. The store is geared mainly to weekend athletes and beginners (children or adults) rather than the serious sportsperson. Brands would be midpriced if sold new. The stores carry some new merchandise and samples. I suggest that hard-pressed parents give this outfit the once-over. And call before coming in, especially if you're bringing something to sell or consign. The staff keeps a list of special requests and will notify you when or if the merchandise comes in.

Safari Sport Zone

1410 Park Street, Alameda. (510) 522-1723.
M–Sat 10–6, Sun 11–5. Cash/Check. Parking: street.
Don't let your children's sports equipment gather dust. Scoop up all that old stuff and bring it in to sell or trade for store merchandise. Or, save a little and buy used soccer balls or basketballs, hockey or baseball equipment, bikes, skates, skateboards, video or board games. Your credits can also be used at Toy Safari (just a block away—see Toys).

Sportmart

1933 Davis Street (Westgate Center), San Leandro.
(510) 632-6100. M–Sat 9:30 a.m.–9:30 p.m., Sun 10–7.
MC, VISA, DIS. Parking: lot.
(Other stores: Concord; Daly City; Emeryville; Milpitas;
Sacramento/Roseville; San Jose; Sunnyvale; Vacaville.)
Wow! These stores offer a great selection in bikes ($60–$400),
skiing, bowling, tennis, golf, water sports (skis, buggie boards),
fishing equipment, and camping, plus sports and workout
apparel, shoes for every sporting activity for the whole family,
and exercise equipment. You'll find brand names, a wide range
of prices representing budget to best in the lines carried, and
an in-depth selection that far surpasses almost all its competitors. Each category is well supported with an endless array
of accessory items. My comparisons show that Sportmart trims
prices to beat the competition from a little to a lot every day.
Competitors' loss leaders may undersell it on occasion, but its
price guarantee takes care of this. Very accommodating return
and refund policy.

Wilderness Exchange

1407 San Pablo Avenue, Berkeley. (510) 525-1255.
Sun–W 11–6, Th–F 11–8, Sat 10–6. MC, VISA. Parking: street.
Wilderness Exchange serves backpackers, climbers, moun-
taineers, campers, and cross-country skiers. It sells closeouts,
sales rep's samples, blems, and overstock from over thirty
outdoor companies at discounts of 15–40% off retail. Another
angle: About 20% of the inventory is used (high-quality,
cleaned and reconditioned if needed), most often sold for at
least 50% off original retail. Buy, sell, or trade your way to
good deals. Call to inquire about availability of any specific
item or brand of equipment you have in mind.

About Bikes—Strategies for Buying New Bikes

Once you understand how distribution works, you'll see why
it's very difficult to select any particular bike retailer as a
source of bargains. Bike manufacturers protect their markets
by creating a carefully balanced network of dealers, insuring
that each store is able to serve a particular market area profit-
ably. To that end, manufacturers "suggest" a minimum selling
price for the dealers. In the Bay Area, it appears that most

dealers sell bikes at the "minimum suggested price." Therefore, the market is very competitive, with no one dealer offering substantially lower everyday prices. Of course, each store holds a few sales during the year, but if a dealer holds too many, or attempts to lower prices too much, other dealers complain to the manufacturer and the offender is in jeopardy of losing the line. So everyone plays along. Since the Bay Area is considered a year-round market, you don't have the predictable end-of-season blowout sales prevalent in ski equipment. Also, since the bikes are expensive, dealers control their inventory so that they can offer a good selection without becoming overstocked. If you're buying a better bike for off-road or heavy street use, you'll want to spend at least $300 to get reliable components. Each step up—to $500, $700, or higher—buys you better braking, shifting, frame materials, etc. Choosing which brand to buy is a very subjective decision. If you're in a good shop, the staff will spend time determining your anticipated use, where you'll be using the bike, perhaps even what trails you plan to ride on, and then you'll need to try several bikes to see how they handle. To buy at a bargain, first spend time evaluating the various models, make your decision, and then watch for a sale. Another option: cycling or bike publications for mail-order companies. Many have discounted prices, but you'll have to forego after-purchase service and support, something you may regret.

If you're not interested in the better bikes, you won't have any problems finding bikes in the $100–$300 range. Sportmart, Wal-Mart, Toys 'R' Us, K-Mart, Price/Costco, Sears, Play It Again Sports (used), and others are likely resources. Don't overlook classified ads or sheriff's department or police auctions. Refer to listings in this section that profile the best sources for used bikes—a good alternative when money's tight and for many out-of-state students who need a bike just for the school year.

Also See

Under Active Sportswear:
Mont–Bell Company Store; Sierra Designs

Under General Merchandise:
All sections

Toys

Applause Factory Store
Factory Stores of America, Vacaville. (707) 451-4677. Daily.
MC, VISA. Parking: lot.
The Applause Outlet is brimming with adorables! Soft, cuddly
stuffed animals; several types of dolls; fabric-covered stuffed
prehistoric animals; collectibles from Precious Moments; teddy
bears including those from Raike; and charming Applause
ceramics. Discounts on discontinued merchandise are 20–40%;
two-for-one offers bring prices down to irresistible levels. This
is a great resource for sentimental bargains!

Basic Brown Bear Factory
444 De Haro Street (off 17th Street), San Francisco.
(415) 626-0781. M–Sat 10–5, Sun Noon–5. MC, VISA, AE.
Parking: street.
Basic Brown Bear's line is known for the quality of its plush
fabrics and the appealing personalities of its critters. Here
you'll find B.B. Bear, Beary God-Mother, and FOBs (friends of
bears) like Chocolate Moose and Mother Goose. Prices range
from $5 to $250 (a gigantic, fully jointed grizzly bear with
leather paws), but the median price is $25–$30. You may want
to return with your children at another time for a captivating
tour and demonstration of bear-making. Call for tour information for individuals or groups. Lots of fun!

Doll Factory Outlet

2150 John Glenn Drive, Concord. (510) 685-6787.
M–F 9–5 (occasional Sats). MC, VISA (over $50). Parking: lot.
This company is a major importer of collectible porcelain dolls, clowns, and Pierrots, water balls, and other gift items. The outlet is spartan, yet it's filled with discontinued, damaged, or sample dolls. Most people who buy these dolls are collectors and showcase the dolls in a cabinet. One line of dolls is moderately priced; the other is a charming collection of limited editions. Some dolls may have broken music box components, accounting for their deeply discounted prices. Doll prices range from $10 to $100. The same pricing (40–70% off retail) and descriptions apply to clowns and Pierrots. Most tags note any problems or flaws. You can also buy doll stands, costumes, furniture, and more. Prices range overall from $10 to $100. All sales final.

Folkmanis

1219 Park Avenue, Emeryville. (510) 658-7677. M–F 9:30–4:30.
MC, VISA. Parking: street.
This factory-second store features some of the most creative puppets on the market—weird and wonderful animals from cuddly to creepy. Poor puppets; some are flawed, discontinued, or production samples, but these lovable creations offer hours of entertainment for the child in all of us because of their appealing, lifelike appearance. Scorpions, iguanas, cockroaches, dinosaurs, dragons, elephants, otters, dogs, raccoons, bears, skunks, and more are far superior to the typical puppet; in fact, they look more like stuffed animals. Witches and other extraordinary "folks" are also part of the family. Prices on seconds with minor flaws are about 50% off retail or wholesale prices of $5–$25.

Lakeshore's Learning Materials

1144 Montague Avenue, San Leandro. (510) 483-9750.
M–F 9–5:30, Sat 9–5, Sun Noon–5. MC, VISA, DIS, AE.
Parking: street.
Lakeshore Learning Materials supplies teachers and educators (preschool and elementary grades) and nursery school and day-care operators with educational toys, games, teaching materials, books, play equipment, and more. Parents are free to shop for their children and find bargains in Lakeshore's large clearance center in the back. Stop by for 25–75% savings

on overstocked, discontinued, returned, and slightly damaged items. You'll find a constantly changing selection of toys, teacher aids, and equipment. I noted many books (some teachers' copies with answers), clear plastic boxes for treasures, little nylon backpacks, even classroom tables, large activity carpets, and miscellaneous small toys. Pick up a catalog when you enter the retail showroom, since many catalog items are not displayed.

Sanrio Sampler

Factory Stores of America, Vacaville. (707) 447-3721. Daily. MC, VISA. Parking: lot.

If you've got little girls, chances are you've had to buy Sanrio's popular "Hello Kitty" line of novelties, school supplies, party goods, lunch boxes, stationery products, cosmetic and beauty sets, craft sets, and other goodies. Sanrio Sampler offers 50% savings on many discontinued items. About 40% of the store is discount—it annoys me no end that the rest is at full price. If you stick to the marked-down merchandise you can stock up on birthday party presents that will save you expensive last-minute sorties to local stores.

Toy Go Round

1361 Solano Avenue, Albany. (510) 527-1363. M–Sat 10–5, Sun Noon–5. MC, VISA. Parking: street.

A consignment and resale store that's well stocked with toys, books, records, games, tapes, and even skates for budget-strapped parents. Nice preschool selection of developmental toys and a wall of books priced to gladden the hearts of parents of budding bookworms.

Toy Liquidators/Toys Unlimited

Factory Stores of America, Vacaville. (707) 448-7314. Daily. MC, VISA, DIS. Parking: street.
(Other outlets: Anderson/Redding, Folsom, Gilroy centers.)

Toy Liquidators is one of the country's largest toy firms, selling large quantities of closeout inventory from a wide variety of toymakers, including Mattel, Fisher Price, Hasbro, Tonka, and Playskool. There are typically about 1,300 different toys, dolls, and games in stock at any one time. Stop by for little treasures or big-ticket items. Prices are kept low because there is no advertising of individual brands or stores.

Toy Safari
1330 Park Street, Alameda. (510) 522-0825.
M–Fri 10–6, Sat 10–7, Sun 11–4. Cash/Check. Parking: street.
Teach your children a little about business and commerce. Have them gather up their toys in good condition and bring them in to sell. The owner is obviously a parent of boys, since much of the inventory is geared toward boy stuff. Lots of action figures, Matchbook cars, Nintendo, models, developmental toys for tots, books, and collectibles including Stars Wars.

Also See

Under Recycled Apparel:
General information

Under Stationery and Party Supplies:
All sections

Under Furniture and Home Accessories—Baby and Juvenile:
Baby World

Under General Merchandise:
All sections

Guide to Outlet Centers

Approach shopping at outlet centers with the right expectations and you'll come away satisfied. If you're unrealistic and expect wholesale pricing or 50% discounts everywhere you shop, then you'll wonder what all the fuss and hype is about. Many stores offer discounts that I can only call modest. When consumers observe that prices are just as good at department store sales, they're often not far off. Yet each manufacturer's store offers far more of its own lines than you'll ever see in any one store, so your choices are much greater. Combined with the overall aspect of value pricing and the concentration of so many attractive factory and off-price stores in one location, it's hard to spend a few hours shopping without leaving with several bags of good buys. Finally, there are usually several exceptional tenants at each center whose discount prices will more than satisfy your thriftiest inclinations.

Unlike conventional malls, outlet malls are usually located away from urban areas to avoid placing manufacturers in competition with retail stores that sell their products. Many manufacturers benefit greatly from their outlet stores. They can make more money selling their merchandise directly to the public than selling it to an off-price retailer or discount store. As department stores have moved heavily into developing their own private-label lines and direct-import programs, many manufacturers have been propelled into the outlet business to maintain their profits and production. Outlet centers have popped up all over Northern California. These are typically destination centers—at a comfortable distance from the major retail stores and shopping malls in the Bay Area, but close enough for a day's outing of shopping thrills, savings, and fun!

For a complete profile of the outlet stores found in the centers closest to the Bay Area (and in most outlet centers around the country), refer to the individual listings under the appropriate category.

Handy hint

For a comprehensive listing of outlet centers across the country, I enthusiastically recommend the *Joy of Outlet Shopping.* This magazine-sized directory is published by *Value Retail News,* the highly regarded industry trade publication on outlet development around the country. The directory includes a state-by-state listing of more than 350 outlet centers; handy cross-reference guides so that you can match stores and brands to particular centers; directions; tourist attractions in the area; national and regional maps; money-saving coupons; and helpful hints and tips. Price: $6.95. Phone orders: (800) 344-6397 for MC, VISA. Send checks or money orders to: Joy, P.O. Box 17129, Clearwater, FL 34622-0129.

For a listing of stores in each center, see Geographical Index.

Anderson/Shasta
Shasta Factory Outlets
1981 State Highway 273, Anderson. (916) 378-1000.
M–Sat 9:30–8, Sun 11–6; winter M–Sat 9:30–6, Sun 11–6.
Parking: lot.
A good stopover on your way north on I-5. Closest Polo/Ralph Lauren Factory Store. Directions: 8 miles south of Redding. 5 North: Anderson-Deschutes Road Exit; 5 South: Deschutes Road Exit.

Folsom
Folsom Factory Outlets (formerly Natoma Station)
1300 Folsom Boulevard, Folsom. (916) 985-0312.
M–Sat 10–8, Sun 10–6. Parking: lot.
Charming and appealing villagelike complex and a convenient detour for Tahoe travelers. More than fifty stores. Directions from Bay Area: 80 to Highway 50 to Folsom Boulevard Exit, turn left.

Gilroy
Outlets at Gilroy
8300 Arroyo Center, Gilroy. (408) 842-3729.
M–F 10–9, Sat 9–9, Sun 10–6. Parking: lot.
Located across the street from Pacific West Outlet Center. Provides shoppers with seventy-five more stores to visit. The stars: Ann Taylor, J. Crew, Lenox, Laura Ashley, and Kenneth Cole. Directions: From 101 South, take the Leavesley Exit left.

Pacific West Outlet Center
8375 Arroyo Center, Gilroy. (408) 847-4155.
M–F 10–9, Sat 9–9, Sun 10–6. Parking: lot.
Noted for its upscale apparel tenants. Located at 101/Leavesley Road (Highway 152) interchange. Going south, take Leavesley Road Exit, turn left.

Lathrop
Factory Stores of America at Lathrop
16954 S. Harlan Road, Lathrop. (209) 858-1989.
M–Sat 10–8, Sun 10–6. Parking: lot.
Located directly off I-5 (Louise Avenue Exit), fifty miles south of Sacramento, eighty miles east of San Francisco. Twenty-five stores and growing. Convenient for Central Valley shoppers.

Milpitas
Great Mall of the Bay Area
447 Great Mall Drive, Milpitas. (408) 956-2033;
tours: (800) MALLBAY (625-5229).
M–F 10–9:30, Sat 10–8, Sun 11–7. Parking: lot.
This was the largest retail center to open in the United States in 1994. The 1.5 million-square-foot project includes 10 anchors and 220 specialty retailers (primarily off-price tenants and manufacturers' outlets). Former employees of the converted Ford Motor assembly plant won't recognize their old workplace.

The Great Mall offers a Wonder Park family entertainment center, restaurants, infotainment on a mall-wide video network, and travel-themed courts featuring autos, ships, trains, and future modes of transportation. Everything about this exciting new development is designed to educate and amuse young and old alike while providing an exhilarating shopping experience. Located off 680 and 880 at the intersection of Montague Expressway, Capitol Avenue, and Main Street.

Napa
Napa Factory Stores
999 Freeway Drive, Highway 29 and First Street, Napa. (707) 226-9876. Daily 10–8. Parking: lot.
An outdoor center in the heart of the wine country, with over forty factory-direct stores. Some manufacturers are making their first outlet appearance in Northern California! Anticipate some deluxe bargains from Ellen Tracy, Cole-Haan, Laundry, Nautica, Timberland, TSE Cashmere, and others!

Pacific Grove
The American Tin Cannery
125 Ocean View Boulevard, Pacific Grove. (408) 372-1442. Sun–Th 10–6, F–Sat 10–8. Parking: lot.
A lovely, airy, enclosed shopping outlet mall with more than fifty tenants. Directions: Easy access from Highway 1, Pacific Grove Exit. Follow signs to Cannery Row and Aquarium. American Tin Cannery is one block past Aquarium.

Petaluma
Petaluma Village Factory Outlets
2200 Petaluma Boulevard N., Petaluma. (707) 778-9300. Daily 10–8. Parking: lot.
A village-themed outdoor center with over forty factory stores. Many new faces, starting with Adrienne Vittadini Direct, Ann Taylor, The Nap Outlet, Petite Sophisticate, Evan Picone, and Villeroy & Boch. Directions: From 101, take E. Washington Street to Petaluma Boulevard, turn right.

St. Helena
Village Outlets of Napa Valley
3111 N. St. Helena Highway, St. Helena. (707) 963-7282.
M–F 10–6, Sat 10–7, Sun 11–6. Parking: lot.
A small center, distinguished by its status tenants—Donna
Karan, Movado, Coach, Brooks Bros., and others. On Highway
29, one mile north of Christian Brothers Winery.

Tracy
Tracy Outlet Center
1005 Pescadero Avenue, Tracy. (209) 833-1895. M–Sat 10–9,
Sun 11–6. Parking: lot.
From 205, exit at MacArthur Boulevard. Convenient for many
who get their thrills from shopping at Anne Klein, Liz Claiborne,
Rockport, Jones New York, and about thirty-five other now-
familiar outlet center tenants. The center should double in size
by the end of 1995.

Truckee
Tahoe*Truckee Factory Stores
12047 Donner Pass Road, Truckee. M–Sat 9:30–6, Sun 10–6.
Parking: lot.
A relatively small center with eleven tenants. The large Villeroy
& Boch and Dansk factory stores are the main attraction.
Directions: Located one-eighth of a mile east of the Agricul-
tural Inspection Station. Donner Pass Road Exit from 80.

Vacaville
The Factory Stores of America at Nut Tree
Nut Tree Road, Vacaville. (707) 447-5755.
M–Sat 10–8, Sun 10–6. Parking: lot.
This huge complex is just across the freeway from the famed
Nut Tree restaurant, halfway between San Francisco and
Sacramento. More than 125 stores—a shopper's shuttle takes
some of the legwork out of visiting this center. Directions:
From 80 East; take 505/Orange Drive Exit at Orange Drive,
turn right to access center entrance. From 80 West, exit at
Monte Vista Avenue, first right onto Monte Vista, left at Nut
Tree Road.

Travel Tip:
Your Best Bets for Southern California Outlet Center Shopping

Desert Hills Factory Outlet Mall (Palm Springs Area)
48650 Seminole Road, Cabazon. (714) 849-6641.
Sun–F 10–8, Sat 9–8.
About twenty miles before you get to Palm Springs on I-10, you'll pass by Cabazon, an almost invisible community until the Desert Hills Factory Outlet Mall opened. More than fifty tenants, including Donna Karan, Perry Ellis Shoes, Coach, Albert Nipon, Patagonia, Spa Gear (La Costa Spas), Adrienne Vittadini, Movado, and more. This center rates high!

Factory Merchants of Barstow (Los Angeles to Las Vegas)
Lynwood exit off I-15, Barstow. (619) 253-7342.
Jan–Mar M–Th 9–6, Fri–Sun 9–8, Apr–Dec daily, 9–8. Parking: lot.
Very nice center situated to capture the Las Vegas traffic. Tenants: fifty-one factory stores including Polo/Ralph Lauren, Lenox, and Eagle's Eye.

Glossary of Bargain-Hunting Terms

Whenever an item is for sale to the public at 20–50% under retail, common sense tells you there must be a reason. I have tried in each entry to give you an explanation; the answer generally falls into one or more categories described by the following terminology used in retailing.

discontinued or manufacturer's closeout: Apparel or products that are no longer being manufactured. In most instances this does not affect the merchandise, but if parts may need to be replaced, it could cause a problem.

floor sample: A model displayed in the store.

freight damage: Even if only one or two items in a shipment are broken, burned, chipped, or marred, for insurance purposes the entire lot is designated "damaged." This merchandise may be noticeably damaged; often, however, it is actually in A-1 condition but part of a large shipment that met with physical mishap.

gray market: Also known as "parallel importing." Refers to the overseas purchase of foreign goods by independent companies who are not authorized U.S. dealers for those goods. The goods are then sold in the United States by off-price and discount retailers who compete with the owners of the U.S. trademarks for those goods. Not having to pay for service, warranties, or advertising, the gray-market merchants can undercut the prices of the U.S. trademark owners.

in-season buying: Whereas most retailers buy preseason, a discounter will often purchase in-season, relieving the manufacturer of merchandise that is old to it but still new to the public.

irregular: Merchandise with minor imperfections, often barely discernible.

job lot: Goods, often of various sorts, brought together for sale as one quantity.

jobber: A person who buys goods in quantity from manufacturers or importers and sells those goods to dealers.

keystone: Traditional retail markup. Based on the wholesale price being doubled, i.e., a $50 wholesale price results in a retail price of $100.

knock-off: A copy of a highly acceptable design. These may be nearly authentic renditions or shabby imitations. Some manufacturers and designers make their own knock-offs in different- or lesser-quality fabrics for off-price stores and chains.

liquidated stock: When a company or business is in financial trouble, the stock it has on hand is sometimes sold to merchandisers, at prices much lower than retail in order to liquidate the assets of the company.

loss leader: An item purposely priced low (sometimes at a loss) to get you into the store.

odd-lots: A relatively small quantity of unsold merchandise that remains after an order has been filled.

off-price retailing: The sale of major brand merchandise at reduced prices.

open stock: Individual pieces of merchandise sold in sets, which are kept in stock as replacements.

overruns: An excess of products, similar to surplus and overstocks, but generally due to a manufacturer's error.

past-season: Goods manufactured for a previous season.

retail: The selling of merchandise directly to the consumer.

returns: Orders returned to the manufacturer by retail stores because they do not arrive on time. Fashion discounters are able to buy this merchandise below cost from the manufacturer, thereby helping to alleviate those losses.

samples: An item shown by the manufacturer's representative to the prospective merchandiser/buyer for the purpose of selling the product.

seconds: Merchandise with more-than-minor flaws, which may affect the aesthetic appeal or performance of the product.

surplus overstock: An excess quantity, over and above what is needed by the retailer.

wholesale price: The cost of goods to the retailer, except in discount shopping, when consumers can buy at or near this price.

wholesale to the public: This term is often used inappropriately by discounters. From my perspective, "wholesale" is the price the seller pays for the merchandise. If that same price were passed on to the consumer, a discount retailer would make no profit. When a discounter is able to buy merchandise for less than the manufacturer's original published wholesale price (at liquidations, end-of-season closeouts, etc.), it is possible for the discount retailer to add a markup and sell the merchandise for the original wholesale price or for even less.

The Attic (Emporium Furniture Clearance Center)

835 Market Street, San Francisco. (415) 764-2375.
M-Sat 9:30-8, Sun 11-7. MC, VISA, AE, DC; Emporium,
Weinstock, and Broadway charge cards. Parking: pay lots.
(Other store: Emporium, Almaden Plaza, San Jose.)
The fourth floor of Emporium's downtown store is where they
send canceled orders, floor samples, discontinued furniture
styles from its warehouse inventory, and some slightly damaged
pieces from the furniture departments of 50 Broadway, Weinstock, and Emporium stores. Initial markdowns are 25-40% off
original retail, but progressive markdowns are taken as needed
(up to 60% off) to keep the stock moving. Upholstered sofas,
chairs, and sectionals get the most floor space, surrounded
with smaller selections of case goods, accessories, area rugs,
and occasionally some very unique accent pieces. Shop the
San Francisco store for more expensive and upscale furniture
lines; shop Almaden's Plaza's smaller clearance center for promotional lines, moderately priced furnishings, and more as-is
pieces. All sales final. Delivery is extra. Note: The Mountain
View clearance center has closed.

Homeware Manufacturer's Outlet

1041 Murray Street, Berkeley. (510) 849-2856.
M-Sat 9-5 during quarterly sales events. MC, VISA.
Parking: street.
Papy Boez and Harvest are two very popular labels that show
up in national catalogs and boutiques around the country.
Designed locally and made in India from cottons or rayons

colored with vegetable dyes, this charming and timeless line is more mainstream than many imported lines that convey an ethnic or avant-garde image. I can picture Martha Stewart and Cal co-eds appearing equally at ease wearing these dresses, jumpers, blouses, and separates. The line is set apart by its detailing (tucks, appliqués, pattern mixing, embroidery, etc.) and original hand-painted or hand-blocked printed fabrics. During quarterly sales usually held in April, July, August (back-to-school), and for the holidays (Thanksgiving to Christmas), past-season styles and slightly imperfect fashions are priced 60–75% off retail. Prices range from $7.99 for blouses to $39.99 for dresses. Sizes: Small/Medium or Medium/Large. Check local newspapers for quarterly sales announcements. Location: Murray is a small side street that angles off from the intersection of 7th Street and Ashby. Outlet is mid block between 7th and San Pablo Avenue.

Jacqueline West Outlet

805 Gilman Street, Berkeley. (510) 528-8698.
Sat 11–5, Sun Noon–5. MC, VISA. Parking: street.
If you're known by the company you keep, then Jacqueline West is riding high. Barbra Streisand relaxes in her French smock dress and Julia Roberts and other celebs have focused attention on her Henry-Ts (named after Henry Miller). This T-shirt, made from the softest knit imaginable, is fitted and flattering—it's a bestseller in stores around the country (Barney's N.Y. and other status stores). Other styles in her line of casual, contemporary weekend wear are made from natural fibers, i.e. washed linens, cottons, raw silks, and merino wools. Everything is made for comfort. Most separates and dresses are loose and shapeless (many designs influenced by military or Chinese apparel) to fit lots of body types. Colors, for the most part, are earthy. Prices at the outlet are 30–50% off retail on past-season overruns and slightly imperfect fashions. Check the bargain boxes filled with assorted leftovers priced at $5, $10, and $15. This easy wear is European-sized: 1, 2 and 3 (fits 6–14). All sales final. Call for weekday hours scheduled for later in 1995.

Martha Egan Company

1127 Folsom Street (bet. 7th and 8th streets), San Francisco.
(415) 252-1072. M–F 10–6. Cash/check. Parking: street.
The line is vintage-inspired with a retro orientation, capturing
the look of the '40s. Dresses (in short or long versions) may be
oversized—some semi-fitted. Some overalls, vests, and pajama
pants, too. Soft European rayon crepes and failles are fabrics
of choice for fall and winter collections (georgettes and sheers
for spring), while unusual buttons provide special accents.
Check the end-of-season racks for 30% to 50% discounts, or
$10 to $20 racks for last-chance super buys. Prices at retail
range from $75 to $150. Sizes: S, M and L (fits 6–14). This is a
small studio outlet offering a very personal shopping experience for the right customer.

Off Fifth (Saks Fifth Avenue Outlet)

Great Mall of the Bay Area, Milpitas. Phone: pending.
Daily. MC, VISA. Parking: lot.
The only Saks outlet between Hawaii and Illinois is scheduled
to open in August 1995. The outlet will feature the best of
American and European designers and brands of women's
career (including Petite sizes) and casual sportswear, dresses,
coats, footwear, and accessories. Men's suits, sportcoats, sportswear, furnishings, outerwear, and footwear should prompt
many couples to plan tandem shopping sprees. This will be
clearance merchandise from Saks's own stores, Folio catalogs,
and direct purchases from manufacturers. Prices will range
40–75% below original Saks Fifth Avenue prices.

Rodolph Fabric Factory Outlet

989 West Spain Street, Sonoma. (707) 935-0316.
M, W, F 11–2, third Sat each month 10–4. Hours subject to
change during holidays. MC, VISA. Parking: street.
This outlet focuses on unusual dye lots and remnants of fabrics
traditionally sold only through interior designers. Fabrics
normally priced from $80 to $120 a yard at retail are offered
via the outlet at $15 to $30 a yard. There are beautiful colors
and textures in a selection of silks, wools, and cottons found
in contemporary and classical motifs. A great resource for
those trying to capture that *Architectural Digest* image in their
decorating projects, as well as a unique source for quilters and
crafters. Also available, for $5 to $10 per yard, is a selection
of Jim Thompson Thai apparel silks and better-quality batiks
from Bali Fabrications (listed in Fabrics—Home Decorating).

Siri

7 Heron Street (alley off 8th Street bet. Harrison and Folsom streets), San Francisco. (415) 431-8787. M–F 10–6, Sat 10–5. MC, VISA. Parking: street.

An out-of-the-way location for an out-of-the-ordinary collection of feminine fashions. Siri's fashion studio is a combination of retail boutique and outlet. Her elegant collection of daytime and special occasion dresses and sportswear is sold to status stores and boutiques. Prices on dresses range from $150 to $500; on sportswear from $90 to $250. The styles are timeless and classic, yet offer originality for those who don't want to look like department store clones. Women in their twenties, thirties, and forties are prime targets for this sophisticated line. Beautiful fabrics (many designed in-house), interesting textures, and distinctive colors are hallmarks of each collection. Expect savings of 30–50% off retail on past-season styles (many one-of-a-kind beauties). Sizes: 2–12.

St. John

Great Mall of the Bay Area, Milpitas. Phone: pending. Daily. MC, VISA. Parking: lot.

Discriminating shoppers will no doubt find that the opening of St. John (scheduled for early summer 1995) is all the inducement they need to finally schedule a visit to the Great Mall. Discounts of 50% will be offered on past-season collections of St. John's apparel and accessories. Slightly imperfect styles will be reduced even more. This maker's enduring styles made from wrinkle-proof knits travel beautifully—a reason why so many women consider these to be wardrobe treasures. Located near the Great Auto Courts entrance and close to Off Fifth (the new Saks Fifth Avenue clearance store).

Store Index

Store Index

353

Store Index

355

Geographical Index

Geographical Index

367

Subject Index

Subject Index

375